The Ford Dynasty

The Ford Dynasty

JAMES BROUGH

W. H. ALLEN · LONDON
A Howard & Wyndham Company
1978

Copyright © 1977, by James Brough

First British edition, 1978

This book or parts thereof may not be
reproduced in any form whatsoever without
permission in writing

Printed and bound in Great Britain by
Butler & Tanner Ltd, Frome and London,
for the Publishers, W. H. Allen & Co. Ltd,
44 Hill Street, London W1X 8LB

ISBN 0 491 02334 0

The Publishers warmly thank the Ford Motor Company for
providing the pictures included in this book

For James Alwyn Brough
(1886–1968)
an engineer whose dreams
were not fulfilled

Contents

The illustration sections fall between pages 88 and 89 and pages 248 and 249

BOOK
ONE

Chapter One

A Simple Wedding

He looked much the same as most properly brought-up young men on their wedding day—tense, vulnerable, trim, and well-barbered, exhibiting happiness mixed with a desire to hide in the woodwork if only he had the chance. The hundred or so guests who filled the downstairs rooms of the bride's home could remark only that Edsel Bryant Ford, five days short of his twenty-third birthday, seemed as shy as ever and not spoiled one bit by the million dollars that had been his father's gift to him when he reached twenty-one.

To impress upon his only child just what that amounted to in gold, Henry had taken him down into a Detroit bank's vaults to show him a million dollars' worth of bullion bars stacked there for the demonstration; at least so the story went, and few doubted it. When Edsel was still in knee pants, his mother Clara had worried over whether they would ever have enough money to spare for themselves. Henry's astonishing automobile—more than half a million Model T's sold in the twelve months ended last July—had taken care of that.

On this first evening in November 1916, waiting in the library for Eleanor Lowthian Clay, the bridegroom had no cause to wonder whether the slim girl with blue eyes and a wistful child's face was marrying him for reasons other than love. They had known each other too long for any doubts to arise, beginning in the days when their families lived within a mile of each other, the Clays in this solid, comfortable mansion on Boston Boulevard East, the Fords in the stone-columned, red-brick house on Edison Avenue; Henry had commissioned the house as an early necessity imposed by escalating riches. Clara had the grounds landscaped with stands of ornamental trees, a sunken garden, a pergola, and her first massive plantings of roses. Henry needed a place big enough to give him privacy from curiosity seekers and supplicants.

Eleanor had been fifteen, with schoolgirl hair hanging down her back, when she and Edsel met at Annie Ward Foster's dancing classes five years ago. It was not too long since she had stopped playing pranks like laying pennies on the tracks for streetcars to squash. Her father was already dead. Perhaps it had been to soothe the grief that she started going down to the Franklin Settlement to give dance lessons to the children of the Germans, Italians, Poles, and other foreign-born who came pouring into the city, drawn by the dream of jobs making automobiles.

A living William Clay could scarcely have afforded the elegance of Boston Boulevard. He had been no more than manager of the Hudson Department Store, which in the judgment of those customers acquainted with a universe beyond Detroit, compared favorably with R. H. Macy's in New York, Marshall Field in Chicago, and John Wanamaker's in Philadelphia. His employment may have owed something to the fact that he was the brother-in-law of the store's founder, Joseph Lowthian Hudson. On William's death, his widow and their two daughters, Eleanor and Josephine (pet-named "Dody"), moved into her brother's home. When he followed William to the grave not long afterward, she remained in the home, in accordance with the terms of his will, much more comfortably provided for than would have been the case had her husband continued breathing.

Through Uncle Joseph, Eleanor had some tenuous ties with the automobile business. In 1909, the year when Henry Ford made what might well have been a pre-ordained decision to go whole hog for the Model T, her relative along with two other partners had belatedly caught on to the potentials promised in manufacturing horseless carriages and embarked on an attempt to amass a second fortune by founding the Hudson Motor Car Company. He had not lived long enough to see the outcome.

For tonight's ceremony, joining her twenty-year-old younger

daughter and the heir to an incalculable fortune as man and wife, Mrs. Clay again demonstrated those standards of taste that singled her out in a raucous community. A church wedding—in St. Anne's, Trinity and Christ, or Woodward Avenue Central Methodist—would be more impressive but less controllable. In her own inherited house, the guest list could be confined to relatives and close friends, the decor could be imaginative, and an example might be set for the predominantly grease-anointed society of what had recently emerged as the automobile capital of the world.

Mother and daughter together settled the style for the event. The tone was faintly Russian, Tsarist Russian, without recognition or knowledge of the surging discontent among the subjects of Tsar Nicholas; next year his subjects would revolutionize his country and fascinate Eleanor's father-in-law. Her embroidered white wedding gown, complemented by the diadem pinned to her hair, would have become a heroine of Tolstoy's, and the bridesmaids were dressed in keeping. The idea and the dresses had come from the New York *modiste* Lucile, a venturesome Englishwoman born Lucy Kennedy, whose career included a fling in London society as Lady Duff Gordon.

Edsel had gone East with Eleanor and her sister for the initial conference with Lucile this past spring, taking leave from his intimidating job as secretary of the Ford Motor Company; he had held the job for a bare four months. Another young man, Dody's intended husband, made up the party. Broad-shouldered, six feet tall, Ernest Kanzler was a Michigan doctor's son, a year and a half older and six inches loftier than Edsel, who like most of those in his circle was impressed by this husky college man—University of Michigan, then Harvard—and future lawyer. Edsel had been too eager to go to work for Father to give much thought about a college education. He had been wondering lately if that was a mistake.

He wrote a dutiful letter home about the days in New York, when the foursome spent every evening in a theater, with supper and dancing to follow. "We had a slick time . . . Eleanor is buying a trousseau, fancy that. . . . The funny part of it was that with all the late hours and strenuousness I felt great. Haven't had a pain or ache since I left Detroit."

At that time, he and Eleanor had reached an understanding,

but they were not yet formally engaged. She had to complete her senior year before she would graduate from the Liggett School, the most prestigious establishment for young ladies in the city, and she still hadn't been presented to society. She contemplated entering Vassar, which would be a breeze for a girl of her quick intelligence.

As it was, she gave up both the debut and thoughts about going to college. The love she felt for her sometimes harassed, always devoted sweetheart established its own order of priorities. He needed her badly. On the June day of her graduation from Liggett, she had their engagement announced to the newspapers and steeled herself to greet the reporters from the News and the Free Press when they came hurrying to ring the front doorbell. She fended off their more personal questions like a veteran of such inquisition. The only quote of any significance that they left with was, "We are going to live very simply." She also allowed that she had been given a diamond engagement ring.

Her mother went along with her daughter's wishes to keep this evening's ceremony in low key and high taste. There must be no displays of glitter or gold, no treasures in jewels dangling on talcum-dusted bosoms. Flowers, masses of them painstakingly placed for optimum effect, would constitute the only decoration. They were banked against the walls of the entrance hall and woven around the chandeliers, their colors chosen to complement the yellow tapestry furnishings in the living room and the paneling of the library, where artful clusters of autumn foliage stood on the mantel of the bronze fireplace.

Kasserine roses in tall silver vases bracketed the candelabra on the table in the solarium, where a buffet supper, centering on three wedding cakes, would be served at nine o'clock. Candlelight contributed a Russian touch, and Mrs. Clay was proud to mention that the tablecloth had been specially woven in New York by seven girl immigrants from Muscovy.

A thin crowd of a few dozen people waited in the shadows outside for the guests to arrive, hoping for a glimpse of the kind of spectacle that accompanied Vanderbilt nuptials or the epochal marriage in Manhattan of William E. Corey, president of United States Steel, who trumpeted the news that taking the actress Mabelle Gilman as his second bride cost him $5,000 for the breakfast and $6,000 for the florist, with $200,000 set aside "for honeymoon expenses" and other incidentals, for a grand total of $499,995. The watchers on Boston Boulevard wasted their time. "I don't think I saw $1,000 of jewels," a *Free Press* columnist sniffed.

Most of the faces were unrecognizable, not excepting the bridegroom's; only one or two blurry photographs of him had ever appeared in the newspapers. A select handful of Ford's seven thousand dealers and their wives arrived—notably the Gaston Plantiffs, in from New York City, and the Dutee Flints of Providence, Rhode Island—but they were no cause for excitement. The Dodge brothers, John and Horace, appeared, creating more of a stir because they, at least, were Detroit people and legendary in their own fashion.

Middle-aged now, the two redheads had built a reputation as roughneck Saturday night brawlers a dozen years back when their machine shop on Monroe Avenue was turning out engines and transmissions for Henry's first automobiles. In some sleazy saloon, they would drink themselves to the sawdust. One night John, four years older and twice as quarrelsome as his brother, pulled a revolver from his waistband to prompt a terrified saloonkeeper to dance a tabletop fandango, which John accompanied by pitching glasses against the fly-specked mirror behind the bar.

John and Horace were still prepared to pick a fight with anybody, but they were buttresses of the industrial establishment these days. Together, they owned one tenth of Henry's company, with a seat on its board for each of them. For the past two years, they had been manufacturers in their own right of cars that bore their name, pumping in as capital their $6,600,000 in Ford dividends and the $10,000,000 in profits made by supplying parts for Henry's automobiles.

They would behave themselves at least until the evening was over, for Edsel's sake. They shared admiration for Edsel. "Henry," John once told the father, "I don't envy you a damn thing except that boy of yours."

Henry himself was easy to spot with Clara at his side when their chauffeur halted at the curb and Henry climbed the steps to the door, fitted in a handsome topcoat, nimble as a cat on his feet at the age of fifty-three. The lean face, lustrous blue eyes, and wavy hair parted just off-center like a dry-goods clerk's had been pictured around the world ever since the Sunday morning meeting in his office of January 1914 brought him to decide that $5.00 a day should be the minimum wage paid to Ford workers, with the laboring day cut to eight hours for good measure. The subsequent press handout forecast that this would launch "the greatest revolution in the matter of rewards for its workers ever known to the industrial world." Henry approved of this kind of hyperbole so long as he wasn't called upon to get his tongue around such words himself. Virtually overnight, he was an international celebrity, a prophet, and among his competitors "a traitor to his class."

He credited Edsel's presence in the plant for opening his eyes to the merit of paying $5.00 a head as a step toward making the world over. Father and son had taken a walk through the place and seen two men battering each other with their fists. Henry was struck with a sense of shame that Edsel, for whom he wanted the best of everything, should be exposed to the sight of brutality. It prompted him to reason, Henry said, that subsistence wages made for barbarous living, and barbarous living bred savagery. He came up with a simple solution: a share in the profits for his employees sufficient to guarantee the $5.00 minimum. As he skipped up the steps to see his son married, Henry had reason to feel pleased. He always enjoyed a wedding, and company profits for the twelve months ended last July 31 were only $5,891.99 short of $60,000,000. He knew exactly what should be done with that bundle of money.

There was one guest compared with whom Henry felt he was moon to the sun. Thomas Alva Edison plowed through the entrance hall, his suit powdered with the perpetual dandruff that flaked off the white bristles of his head—in consequence, he would explain, of the brain waves that forever surged within his skull. At Henry's urging, Edison had come for the celebration from his home, Llewellyn Park, in West Orange, New Jersey, bringing Mina, his second wife, eighteen years younger than he; Mina was known to complain that Old Tom labored so long in his laboratories that he occasionally stumbled into bed fully clothed and fell asleep with his boots on.

Henry revered him. Edison was his friend, companion on a dozen motorized and highly publicized camping trips into the wilds of the West, the undoubted genius that Henry aspired to be. The old man's cut-and-try methods had begotten a new America with the invention of the telephone, the phonograph, microphones, incandescent electric lamps, the alkaline storage battery, and film for movie cameras in similar fashion as Henry's intuitive tinkering had produced the best-selling automobile in the world.

Henry had absorbed a great deal from Edison: belief in an infinitely improvable future for mankind, provided human frailty was sublimated and the law of reason permitted to rule; faith in the ability of gifted men, Tom and Henry foremost among them, to reshape civilization; conviction that the use of tobacco was a curse to be eradicated, and that it was the duty of men of enlightenment to combat the arcane forces of international Jewry, which conspired to enchain the universe.

The team of ushers, sparked by Kanzler, opened a path through the throng for Edison and other venerated guests to make their way into the library. As best man, Edsel had chosen his closest friend, Tom Whitehead, who had driven with him across the United States to San Francisco the previous year—in a Ford, of course. They wanted to see the Panama-Pacific International Exposition in the city, which was emerging from the rubble of the earthquake nine years past. Edsel muttered praise for the product at every stop for gasoline to pour into the ten-gallon tank and on the single occasion when one of the thirty-inch tires had to be changed.

In a grimy khaki shirt and pants, leggings, and an old cap, he turned up at the Golden Gate toting his camera, eager to be off on a tour of the Barbary Coast and Chinatown, where a co-operative police sergeant slipped one pigtailed inhabitant $1.00 to persuade him to light up an opium pipe and provide a snapshot for Edsel. Then Edsel was off to change his clothes and present himself as the heir apparent at the exposition's Palace of Transportation, where the crowds gaped in wonderment at a working replica of Ford's Detroit assembly line, giving birth to Model T's before their very eyes.

To describe the earthy dependability—its supreme virtue, in his opinion—of the car that Americans had christened "Tin Lizzie," one of Henry's favorite slogans was, "Built to take you anywhere

you want to go and bring you back on time." Edsel had joined the
multitude who found positive evidence that this was no advertising agent's pipe dream.

Now the clocks in the house began chiming the half hour past
eight. With his long-fingered, bony hands clasped behind his
back, Henry stood at his son's left side while the hired string orchestra started into the wedding march from *Lohengrin*. The mus-
ing glimmer of a smile with which he often confronted all
strangers creased his face. In a gown of apricot velvet and tulle
that flattered her dumpy figure, Clara was a model of matronly re-
straint. Then Eleanor made her entrance with Josephine, her maid
of honor, and the bevy of bridesmaids; Eleanor looked for all the
world like Natasha Rostov on her way to the altar. The Reverend
H. Lester Smith of the Central Methodist Church smoothed his
vestments.

"A Ford will take you anywhere except into society," another of
Henry's pet summations of his product, carried a caustic note that
expressed his deepest feelings about most social folderol. The present gathering contained a sprinkling of two classes of people he
disdained. He shunned rich idlers and mere money-grubbers, neither of whom appreciated the moral value of working for a living.
These recent boomtime years had multiplied both categories of
parasites.

The city had more than doubled in physical size since he and
Clara moved there, a dissatisfied twenty-eight-year-old mechanic
and his trusting wife, bringing their chattels aboard a hay wagon.
Today it sprawled haphazardly for more than forty square miles,
chewing up woods and farmland north, south, and west of its original site on the misnamed Detroit River, in actuality an oil-slicked
strait joining Lake Erie with Lake St. Clair. Next year, local
boosters would proclaim that it had attained the status of fifth-
largest city in the land, preceded only by New York, Chicago,
Philadelphia, and Boston. The way things were shaping up, the
population, too, would double itself every decade, swollen by the
influx of job-hunters lured by newspaper advertisements placed by
the automakers, calling desperately for more hands to work in the
dinning machine shops.

Queer-looking objects had recently appeared at intersections
along Woodward Avenue, which performed double duty as main

business street and residential boulevard, and divided the city in two. Round disks, painted green on one side, red on the other, stood perched on poles at head height, to be revolved by a police-man's hand. The first traffic-control signals in America were fittingly born on the streets of Detroit, the fibrillating heart of what had currently grown into a billion-dollar industry exactly twenty years since the first horseless carriage had come jouncing down those streets, followed by a sharp-eyed Henry, tagging along on his bicycle.

The highway to automobiling glory was littered with the debris of companies that had met defeat in the race. Two thousand, three, four—there was no knowing how many men with no better qualifications than ambition and a toolbox had gone broke in a business where rewards were uncertain and odds on failure long. The industry could count roughly one hundred survivors, but no more than a dozen of them cleared real money, and of every five cars sold, two were Lizzies, their price slashed by Henry last August to a bone-bare $345. No competitor could come within $200 of that figure.

His closest individual rival in the marketplace was a former sporting-goods dealer, John North Willys, who had flirted with bankruptcy in the financial panic of 1907 to make over the Willys-Overland Company; its cars were selling these days for up-ward of $600. In the next price bracket, the Hudson was having no difficulty finding customers, and the boss, Roy Dikeman Cha-pin, had made a fortune, a reputation as a lady-killer, and a career that ultimately saw him appointed Secretary of Commerce in the terminal months of Herbert Hoover's administration.

By some quirk of history, a remarkable percentage of brothers had contributed to building the industry, sweating together to fab-ricate a car and simultaneously scrape up financial backing for it. Charles and Frank Duryea won their place in the record books by producing the country's first gasoline-powered automobiles in their Springfield, Massachusetts, workshop in 1895. Now the two Dodges' new entry—twenty-four horsepower against Lizzie's twenty—was beginning to sell like popcorn in a ball park. Be-tween these two benchmarks, other brotherly teams waxed and waned.

Edgar and Elmer Apperson had been in business and out again

in a grubby little factory in Kokomo, Indiana. Francis and Freelan Stanley had put their name on a respected line of "steamers." The three Studebakers—John, Henry, and Clem, former carriage makers—were succeeding to the point where their cars threatened to outsell Willys-Overland. Fred and August Duesenberg would manufacture a superb vehicle that its owners rated the best in the world. The Briscoe Manufacturing Company (Benjamin and Frank) had a healthy share of the market before the company collapsed. Three more siblings—Fred, Edward, and Charles—organized themselves as Fisher Body Corporation in 1916. Another trio, the Grahams, who had once farmed together in Indiana, controlled the Graham-Paige Company. The Packards, John and Warren, had been making automobiles since the turn of the century.

Henry was different. His empire must be his alone, to be run as he, in his brooding, saw fit. His two surviving, younger brothers, John and William, were not invited to his house. For reasons of envy or neglect, they hated him.

Lately, a new family name borne by three immigrant brothers had been all over the headlines of Detroit's financial pages. Louis Chevrolet arrived in the United States from Switzerland in 1900, looking to market a wine pump that he had invented. Instead, he subordinated his engineer's talents to earning a perilous livelihood racing cars down the roads and around the circuits that were introducing a deafening new spectator sport to America. His brothers Gaston and Arthur joined him in the same devil-may-care calling.

Louis soon developed ideas of his own for an improved motor and aspired to launch into automobile manufacturing. Now, the Chevrolet Motor Company had just been integrated into the mammoth General Motors Corporation that was challenging Ford's supremacy as a money-maker with cars in an assortment of prices from Buicks ($600 and up), Oaklands, Cadillacs, and Oldsmobiles at anything up to $2,000, and now Chevrolets, which were nibbling away at Lizzie's sales with Baby Grands at $625, Royal Mails at $750, and the latest entry, Model 490.

Henry remained no more concerned than he had been by news of the $50 cash dividend, its first, paid out on each share of common stock by General Motors the previous September. He was content, too, to give Chevrolet a clear profit of $278,000 in selling him a parcel of land it had bought with the idea of building its main factory there across the highway from his plant at Highland Park, out on Woodward Avenue near the city limits. He had more important matters on his mind, like war and peace and his niche in the annals of homespun philosophy. Chevrolets were being built in Flint, an hour's drive north from Detroit.

Like most fresh-made rich, the men who owned the plants attributed their success to an amalgam of manifest destiny and unique personal qualifications. So far as this explained the city's role, they were correct. It was the logical point at which the boom could be nurtured. Before the new century opened, a picket fence of factory chimneys gushed smoke over the Detroit River. Lathes and drilling machines in close to a thousand locations cut iron and brass and steel. Carriage works, iron foundries, and marine engine manufactories all provided a labor force of skilled craftsmen and their apprentices.

But the era of craftsmen was dying fast, to the sorrow of the veterans who had taken pride in their accomplishments. On the shop floors of the new factories, assembling the five thousand or so parts that comprised an automobile called for a man to work like a machine himself, required only to perform a single, endlessly repeated action like turning a screw or tightening a bolt. Anybody who could stand the monotony, the clatter of the conveyor chains, and the nonstop whine of leather belting overhead that drove the machinery below was qualified as an auto worker; a man felt chronically insecure in a job like this.

It was the year in which Carl Sandburg wrote: "I am the people —the mob—the crowd—the mass. Do you know that all the great work of the world is done through me?" The sentiment was not too remote from Henry's way of thinking, though his interest in poetry stopped short with Henry Wadsworth Longfellow. Henry was appalled by the practice of most parts suppliers, who paid their machine-shop hands pinchpenny piecework rates—and suffered the penalty in shoddy workmanship. These jobs were often all that the foreign-born could find. He had already taken an initial step toward upgrading their opportunities by opening a company school to teach English. His latest effort to preserve an inheritance of craftsmanship was a technical school, where youngsters received a thorough training in engineering. Ford executives didn't go for the idea. As usual, Henry overrode them.

At a later date, Sandburg, who was an early customer for a Model T, was invited to meet Henry. "One feels in talking with Ford," wrote the shock-haired poet, "that he is a man of power rather than of material riches."

Detroit was endemically overcrowded. Incoming job-hunters packed themselves and their families into shanties, tenements, and multiple-family houses that a map would show like a fever rash spread over sections of streets dotted with beer parlors, gambling dens, and bawdy houses. There were few true slums to be pinpointed as such. The pace of growth had permitted little time for areas to congeal into the scabby poverty that shamed older cities.

The wealthier families were more closely concentrated, with addresses on Grand, Boston, and Chicago boulevards, along stretches of Cass Avenue, in Virginia Park and Arden Park. Lately, more and more businessmen had migrated northeast along the lakefront, beyond the city limits to the clearer, quieter air of Grosse Pointe. At the end of long, tree-shaded driveways, construction was proceeding at a spanking pace in a heyday of architectural whimsy—chateaux, manor houses, baronial halls, and villas that would do credit to Biarritz. Older money had bought estates there in earlier days, accumulated by speculators whose profits from land, ore, or timber had elevated them into what passed for aristocracy.

When his almost new Edison Avenue house failed dismally to provide the seclusion he insisted on, in spite of a guard mounted at the door, Henry had been sufficiently attracted by the charms of Grosse Pointe to buy some three hundred acres there on Lake St. Clair. The architects had undertaken to draw up building plans when he and Clara shied away. A neighbor had offered to take them along to a meeting of other property owners and introduce them to the community pleasures of life in Grosse Pointe. For Henry, that amounted to inviting a cat that liked to walk by itself to join a pack of bull terriers.

"I'd like to build out in Dearborn," Clara said. Since her wishes had usually prevailed in the Ford household from the day they were married, that is what they had proceeded to do. They held onto the land, however; it would make a future gift for Edsel.

Henry liked to keep himself apart from almost everyone—his fellow motor magnates, his staff, the rich, and the poor. "You know me too well," he once told an intimate of his who had worked alongside him on designs for Lizzie. "Hereafter I am going to see that no man comes to know me so intimately."

He stayed out of the downtown clubs, avoided contact with his peers (if there were any), and cared nothing for the high living that the boom had brought. On a more expanded time scale, Detroit had undergone a similar kind of frenzy as the Klondike in the gold rush. The proprietors and shareholders of a flourishing automobile business found that they had the next best thing to a license to print treasury bills.

Thomas Edison, prone to pontificate, once remarked, "The automobile has done more to make America a nation of thinkers than any other invention or agency." It also contributed to giving Detroit the flavor of a western town where men strode the sidewalk in shirtsleeves and women tended to the cook stove, children, and church socials. For the most part, this latest generation of new rich knew what it meant to work with their hands, run a lathe, adjust a carburetor, and relish the pungent scent of hot oil and metal. They were as smitten with the mystique of the internal-combustion engine as schoolboys hanging around a garage to watch a mechanic changing the spark plugs. They were hellbent on building an automobile that would outperform and outsell the competition.

They comprised a different breed from the past generation of titans who had put wheels under America. The men responsible for straddling the continent with railroad tracks had operated as absentee proprietors, remote from the crews who laid the ties. Shares in Union Pacific, Illinois Central, Great Northern, and the rest were stakes on the gambling tables of Wall Street. Men like frail, mousy Edward Henry Harriman, who started as a broker's office boy at fourteen, sat behind their desks, buying and selling the pieces of paper that constituted ownership of the monopoly in national commerce and transportation that railroads exercised. Their interest lay in the figures on a profit-and-loss statement, not in the engines that hauled the coaches and boxcars.

There was no more community of spirit among them than would arise among crows pecking at a dying horse. No single city qualified as the railroaders' Mecca. In 1916, when the tracks stretched for 254,000 miles crisscrossing the country, they gave no sign of awareness that their era had peaked out. Soon, most railroads would start abandoning branch lines and boarding up depots. When Harriman died in 1909, his estate was estimated at something approaching $100,000,000. Henry was worth more than that already, and the greenest years would seem to wait ahead unless the government, which had just scandalized the rich by levying the first federal inheritance tax, continued going hog-wild, spending billions on guns and battleships.

In the hush of the library as bride and groom murmured their responses, a sharp ear could catch the rumble of streetcars on Woodward Avenue, traveling past Highland Park and back. They would run until the early hours of tomorrow morning, overflowing with Ford workers after shifts changed at midnight. The buildings of the home plant spread over the fifty-seven level acres of what had once been a race course, snapped up by Ford at a bargain price of $81,225 nine years ago. The whole $7 million worth of plant, which included the biggest building in Michigan, had been erected for a single purpose, the manufacture of Model T's. In the estimation of experts who came from around the globe to tour the place, it was the pre-eminent wonder of the engineering world, putting Henry so far ahead that no other automaker could overtake him.

Here, Ford's crew of hard-driven technicians had perfected the assembly line. Like streams feeding into a river, every component unit was channeled in by mechanical conveyors at that split second of time when the workman reached out a hand for it, to add it to the embryo that would be a full-grown car ninety-three minutes from the moment of conception. The great majority of parts were made on the premises. Machines shaped crankcases from sheets of steel, curled gas-tank heads, and drilled forty-five holes in a cylinder block at a time. Presses produced a radiator's ninety-five tubes in one stroke. Any one of the fifteen thousand items of contributory machinery that churned out axles, wheels, brake bands, gears, and the rest would be scrapped after as little as a month's use if the design departments could devise something better, something to shave an extra fraction from time spent in assembly. No other manufacturer sold enough cars to afford to follow suit.

Currently, Henry was producing at the rate of more than 750,000 a year, yet customers' demand could not be met. The product was invariably oversold. No car was kept at Highland Park for a single day after it had rolled off the line. Not an acre was left for storage, and nine out of ten Lizzies were shipped out carrying their own bills of lading, cash on delivery.

Five dollars a day elevated Highland Park's eighteen thousand workers into a corps of élite. Henry could not give up nosing around every department, which he much preferred to being cooped up in his fancy office—the first of its kind he had ever given himself—with its carved oak desk in the far corner, oriental rug, antique wall clock, and a telescope for bird watching, a hobby that had fascinated him from the age of three. The payroll was far too big, of course, for him to know more than a few dozen men by name, but working for Ford gave a man the satisfaction of having a boss who knew the business and cared about more inspiriting things than profits.

You earned your money on your eight-hour shift for Ford, whether you sweated in the foundry, operated a drilling machine, assembled magnetos, or swept the floor. The noise everywhere was enough to split your eardrums, and the foremen pushed you to your physical limits. Smoking on the job was cause for firing. Talking was frowned on, too. You had fifteen minutes for your mealtime break, which usually meant buying a $.15 box lunch—a sandwich, a piece of fruit, and a cake—from one of the wagons the company allowed into the plant; coffee cost $.05 more.

But men wore Ford badges with a certain pride. It was the best place to work in the industry, and morale and co-operativeness soared high. The turnover rate used to waver close to 400 per cent a year—four men hired, then quitting or fired to keep one job filled. Most of the present workers, veiled in grease, who would catch the streetcars home long after the wedding party broke up this night were glad to do their bit in contributing toward an industrial miracle.

"I now pronounce you man and wife," and after the rounds of kissing were over, an unexpected change came about among the guests. It could have been young Eleanor's influence; it was impossible to tell. The older people, even Edison and Henry, found themselves delegated to the background, to chat with each other. The younger ones, centering on the bride and groom, set out only to enjoy themselves. The house suddenly lit up as if this were not the solemnization of matrimony but a coming-out party for Eleanor, signaling that she was no longer one of Liggett School's more promising students but an adult, quite capable of taking care of the son of the couple she could bring herself to address only as "Mr. and Mrs. Ford."

The father exchanged a few words with old friends—Edison, John, and Horace among them. Henry had nothing in particular to say that anyone recalled. He had not expected Edsel to be married so soon, but perhaps it would speed his son's growing up to Henry's expectations of him, the right kind of man to fulfill Ford's mission in the company that he preferred to call "the institution."

Henry had already said his piece for the newspapers this week. He had a weakness for sounding off on whatever subject sprang to mind if a reporter was in earshot. Critics called it his "madness for publicity," but he justified it to himself as free advertising, preferable to paying for it any day. Twenty-four hours ago, he had offered a thought in the running debate that engrossed the nation: whether or not the entire United States should be voted "dry." There was no doubt where he stood when nothing headier than grape juice was served at his table, but one of the arguments of the "wets" held that Prohibition would create mass unemployment. Henry essayed to lay that scare to rest.

"Denatured alcohol," he declared, "is a cleaner, nicer, better fuel for automobiles than gasoline, and I believe denatured alcohol is the coming fuel for internal-combustion engines." He went on to picture an evil industry converted to something closer to sanctity under headlines that shouted:

FORD SAYS BREWERIES
CAN MAKE DENATURED
ALCOHOL FOR AUTOS
*Employees Need Not Be Thrown
Out of Work by Prohibition Vote*

He was a hero of the Prohibition Party and the Anti-Saloon League, whose pressures up to the present had succeeded in drying up twenty-four states, forcibly putting more than 32,000,000 citizens on the wagon or driving them to the bootleggers. At that time, the country's production of gasoline was an adequate 300,767,000 tons a year. Little more than half a century later, when 17,000,000 barrels of oil were consumed every day in the land and the Arabs clamped down on exports from their wells, scientists would return to Henry's thinking about the uses of denatured alcohol.

His reputation as a dry was such that among fellow Prohibitionists he was boosted as a write-in candidate for the cause in the presidential elections that would be here next Tuesday, with Charles Evans Hughes fatuously confident that he would oust Woodrow Wilson from the White House. Henry, otherwise a Republican, was for Wilson, principally on the strength of Wilson's campaign slogan, "He kept us out of war." As a political apprentice, Wilson had publicly denounced the automobile as a rich man's plaything, ruinous to the morale of the workingman, but Wilson had been persuaded otherwise as President.

The automakers had learned the tricks of the railroad tycoons in cajoling congressmen into providing government nourishment for the industry. That summer, Wilson signed the Federal Aid Road Act, matching dollar for dollar all funds spent by the states on highway construction. Henry was not impressed. If his rivals in the business wanted to get involved with lobbying and road building, that was their affair. Any time he had something to tell the President, he would go to Washington himself.

"He kept us out of war" appealed to the Germans, too. The stalemate on the Western Front in the War of the Nations had been broken at last, and Germans and French were joined in annihilating battle east of Verdun. Kaiser Wilhelm's statesmen, fearful that the United States would abandon neutrality, had asked Wilson to mediate earlier in the fall. He declined to make any move until after Tuesday's election.

Henry was less circumspect. The country continued to resound with one of his recent *obiter dicta*. "We've got the war fever over here because they've got a war over there. We are crazy about spending millions of dollars on an army and navy . . . and somebody has got to pay the bill. Who? The workingman."

His personal crusade for peace was a little more than one year old. It dated back to an afternoon in August when a reporter called on Henry and was taken off by him for a walk in the woods. The conversation turned to the war, the piling up of pointless casualties, the Cunarder *Lusitania* sunk by U-boats, with 128 Americans among the drowned, German poison gas drifting over the mud of Ypres.

"I'd give all my money—and my life—to stop it," Henry said.

"How about quoting you?"

"Go ahead."

"What shall I say?"

Henry's speech was always laconic, but he trusted his visitor to dress it up. "You know how I feel. You say it for me. Make it as strong as you like." On August 22, 1915, he picked up the Sunday newspaper and read:

HENRY FORD TO PUSH

WORLDWIDE CAMPAIGN

FOR UNIVERSAL PEACE

*Will Donate Life and Fortune to Combat
Spirit of Militarism Now Rampant*

The quotes would not have sounded out of place coming from the lips of Eugene Victor Debs, champion of 500,000 Socialist voters; Debs would be handed a ten-year jail sentence before peace was finally written: "War is murder—desolating, destructive, cruel, heartless, and unjustifiable. . . . Militarism draws its foul sustenance from the blood, labor, and toil-earned goods of common people. . . . It is a pity that most men who pose as standing for the best things and pray in the churches to God for peace on Sunday are busy Monday getting contracts to make shot and shell to destroy the loftiest thing in the world—human life, happiness, and prosperity."

In the middle of the week, when mailbags filled a room of the house, Henry recalled the reporter, Theodore Delavigne. "You got me into this. You'd better go back to your office and resign. Then come and get me out of it."

Not even Henry was always certain that he meant what he said; in this instance, he did not. He showed no sign of wishing to be extricated from the crusade when a determined, dowdy journalist from Budapest named Rosika Schwimmer, who had pawned some jewelry to buy her steamship ticket, arrived in Detroit low on cash but high in resolve and contrived to be invited to lunch in the executive dining room at Highland Park.

In her high-button shoes and shiny serge costume, the Amazonian Jewess was a battler for the causes of votes for women, birth control, and peace by mediation. She had come, she said, to lay before Mr. Ford her private memoranda proving that the Allies and the Central Powers were both ready for a negotiated settlement.

"I think I'd like my wife's judgment on this," he said and asked Madame Schwimmer over to the house to meet Clara and see her geraniums. He left the two women alone "to talk things over." When he returned, he found Clara converted. She would pay for a deluge of telegrams to President Wilson, demanding continuous mediation until hostilities ceased. Henry approved what they thought it would cost: $10,000. He could follow Rosika to New York tomorrow afternoon, Saturday. "Whatever we decide to do," he said, "New York is the place for starting it." He had shaken the axis of the earth three times already: with Lizzie; a revolution in mass production by way of the assembly line; and the $5.00 day. He was bubbling with anticipation, ready for an even greater *coup de main*, but he had no notion yet of the form it should take.

As a companion on the journey East, he had another believer in continuous mediation: Louis Lochner, fragile young Middle West director of the pacifist American Peace Federation and a visitor to the Fords' home at the same time as Madame Schwimmer. Henry used him as a sounding board for some of the fancies that were spinning in his head. "Men sitting around a table, not men dying in a trench, will finally settle the differences." This went over well with Lochner. "Make a note of that," said Henry. "We'll give that to the boys when we get to New York."

He checked into his favorite Manhattan hotel, the Biltmore, next door to Grand Central Station. He left there for a Sunday luncheon farther downtown at the Hotel McAlpin. At the table,

Rosika, Lochner, and other more distinguished enthusiasts began to shape a plan of action. It should be highlighted, they decided, by sending a commission to check out the situation in Europe with the President's blessing if that were obtainable.

"Why not a special ship to take the delegates over?" Lochner suggested. Henry rose to that like a kite lofted by a gale. At the first opportunity, he summoned steamship agents to work out for him the cost of chartering an ocean liner, while he fixed a Tuesday appointment at the White House. The pace of it all alarmed most of the group, notably Jane Addams, the resolute founder of Hull House settlement. He left Rosika to negotiate the terms of hiring *Oscar II* of the Scandinavian-American Line, which would sail as his peace ship nine days later in a campaign that ultimately cost him $500,000.

In the presidential study, Henry sat himself unasked in an armchair and swung his left leg over its arm. Wilson could do little else but relax, too, unbending so far as to confess that he enjoyed hearing a good story or two after office hours. Henry proceeded to tell one of his own creating.

Every vaudeville comic had an armful of Ford jokes. "What's the matter?" asks a farmer, coming upon a motorist peering up a tree. "I was cranking my flivver and the darned thing flew off the handle." . . . This geezer goes looking for a job, and he says, "I'm the guy who used to put part No. 453 on all cars at the Ford factory." "Why did they fire you?" "One day, I dropped my monkey wrench, and by the time I'd picked it up, I was sixteen cars behind." . . . "You don't need a speedometer on a Model T. At ten miles an hour, your lamps rattle; at twenty, the fenders rattle; at twenty-five, the windshield starts to rattle; and faster than that, your bones join in."

Henry spun a tale for Wilson about driving past a cemetery, where the sexton was spading out an enormous grave. Why so big? It was for a fellow who'd given the order in his will that he must be buried at the wheel of his Ford. And why was that? "Because it had never gotten him into a hole it couldn't get him out of."

The President chuckled, and Henry explained what he wanted of him. The atmosphere suddenly chilled. Wilson reiterated his position: The time was inopportune for mediation. He could not commit himself to the peace ship enterprise.

"If you feel you can't act, I will," snapped Henry. Leaving the White House, he shook his head. "He's a small man," Henry lamented.

At ten o'clock next morning, Henry presided over a press conference at the Biltmore in what the reporters would quickly label "the stop the war suite." He fumbled with a few introductory words himself before he had Lochner and others supply the details. "A man should always try to do the greatest good to the greatest number, shouldn't he? I want to crush militarism and stop wars for all time. I intend to get the boys out of the trenches by Christmas."

It was a season of ambiguity in the mood of the nation. U-boat attacks in the Atlantic had heightened the hostility many Americans felt toward Germany, and British propagandists headquartered in their country's embassy in Washington played on that feeling. But the average citizen's overwhelming desire was to stay out of the conflict and avoid anything that smacked of interference in what was seen as a strictly European problem. From the onset of his crusading, a chorus of newspaper editorialists and speechmakers who counted themselves as shapers of public opinion poured scorn on Henry as a meddler—well-intentioned, maybe, but potentially dangerous. Theodore Roosevelt, aching from old wounds and lust for a new war, grunted, "Mr. Ford's visit abroad will not be mischievous only because it is ridiculous."

Henry put some of his New York staff, Lochner, and above all Rosika in charge of arrangements and went back to Detroit. Clara was appalled by the surge of criticism that was splashing over her husband's head. Edsel expressed no strong opinion either way, but his mother urged Henry to abandon ship. For once, he paid no attention to her.

On the eve of sailing, she spent half the night in the Biltmore suite in a last weeping effort to dissuade him. It was useless. In a Model T touring car, the three Fords set off for the Hoboken pier. Supposing the expedition failed, one reporter asked.

"I'll start another. . . . We've got peace talk going now, and I'll pound it to the end."

Fifteen thousand people had gathered on the pier. A band was blasting out, "I Didn't Raise My Boy to Be a Soldier." There stood William Jennings Bryan, Wilson's first Secretary of State

and a confirmed pacifist himself, clutching a caged squirrel that
someone had handed him. But he would not join the eighty or so
delegates and score or two of pressmen due to voyage with Henry,
who was tossing American Beauty roses at the crowd. Neither
would Edison, who went aboard to say farewell, even though
Henry promised, "I'll give you a million dollars if you'll come,"
then repeated the offer because Tom was so deaf he hadn't heard
him the first time.

Tom and Mina watched from the pier next to Clara and Edsel
as *Oscar II* pulled away. Clara began to cry once more.

Henry walked the decks for exercise no matter what the winter
weather. One morning, a wave drenched him, and he retired to
the seclusion of his stateroom with a heavy cold for the rest of the
crossing. Rosika filled the gap in the ranks by quarreling with the
corps of newspapermen, who suspected that she was censoring
their outgoing Marconigrams. She retaliated by charging them
with passing word to Henry that she eavesdropped at keyholes.

When the ship docked at Oslo, he vanished into a hotel bedroom. Four days later, in Christiana, he summoned the local press
to talk not about the peace mission but about the new tractor he
was working on, whose secrets he would gladly donate to arms
manufacturers so that they could make more money than by pro-
liferating weapons of death. The following day, forty-eight hours
before Christmas, he slipped away to Bergen, where he could
hurry aboard a liner that was sailing for the United States.

"Guess I had better go home to mother," he sniffled through
his cold. "You've got this thing started and can get along without
me." By the time he reached New York, all trace of the sniffles
had disappeared. The unabated tide of ridicule didn't bother him,
he said. "The best fertilizer in the world is weeds." Somewhere on
his travels, his eye had caught a broken-down antique clock, which
he contrived to have shipped back with him to add to his collection. It would be well worth fixing, with its jeweled movements,
dials that included a perpetual calendar, and a verse cut into its
metal that appealed to him:

> *Slowly, slowly, always on,*
> *Regrets are vain*
> *When time has gone.*

Two weeks before Edsel's marriage, Rosika arose from what had become the grave of continuous mediation with a fresh accusation. She was living "ill and in want" in Sweden, said a news agency dispatch from Stockholm, and insisting that for all her trouble she had received not one red cent from Henry.

This was the very least of the matters exercising his brain as he meandered among the more elderly wedding guests at the Clays', less important even than the lawsuit he had filed against the mason contractor who, he claimed, had overcharged him for work done in building the Fords' latest home, "Fair Lane," in Dearborn, fifteen miles from Detroit's center, in which they had been living since December. Henry would shortly enjoy the brief satisfaction of hearing a judge knock several thousand dollars off the bill, which brought the total down close to a million dollars.

Such amounts of cash were common currency for Ford. It happened to be the sum he was demanding in a much weightier action filed less than two months ago, for libel against the Chicago *Tribune*. It had come about as an indirect result of the call-up of U.S. troops to patrol the border with Mexico, where Pancho Villa's raids and General "Black Jack" Pershing's retaliations threatened war. When a *Tribune* correspondent questioned a Ford director, Frank Klingensmith, about the fate of company employees who answered the call to duty, he was told—incorrectly —that they would automatically forfeit their jobs. Henry had no such intention.

FLIVVER PATRIOTISM, the *Tribune*'s headline jeered, and an editorial, "Ford Is an Anarchist," recommended that Henry should move his operations to Mexico. "If Ford allows this rule of his shop to stand," thundered the writer, "he will reveal himself not merely as an ignorant idealist, but as an anarchistic enemy of the nation which protects him in his wealth."

So the bridegroom's father, swimming in a sea of trouble, hadn't much cause to celebrate. "It is the fashion," one observer noted, all too accurately, "to make fun of Ford, to decry him and belittle him." The company's thirteenth birthday had fallen in the same week that Edsel and Eleanor announced their engagement. At that time, Henry was undecided about whether or not to quit the automobile industry for good. Should he sell out to the House of Morgan, which he had scorned all his working life? But if he did, what would he and Edsel do to occupy their time?

Young Mr. Ford and his twenty-year-old bride left at midnight. They would be gone for two months while their new house—unimposing by big-rich standards—was finished on Iroquois Avenue. Their first stop would be San Francisco, driving there not in a Ford but in a more luxuriously equipped Mercer, such as Wilson used. Then the Fords would be off to Honolulu. The self-effacing man, whose name nearly half a century hence would be equated with corporate blundering, and the wife whose character was as yet unknowable, looked more like bourgeoisie than participants in a great fortune as they waved good-bye.

Readers the following morning had to hunt through their newspapers to find an account of the wedding. The front pages were dominated by a different story, told under black type two inches high. John and Horace, hungry for cash for themselves and their new business, were demanding that Henry disgorge three quarters of the company's cash surplus, amounting to about $39,000,000, in dividends even if this spelled disaster for him.

DODGE BROTHERS SUE FORD, said the headlines. They hadn't mentioned a word about *that* as they nibbled wedding cake last night.

Chapter Two

The Farmer's Boy

Winter came early to Detroit in 1893. The cold set in by the beginning of November, and the long walk home over slithery sidewalks at six in the morning from his job as night engineer at the Edison Illuminating Company's power station chilled Henry to his sparely covered bones. The pay, $45 a month and no raise since he started, did not amount to much either when a third of it went in rent for his lowly flat at 570 Forest Avenue, and there would be new expenses when Clara had her baby, expected any day.

For more than 5½ years of married life, she had been compelled to count pennies to keep him suitably dressed for work beneath the curl-brimmed derby that marked his superiority over a common, cloth-capped workingman; to buy the odds and ends of hardware required for the contraptions he was forever tinkering with; to pay for the succession of moves from one address to another—this was at least the fourth place they had rented in the city.

She didn't complain because she had married him believing that one day he would make something of himself, even if so far he had no sharply defined goal in mind except to make more money. One advantage his job provided was the hideout he made for himself in a storage room back of the Edison plant. Here he spent his unoccupied hours figuring how to make a one-cylinder gasoline engine out of scrap. He took care not to push himself too hard. There was always time to spare for joking with the cronies who hung around, especially on Saturday nights, strangely drawn by his sheer presence. He had no trouble getting one of them, Fred Strauss, whose friendship went back to days when they were boys employed in a local machine shop, to do the bulk of the work on his latest brainchild. After six weeks of desultory labor, the little gimcrack motor, with an ignition that sparked like a cigar lighter, was about ready for testing.

Henry kept calm when Clara's pains began, and he went hurrying for Dr. David O'Donnell. The doctor's fees—$10 for a confinement—were as meager as his practice in this working-class neighborhood. He could not afford a horse and buggy like his more prosperous colleagues. Dr. O'Donnell arrived by bicycle, with his black bag strapped to the handlebars.

Clara made no complaint, though the birth was difficult enough for a nurse to be kept in the flat on round-the-clock call for two weeks after the baby was delivered on November 6. Finding the $4.00 a week for her wages imposed an unexpected strain on Clara's budgeting. She was either unable or unwilling to bear further children. An operation she underwent a few years later in Detroit General Hospital may have had some relevance in this. Or perhaps one child was all that her husband, mindful of his mother's death, really wanted. Henry, who liked to settle all scores for or against him, remembered the doctor's solicitude. From the time he finally bought a car to the day of his death, it was serviced free of charge.

Edsel was Henry's choice for his new son's name, not William for his own father or John or Robert for his brothers. Long-nosed Edsel Ruddiman and he became best friends after seven-year-old Henry started in at the Scotch Settlement School, a 1½-mile walk from the Ford family farmhouse. They struggled together through McGuffey Readers under the eyes of their seventeen-year-old teacher, Miss Emily Nardin; slipped notes to each other, written in their secret code; and went skating when the ponds froze. As adolescents, they spent Sunday evenings trying out a dozen different churches, searching the congregations for likely looking girls more than for inspiration to faith.

Young Ruddiman went on to high school and college, which Henry never did, and their paths crossed less and less frequently.

His friend was a degreed pharmacist and still single when Henry and Clara were married. He did not bother to let Ruddiman know anything of that. For his part, the older Edsel confessed years afterward, when Ford had become an international celebrity, he found him to be "just an ordinary person." Even in the matter of naming his son, the workings of Henry's mind were mysterious.

Bryant, the baby's middle name, was a more obvious choice. That was in honor of Melvin Bryant, Clara's parent, who farmed forty acres in the township of Greenfield, adjoining Dearborn.

During the second postnatal week, Clara's anxiety about paying the bills was eased. Henry came home with the news that he had been promoted. He would not have to use the letters of recommendation that he had been soliciting from people since Clara was halfway through her pregnancy to help him get the position of chief engineer. He had done such a commendable job fixing the steam boilers at the Edison Company's main powerhouse that he was being transferred there, his salary almost doubled. As part of the celebration, he ordered a player piano, bought on time for $355 with seven years to pay, and set off househunting again, looking for something nearer his place of work, a few blocks from City Hall.

In mid-December, the Fords moved into a two-family house at 58 Bagley Avenue, five minutes' walk through the snow from the generating plant. Clara was spared the work of packing and unpacking this time; moving men were hired for the task. Behind the house there was a storage building for coal, to be shared with the other tenant, old Felix Julien. It would make a handy replacement for the hideaway Henry had been forced to abandon. He brought home with him the engine Fred Strauss had put together, using a length of gas pipe as a cylinder and a flywheel stripped from an old lathe.

The first primitive motor stirred to life seven weeks after Edsel had gone through a similar process. After supper on December 24, Clara was in the kitchen, making an early start on tomorrow's dinner for themselves and her family, who were coming in to spend Christmas with them. Henry interrupted her. He wanted to try out the engine, whose spark plug consisted of two ends of bared wire. The coalshed had no electric light, and he had no battery. He needed the kitchen power plug, and Clara would have to help by dripping gasoline into the metal cup that functioned as a makeshift carburetor.

The turkey stuffing, if that was what she was preparing, was put aside. He clamped to the sink the wooden board on which the contrivance was mounted. Clara followed directions, and Henry spun the flywheel. Edsel was asleep in his crib in a bedroom next door. She was afraid that the fumes of the gasoline would choke him. Her alarm grew when the engine began to shudder, shooting out flame and shaking the sink. Henry had her shut the intake valve to choke off the fuel supply. It was enough that it worked for a minute or so. He fancied now that he would get going on a new two-cylinder model that he could use to propel his bicycle.

He had no patience with anybody's fears about the perils of gasoline engines. When the original Ford factory was finally started, carburetors were tested in an airless shanty with no ventilators. Many a workman would have to be hauled out unconscious, overcome by exhaust fumes, and dumped on the grass or in the snow until he came to. Henry did nothing about it. He considered carbon monoxide the best treatment in the world for a case of tuberculosis or a heart condition.

Both parents doted on the baby. Providing security and comfort for Edsel took precedence over everything else in the household. To make extra dollars to spend on the child, Henry taught classes in metalworking at the YMCA—with no great distinction, in one student's estimation—and sold his little engine to a man who installed it in his boat. He lingered after breakfast to play with his son, which made Henry notoriously late for work in the mornings. The two-cylinder version for his bicycle was never built. For two years, Henry's fitful experiments were at a standstill, the impetus all but spent when he received another raise, to $100 a month.

He bought a camera, and pages of the family photo album overflowed with pictures of Edsel. A fat-cheeked cherub in fresh-ironed white, looking uncannily like his own firstborn son twenty-five years later, sits contentedly on the knee of his mother, who is wearing finger curls and bombazine. Edsel, hair to his shoulders, glances backward as he pedals his tricycle around a clutter of toys. Under a big straw hat with a Tom Sawyer rake to it, he stands holding a rod and line, "after having caught his first string of fish, Orion Lake," as Clara's inscription testifies. Every Christmas, there was a tree until Henry's ambition caught fire again and an end had to be called for the time being to such luxuries.

His son must enjoy a childhood and more particularly a father different from Henry's, a man he invariably spoke of in later years as having been antagonistic and blind to Henry's potential.

Bearded, blue-eyed William Ford, an Irish immigrant of English Protestant stock from County Cork, was thirteen years older than his wife, Mary, *née* Litogot, an orphan adopted by another family from the same part of Ireland, childless Patrick and Margaret O'Hern. She was married at twenty-two in 1861, two weeks after Confederate cannons' pounding of Fort Sumter in Charleston Harbor set off the Civil War. Her firstborn child, a son, was born and dead before the year was over.

So Henry's arrival on July 30, 1863, in the clapboard farmhouse that stood on ninety acres of still only partially cleared land by the village of Dearbornville was tense for Mary and the midwife. At Gettysburg, the count of the Union and Rebel dead had scarcely been completed. During the next decade, Mary Ford was delivered of five more children, beginning with John, born nineteen months after Henry, then Margaret, Jane, William, and Robert.

"The first thing I remember in my life," Henry reminisced in a diary entry much later, "is my father taking my brother and myself to see a bird's nest under a big oak twenty rods east of our home and my birthplace. John was so young that he could not walk. Father carried him. . . . I remember the nest with four eggs and also the bird and hearing it sing." Henry was then on the verge of three.

He recorded no further fond recollections of William Ford. The parent Henry idolized was his overworked, bird-quick mother —sewing, knitting, making soap, butter, and candles, tending to the chickens and the vegetable garden, looking after her increasingly feeble foster parents (who lived with the Fords), and teaching her eldest child to read before he entered school.

Henry's second memory of childhood took him back to the summer when he was six and suffering from "the ague." "I would be all right in the forenoon and would have chills, fever, and shake in the afternoon. I remember my father hauling wood and seeing the red-head woodpecker, swallows, bluebirds, and robbins

[sic]." It was "Grandfather" O'Hern who "told me the name of all these birds." Either William Ford was too busy, or Henry felt neglected.

William felled stands of virgin woodland with the help of ox teams and hauled the cut trees down the splintered plank road to the city on Saturdays for sale as fuel and lumber. He harvested wheat, oats, corn, hay, and crops of apples and peaches, selling the surplus. He kept cows, pigs, sheep, and horses; care of the horses was one of the jobs he allotted his oldest son. William hired out his skills as a carpenter, equipped with a workshop and the tools of a former trade, to add to his savings and more acres to his holding.

"I never had any particular love for the farm," Henry recalled; "it was the mother on the farm I loved." It was she who "presided over it and ruled it. She made it a good place to be."

Shoveling out the stables repulsed him. "I don't want to," was his constant complaint, which, coming from the eldest of their children, won little sympathy. "My mother used to say, when I grumbled about it, 'Life will give you many unpleasant tasks to do; your duty will be hard and disagreeable and painful to you at times, but you must do it. You may have pity on others, but you must not pity yourself. Do what you find to do, and what you know you must do, to the best of your ability.' "

The advice ran off his back like water. Rebellion showed itself in his behavior at the Scotch Settlement School, where throwing a dart into a boy's leg (and being jabbed with a penknife in retaliation) had to be condemned as more than a boyish prank. He spent hours on what the pupils knew as the "mourner's bench" at the front of the classroom directly under the teacher's gaze. He could do arithmetic on paper or in his head well enough and memorize poems from McGuffey, but he never did learn how to spell.

No Ford child felt the swish of a cane at home. His sister Margaret, four years younger, who would become the bride of Edsel Ruddiman's brother James, thought of her father as a strict disciplinarian and Henry an obedient son, which did not gibe at all with his own impressions.

To him, the figure of respected authority was Mother. "I was never whipped, but I was punished when I deserved it. . . . I was made to pay the penalty of my misconduct. I was humiliated. Shame cuts more deeply than a whip. Once, when I told a lie, Mother made me suffer the experience of a liar. For a day I was treated with contempt, and I knew I had done a despicable thing. There was no smiling at or glossing over my shortcomings. I learned from her that wrongdoing carries with it its own punishment. There is no escape."

If anything, he was favored instead of being burdened with a growing boy's chores on a family farm. He found how to coax his brothers and his school friends into doing his jobs for him. His father laid down no hard-and-fast rules for Henry. William was up at six most mornings to make a start in the barn. His son was allowed to stay in bed.

"There was no particular reason for it," Margaret Ruddiman recalled, "except that he was sleepy. The rest got up and went about their duties, and he stayed in bed. That didn't happen every day, but it was a habit that he formed."

It was Mother "who always said that I was a born mechanic," he wrote half a century after the event, identifying with her. It seemed to him that she was able to read his mind to tell what he would do next. Margaret confirmed that. Mother and son both operated by intuition. "I've answered questions before they were asked," he would boast; she had the same ability to divine intentions. "Henry," she would say on a May morning, "you are not to think of going swimming with the other boys after school. It is much too early, and the water is still too cold."

Following the inclination of self-made men to predate the achievements of childhood, he set seven as the age at which he developed what he called his "mechanical turn." He was at least three years older than that and had been transferred from the Scotch Settlement to the Miller School when he dammed a ditch to work an improvised water wheel, connected by a rake handle to a rusty coffee grinder, which chewed up potatoes and hunks of clay.

More accurately, he supervised his schoolmates' labor on the project. "He didn't do much," Margaret remembered. "He only told them what to do, and they very willingly did it." Overnight, by his account, the dam overflowed, flooding a field, and the farmer ran raging to the schoolmaster. His sister corrected the perspective. "It was just a small dam."

He was the straw boss again in making a steam engine with turbine blades of tin, wood blocks for couplings, and a ten-gallon can serving as the boiler. He had ten other lads down at the railroad tracks picking up coal for the fire. The turbine spun faster and faster until the boiler exploded. Three apprentice engineers were scalded, one boy was knocked cold by a metal fragment hitting him in the belly, Henry suffered a hole in his lip, and the school fence caught fire.

Though it fell to William to fix the fence, he gave his son a free hand with the tools he kept at the farm. "I had a kind of workshop with odds and ends of metal for tools before I had anything else," said Henry when the time came to write his autobiography. The total omission of his father's contribution was another correction of Margaret's. "Since Father was handy with tools, he was very proud that Henry had inherited his ability to fix things. . . . He was very understanding of Henry's demands for new tools for the shop, and ours was one of the best-equipped in the neighborhood."

Henry forged hinges for the gates and concocted a device for opening and closing them without dismounting from a wagon. He repaired harnesses, helped the neighbors with their repairs, and continued complaining that there was "too much work on the place."

Mary Ford became the inspiration and symbol of all virtue for her son on the day she died, March 29, 1876, twelve days after the birth and death of her eighth child, an unnamed boy. She was thirty-seven years old, a seemingly healthy woman. Stirred by the passions and inchoate reasoning of impending adolescence, Henry could only have blamed his father, who from now on must be the focus of his hatred. The house was like a watch without a mainspring. "I thought a great wrong had been done me," Henry remembered. He could foresee no possibility of future happiness.

He always thought of the house exclusively as his mother's. "My father just walked into that place. That belonged to my mother. That was my mother's home." She was buried in the little cemetery on Joy Road. Her youngest surviving child, four-year-old Robert, followed her there within the next twelve months. William's sister Rebecca and then her daughter Jane helped him care for his family until Margaret was old enough to take over.

The habit of order and prescribing a place for everything, which he attributed to his mother, would grow into an obsession. "People often ask," he commented long afterward, "why we keep our shops immaculately clean. My mother was a great woman for orderliness and cleanliness. I want my shops to be as clean as my mother's kitchen." Violations of the rule were cause for a Ford worker's dismissal.

Turbulence of emotion made the mind of the thirteen-year-old boy like soft wax, ready for imprinting. Two events that summer marked him for life. Mary's death, coinciding with the hardest season of work on a farm, increased the load on everyone in the family. It might have been then that Henry had his first taste of spring plowing. "I have followed many a weary mile behind a plow," he would say afterward, "and I know all the drudgery of it. What a waste it is for a human being to spend hours and days behind a slowly moving team of horses. . . ."

Just before his birthday, he was riding with his father on the weekly wagon run into Detroit when they overtook a steam engine coughing along under its own power. Neither of them had seen anything like this before. Similar engines, used for threshing grain or sawing timber, were pulled into the fields by dray horses. The engineer stopped to make way for the wagon.

Henry's account of what happened next contained the usual implied denigration of William Ford: "I was off the wagon and talking to the engineer before my father, who was driving, knew what I was up to." He wanted to know how fast the engine turned over. "Two hundred times a minute," said the soot-streaked man on the iron platform behind the boiler. Curiosity was not satisfied until he had promised Henry that one day soon *he* could try his hand at shoveling coal into the firebox, sliding open the throttle, releasing the brake, and steering the marvelous machine up and down the road.

That summer and next, the engineer often let the enraptured boy take over for a drive. Henry learned his name, Fred Reden, "a good and kind man," who convinced him "that I was by instinct an engineer." The seeds of an outrageous ambition were germinating: Abolish the despicable beasts that to him exemplified the drudgery of farm living that had helped kill his mother! As an act of atonement, to vindicate her faith in him, he would engineer machines to obliterate the horse.

Within a few days of his encounter with the miraculous steam engine, a second act of revelation occurred. He was given a watch, probably as a birthday present by his father. Its importance for him lay not in telling time by it but in his taking it apart and assembling it over and over again until he knew every piece and its function. Books were useless for learning how things were made, which was what he had to know to become a self-taught engineer, to liberate himself and honor his mother's memory.

It took two years before he felt qualified as a watch repairer, using miniature files homemade from knitting needles, and tweezers shaped from a steel stay in a woman's discarded corset— could it have been Mary's? He could pick up the scattered cogs and springs of a watch and have it in working order within thirty minutes. Friends and neighbors heard of his expertise and invited him to repair their clocks and pocket timepieces. Taking money for his work was unthinkable; the cause was sacred.

Later, he was to weave all this into the impelling legend of the harsh father, who, said Henry, forbade him to go calling around the neighborhood after his chores were done for the day, fixing clocks as a courtesy, because William insisted that his son should be paid for his labors. "I couldn't quit, so I used to go to my room at nine o'clock at night and wait until I thought my father had gone to sleep. Then I used to creep out of the house, go to the barn, saddle a horse, and ride away—sometimes many miles—to a place where I knew there was a watch or a clock to repair. Many a time I did not get home until three o'clock in the morning. Yes, I always worked on the farm the next day just the same. The loss of sleep did not seem to hurt me any."

Again Margaret amended the record. "Father never forbade him to repair neighbors' watches. I never knew of him going out at night to get watches and bringing them back to repair them. . . . I know that Father never told Henry he should charge for the work he did."

Henry gave the myth verisimilitude in three-dimensional form when he set about restoring his birthplace as a museum exhibit. Up there in his bedroom, he had a workbench built, identical, by his account, with the original at which he sat working in secret on the forbidden watches, with the lantern set between his legs to ward off the cold on wintry nights. That was the wrong place for it, Margaret said.

"There was nothing upstairs except his dresser and a little stand that he kept trinkets in, and his bed, of course." The workbench, in truth, had stood under the east window in the kitchen, the window with a clear view down the road, where his mother used to watch for William coming back from town. The orphan's love for her husband had deep roots. Henry wanted nobody, especially himself, to be reminded of that.

Weeks into months, months into years. It was a matter of counting time before he could finish school and leave home. A job in a machine shop must be the next step in educating himself for his mission. In the family, it was taken for granted that some day he would go to Detroit to learn more about steam engines and their making. His father left the date of departure up to him, once Henry was through at the Miller School when summer recess began in 1879.

"Of course Father was disappointed that Henry did not wish to continue life on the farm," said Margaret, "but if learning about machinery was what he wanted to do, Father would not hinder him." Her brother told a different story, of quarrels and frustration that drove him to ignore William's commands and slip out through the front gate on the first day of December without saying a word to anyone, then walk the nine miles to Detroit, find a room to sleep in, and look for work that would speed his search for the Holy Grail.

He chose to depict himself as a man of impulse, playing hunches, intuitive like Mother. In fact, it was against the grain of his nature to hurry into any unknown situation or put himself at strangers' mercy. Though he would suppress the fact, a job was waiting for him with the Flower Brothers. His father had lined it up in advance for him; the brothers, James, George, and Thomas, were friends of his father who had come out to the farm to buy fresh fruit and vegetables.

Fred Strauss was already employed in their machine shop. "One morning I brought some valves into the office, and while there I saw Henry Ford's father, and Henry was with him. I didn't know who they were, but the next day Henry came to work. . . . He never wanted anybody to know that he had worked at Flower Brothers."

Neither did he have to walk the streets, trying to rent a boardinghouse room affordable on the $2.50 a week he drew in wages. A bed was waiting for him in the home of Aunt Rebecca Flaherty, William's sister, who had stepped in as temporary housekeeper when Mary died. The next time he drove in from the country, William called on his son.

An apprentice in engineering had to serve for four years at pittance wages, and Henry was in too great a hurry to stay that long at any one place. He switched jobs as he switched lodgings "so that I could learn more about different things," and he made extra money in the evenings, repairing watches in a back room at the McGill Jewelry Store on Baker Street. He knew as much about them as about engines. Maybe one could be substituted for the other in the dream of fulfilling his mother's desires. "I thought that I could build a good serviceable watch for around $.30 and nearly started in the business. But I did not because I figured out that watches were not universal necessities. . . ."

To get the price down to $.30, he calculated that he would have to turn out two thousand of them a day. How could he ever hope to sell that many? He discarded the fancy. According to the legend, William had fallen ill and demanded Henry's return to manage the farm. Not so in the testimony of Margaret, who by now was in charge of the household. Their brothers John and William, together with a hired man, were helping Father. Henry came home in 1882, nineteen years old, because he "wanted time to plan and think," she said. He avoided taking on any regular duties in the fields or around the barn. Instead, he hired out as an itinerant driver-mechanic of a threshing crew, traveling through southern Michigan with a steam traction engine like the one Fred Reden operated. Henry, by his own word, was now an "expert."

In Europe, meantime, wholly different means of making a vehicle's wheels turn on a road were being hastened to fruition. "I have created the basis for an entirely new industry," Gottfried Daimler bragged the year after Henry's withdrawal to Dearborn. Karl Benz, too, glimpsed the potentials of the internal-combustion engine. A third German, Nicholaus August Otto, had built and sold hundreds of gas-driven units at home and overseas. Henry carried out some repairs on one of them in 1885. Otherwise, what he learned about this incipient rival to steam propulsion came from copies of such magazines as *English Mechanic* and *American Machinist*, which he read whenever he could lay hold of one.

The farm was his permanent postal address and out-of-season retreat when harvesting was over for another year. He bought a cheap violin and taught himself to play a tune or two. He learned the steps of the waltz and the patterns of square dancing and found to his delight that girls rated him a light-footed partner at any party.

The Greenfield Dancing Club gathered on New Year's Day to celebrate the start of 1885. Henry, unattached, entered the hall as the fiddler was in the middle of an old quadrille and the caller was shouting, "Last gentleman, lead to the right, Around the lady with a grapevine twist," and so on up to, "Promenade to your seats." A dance or two later, Henry asked to be introduced to a tiny, round-faced girl with chestnut hair who had caught his eye. Clara Bryant, aged eighteen and the eldest of ten, had more sense than the other nine children put together, in the opinion of family friends, including Margaret. Clara saw no point in adding one more admirer to her string.

"He made no impression on me at the time, and I didn't see him again for a year," she reported later. She interested him enough to keep him from courting any other girl.

Twelve months and more afterward, he ran across her again at a dance at the Martindale House, a hotel-restaurant on Grand River Road, where crippled George Race tapped out music on a dulcimer and called off the dances in the dim room lit by suspended kerosene lamps and candles in wall sconces. His friend Albert Hutchins, whose pocket watch was the second after his own that Henry ever fixed, was there and happy to reintroduce him to Clara. She was sufficiently taken with this serious young man this time to allow Henry to escort her in to a supper of oyster stew.

Winter was the season when William cleared more land for the plow. Pulling tree stumps from the earth normally required a team of oxen, straining under their yoke. This year, Henry borrowed a Westinghouse traction engine to do the job and coaxed Margaret into bringing Clara to watch. The invitation to take a

ride on the footplate with him was a test. The girl he chose as his
wife must share his fascination with engines. Clara allowed that
she would be glad to climb aboard.

The courtship got under way with no further waste of time.
Mythmakers would claim that the green sleigh he gave her was
made by himself (he bought it from his savings). On Valentine's
Day, a pink satin heart arrived in a frame of varnished walnut
shells, which did appear to be his own handiwork. The letter of
the same date was unmistakably his own:

> Clara Dear, you can not imagine what pleasure it gives
> me to think that i have at last found one so loveing kind
> and true as you are and i hope we will always have good
> success. . . . May Floweretts of love around you bee
> twined And the Sunshine of peace Shed its joy's o'er
> your Minde From one that Dearly loves you H.

He was, Clara thought, "one of the most sentimental men who
ever lived." Margaret approved completely of the match. Her
brother needed a wife who understood his opaqueness, who would
encourage him in his obscure dreams, have patience with his
pranks, and lead him as Mary Ford had done.

William opened the way for his son to marry by giving him the
use of the eighty-acre Moir place, which William had bought
twenty-one years previously. A little house was waiting there—ad-
mittedly a poor kind of dwelling, but it would serve—and the
stands of trees could be cut and sold at a profit. Henry told another story. "My father offered me forty acres of timber land, provided I gave up being a machinist," he said in 1923.

He set up a sawmill to cut planks and cordwood to make the
money he would need for marriage. Clara sewed a wedding dress.
Margaret with the other Ford boys scrubbed and cleaned the
Moir farmhouse. He took Clara to the Johnson's Minstrels show
at the city's Whitney Opera House, and treated her to dinner at
the Martindale to celebrate his acquisition of a special new watch.
He had equipped it with an extra set of hands to keep railroad
time, while the other told the hours in accordance with "farmers'
time," the movement of the sun.

They were married on the bride's twenty-second birthday, April

11, 1888, standing in the bay window of the Bryants' new brick house in Greenfield, which was chockful of guests. "If I were asked to name the most important single factor in his success," Margaret reflected, "I should say that it was his marriage to Clara Bryant." They spent their honeymoon in the freshly furbished Moir cottage, too cramped to suit Clara, who soon was planning a new home, to be built on the farm from lumber cut at Henry's sawmill.

Next to the site, he erected what he later described as "a first-class workshop" where, he said, he assembled first a gas engine similar to the Otto, then another designed for installation on a bicycle, and finally a steam engine that was supposed to haul a wagon or a plow. He gave the first away, he said, and destroyed the rest. Neither Clara nor Margaret could remember his making anything of the sort. He did sow and harvest a few crops, and he did go off to repair engines whenever he was called to Detroit. Clara opened a bank account.

A dozen years had slipped away since the seeds of ambition were planted. Germination resumed on a trip to fix an Otto at a Detroit bottling plant. He came home to tell Clara that he could see how it could be adapted to drive a carriage in place of horses. How could that be? she asked.

"Get me a piece of paper and I'll show you."

On the back of a sheet of organ music, he penciled a rough sketch. Clara thought she understood. Even if she didn't, she had confidence in him. Moments later, she was stunned to hear what else would be involved. Without telling her, he had taken a job that a former shopmate at Flower Brothers' had obtained for him as night engineer at the Edison Company.

Leaving the farm, she said, "nearly broke my heart," but to do otherwise would be a breach of faith. A wage of $45 a week was the main attraction for her husband. "That was more money than the farm was bringing me, and I had decided to get away from farm life anyway. The timber had all been cut." In the late summer of 1891, they loaded the harmonium, the armchair that her mother had brought over with her as an immigrant from England, and the rest of their pieces onto a wagon for the drive into the city.

The "entirely new industry" that Gottlieb Daimler had exulted about was sprouting on both sides of the Atlantic, beyond the scope of Henry's knowing. In France, René Panhard and Emile Levassor had more orders than they could fill for their horseless carriages—"automobiles," as the French called them—which had a Daimler engine in front to propel them. In Lansing, Michigan, the Olds Gasoline Engine Works (founder: Ransom Eli Olds) was in the process of gestating the curved-dash runabout that was due to be the most popular car in the land in the next dozen years. Charles and Frank Duryea were wrestling with the problems inherent in designing and producing a successful gasoline-powered carriage, complete with four-horsepower motor, and socket for a buggy whip.

"It had become apparent," wrote one pioneer, Hiram Percy Maxim, who was about to enter the bicycle business as a prelude to enlisting in these bigger ventures, "that civilization was ready for the mechanical vehicle." Some fifty men in the United States, most of them totally unaware that they were not alone in their endeavors, were contending for the same prize: production of a car that would run and keep on running on roads ankle-deep in summer dust and knee-deep in winter gumbo. As yet, Henry could not be counted as a starter in the race.

The issue of *American Machinist* that went on sale twenty-four hours after Edsel's second birthday inspired his father into edging toward the starting gate. One of the students Henry had taught at the YMCA, eighteen-year-old Oliver Barthel, showed him the magazine. It gave detailed instructions, including illustrations, for making a gasoline engine from bits and pieces of machinery, with further directions to follow in a future issue. Henry took it to work with him to show a fellow Edison employee, George Cato, an electrician. There was, said Henry, "a barrel of money" to be picked up in building a motor like this. Would George like to take a shot at seeing what might be done?

Cato was willing. The skinny chief engineer with the military mustache had a knack for drumming up assistance when he needed it. He enlisted other willing and unpaid help from Barthel; Jim Bishop, who was another Edison Company hand; and Ed "Spider" Huff, a mechanic even skinnier than Henry. By early January, after *American Machinist* published the second installment, they were ready to go. Henry rented a basement room next to the power plant for $.75 a month to provide them with a workshop.

He also paid two months' rent, $30, and invested $94.82 of a total $268.50 spent on tools to set up Fred Strauss in business as part of a long-term plan. Fred would manufacture engines like the first experimental model for sale and also machine parts for the new motor as required, though Fred was not told they were intended for a car.

Like so many of Henry's efforts, progress was fitful at first and punctuated by his prank-playing. One day, his crew began to gasp for breath. Hurrying outside, they found Henry there with a companion, tossing handfuls of sulphur onto hot coals and pumping the sulphurous gas into the room through a knothole. Another time, Henry's ingrained passion for neatness prompted him to spike to the floor the pair of shoes one of his workmates had left behind to litter up the place. Henry was known to do the same to a man's forgotten derby hat. Henry brimmed over with fun, but only when he was the joker. Put on the receiving end, he clammed up, affronted.

Another would-be pioneer was more single-minded in his purpose. George Baldwin Selden, a gray-bearded patent attorney of Rochester, New York, was an engineer *manqué*. After he had tried and failed repeatedly to construct a successful working engine to call his own, he used his professional knowledge to take him along an easier road. In precise legal language, he described the motor and carriage that had eluded him and, with accompanying diagram, filed it as an application to the United States Patent Office. For nearly twenty years, while he kept abreast of developments in Europe, he had added changes to the documents on file so that they might cover any "road carriage" powered by a gasoline engine that an American might devise. In Edsel's birthday month, the deliberately delayed patent was finally issued in Washington. In Selden's hands, it would serve as a pistol aimed at the head of the infant industry to exact a toll in royalties to be paid to him.

Fred Strauss turned out two more engines, one for a friend of Henry's, the other for another boat, but work on the two-cylinder power unit and chassis for Henry's first car was transferred from the rented basement to the coalshed behind No. 58 Bagley Road when the hazards of dripping gasoline into an open carburetor became all too evident. Old Mr. Julien moved his coal and kindling inside to his half of the house, and he let Henry knock out the partition in the shed to provide more space.

As soon as Edsel had fallen off to sleep after supper, Clara would slip out to check on the job. With visitors other than his workmates, she was as guarded as her husband. "Henry is making something, and maybe some day I'll tell you."

The pace increased after he had actually seen a horseless carriage in action on the dark streets in March, steered by another frustrated enthusiast, Cornell-trained Charlie King. King supplied him with four valves from its engine when he stripped it down, which did a little to ease the drain on Henry's pocket. Bills were piling up for lumber—the frame was mostly wood—ironwork, an upholstered bicycle seat, springs, nuts, and bolts, all bought from local suppliers on limited credit. Equipping what he now named his "quadricycle" left Clara short of cash above bare expenses. She struggled to make sure there was enough money left in the bank to keep him going. For the wife who mothered him and felt he could do no wrong, he had undiminished admiration. "She is," he would grin, "the best-looking woman in the whole crowd."

Everyone in the gang of half a dozen men furnished ideas, major and minor, for improving on the *American Machinist* specifications. Cato solved ignition problems. Bishop, cycling over to work in the coalshed every evening, had Ed Huff's help in putting together the chassis. King passed along some thoughts for the transmission and laid hold of a ten-foot length of chain to link the sprockets of the drive shaft with those on the rear axle. Henry made the four wire wheels himself.

In the first nights of June, he caught only an odd hour or two of sleep as their labors neared completion. Around 3 A.M. on the fourth, he and Bishop tightened the last bolt. Rain beat on the roof, but the quadricycle's first run must not wait. A sudden, unforeseen problem threatened to thwart them. Like the classic home hobbyist of later years assembling a boat in the cellar, Henry had built too big. The creature of his efforts would not fit through the door.

He grabbed an ax and demolished part of the front wall. The cascade of bricks brought Clara, who sat up waiting for Henry, on the run under an umbrella. He spun the flywheel to bring the motor to life, cocked a leg over the saddle, and emerged into the downpour, clutching the steering tiller. Bishop mounted his bicycle and pedaled on ahead, ready for emergencies.

Up the road they went as far as Grand Avenue, then made a right turn down to Washington Boulevard. The quadricycle rolled to a halt, its smoking engine sputtering into silence. One of Cato's improvised make-and-break gadgets that fired the mixture of air and gasoline in each cylinder was in want of a new spring. Ford and Bishop trotted off to the Edison powerhouse around the corner to help themselves. They installed a commandeered spring, watched by guests from the Cadillac Hotel who, aroused by the clatter, had come out to investigate.

Clara had a bed ready for Bishop when the pair got home. She was up again to serve breakfast for Edsel and the two men before they went off to the plant, exuberantly planning in the fashion of all amateur devotees what might be done to polish the performance of the homemade wonder.

The first priority, set by Henry for private reasons, was to strengthen the chassis by substituting iron for its wood. Henry hired a new hand at Edison as soon as Henry heard that here was a trained blacksmith who could tackle the job in his spare time. The new frame would support two people. Henry replaced the bicycle saddle with a carriage seat. It was time to show off the machine to his father and impress him with what he had achieved at last at the age of thirty-three in giving shape to his mother's hopes for him, instead of continuing enchained by William as a farmer.

Clara put his best long dress on Edsel and clutched him on her lap for the Sunday ride to the farm, the quadricycle's first venture into the countryside. The car weighed only five hundred pounds, and its wheels were more closely set than a wagon's, which meant driving at an alarming angle, with one side dipping into the ruts, the other tilted high above them. Margaret took a spin and felt bewildered at the speed. "I wondered more than ever at the cool confidence and nerve which Clara displayed," she remembered.

William Ford came out to watch, and the neighbors joined him. He was as fascinated as they were as he looked the car over, listening to his son's explanations of what made it tick, but today he didn't care to risk his neck in a carriage without horses. That came later. Meantime, Margaret reported he could only tell his family and friends how proud he was of Henry.

This was one more episode that had to be rewritten when Henry reconstructed his past to conform with his fantasizing. One employee of a future date recalled Henry's saying, "His dad got mad about it. He didn't like it at all. He thought it was something that would scare all the horses off of the road. He could never get his father interested in his idea."

Some lapse of memory or half-forgotten anecdote led Charles King to claim long afterward that it was he who had been Henry's passenger that Sunday. "I could see that old Mr. Ford was ashamed of a grown-up man like Henry fussing over a little thing like a quadricycle. We'd gone and humiliated him in front of his friends. Henry stood it as long as he could, then he turned to me and said, in a heartbroken way, 'Come on, Charlie, let's you and me get out of here.'"

Yet William had already offered to put money in the car before it was completed. Henry, of course, refused it. "I don't know why my brother told my father not to invest money in the first car, but he just did," Margaret said. Internal conflict impelled Henry to go it alone. He had convinced himself that William's hostility had driven him from the maternal nest. Now that he was in a position to retaliate, on the way to self-achievement, proving his independence of everything represented by William, his father was abandoning *him*, proving that he needed him no longer by dangling cash in front of his nose to keep him working as an engineer.

The tension surfaced in Henry when he displayed his zippy little carriage on the streets of Detroit. He made a practice of chaining it to lampposts in fear that somebody would take off in the frail machine, which symbolized his present aspirations. There was at least one ugly incident when, with gong clanging, he chased a pedestrian down Woodward Avenue.

In August, he and Clara were both feeling less than well when he was sent on a train to New York City as a delegate to the Association of Edison Companies' annual convention. Clara took Edsel to stay with her parents and wrote from Greenfield to "Darling Henry":

It is 5 P.M. now and the baby is having a glorious time
on the lawn. They have been cutting the grass and he
enjoys it, I can tell you. I asked him if he would like to
send Papa a kiss and he said yes paper him one over. Just
like one of his speeches isn't it? . . . I have not been a
bit well since I came out here. I expected it, as I felt so
played out the last few days at home. Am feeling better
this afternoon. Guess I will be all right now. . . . I want
you awfully bad. Edsel's cold is not much better. He
keeps getting a little more. It is supper time so I guess I
will stop. I hope this will find you much better than you
were when you left me Saturday. Dearest husband Good
bye Clara.

At the convention's wind-up banquet, held in the Oriental
Hotel, Manhattan Beach, Long Island, Henry was introduced to
the great one himself, Edison, as "a young man who's made a gas
car," thereby marking himself as something of a curiosity in this
gathering. Hadn't battery-powered "electrics" proved themselves
quieter, more comfortable, and superior in every way to those
coughing, bone-rattling automobiles? Tom, his jacket sprinkled
with snuff, beckoned Henry to sit beside him while he peppered
him with questions about how his ignition system worked. Henry
tried to explain, drawing rough sketches on the back of the menu.
When he had finished, Edison pounded the table. "You have it—
the self-contained unit carrying its own fuel with it! Keep at it!"
On Ford's side, the bond between them was forged on the spot.
Encouragement from the self-taught genius of Menlo Park was exactly what was prescribed to treat Henry's present nervous depression. The more he came to learn about Edison, the closer he felt
drawn to him. Tom, too, had a mother whose qualities impressed
him above his father's, and at forty-seven he was just old enough
—and certainly prestigious enough—to be the father figure Henry
was seeking.
Henry could scarcely wait to pour out news of his meeting to
Clara. "You won't be seeing much of me for the next year," he
warned her. The expectation did not come true. He was looking
ahead to producing cars by the dozens, not in single numbers.

"But before that could come," he acknowledged in a rare moment of frankness, "I had to have something to produce."

He tried shopping around Detroit for men to back him now that most of his own expendable cash was spent. It was a hopeless search. Nobody who knew anything about sound investing would put up a nickel in a venture so chancy. After a thousand miles on the road, the quadricycle, product of half a dozen men's labor, was sold for $200, which Henry kept as seed money for a second try. He consoled himself with the thought that "I had built the car not to sell but to experiment with." He and the buyer "had no trouble agreeing on a price." Henry was far from content with what he had accomplished so far. He had to impress the world with some exemplification of himself worthier than this. Meanwhile, he had to go on casting around for a financial angel.

The pursuit influenced everyone's behavior in the Ford household, as Edsel's own reminiscences testify. "Of course, I don't remember the first automobile that my father made, for he got it running to his satisfaction the year after I was born and sold it two years later. But I do well remember that the mayor of Detroit came to see . . . because I was standing at the window, watching for him to come. It must have been around election time. We had a picture of him in the window."

Mayor William Maybury, an old family friend, was pleased to grant his attentive supporter permission to drive the streets as he wished and never mind about scaring the horses; Henry afterward asserted that this gave him the "distinction of being the only licensed chauffeur in America." Beyond that, Maybury exerted his influence to get loans of a lathe, shafting, and gears to expand the resources of Henry's rented basement, and then rounded up three other interested parties to chip in a skimpy $500 apiece with him to form a company "to manufacture the inventions of said Ford," as the contract among the five of them stated.

Building the second car was still only a part-time preoccupation; Henry held onto his job at the Edison Company, where his pay had been upped to $1,900 a year. The company contemplated in the contract was never organized, since said Ford had no inventions for manufacture. He did, however, uproot his family again to move into new rented quarters in a clapboard house on East Alexandrine Avenue, possibly because of complaints about the nightly racket that emerged from the coalshed on Bagley Road. Edsel was entered in Miss Harriet Lodge's kindergarten, some eight blocks' walk away.

The first quadricycle had been finished in six months; the second, almost identical in appearance except that there was a cover over its motor, took almost two years. It seemed as though Henry was missing the tide. The brief era of the horseless buggy was already over. "Automobile" was the accepted label these days, and the first death under the wheels of one of them was recorded in New York City, when a Mr. H. H. Bliss was struck as he alighted from a streetcar. Investment capital was easier to come by now that the urge to travel on four rubber-tired wheels was proving to be more durable than a rich man's fad.

The first months of 1899 saw eighty factories in operation with combined capital of $388,000,000. Haynes-Apperson, Oakland, Locomobile, and Packard were a few of the shinier names on domestically manufactured models. On East Jefferson Avenue, Olds was building what it claimed, in the usual braggadocio of the infant industry, to be the biggest factory of its kind in the world. The Automobile Club of America was in its birth throes. Scots-born Alexander Winton was pushing sales of his line of vehicles with weekly advertisements under such catch lines as "Away with the whip!" An anonymous versifier spelled out the merits of the latest mode of transportation:

It doesn't shy at papers as they blow along the street;
It cuts no silly capers on the dashboard with its feet;
It doesn't paw the sod up all around the hitching post;
It doesn't scare at shadows as a man would at a ghost;
It doesn't gnaw the manger and it doesn't waste the hay;
Nor put you into danger when the brass bands play.

The most important passenger to be given a ride up on the seat of quadricycle No. 2 was William H. Murphy, a Detroit lumber merchant with money to spare. He termed himself satisfied when Henry dropped him at his front door. "Now we will organize a company," Murphy said. On August 5, the Detroit Automobile Company, with Mayor Maybury among those paying in its $15,000 of working capital, was established. Henry invested nothing but "his whole time and attention" under an employment contract at $150 a month to superintend production of his car.

He let ten days pass before he resigned from his other job. The leave-taking had to be dramatized in his memory. "The Edison Company offered me the general superintendency of the company, but only on condition that I would give up my gas engine and devote myself to something really useful. I had to choose between my job and my automobile. I chose the automobile . . . for already I knew the car was bound to be a success."

His gas-engine experiments, he explained, "were no more popular with the president of the company than my first experimental leanings were with my father." The president, Alexander Dow, related a conflicting version. "Henry even at this time had the dream of an American-made automobile to be in common use." Dow outlined the Edison Company's expansion plans in a friendly talk with Henry; "there was no threat to discharge him . . ."

The Detroit Automobile Company signed a three-year lease on a multi-story building with an option to buy it, installed machinery, began hiring on a payroll that was expected to top one hundred before the year was past, and promised finished cars by October 1. But Henry was not ready. He had no workable design for an automobile.

To get things started, he sketched some axle shaftings, "but they didn't belong to anything," said Fred Strauss, who was one of the first mechanics enrolled. "It was just a stall until Henry got a little longer into it." The superintendent put in only a few hours a day at the plant. He preferred going off into the woods to brood over what to do next.

For the next four months, nothing whatever emerged from the factory as a finished product. The twentieth century dawned, which Americans were confident would be the greatest the world had ever known, and still there was no car. The country believed that soon men would fly, wars would end, diseases would be eradicated, but where were the promised quadricycles? What came forth in mid-January was as surprising as a spider spinning a brick —a boxy delivery wagon weighing more than half a ton, which Henry demonstrated in helter-skelter fashion for a *News-Tribune* reporter. The machinists went on turning out parts for a car that never was.

Just how many vehicles the company completed was uncertain. One mechanic counted three, but Henry subsequently estimated nineteen or twenty, this before the directors called it quits in November. He ducked the crucial meeting. "If they ask for me," he told Fred, "you tell them that I had to go out of town." The next morning, following management orders, Strauss and his workmates fetched every car body to the boiler room, broke them up with a sledgehammer, and fed the wreckage into the furnace. A junk man bought the machine parts, steel castings, and bronze gear wheels that had piled up by the hundreds.

Henry branded the directors as speculators, out to exploit him. "The main idea seemed to be to get the money. . . . I found that the new company was not a vehicle for realizing my ideas but merely a moneymaking concern." The fact was that in its fifteen months of existence, the Detroit Automobile Company lost $86,000, and Henry had lost his only paying job.

He could not see where he could scrape up house rent when he was bent on designing and making cars, not bowing his head and working again for men who didn't appreciate him. There was one place where he might take his family to stay rent-free. Too old for farming at seventy-two, William Ford had moved into the city, with his younger daughter Jane to keep house for him after Margaret was married. On January 8, the Henry Fords went unashamedly to live under his roof.

A student of the human mind would have no trouble in probing the subsurface reasons that drove Henry to this step, ostensibly only a move to cut down expenses, seemingly a reversal of all that he felt toward his father. Ambivalence was basic in his character. Failure in building cars represented a loss comparable in its impact on him with the death of Mary Ford. He had to heal the wound and protect himself from further hurt. He could do that by acting out the role of the good son, prepared to forgive his parent for the imagined wrongs that William had done him. William symbolized the hostility of the universe.

Chapter Three

Up the Hill to Easy Street

There was a hint in Clara's diary that their lease at East Alexandrine Avenue had expired before the end of December, but if that were so, no clue survives as to where they spent the intervening days before they descended on William or what they did with their furniture.

Wednesday, January 9, 1901: "Edsel found lots of his playthings *that he had not seen for some time* [author's italics]. Decorated rocking horse with Xmas tree trimmings."

Friday, January 11: "Snowed all day. Edsel got soaking wet. He and Grandpa played checkers. Edsel cheated awful and beat every game. Went to bed so full of laughs he could not say his prayers."

Saturday, January 12: "Went downtown, got Edsel shoes and leggings. Went to Sheaffers store to hear the music. After supper we tried to learn Grandpa to play cards. Henry got pattents of entire machine."

Sunday, January 13: "Edsel and I went to Sunday School. Met Mrs. Gore. Came home, had dinner, then Henry fixed Edsel's old sleigh to take him coasting, but Edsel would not go, said sleigh was no good. He was sent up stairs for punishment for his pride. He was sorry."

Tuesday, January 15: "Edsel started lessons for first time this morning."

Edsel was seven years old, his mother's evident darling, and this was his first taste of public education; the deceptively titled Farrand Training School was maintained by city taxes. Perhaps it was

Clara's wish to continue the private schooling that was all he had known to date. But finances were too tight for that when Henry's restive imagination had taken a new turn. He was looking to create a totally different kind of automobile. A fast, high-powered car would transform him into a race driver, competing for cash prizes and trophies, too, freed from the onus of working for other men's profit.

Once again, he anticipated earning "a barrel of money." "I expect to make $," he shortly wrote to Clara's brother Milton, "where I can't make ¢s at manufacturing."

After two weeks of school, his mother took Edsel with her when she left to attend to her sister Kate in childbirth. Henry's health often faltered under pressure; he fell ill in her absence. He was growing as thin as Jack Sprat, while Clara had gained so much weight that her feet hurt if she stood too long. "Very nervous about Henry," said her diary. And later: "Got home, and before the train stopped Henry got in. Was never so glad to see him because I expected he would be in bed."

Murphy, the lumber merchant, was the only readily accessible source of fresh risk capital. In spite of the collapse of the Detroit Automobile Company, Henry courted him, and he agreed to back the racer, which at the moment existed only in Henry's head. By May, Henry could make a start and hire Spider Huff and, on part-time, Oliver Barthel, who was to assert that it was he who actually designed and oversaw construction of the twin-cylinder, twenty-six-horsepower car.

"I never knew Henry Ford to design a car," Barthel said half a century later. "I don't think he could. Mr. Ford had no draughting experience at all. He even had difficulty reading a blueprint."

On October 9, with Henry steering and Spider clutching the seat beside him, the latest Ford covered ten laps of the one-mile Grosse Pointe track at an average time of a fraction more than 1.20 minutes for each circuit. The only other starter, Alexander Winton in his forty-horsepower "Bullet," was ahead until blue smoke began streaking from his engine. Henry, better off by something in the region of $1,000 and visibly shaken, declared that once was enough for him, but two weeks later he had his car out again, to try to better Winton's attempt to set a world's speed record at Grosse Pointe that day. On the first turn, Henry lost his nerve and cut the motor.

But winning the first race had the effect he was searching for. The ever-optimistic Murphy and four former stockholders in the defunct Detroit operation incorporated the Henry Ford Company in November, giving him as chief engineer one sixth of the business, with a thousand shares valued at $10 each.

Life with Father could be dispensed with. The Henry Fords moved out, to 332 Hendrie Avenue, a yellow brick house rented for $16 a month, little more than a stone's throw from the Michigan Central Rail Road tracks, and Clara bought her husband and son a new raglan overcoat apiece. "We are keeping house again and very glad to be alone," she wrote to brother Milton. "We have a very nice cosy little house. We did not build on account of Henry building the racer. He could not see to anything else. So we will have to put up with rented homes for a little longer."

Edsel had hopes, too, that the lean times were over. On December 24, he wrote: "Dear Santa Claus—I haven't had any Christmas Tree in 4 years and I have broken all my trimmings and I want some more. I want a pair of roller skates and a book and I can't think of any thing more. I want you to think of something more. Good by—Edsel Ford."

The new company settled into premises on Cass Avenue to manufacture what five of its half-dozen owners believed would be a line of small cars to market. Henry was not interested. He was suffering from an intractable attack of racing fever. To Oliver Barthel, whom he persuaded to come to work full-time on designing, he talked only of building a bigger, faster racer and somehow acquiring a larger share in the business.

Clara shared Henry's acquisitiveness, at least. She considered that "Henry has worked very hard to get where he is." She foresaw a struggle ahead to wring money out of the company. "You know rich men want it all."

The pattern of perverse independence repeated itself. "My company will kick about me following racing but they will get the advertising," Henry said in self-justification. He had Barthel design another speed machine, this time with four giant cylinders, powerful enough to outperform any known rival. Murphy, outraged, threatened to fire Barthel if he took heed of the chief engineer when there was no sign of a commercial, salable automobile anywhere on the horizon.

In an effort to set Henry's thinking straight, Murphy engaged as a consultant to the company an engineer who was regarded as perhaps the finest technician in the entire industry. Henry Martyn Leland, with the beard and bearing of a Confederate colonel, was a perfectionist whose machine shop could turn out engine parts to tolerances of .0001 inch as a matter of routine. Nowhere in Detroit—or anywhere else in the country—was there a factory more superbly equipped than Leland & Falconer's.

With Murphy and the rest of the management backing him, Leland sought to take over the reins from Henry, whose qualifications as a craftsman were skimpy by Leland's standards. When the inevitable showdown came, Henry as usual sloughed off all responsibility. "The main idea seemed to be to get the money," he remembered. "And being without authority other than my engineering position gave me, I found that the new company was not a vehicle for realizing my ideas but merely a moneymaking concern that did not make much money." Leland's name was added to the list of those he would settle with some later day.

As the price of leaving, Murphy gave Ford $900 and Barthel's unfinished blueprints, and willingly consented to drop Ford's name from the title of the business, which was reorganized as the Cadillac Automobile Company. Henry had lasted sixteen months this time around, but a new backer had already showed up in the city.

At twenty-five, dashing Tom Cooper, with thighs like tree trunks, had saved something close to $100,000 from his earnings as America's champion racing cyclist. The only other rider in his class was the equally chunky Barney Oldfield. Itching to get into automobile racing, Cooper provided the funds for Henry to set up shop on Park Place to conceive two cars—the *Arrow*, painted red, and the yellow 999, named after the crack New York Central train that took only eighteen hours to steam between Manhattan and Chicago.

Spider was willing to switch jobs, but notwithstanding Henry's offer to give him 10 per cent of everything he made in the future, Barthel refused. Who could then design the cars? Henry lit on the man he needed in Harold Wills, a young draftsman with ambition burning in his belly, who agreed to come in before breakfast and after supper while he held onto his steady employment at a local machine company.

The two racers they built were flame-spewing monsters, nearly ten feet long, with four cylinders that looked as big as oil drums set on top of the naked motor. Their roar, Henry admitted, "was enough to half kill a man." Thirty-six-inch pneumatic tires, eighty horsepower at 13,000 revolutions per minute, and steering by means of an iron bar with hand grips at either end—all were part of the incredible specifications. Over the rear wheels, a black leather bucket seat was bolted to wood that might have been wrenched from an orange crate. A pair of goggles was the driver's sole protection from death, track dust, and hot oil.

"There was only one seat," Henry recalled. "One life to a car was enough. . . . Going over Niagara Falls would have been but a pastime after a ride in one of them."

Both he and Cooper hesitated to drive the suicidal machines, so Cooper brought happy-go-lucky Barney Oldfield from Salt Lake City. Oldfield had never driven any car, but he was game to try. Spider gave him his first lesson on the Grosse Pointe circuit after 999 had been towed there by a horse.

Arrow had proved a flat failure. "The engine," Barney said, "was as hot as Mother's cook stove." Henry was so disgruntled that he turned it over to a Detroit piano tuner without saying a word about it to Cooper. That would help provide the necessary leverage to terminate the partnership. Ford wanted as soon as possible to get out of yet another situation he had placed himself in.

Two weeks before 999 was scheduled to make its October 25 debut competing against Winton at the wheel of a pepped-up *Bullet* for the five-mile Manufacturers' Challenge Cup, Henry broke with Cooper. He sold him both cars for their cash value and maneuvered him into assuming all debts incurred in their enterprise and paying for the machinery in their shop. Inevitably, he blamed his backer for the sorry outcome.

Her husband, Clara wrote to Milton, "thinks himself lucky to be rid of him. He caught him in a number of sneaky tricks." Tom "was looking out for Cooper and Cooper only. I am glad we are rid of him. I would not like you or Henry to travel with him. He thinks too much of lowdown women to suit me."

On race day, Henry went to the track to beg Barney to stay out of the race to save his skin. "I might as well be dead as dead broke," was Oldfield's response. As he climbed up into the seat of 999, he grinned at Ford. "This chariot may kill me, but they will say afterward that I was going like hell when she took me over the bank." The starting flag sent him off in a fog of oily smoke and flame, slamming into the turns with the throttle wide open, to leave Winton and two other contestants well behind and set a winning record of under 1.06 minutes a mile.

When Edsel was old enough to handle it, he drove 999, but never at full speed. "Nobody knows how fast it will go," he said. Two years after Barney's triumph, Henry personally learned that *Arrow* could hit at least 91.4 miles an hour when he steeled himself to take the reconstructed racer over the cinder-strewn January ice of Lake St. Clair with Spider clinging to the frame behind him and Edsel watching starry-eyed among the crowd. Henry did that not for thrills but to generate publicity for the Ford Motor Company, which by then was a healthy seven months old. Spider was handed a $50 bonus.

Ford had been careful not to leave himself stranded again when he split with Tom Cooper. He had already found another partner and signed a contract with him, which included the employment of Wills, his indispensable designer. Muttonchop-whiskered Alexander Malcolmson was the Sunday school superintendent at the Episcopal Church, which Clara attended regularly. Malcolmson was also the coal merchant whose wagons, emblazoned with his slogan, "Hotter Than Sunshine," delivered fireplace fuel to the Fords.

Henry had to bury his determination never again to take orders from other men. The August agreement stipulated that Ford would "devote his time to the construction of a Commercial Automobile," while Malcolmson would "have charge of the financial and commercial departments." Malcolmson was to contribute a cautious $500 immediately, with further sums to follow until the car was completed, when capital would be raised to form a company. Wills was to be paid $125 a month, which he apparently split with Henry, who was provided with no salary and was living off what Clara had managed to save.

To guard his investment, Malcolmson delegated his managing

clerk-bookkeeper, hard-working, trigger-tempered James Couzens, who could never forgive his mother for giving birth to him in Canada. "I can never become King of England," he once chided her, "but if I had been born in the United States, I could be President." In due course, he elevated himself to the highest office that the Constitution allowed him, a seat in the Senate in Washington, D.C.

Barney's success with 999 inspired the moneyed partner of Ford & Malcolmson to feed only dribbles of extra cash into their venture. Henry hired Fred Strauss to take charge of the shop. When Fred grew uneasy after three months had gone by with only one engine and a transmission completed, Henry promised him $2,000 in future stock if he would stay on for two more years. "I couldn't wait," Fred reported. "I had to go and get a job."

One of the coalyards that Malcolmson leased contained an old wagon shop, owned like the rest of this place on Mack Avenue by Albert Strelow, a painting and carpentry contractor. The coal dealer called at the office to ask him to remodel the shop into an assembly plant for automobiles. Who was in it with him? "A fellow named Ford," Malcolmson answered, leading Strelow to the window. Henry was waiting outside, forlorn and shabby in a patched yellow overcoat.

"If you want me to put up a factory for him, I won't do it," said the contractor, contemptuously. But the pledge of $75 a month in rent for three years won him over.

By November, the drain on his pocket prompted Malcolmson to think about forming the Ford & Malcolmson Company, Ltd., with 15,000 shares of $100 each. Together, the two would hold half of them, leaving the rest to be sold. The stumbling block was Ford's dismal reputation as a businessman who had walked out on every commitment. Henry was turned down flat when he approached Alexander Dow. Couzens ran into so many rebuffs that he came close to tears.

It was June 16 before enough capital had been scraped up for the company to file for incorporation, and Malcolmson, its designated treasurer, had almost single-handedly performed the scraping. His old banker uncle, John S. Gray, put up $10,500 in cash with the proviso that he must be appointed president and could pull out in twelve months with his money repaid in full. One of

Malcolmson's attorneys, John W. Anderson, came up with $5,000, and another, Horace H. Rackham, with $3,500 plus a note for $1,500. A cousin of coal merchant Vernon C. Fry, a real-estate promoter, also wrote a note, for $2,000, in part payment for his fifty shares.

A second Malcolmson cousin referred Charlie Bennett, whose firm manufactured Daisy air rifles, to Henry when he heard that Charlie was looking to buy a new car for himself. He asked Ford when he would have an automobile ready for sale. That was a question Henry had to duck when a blueprint contained such little meaning for him that he had to have a part made to hold in his hands before instinct told him whether its design was right or wrong.

"I don't know," Henry hedged. "That's really my partner's department."

Bennett learned from Malcolmson that he already had engines, transmissions, axles, and wheels on order, though no delivery dates had been guaranteed, and if by some mischance the suppliers shipped everything cash on delivery tomorrow, he could not nearly pay for it. Nonetheless, Bennett still wanted a Ford, and he gave a personal pledge to buy fifty shares of stock, payable in two installments the following year.

Couzens' initial skepticism about the chances of the undertaking had disappeared. He was going to invest "all the money I can beg, borrow, or steal." For the time being, that amounted to $1,000, of which $100 came from his schoolteacher sister Rosetta, with the balance of the price for twenty-five shares to be forthcoming fourteen months later. An assistant of his in Malcolmson's bookkeeping department, Charles J. Woodall, gave a four months' note for ten shares in the company.

The dozen $1.50-a-day workmen in the made-over wagon shop were hired only to put the little cars together, tires to wheels, wheels to axles, bodies to chassis, and then paint and test what Malcolmson had prematurely christened "the Fordmobile." Every part would be made by outside contractors, which was Couzens' idea, not Henry's. To defer the day of judgment when a car of his faced trial on the open market, Henry had hoped that the peanut of a company would undertake to produce the whole automobile, from front end to rear.

The key ingredient was the two-cylinder, eight-horsepower engine, which was Henry's prime concern. What they saw of the working prototype convinced John and Horace Dodge that they could forego a contract for their spic-and-span machine shop to manufacture power units for Oldsmobiles, four thousand of which were sold that year. Instead, they would produce for Ford, including axles and transmissions to complete 650 whole chassis, all on piecework, at $250 each. If Ford's fell behind on the schedule of payments, the Dodge brothers could repossess all stock.

To tie them more tightly to the business, Malcolmson allotted John and Horace fifty shares apiece, paid for with $7,000 worth of Fordmobile parts and a note for $3,000. Couzens' arithmetic indicated that this shoestring financing should show early profits. All components for a car could be bought for $384. Add $20 for assembling, and selling expenses of $150, and the basic vehicle, costing $554, would be retailed at $750, with the back seat extra.

But by July 10 payments for the Dodges' motors and other outlays saw the infant firm's bank balance down to $223.65, and not a nickel had arrived from any customer. Strelow, the landlord, saved them from imminent bankruptcy. Malcolmson had talked him into subscribing for fifty shares. The next morning, Strelow wrote his check for $5,000. Four days later, Couzens recorded the first sale, to a Chicago doctor who paid $850 in advance for a car with the optional back seat attached.

By mid-August, a few cars had been assembled but none shipped out. Henry's obsessions would not countenance that. The $3,600-a-year vice president pictured himself as a man incapable of error. As an extension of himself, his car must be perfect, too, and it was far from that. The radiator was so small that the water boiled over. The transmission bands slipped. The carburetor was a plain disaster. The drive chain rapidly wore thin. The cranking handle held enough kick to break a man's arm.

Couzens, who exhausted himself and his temper as the $2,500-a-year manager, faced Henry down again. "Profits" were the real name of the business. He bullied Ford into helping him and Harold Wills, coats off and sleeves rolled up, to crate the cars that were ready and deliver them to the railroad. Whether it was Henry or Clara who first developed their antipathy for Couzens was impossible to determine. The Ford that Couzens got along with best was Edsel.

"The business went along almost as by magic," Henry wrote in retrospect. "The cars gained a reputation for standing up." Neither statement was remotely true. Couzens was a tyrant who rode roughshod over everyone. Henry took the opposite tack, the hero contrasted with the villain, addressing every hand by name, engaging occasionally in a friendly wrestling match with one of his favorites, up to his mischief again in electrifying doorknobs, nailing down hats, and handing out trick cigars.

Not all of them were taken in by displays of amiability. Oliver Barthel, who finally rejoined Henry, thought, "In order to get along with Mr. Ford, you had to have a little mean streak in your system. You had to be tough and mean; Mr. Ford enjoyed that."

The trickle of orders and incoming cash grew into a steadier flow—no flood yet, but enough for Couzens to report that up to October 1, they had shipped 195 cars and made a profit of $36,957. A 10 per cent dividend would be forthcoming in three more weeks. Before it was paid, George Baldwin Selden and the newly created Association of Licensed Automobile Manufacturers —Olds, Winton, Packard, and Cadillac among them—moved to trample the life out of the infant company.

Ford, said the lawsuit filed in New York, was infringing the Selden patent, to which the twenty-six member firms of the association had exclusive right since they paid royalties of 1.25 per cent of the sales price on every vehicle they produced and were vested with the legal power to deny further licenses to anyone. That summer, Henry had approached the association's president, Fred Smith, of Oldsmobile, to ask whether he would qualify if he applied. Probably not, came the answer, since the Ford factory was nothing but an inglorious assembly plant.

Like any other cagey banker, John Gray tried negotiating with the enemy before the company committed itself to retaliate. He had Smith brought to lunch with himself, lawyer Anderson, Henry, and some other shareholders. They listened to the spokesman from ALAM present his case; then Couzens was the first to speak: "Selden can take his patent and go to hell with it."

Henry, feet swinging from a chair that was tilted against the wall, snapped at Smith, "Couzens has answered you."

"You men are foolish," warned their visitor. "The Selden crowd can put you out of business—and will."

Couzens sneered, and Henry swung up onto his feet. "Let them try it."

The fight began as a contest of nerve and advertisement copy. The association weighed in with notices listing its member firms and warning that "No other manufacturers or importers are authorized to make or sell gasoline automobiles, and any person making, selling, or using such machines made or sold by any unlicensed manufacturers or importers will be liable to prosecution for infringement."

The company responded with a promise to dealers, agents, and buyers: "We will protect you against any prosecution for alleged infringements of patents. . . . We have always been winners." Over Couzens' signature, a letter went out to every major trade publication, repeating the pledge to defend any suit and undertaking to make and sell to maximum capacity. "We cannot conscientiously feel that Mr. Selden ever added anything to the art in which we are engaged," Couzens added. "We believe that the art would have been just as far advanced today if Mr. Selden had never been born."

In all its ramifications, the action dragged on for more than seven years, a perennial hazard to the fortunes of the company, draining off more than $500,000 in legal fees, cramping the plant expansion that soon seemed mandatory when nearly $2,000,000-worth of Fords were sold in the second year, ending September 30, 1905, for a net profit of $290,000. Henry was still unhappy with the product.

His engineers found that the only way to please him in redesigning a part was to try to guess what he had in mind and then keep on machining samples until he pronounced himself satisfied. A similar procedure was applied to a car. The first, labeled Model A, was superseded by the fancier and much bigger Model B, which sold for more than twice as much. Model B would be followed to market by six more tries—larger or smaller, with more horsepower or less, more expensive or cheaper, and all alphabetically identified—C, F, N, R, S, and K—as Henry wrestled with the problem, insuperable at present, of giving effect in metal and wood to the fancies of his brain. There was a direct parallel in the effort of a sculptor, chisel in hand, striving to release the image that only he can see buried in a granite block. Nothing running on wheels came close yet to fulfilling Henry's inarticulate imagining.

Virtually every other manufacturer, Malcolmson included, foresaw the future in terms of heavier, more expensive automobiles. The former playthings of the rich were becoming luxuries affordable by the well-to-do in the current burst of prosperity that the nation was enjoying with Theodore Roosevelt established for a full term in the White House. The Vanderbilts, the Astors, and the Harrimans had set the style, in the industry's general opinion, by flaunting fancy limousines, and so had Britain's Prince of Wales. Windshields and closed bodies for protection from the weather, shock absorbers to iron out the bumps, straight-eight engines— they were no longer the stuff of inventors' hopes but realities, waiting to be incorporated, at a price, into manufacturers' designs. Maybe Edison was not far wrong in extolling the automobile as the biggest spur yet to the creativity of Americans.

One dissenter from the belief that the way ahead lay along the path of luxury was Ransom Olds. Quarreling within the business he had founded put him into temporary retirement, forty-one years old and the industry's original self-made millionaire. Henry drew encouragement on two counts. Olds had picked up a personal fortune on sales of his $650 runabouts, with the worth of the company soaring to $2,000,000 in three years. And in his absence, Oldsmobiles were swelling in size and price like everyone else's output. What would be left for the average man to buy? Certainly not Ford's Model B at $2,000, or the Model C runabout —$1,000 with back seat—or the Model F, which went for the same price.

By the end of 1904, the Mack Avenue plant was strained at the seams. Three hundred men worked there; orders and paid-out dividends increased together. Couzens had accumulated enough in the bank to have a new, three-floor building erected on Piquette Avenue. Henry's second-floor office there was empty more often than not. Either he would haunt the assembly floors, drafting room, and experimental shop, or else stay away altogether. His mail—checks, bills, business correspondence—piled up until it filled two wastebaskets, at which point Couzens delegated a clerk to open every letter. Henry was searching his soul again.

The following spring, the conflict was resolved in an upstairs bedroom in the house on Hendrie Avenue. The failing health of William's daughter Jane, his housekeeper, had left no alternative but for the old man to take shelter with his eldest son. On March 8, William died, and Henry was liberated from the frustrations of the past. Father alive was a detested figure who bore responsibility for his wife's death. Father dead became an idealization of the virtuous farmer, the very essence of nineteenth-century America, to whose service Henry could dedicate himself and so assuage his guilt.

He would create a car tailored for a farmer's pocket and a farmer's needs, a light, nimble car that could ride over rutted roads and plowed fields, easy to repair with any workshop's tools, strong enough to enjoy indefinite life. He let precious little time go by before he called Detroit newspaper reporters into his office. "Plan Ten Thousand Autos at $400 Apiece," said one headline.

"It will take some time to figure out what we can do," Henry allowed, "and we do not care to say much until we know what the result will be."

He spoke without apparent reference to Gray, Malcolmson, or any other stockholder or executive except, in all probability, Couzens. Malcolmson's thinking was poles apart from Henry's. The treasurer, rarely seen at the plant, pressed hard for cars priced as high as $4,775, and the two Dodges did not argue with that. But here in May, Ford was a man transformed, decisive, where he had procrastinated before, iron-handed, determined to have his way.

The house on Hendrie Avenue was no longer tolerable after William had died there. As soon as possible, Henry took the family to a new, $60-a-month address, still nothing but a single-fronted brick house with one bathroom upstairs and a little covered front porch, at 145 Harper Avenue, but it lay closer to the Piquette plant. He bought Edsel a bicycle so that he could ride to and from school and stop by at the office on his way home to help stamp the mail.

Edsel was more his mother's boy than Henry's, a conscientious scholar whose careful handwriting put his father's farmhand scrawl to shame. Edsel liked to read, as Clara did, whereas Father seldom opened a book and devoted his spare time to newspapers and technical magazines. One visitor was surprised to find that, in light of Clara's churchgoing, there was no Bible on the bookshelf. Edsel had an artistic streak that showed itself in sheet after sheet of crayon and pencil drawings—of automobiles, of course, and flowers and characters from fairy tales. Clara saved all he did, from homework essays to jottings in a diary. He caused no trouble, played no pranks. He was so eager to please that the neighbors could be forgiven for wondering whether he wasn't too docile.

Board meetings at Ford Motor broke up in shouts of anger and fists hammering the table. The sides were neatly drawn, Ford and Couzens vs. the rest. Since the two of them *were* the company, they exercised more muscle than the others combined. One of Malcolmson's opening moves was an attempt to isolate Ford by demanding that Couzens be sent back to the coal business.

"I don't want you, but I want your man" was the gist of Henry's reply. Then the treasurer wanted his ungrateful steward fired. Henry countered by contriving to have the directors boost Couzens' salary to $8,000 a year. This was only a holding action in the war. A devastating attack had to be devised. If Malcolmson stood in Henry's path, Malcolmson must be disposed of.

The first stratagem was to set up a separate operation on new premises, ostensibly to manufacture engines and other components for sale to Ford Motor for less than the Dodge brothers and outside suppliers charged. When the Ford Manufacturing Company was incorporated in November—with Henry as president, Couzens as treasurer, and $10,000 in cash—Malcolmson was excluded as a shareholder. Ford had unchallengeable control with 2,900 of the 5,000 issued shares. At first, the embattled coal merchant threatened to sue. Within two weeks he cut the ground from under himself by forming a new corporation, Aerocar, intending to market a competitive automobile with an air-cooled engine and feed the enterprise with his dividends from Ford Motor.

To Henry's codirectors on Piquette Avenue, this was an act of unpardonable treachery. They asked for Malcolmson's resignation. Henry's luck was as good as his strategy. During lulls in the campaign, he occupied himself at the farm he had inherited from William, pondering how a gasoline engine might further serve the honest farmer and lighten rural drudgery.

He posed the problem to a young Hungarian engineer, Joseph

Galamb, who had been hired by Ford Motor. "Joe, we have to build a light tractor that we can use out on the farm where the wheat is growing, and we need a binder. We have to build a tractor in three days." It took a week to construct a full-size working model, but it was nothing for anyone to be proud of. Henry would have to let his instincts simmer some more.

Deprived of all managerial control, Malcolmson wanted to pull out of the company that owed its start to him. Couzens did the negotiating to determine how much would be paid for his 225 shares, 25 per cent of all Ford Motor stock. Henry enforced a vindictive bargain. In return for Henry's note for $75,000, Malcolmson gave him an option to buy and immediately discounted the note at his bankers, adding the proceeds to the $90,000 he had already put into Aerocar. He also borrowed the 100 shares of Charlie Bennett and Vernon Fry.

When the note was about to fall due, Henry announced that he would neither pay nor take up the option unless Malcolmson included Bennett's and Fry's stock in the deal. The erstwhile Episcopal Sunday school superintendent was trapped. In return for the $175,000 he finally paid Malcolmson in July 1906, Ford owned more than half a company that was on the threshold of registering its first annual profit of more than $1,000,000. Thirteen years afterward, Malcolmson, temporarily in sad financial straits, went to Ford for help. It was refused.

The shares of Fry and Bennett were probably put up as collateral for the bank loan, cosigned by Couzens, that Henry needed to buy out Malcolmson. As soon as it was repaid and the shares released, they were snapped up, Fry's fifty by Henry, plus fifteen of Bennett's, leaving thirty-five of those for Jim Couzens. Henry had already paid off Charles Woodall, another Malcolmson supporter who read the danger signals, to pick up his ten, while Jim bought Albert Strelow's block of fifty at a fire-sale price of $25,000. The painting contractor was greedy to make a speculator's killing in Canadian gold mining stock. The day would arrive when he came back to the company, begging for a job.

Ford and Couzens, well matched in ruthlessness and the will to dominate, stayed a respectful distance apart from each other except to connive or cope with a crisis, Couzens with his quarters and staff of perpetually overburdened clerks at one end of the building, Ford at the other. Henry never could see the point of all the paperwork involved in selling cars. Once he could get the design frozen for the quintessential automobile, he felt certain that the world would come pounding on the door.

He was boss of both companies now in title as well as fact. The death of John Gray had cleared the way. At the next board meeting of Ford Motor, Couzens proposed that Henry succeed to the presidency, with John Dodge as vice-president. Ford had to wait thirteen years more before he acquired the shares that the banker bequeathed to his heirs. Henry paid $26,250,000 for them.

In the summer of 1906, he consolidated his triumphs by bringing the decoy company, Ford Manufacturing, back under the parent's wing, its purpose fulfilled in terms of the original plan. No more than a week or two after the deal with Malcolmson was concluded, Henry had another story for the trade papers. "To Make It All Ford," was how *Motor Age* announced it. The Piquette Avenue factory had a five-month backlog of orders for the latest Model N, a peppy little runabout whose fifteen-horsepower engine would make forty-five miles an hour, the fastest Ford yet produced. Henry fought to hold the price down at $500, but it eventually cost $100 more.

He was talking about turning out cars on "the same basis as sewing machines and typewriters." There was a missionary ardor in him nowadays, for which he gave credit to Clara, who at last had loftier things to think about than how to make ends meet. It was she, he declared, who had maintained his "faith in God and man." He called her "The Believer." His workmen came to know her as "The Empress," a remote presence to whom they sometimes addressed their written appeals when they found Henry unapproachable. Her influence with him was nobody's secret.

"If you get people together so that they get acquainted with each other," he confided to a mechanic who was driving him home, "and get an idea of neighborliness, the car will have a universal effect. We won't have any more strikes or wars."

Merging Ford Manufacturing with Ford Motor made Henry, the controlling shareholder in both companies, richer by $261,000. Couzens had the details of the exchange of stock that united the two businesses cut and dried in advance, like everything else on the agenda these days. The directors applied their rubber stamp, as they did when Henry presented them with another *fait accompli.*

He and John Dodge had been shopping around for space on which to erect the world's most advanced auto factory, where *the* car could be built in its mechanical entirety, parts and all, just as Ford had desired in the first place. *The* car was in sight already in Henry's convoluted brain. They had found the site in the old Highland Park racetrack. There he chose to build as no man had done before, and never mind about the Selden suit that was dragging through endless lawyers' conferences. Highland Park's new plant would cost better than $500,000 for a start, but that was worth only a moment's consideration. "I have never known what to do with money after my expenses were paid" was a standard remark of Henry's.

One recent newcomer to the industry had a less disarming view. Wheeling and dealing in fortunes was the essence of life for William Crapo Durant. The soft-spoken, immaculately tailored little man had a deserved reputation as the greatest living promoter outside of prison bars. Two years older than Ford, Durant also cherished an impression of tomorrow's potentials that equaled Henry's in its intensity.

Durant sensed that the turning wheels of an automobile fed the hunger for new things and new places inherent in the restless spirit of Americans. Cars would create their own market, advertising themselves as they rolled along the roads or stood at the curb with their promise of freedom from the commonplace. His focus, however, was diametrically different.

Durant envisioned a mighty industry offering models for sale in every imaginable range of price and contour, plushy cars to sell to the rich, more utilitarian vehicles at progressively reduced prices to suit middle-class pockets. As for the struggling farmer and the sweating factory hand, in the perspective of those times they were too poor to amount to a profitable market for anything much beyond such staples as soap, patent medicines, and groceries.

Will had made his first million in stake money by the time he was thirty-nine, peddling insurance policies through the Boston agency he had started nineteen years previously. His next achievement, in November 1904, was to take over the starving Buick Motor Company in a *coup de main* that saw him sell $500,000 worth of stock in a single, calm working day. When Henry pulled off his scheme to depose Malcolmson, Buick was earning profits of $400,000 on sales of $2,000,000, which were figures nowhere near as good as Ford's.

The following year brought financial panic to the United States. It was precipitated by Theodore Roosevelt's vendetta against the "malefactors of great wealth," the trust companies that dominated the commerce of the nation, which brought him a fleeting victory when a Chicago judge levied a fine of $29,240,000 on Standard Oil of Indiana for extorting freight rebates from railroads ferrying its cargoes.

The boom-or-bust automobile industry was hit hard, with the most crushing losses suffered by those manufacturers who had demonstrated the same inability as generations of their successors to read a crystal ball. Luxury cars languished in the dealers' showrooms. Malcolmson's Aerocar Company was one of the many casualties that finished in bankruptcy court, but Durant's Buick sales surged by 50 per cent.

Keeping the cash flowing in was Couzens' principal problem. Contractors' bills for Highland Park were a heavy drain. Fridays came when the Piquette plant payroll couldn't be met until he found a pitiless way out of the quandary. He ordered cars to be shipped out with cash-on-delivery bills of lading. That compelled Ford dealers to scrounge up instant money for them or be squeezed out of business. In any event, the discounts of 10 per cent that Couzens allowed them, an essential factor in keeping down the price a customer paid for a Ford, made them the hardest pressed in the trade. Unless they sold in volume, they could not stay afloat.

Financial thunderclouds piling up overhead concerned Henry no more than a summer shower. Early in the year, he had told Galamb, "Joe, I've got an idea to design a new car. Fix a place for yourself on the third floor 'way back, a special room. Get your board up there and a blackboard, and we'll start work on a new model."

For "good luck," as Henry said, he brought in his mother's comforting old rocking chair, in which he would sit by the hour evenings after seven, studying the designs that Joe transferred from draftboard penciling into blackboard chalk, changing features that did not seem right to him. Lizzie was coming to life behind the locked door of the little room next to his office.

Next, "Joe, you get a small brass model made." Every part of the motor was made half scale in the shops downstairs for Henry to satisfy himself that it would work. Once it had passed that test, he earmarked more space adjoining his office, a room twelve by fifteen feet, big enough to hold a lathe, milling machine, and drill press, and still leave space for assembling a full-size chassis. Henry was there every day, straining his voice to make himself heard above the whine of machinery. There were days when he would have the engine torn down, reassembled, and then stripped again to install fresh gears. His method was to coax the crew, never to bully. "I wonder if we can do it. I wonder," he would muse. The men were prepared to work all night with him if need be, and he would pick up a monkey wrench to help.

Something like rapture lit his face the morning the handmade Model T was wheeled out of the experimental room. After a minute or two to adjust the transmission, the motor roared at a turn of the crank. Every man within range received a thump on the shoulders or a joyful kick in the pants. "Well, I guess we've got started," he beamed, as if this were the very first car he'd conceived. In the depths of his heart, perhaps it was.

He asked George Holley, whose specialty was carburetor design, to take him on a tour of the city, choosing a route that took them under Malcolmson's office windows. The defeated enemy must be shown what Ford had wrought. When Lizzie returned to her womb, she was taken to pieces for a check to be made of every wearing part. "I wonder if we'll get up to No. 10," said Henry of the car whose sales would exceed fifteen million.

By the following March, Lizzie was ready to have her picture taken, and birth announcements went out to all Ford dealers. They must do their damnedest to sell everything they had in stock to clear the decks for Model T before she went on sale on October 1. She would prove to be bony, graceless, but tough as nails, a skittish creature who nevertheless endeared herself to a generation of customers. Nearly seven out of ten of them lived on farms or in small towns. Henry's compulsions served him well.

She was as near perfect as he could have her be in everything except price. For $850, the only equipment supplied was a horn, three oil lamps, and an iron frame for an optional folding top. No spare wheel or tire was provided, which was a hardship when country roads wore out the tread in a few thousand miles and flints and cobbles made blowouts a certainty. Buicks were selling like nickelodeon tickets for only a few dollars more—8,487 of them this year, compared with 6,181 Fords.

But the volume of early orders swamped Couzens' skimpy staff. Double shifts were instituted at Piquette Avenue, floor layouts streamlined for efficiency, and extra hands hired. New machines were installed to make possible the building of a hundred cars in a ten-hour day, one every fourteen minutes.

Ford branch managers, two of them from Europe, were brought to Detroit to see the car they had heard so much about during a three-day sales meeting in September. From the huge rolltop desk, its pigeonholes crammed with papers, that was his command post, Couzens whipped them into shape like a drill sergeant. Before they went home again, Will Durant—the "Little Giant" of newspaper stories—took over the headlines.

Using Buick as its base, he incorporated General Motors Company of New Jersey, with authorized capital of $12,500,000. Before the year was over, he added Oldsmobile, then—in 1909—Oakland, Cadillac, and AC Spark Plug. Here was a baby that grew like Alice biting the magic mushroom, a giant ready to challenge Ford. Frenetic expansion, Durant thought, held the key to supremacy. Couzens' response was fast. In October, Ford Motor's capital was boosted to $2,000,000 and a stock dividend declared amounting to all but $100,000 of that sum. Durant did better. "The lustiest industrial infant ever born in America," as General Motors was described, declared a 150 per cent dividend when it reached the age of fourteen months.

Henry was secretive about what he did with his deluge of cash. "Money for purposes outside of the business," Edsel said later, "is a subject that our family never talks about." His father would continue to be haunted for the rest of his life by an irrational fear of debt when so much money came flooding in that Clara would discover checks—one for $75,000—stuffed and forgotten in his suit pockets. She knew one thing that she wanted after waiting so long, and that was a home of her own. She also felt that Couzens was getting way too big for his breeches.

Driving a distant relative of hers around town one day, Henry stopped at a lot on Edison Avenue where a new house was going up. "I want to go through it," he said without further explanation. The two of them prowled through a living room and dining room, a library, kitchen, servants' quarters, and butler's pantry. Upstairs, they explored three bedrooms, freshly tiled bathrooms, and wide hall. Only then did Henry reveal that the place was his and Clara's. The landscaping that she specified brought the total outlay to $293,253, as she noted in her records.

For shopping trips, he bought her a Detroit Electric—Lizzie was too much for her to manage—and they engaged two maids, but no chauffeur. Clara turned out to be a demanding mistress. Turnover was high. When a cook was added to the domestic staff, Henry complained, "My wife doesn't cook any more, or not much. We hire cooks, but none can hold a candle to her."

Fifteen-year-old Edsel was given his first car, a Model N, to drive, and he returned to private education at the Detroit University School, a prepping establishment at the foot of Woodward Avenue, within sniffing distance of the waterfront. In knickerbockers and wool stockings, he would drop in at the plant after school, carrying his homework books in a strap over one shoulder, depositing them quietly on a desk by his father's office and heading straight toward the magical experimental room.

If Henry was there, he would unlock the door to welcome his self-effacing son, then take him inside until long after the staff had left, giving him lessons in running the business. If he spotted the telltale books without seeing Edsel, he would ask, "Have you seen Ed?" Employees who saw them together thought they were extraordinarily close, "twins in knowledge," as one of the clerks said.

Edsel was crazy about automobiles. He pasted up pictures of all kinds of makes as a frieze around his new bedroom's walls, and before long he was given an allowance big enough to buy any kind of new car that came onto the market. A Locomobile, a Marmon, a Packard, and the pick of the crop, a slick Hispano-Suiza—he tried them all in his salad days. "They must have cost a great deal," he thought, but nobody spoke of such things. Very little was too good in the upbringing of the son of Mr. and Mrs. Henry Ford, the principal proprietors of the project.

At nineteen, the boy's thinking was more flexible than the father's. Edsel bought a French-made Renault. "We hope to find ideas from this machine which we can use in our work," he said ingenuously. "Foreign cars help us." He was careful to swap it for a Ford whenever he drove to Highland Park. "Someone might not understand." Did he mean Henry?

Henry made an almost pathetic attempt to duplicate for Edsel some aspects of his own boyhood. Over the garage, he fitted out a workshop, but the tools were not homemade or borrowed from a barn. Father and son ran the new power lathe and other high-speed machines together. One evening, Edsel lost the tip of a middle finger to a spinning steel blade.

Lizzie had been available to customers for less than a year and $9,000,000 worth of the cars had been sold with no royalties paid to anyone when the trial judge, Charles Merrill Hough, announced his decision in the Selden case. Patent No. 549,160, he ruled, was valid. Every manufacturer, importer, and owner of an automobile owed tribute to the scheming attorney of Rochester, New York, and his assignees under penalty of law. At Ford's, which was threatened by crushing infringement suits, it seemed like the end to almost everyone but Henry. Even Couzens' nerve snapped, and he resorted to querulous arguing about the size of the bills the defense attorneys had run up in an apparently lost cause.

Henry chose to press the battle to the Court of Appeals and, if necessary, on up to the Supreme Court itself. "There will be no letup in the legal fight," he promised, even if it obliterated all $6,000,000 in assets, together with the same sum that a bonding company had guaranteed. And then, characteristically, he wavered. Will Durant took prompt heed of the judge's ruling and paid out $1,000,000 in back royalties to clear General Motors. One week later, Henry and Jim Couzens caught a train to New York for what the circumstances indicate was a prearranged conference with Durant.

The tensity of the overall situation produced the usual psychosomatic symptoms in Ford. He was stretched out on the carpet, trying to ease an attack of lumbago, when the house phone rang in their Belmont Hotel suite. Couzens answered. "This is Billy Durant. I'd like to see you." He was in the lobby.

"I'll come down," said Couzens. "Henry's not feeling good."

He returned in half an hour. "Billy Durant wants to buy the Ford Motor Company."

"How much will he pay?"

"Eight million dollars."

"Tell him he can have it if the money's all cash. Tell him I'll throw in my lumbago."

"He's gone. He's coming back tomorrow for an answer. You want to let it go for that?"

"What do you think?"

"I'd say yes."

"If we get cash," Henry repeated. He could always pour the money into developing the farm tractor that lingered, befogged, in his mind.

The following day, Couzens arrived alone at Durant's office. Henry, he reported, was suffering from "nervous dyspepsia," but he had authorized the deal. The terms were clinched on a hand-shake—$2,000,000 cash, the balance payable in one to two years, Couzens to retain a 25 per cent interest in the company. Durant went to talk to his bankers.

"We have changed our minds," they told him. "The Ford business is not worth that much money."

Within twelve months, Durant lost General Motors. He was running too fast, a visionary who, with the fallibility of his kind, did not know when to slow down and consolidate, while Henry simply concentrated on turning out nothing but Lizzie to block out competition in her price field, aiming to blanket the universe. "No factory is big enough to make two models of cars," he ruled. "Let them concentrate on one."

There had been cause to wonder whether Will was trying to outdo two monopolists of an earlier generation: John D. Rockefeller, whose Standard Oil of New Jersey once controlled 95 per cent of all the oil pipelines and refineries in America, and J. Pierpont Morgan, who assembled an even bigger monster in the United States Steel Corporation, capitalized at the moment of its inception at $1,403,000,000.

It was not the Sherman Anti-Trust Act that nobbled Durant, as it did Rockefeller, but his own passion. Reckless cash commitments and vanishing profits promised to thrust General Motors into receivership in the summer of 1910. Shrinking like Alice after tasting the opposite side of the mushroom, the Little Giant had to mortgage every brick of the corporation's property in Michigan and agree to pay what amounted to a fee of $2,500,000 before he could borrow $12,500,000 at upward of 7 per cent from two merchant banking firms, J. & W. Seligman of New York and Lee, Higginson & Company of Boston. By Henry's scale of values, those were Shylock terms. He had followed the rule of good husbandry and plowed back its own earnings to pay for Ford's growth.

The new satraps of General Motors made a clean sweep of the board of directors, including Durant. Will looked for the means of requital. There was Louis Chevrolet, the onetime Buick racing driver, who might be worth establishing in business with the six-cylinder engine he was developing in his Detroit workshop. Durant followed through, but it was Louis' name that went on the radiators of the line of bargain-price automobiles they started to build.

The debut of Chevrolet, an inferior piece of work, gave Henry nothing to be concerned about when output of Lizzie was climbing fast toward 100,000 a year. As the battle to reverse the Selden decision approached its climax, his attention was concentrated on the niche he was shaping for himself as a hero combating an attempted monopoly on behalf of everybody who bought an automobile. As reclusive as a lynx in private, he liked to pose for public attention as a resolute lion. Advertisements placed by the company contributed to the picture. "Henry Ford," declared one of them, "has been the greatest factor in the development of the automobile industry, greater than any other man in the world. . . . He is as well known in Europe as in America." Henry "stands out, independent and alone, clear and strong, as the most dominant factor in the automobile industry of today."

Other advertising copy argued that customers should not buy cars licensed under the disputed patent because that encouraged "trust methods" and the production of "high-priced and poor-quality cars." Any Ford buyer who wanted a protective bond could have it for the asking. If bouquets were going to be tossed at the Ford Motor Company for its trust-busting effort in the courts, Henry was out to catch them. There were no longer other spokesmen. When the company had news to announce, only Henry met the reporters.

After hearing out the battalion of lawyers employed by both sides, three judges awarded final victory to Ford on January 9, 1911. As for Selden, their unanimous opinion said, the defendants "neither legally nor morally owe him anything." Henry gave a celebratory banquet at Rector's Restaurant, where the swells of New York went to dine. Edsel was granted time off from school to join the fifty guests at table. It is possible that something more inspiriting than grape juice was served that night, and smoking was permitted. The host had not yet succumbed to Edison's persuasions or jumped into print with such pronouncements as "Brains and booze will not mix" and "Study the history of almost any criminal and you'll find an inveterate cigarette smoker."

With the legal ground firm under his feet, Henry straightway turned his attention to realizing the second, complementary half of his obsession with Lizzie. What he had created must be shared with the utmost number of other men. Highland Park had more orders than could be fulfilled on the overstrained premises, but Henry cut prices to attract more and ever more customers. Over the next five years, the tag on the runabout, for example, fell progressively from $590 to $525, then $500 and down to $440 before it hit $390.

"Every time I reduce the charge for our car by $1.00," Ford said, "I get a thousand new buyers." When Edsel was married, Lizzie was selling for $345.

Henry canceled advertising programs that Couzens had approved; Lizzie was her own best promoter. More than any other single factor, it was she who tempted farmers to convert from horsepower to enginepower in a dozen, previously inconceivable ways. They mailed Ford the evidence, snapshots showing Lizzie at her workaday labors—dragging plows and wagons, and supplying power for threshing machines, circular saws, and vacuum cleaners —and at her Sunday glory, off on a family outing. In the face of this, he saw no reason to fritter away good money on advertising when it could be spent to better purpose.

In the summer of 1912, he felt secure enough to take his wife, son, and brother-in-law Marvin on the Fords' first Atlantic crossing, mixing a vacation with a look at the company's subsidiaries in

England and France; Couzens had made two earlier trips. What she saw of country houses and gardens after the *George Washington* docked at Plymouth set the pattern of Clara's social style from then on: She would model herself on English gentlefolk and behave as befitted a lady of the manor, surrounding herself with flowers and an ever-expanding collection of Staffordshire, Leeds, Whieldon, and Wedgwood china. If Edsel was impressed by anything at all, there was no mention of it in the few vapid words of the diary he kept for his parents' sake on the journey.

Whatever pleasure Henry had found went up in smoke the evening he made his reappearance at Highland Park. In the two months he was gone, Wills and a crew of engineers decided to surprise the boss with a fancied-up version of Lizzie, handmade with four doors on a chassis stretched a foot or two and painted a dandy-looking red instead of the black that Henry had recently ordered as his cars' standard color to pare a dollar or two off the price. The new beauty stood in the executive garage, awaiting Henry's approval after he had been welcomed home by his top staff. That, at least, was the plan. He foxed them by slipping into the garage without bothering to use the main entrance.

One of the welcoming group found him there by accident. "Ford car?" Henry asked, staring at his gift.

"Yes, sir."

"How long has that been standing there?"

"Well, about two weeks. They just finished it. It's just going into production."

"It *is* going into production?"

"Yes, sir, it's all tooled up; the bodies are ordered; the orders are all placed for that car."

The staff man remembered that Ford "kind of smiled" as he walked over to take a closer look. Hands in pockets, he circled the spotless new model three or four times, then grabbed hold of a door. One frenzied jerk and it came off in his hands. He scrambled across the front seat to wreak the same damage on the other side before he smashed in the windshield. In blind rage, he clambered into the back and ripped the folded canvas top with his shoe.

He raced up the stairs to the second floor to hunt down the men responsible. With arms and legs twitching, he cursed them out, ready to fire the lot of them then and there for daring to imagine that Lizzie was less than perfect in her everyday glory.

At Highland Park, a revolution in manufacturing was taking shape under the iron-handed direction of the company's latest *wünderkind*, thick-shouldered Charles Sorensen, a Dane by birth and explosive by nature, who seldom hesitated to tongue-whip any workman if he crossed him. With the backing of Henry and protests from Couzens about the expense, Sorensen had been experimenting with methods of keeping embryo Lizzies rolling along continuously down a production line instead of having teams of mechanics close in to complete a hundred stationary chassis. From its beginnings, when two men tugged a car at the end of a rope, mass production was now an accomplished fact. Endless chains, specially designed conveyors, chutes, and mobile platforms kept every piece of work on the move toward the work crews, standing at their appointed places. A complete automobile could be assembled in less than six hours already, and the pace was quickening.

John and Horace Dodge concluded that the hour had come to break away with a complete car of their own manufacture, before Ford monopolized the low-price market. He was the only customer they had nowadays, and his insistence on penny-squeezing made renewal of their annual contract for supplying transmissions and other components a stormy negotiation. They grew increasingly uneasy, too, about his arbitrary ruling, in advance of any board meeting, that in order to accumulate funds for expansion, payment of anything beyond nominal dividends was to be suspended. In much the same way, he was spending unauthorized millions on making over Highland Park and committing the company to put up a miniature skyscraper as combined hotel and eastern headquarters in New York City. He would never countenance their holding onto directorships while they produced rival cars labeled Dodge. They resigned in August 1913, with no ill feeling shown on either side. Their Ford stock remained intact. They counted on the new vice-president, Jim Couzens, who shared their hunger for dividends, to hold Henry's spending in check.

Couzens' range of interests broadened where Ford's absorption with himself and Lizzie as an extension of himself came close to monomania. Couzens was thinking about a public career. He had

acquired more than a bookkeeper's knowledge of cash flows
and balance sheets these days; he had opened a bank across the
street from Highland Park and argued Henry into depositing
$12,000,000 there in an interest-bearing account. It stayed a few
brief weeks until Ford told his Teutonic secretary, Ernest Liebold,
"We're going to build a tractor plant in Dearborn. It may cost as
much as $7,000,000. Get ready to take care of it."

Liebold, whose first job under Couzens had been to help organize the bank, mentioned that the $12,000,000 was on long-term
deposit. "If so," retorted Henry, "Couzens put something over on
me. You get it—I need it." The only course for the dumfounded
executives of the bank was to liquidate a portfolio of investments
as fast as they could.

Coming back from one out-of-town trip, Couzens saw a steam
shovel scooping out a pit in the grass outside the factory walls.
Ford pushed some papers across the desk by way of explanation.
"I read that money is going to be tight, so I got the boys to get up
these figures for me. We've got $33,000,000 around in the banks,
and I'm going to pull it in and put it down in that hole until the
squall blows over."

It took Couzens the better part of a day to bring Henry around
to seeing that such massive withdrawals would rock the financial
institutions of the land. Henry had the excavation filled in and
the earth reseeded.

Disenchantment overcame all his previous admiration for Couzens. Henry had a check kept on his treasurer-vice-president's
comings and goings to California, White Sulphur Springs, and
elsewhere. He was satisfied with the result: "He has been at the
plant only eighty-four days during the past year."

The round figure of one million Lizzies produced every year
had an irresistible appeal for Henry, making the current 300,000
pitiful by comparison. Attaining that target would call for an
infinitely bigger layout than Highland Park's. A few months before Edsel's twenty-second birthday, his father began buying land,
hundreds of acres of it, southeast of Detroit on the banks of what
was little more than a sizable rivulet, the Rouge River, downstream from the thousands of acres he had been picking up in
Dearborn. The vast factory complex he intended for the new site
was his own secret. He led Couzens to believe that no such ex-

penditures would be needed for three or four more years. He bamboozled the Dodges into imagining that all he planned to produce on the Rouge was farm tractors. He set up a plant in Dearborn to experiment with prototypes, funneling into it hundreds of thousands of dollars' worth of Ford Motor man-hours and materials. The tractor, he explained, was to be a strictly family business, with the Fords—father, mother, and son—the only shareholders in a new company.

The war in Europe, almost one year old, had become a battle of attrition on land and sea. In his latest role as international oracle, Henry had pronounced that he would sooner set fire to Highland Park than supply war materials to anybody. "I hate war because war is murder, desolation, and destruction." Madame Schwimmer was waiting in the wings.

As a firm supporter of the Allied cause, Couzens was incensed. When Henry wanted his pacifistic tirades reprinted in the company magazine, *Ford Times*, Couzens would stand no more. He struck out the offending article in the galley proofs and grated to Ford, "I want it killed or I quit."

"You can't stop anything. I'm going to print it."

"Then count me out," Couzens shouted as he marched out the office door.

Henry confided afterward that the thought crossing his head at that moment was, "Fine. That's a dandy way out of it."

Couzens' curtain speech to the newspapers ran longer. "I could not agree with Mr. Ford's public utterances on peace and preparedness," he raged. "I disapproved of what he said. Disagreements have been more violent daily. I cannot be carried along on his kind of kite. We started in the business thirteen years ago, and it was through my efforts the Ford Motor Company was built up around the man Ford. I never worked for any man. Even as railroad car checker in my early days, I had no boss. I was, and am today, willing to work with any man; I am willing to work with Ford, but not for him."

In the reshuffling that followed Couzens' walkout, Edsel came in with the title of company secretary, with more experienced men like power-thirsty Liebold to guide him. Henry would delegate his son to work out the terms for buying back Couzens' 11 per cent. Jim Couzens, who had put in $900 cash as a start, sold his stock for $29,308,858 in 1919.

When the blowup with Couzens became inevitable, Henry was half inclined to hand over the business to other people and concentrate on his elusive tractor. He had Thomas W. Lamont, Harvard 1892 and partner in the House of Morgan, come to Detroit to talk about it. A subsequent letter from Lamont summed up their discussions:

"When you said to me that you would like to have me think about some plan that would embody the 'best ideas of Ford and Morgan,' you gave me a great deal to think about. . . . You have in mind, and are working upon, a wonderful development for the benefit of the farmers of America and in fact of the world. You wish to be able to carry out in splendid fashion your fine ideas along this line. You have some question in your own mind as to your ability to do this and, at the same time, to carry the full responsibility of the present motor car business. There must, it seems to me, come to you moments of almost deep oppression for the responsibilities that you have to carry day by day. . . ."

As in the approach by Durant and then in a $500,000 offer from Hornblower & Weeks of Wall Street, Henry could not bring himself to take the jump. Life would be left too empty without Lizzie. When he brought up the subject with his son, Henry must have repeated the argument he had used to explain why he set such stiff terms, that any deal was bound to fail: "Supposing we do sell. Supposing we do get these millions. What will we have? We wouldn't have a job!"

Five months in advance of Edsel's wedding day, his father had made himself the laughingstock of American intellectuals with a remark that would long outlive him. They seized on it as proof that Henry Ford, in spite of his enviable fortune, was an untutored country hick at heart. Yet the fifty-two years of his own inner life had taught him to believe what he tried to tell an inquiring reporter—that a man must not allow himself to be constrained by the limitations of his past. Only Henry put the thought with less finesse.

"History," he said, "is more or less bunk."

Chapter Four

The Master of Fair Lane

If young Mr. and Mrs. Ford discovered joy on their honeymoon, it was only in each other, and references to that were subdued in the letters that Edsel wrote home week by week. For the rest, they were as bland as a schoolboy's. The roads, he thought, were better in California than around Detroit. It was a relief to know that Charles Evans Hughes had finally, in mid-November, conceded victory to Woodrow Wilson—his telegram to the White House arrived two weeks after the election, "a little moth-eaten," the President commented, "but quite legible." Henry wired congratulations. With only a handful of off-season tourists about, San Francisco was too quiet for the honeymooners, Edsel admitted, and the *Great Northern* had rolled so much on the crossing to Honolulu that Eleanor and he could not sleep. They would change their bookings for the return voyage.

Clara hoarded every letter and its envelope, too, as they arrived at Fair Lane, together with every scrap of a story about the Fords and their friends that a newspaper or magazine published. She engaged a press clipping service to cut and send her fat bundles of the stuff, which she set aside until a couple of college girls could be given vacation jobs pasting them higgledy-piggledy in her scrapbooks.

The fifty-six-room house was too big for them now that Edsel was married, but Clara was finding herself more at home than Henry. The number of servants kept growing. A head butler, second butler, chauffeur, cook, ladies' maid, and laundress lived on the premises. A houseman came in every day, and before she was finished with her array of gardens, she would have twenty-seven men working in them. The staff had no doubt about who ran the place. "Mrs. Ford is the boss around here" was the catchword.

Henry would have preferred to cut back on the help. "I still like boiled potatoes with the skins on," he said, "and I do not want a man standing back of my chair at table laughing up his sleeve at me while I am taking the potatoes' jackets off." But what went for Clara's domestics went for her husband, too. He never quarreled with her. They did not always see eye to eye, but as someone acquainted with both of them said, "They shared their minds."

Fair Lane had been built in the hope that Edsel would be staying there for years to come. It was for his sake that the billiard room, the bowling alley, and the recreation room were included in the plans and the majestic pipe organ installed to cover half a wall. They refused to accept that perhaps he had married early to escape their smothering attention to what they imagined to be his needs. Neither the billiard room nor the bowling alley saw a game played, and the organ was dismantled and removed.

A Thoreau quotation, "Chop your own wood and it will warm you twice," appealed so strongly to Henry that he had it carved in the cypress wood mantle of the fieldstone fireplace in the recreation room. But with Edsel gone, the door was seldom opened, and the place ended up cluttered with storage.

His upstairs quarters equaled theirs in size and sumptuousness of furnishings—a bedroom big enough for a party of two dozen people, and private dressing room and bath. His parents had provided themselves with a dressing room and a bathroom apiece and a view of the trickling Rouge River, which flowed through the estate. Before long, they chose less imposing accommodations and something more congenial than their massive twin beds. They took to sleeping in an old-fashioned double, made of wicker, on the porch outside. They retired to it most nights at ten unless they were going out or entertaining at home, both of which were rare occasions.

Henry's favorite daytime spot was another porch room, where he kept a telescope on a stand for sighting the deer he turned loose in the woods of more than two thousand acres and peering at the nearest of the five hundred birdhouses to see the cardinals, goldfinches, flickers, and imported English thrushes feeding there.

He had courted Clara in these same woods. They could glimpse the cottage that had been their original home. In those days, they used to greet each other by bird calls, and the habit had not died. When Henry came in, he would whistle to Clara and she would reply in the same fashion, wherever she happened to be in the house.

He would have dinner served in his sentimental sanctuary and invite infrequent guests there. Sometimes, Clara read aloud to him in the evenings before bedtime—collecting books in leather bindings was one hobby of hers. Otherwise, he would mostly sit ruminating. "Thinking," Henry insisted, "is the hardest work anyone can do." Books only "mess up my mind." People read them "to escape thinking; reading can become a dope habit." And, sealed in his own assumed infallibility: "No one has ever yet found it worthwhile" to "know everything."

Rummaging through his ego turned up thoughts as mundane as the aphorisms in *The Old Farmer's Almanac*. Those that especially pleased him he jotted down in his well-thumbed notebooks: "Don't find fault: Find a remedy. . . . Anybody can complain." In conversation, he was as sparing with words as a Yankee storekeeper. He cherished a basic distrust of any man who spoke in more elegant terms. He relied on sycophants, on or off the company payroll, to polish his utterances for publication in his desire to emulate Edison as a global philosopher. "I have definite ideas and ideals," Ford was quoted as saying, "that I believe are practical for the good of all."

No theme was too grandiose for him to tackle. Fear? "The result of the body assuming ascendency over the soul." Money? "Part of the conveyor line." Tradition? "If it stands in the way of real progress, it must be broken down." A vein of arrogance ran through most of his maxims. "The world," he pronounced, "has been, is, and will be run by mediocre men."

Henry himself emerged unretouched when a correspondent for the New York *World* asked him, though the question was premature, how he felt "to be the world's first billionaire."

He squirmed and cocked a thin leg over the arm of his chair. "Aw, shit!" was his only answer.

He arose with the dawn and waited for a hunch to tell him how to occupy the day. He assured visitors who caught him in his office that "I have no job here—nothing to do." One notebook entry gave the reason why. Like the rest, it bore no date, but the period, 1916, was established by seven words on an earlier page, "Learned a lot on the Peace Ship." The telltale comment was even briefer. "The motor car is finished," he wrote. Lizzie was enshrined in his thinking. He could recognize her every nut and bolt. Handed a washer one day and asked where it fitted her, he took one look and tossed it out the window. "Doesn't belong in a Ford at all," he growled.

He had temporized over the form that Fair Lane should take, since nothing of this sort had figured before in his fantasies. The original Chicago architects' plans pictured a marble mansion. "What on earth would I do with a palace like that?" he asked, shying away. He figured on spending around $100,000. When all the bills were added up, they totaled twenty times as much.

Downstream from the chosen spot, he had an eight-foot dam and a four-story powerhouse erected for a start, to give him light, heat, and softened water, with so much capacity in reserve that he would supply all Dearborn with electricity, too. A swimming pool was dug; its surrounding marble benches would be electrically warmed for the comfort of its patrons' posteriors, as were the birdbaths, to prevent icing up in winter.

Fresh architects that he found in Pittsburgh satisfied him with a house of Kelly Island limestone two feet thick in a mishmash of styles fondly identified as "Scottish baronial." To provide him with precious privacy, it was positioned at the end of a driveway that wound for a mile through the woods from the guarded entrance gates on Michigan Avenue; Clara had the roadsides massed with her favorite blue woodland scilla. Between the main structure and the new artificial lake, dredged to attract wild fowl, lay a golf course designed for Edsel. Father had no use for wasting time by swinging golf sticks, but his son could be indulged in whatever he fancied. The green sward went the way of the billiard room and the bowling alley.

Once he had settled in on Iroquois Avenue, Edsel's visits to Fair Lane tapered off to the point where, after seven years of hopeful waiting, Clara commandeered part of the course for her

2½-acre rose garden, planted with bushes and climbers in the tens of thousands. "So large a garden is a great problem with all the *pests* we have to contend with, but withall a great joy," she wrote in a paper presumably prepared for fellow members of a horticultural club.

Clara held ostentation in check as best she could, for gentlefolk should not expose themselves to ridicule by flaunting aristocratic airs. Wrought ironwork for her gardens of peonies, iris, and rock flowers was shipped in from England, but she set a firm rule for the landscape artists: "No statues, thank you!"

Eleanor was pregnant when she returned with Edsel to Detroit on the train from San Francisco. There was no guessing what might happen to Edsel by the time the baby was born in the fall when the President announced in February that he was severing diplomatic relations with Germany because its U-boat fleets were once again making piecemeal attacks on merchant shipping. If this was a long step toward war, might Edsel not find himself in the Army?

Henry executed a smart and immediate about-face. He had gone on record with a proposal that soldiers in the trenches of France should call a general strike to celebrate Christmas 1915. On the day of Wilson's action against the Germans, Henry declared, "We must stand behind the President." Pacifism had been no more than a mask for the belligerence Ford felt for whatever target his fancy selected.

He promised to put his factory at the disposal of the United States Government and operate "without one cent of profit." Turnabout enthusiasm filled his brain with new notions as he sat with Clara at Fair Lane. In April, when Wilson went to Congress to ask for a formal declaration of war, Henry repeated his pledge: "Everything I've got is for the government and not a cent of profit."

That spring, he bought the steam yacht *Sialia* ("bluebird" in an Indian tongue), whose smartly uniformed crew would draw $5,000 a month in wages and rate themselves the best fed and best paid in any man's service. Always the dominator, he would challenge his guests aboard to race around the deck, then after a lap or two change the rules with a shout of "Now on one foot!" Rough weather made him queasy; his remedy was to eat. When mealtimes approached, he would haunt the galley to see what was in store. Hash was perennially popular with Henry. "Jiggs, eh?" he would exclaim, linking the aroma floating out from the iron stove with a comic-strip hero of his in George McManus's "Bringing Up Father."

Sailing was too confining to appeal much to him. He idled away the time dozing, playing the phonograph, or sitting in the engine room, watching the wheels go around. *Sialia* was more to Clara's liking, and she tolerated slapdash housekeeping at sea no more than at Fair Lane. Specks of spray on the windows meant that they must be washed as often as three times a day.

He came up with a thought for a one-man submarine to "run out below the biggest battleship afloat, touch off a bomb beneath it, and blow the ship out of existence." Young Franklin Delano Roosevelt, the bustling Assistant Secretary of the Navy, jeered. Henry, he said, always believed that a submarine was something sold across a delicatessen counter until he saw another chance to get his name into the papers.

Henry tried again, remembering Edsel's teen-age fascination with flying machines. That had prompted his father to have a Model T engine bolted into a shop-built fuselage to try providing competition for Orville and Wilbur Wright, but trials were called off when pilot and kite blew into a tree. What he proposed now was to manufacture 150,000 planes, at $.25 a pound, to bomb Germany into surrender. Of course, he disclosed his scheme to the newspapers first and added a sentence or two for his audience's benefit about how essential it was for a seer to keep his calendar clear.

"Suppose a man gets an idea," Henry said. "How is he going to develop it if the program calls for his seeing somebody at five minutes to three or sixteen minutes past four? A man with a program is like a dead fish floating down a stream." Washington was not interested in Ford's prognostications, which would become a reality only in the war after this.

One of Edsel's strengths as company secretary and founding member of the company's executive committee, which Henry tolerated for the present because it was his son's brainchild, was recognition of his own shortcomings. Looking for help when it was needed, he introduced his new brother-in-law, Ernest Kanzler, to Fair Lane.

Young Kanzler was a novice attorney now, employed by the law firm—Stevenson, Carpenter, Butzel, & Backus—that the Dodges and the Chicago *Tribune* both had engaged to represent them in their forthcoming jousts with Ford. Henry made a habit of pretending to be indiscreet: It was a good way to test a man's capacity for keeping secrets.

"Please, Mr. Ford," Kanzler would beg him, "don't talk about your affairs when I am here."

Henry only grinned. "You ought to be on my side. Why do you want to be a lawyer, anyway? They're parasites. Come to Highland Park, and I'll give you a job."

Ford was determined to thwart John and Horace. On the day after Edsel's wedding, the same morning that their $39,000,000 lawsuit against his father was announced in the newspapers, Henry called a meeting of his rubber-stamp board. The directors hastily approved the spending he planned to do, some $23,000,000 worth of expansion at Highland Park and construction at the new location on the Rouge. Even if they won in court, there would be that much less of the present $131,500,000 surplus for the Dodges to share in.

Then he had the Detroit *News* send over a reporter so that he could loose off a few preliminary shots at his latest adversaries. He could not understand why they failed to share his apostolic conviction that there was no limit to the demand for Lizzie if he kept cutting prices. "They say my course is likely to injure them. They own 10 per cent of the stock, and I own 58 per cent. I can't injure them $10 without injuring myself $58."

He doubted that Ford Motor's surplus was any too large. "I have always wanted to swing our purchases without borrowing. I have always been opposed to going to Wall Street because I don't want them to get our hide. We are not afraid of them because we have the cash assets." The conferences with Tom Lamont of the House of Morgan were conveniently forgotten.

He let a few days pass before he took aim again in the columns of the same newspaper. "Let me say right here that I do not believe that we should make such an awful profit on our cars. A reasonable profit is right, but not too much. So it has been my policy

Henry Ford, founder of the Ford Motor Company

Henry Ford with Barney Oldfield at the controls of the old Ford racer "999"

Model T owners did more than just drive their cars in the late teens and early 1920s. They even used their "Tin Lizzies" for camping

Henry Ford in 1919

Above: Thomas Edison and Henry Ford on one of their frequent camping trips.
Below: Henry Ford, himself an aviation pioneer, with Charles Lindbergh

Edsel Ford

With shovel in hand and about four years old, Henry Ford II is pictured here with his younger brother, Benson, as their grandfather, Henry Ford, looks on

Young Benson Ford with brother Henry Ford II, who sits behind the wheel of a British MG at their grandfather's Fair Lane estate in about 1930. Their sister, Josephine, is in her small car

to force down the price of the cars as fast as production would permit and give the benefits to users and laborers, with resulting surprisingly enormous benefits to ourselves. The men associated with me haven't always agreed with this policy."

Will Durant stuck to his opposing philosophy. He had made his comeback as a Goliath of the industry, riding astride the Chevrolet Motor Company. After its rapid expansion into a successful, nationwide selling operation, Will had reorganized it as a Delaware corporation, pulling in capital of $20,000,000 in the process. In a financial maneuver as dazzling as a fireworks shoot, he settled his old score with General Motors almost simultaneously. Of GM's total 825,589 shares of stock, Chevrolet had laid hands on 450,000. Chevy was now the tail that wagged the dog. Durant reinstituted himself as president of General Motors, intent on catching up with Henry with another galloping round of acquisitions of companies in the field.

Durant would shortly have a new vice-president in the long-nosed, cold-eyed personage of Alfred P. Sloan, Jr., who had known Henry since the turn of the century when Sloan started supplying Ford with the product of Sloan's Hyatt Roller Bearing Company. He had a higher opinion of Harold Wills' skills as a designer than of Henry's as a businessman. Lately, he had merged Hyatt into a new car-manufacturing business, United Motors Corporation, which Will had his eye on. Possibly the most momentous step for the future that Sloan had taken to date had passed unnoticed by anyone but himself. When he bought his first car, a Cadillac, he didn't much care for its appearance, so he ordered smaller-size wire wheels to bring the chassis closer to the ground.

Orders for war work were slow in arriving from Washington to Highland Park: 2,000 chassis for ambulances in May, 820,000 steel helmets in October. The Army asked not for Lizzies but Cadillacs, which were adopted as standard military equipment after they passed torturous testing in Texas. Ford's biggest order came from England, where fallow land had to be put under the plow to beat the critical food shortage brought about by the U-boat blockade. The British wanted tractors—urgently. Edsel had been commissioned in the first place to take care of the deal, but Henry took over. WILL COMPLY WITH EVERY REQUEST IMMEDIATELY, he cabled. WE WILL WORK NIGHT AND DAY.

Producing 7,000 tractors would be a Henry Ford, not a Ford Motor, enterprise. On his fifty-fourth birthday, he was unanimously elected president of Henry Ford & Son, which was no cause for surprise, since he, Clara, and Edsel were the sole owners of its $1,000,000 worth of stock. Edsel persuaded Kanzler to enlist with that company. Henry took him to the plant and sat him opposite Sorensen. "Charlie, show this young fellow the business." Edsel had secured his first wholehearted ally in his brother-in-law.

Before a single tractor was delivered, Henry vacillated again. He had long since had Joe Galamb fired for failing to divine just what the boss was after. The present designer, Eugene Farkas, Joe's former assistant, was doing little better. Ford wanted to postpone production until his tractor was as *right* as Lizzie. It took a campaign of flattery and a visit to Dearborn by Lord Northcliffe, British pioneer of halfpenny newspapers who was currently his government's expediter in Washington, to win Ford around. Only 254 machines had been finished by the close of the year.

By then, the main company was grappling with the problems inherited when Henry accepted a government order for cylinders for the Liberty aircraft engine that was the brainchild of the Packard Motor Car Company—a total of 700,000 in all. The forces officer who enrolled Henry into taking on the assignment would undoubtedly have failed if he had told the whole truth.

"Are you sure of exactly what you want?" Ford probed, equivocating. "Certainly," he was told. "All right. We'll do the job." The officer, a Detroit lawyer in civilian life, left no room for shilly-shally, but he knew that machining the cylinders to cobweb-thin tolerances would be a horrendous undertaking.

It seemed as though whatever contribution the two companies made toward winning the war would be concluded without Edsel. Eleanor gave birth to their son on September 4, and he was named for his grandfather. One month later, a Detroit draft board rejected her husband's appeal for exemption from serving in uniform.

Autumn brought misery all around. It gave the Dodges victory in a decision by a justice of the Michigan Circuit Court, ordering Henry to pay out a special Ford Motor dividend of $19,275,387.96 within ninety days—half the remaining nest egg stored in the banks. Henry's performance on the witness stand had done no good.

Two chameleons met when he was cross-examined by the attorney for the plaintiffs, Elliott G. Stevenson, of the prestigious Stevenson, Carpenter, Butzel, & Backus. The witness by turn was evasive, responsive, forthright, and forgetful; the lawyer coaxing, frustrated, truculent, or fulminatory. No matter how the dueling went, Henry stuck to his story.

"You're not satisfied with producing half a million cars a year?" asked Stevenson with the air of a church deacon conducting a meeting of the ways and means committee.

"The demand was not satisfied," Henry answered.

"So far as your experience of 1915–16 is concerned, you had good reason to believe you could duplicate that production and sell it at the same price next year, did you not?"

That was not Ford policy, said its master.

"You are satisfied that you could do it, aren't you?" Stevenson pressed.

"No, we couldn't and keep the same price. . . . The only thing that makes anything not sell is a too-high price."

"Yet you say you could not conscientiously think of making as much profit as you were making in 1916, didn't you? Your conscience would not let you sell cars at the price you did last year and make such 'awful profits.' Is that correct?"

"I don't know that my conscience had anything to do with it." Conscience was the wrong word, and nobody spoke of obsession. "It wasn't good business."

"You also said Dodge brothers claimed you ought to continue to ask $440 a car and that you didn't believe in such exorbitant profits. Does that express your sentiments now?"

Henry ducked. "Haven't thought of it since."

"You don't know whether these are your sentiments?" There was the bite of irony in the lawyer's voice.

"Not altogether."

"Now, I will ask you again. Do you still think that those profits were 'awful profits'?"

"Well, I guess I do. Yes."

"And for that reason you were not satisfied to continue to make such 'awful profits'?"

"We don't seem to be able to keep profits down." The witness looked genuinely puzzled by that failure.

Was he trying to keep them down? "What is the Ford Motor Company organized for except profits? Will you tell me, Mr. Ford?"

"Organized to do as much good as we can, everywhere, for everybody concerned."

The spectators in the open courtroom approved the sentiment. So far as they were concerned, Henry had personally invented Lizzie and deserved the fortune she had made him. But he had not blinded himself to the needs of his fellow man like other mogul millionaires, not caring a damn about where the money came from or how it was spent. His seeming ordinariness was an inspiration in itself. If he could succeed, then so could any workshop tinkerer. In this astounding twentieth century, a fellow who worked as hard as Henry might stumble on something along the lines of the telephone, radio, electric light, or moving pictures, to make a pile for himself, too. Henry Ford, a model for all to follow, was losing the lawsuit, but he was reaping a harvest of public sympathy.

"You did not object in the beginning to pretty satisfactory profits?"

"We needed them."

"You started in to make money, didn't you? That was why the company was organized?"

"I didn't give it much thought. The best way to make money in business is not to think too much about making it." Tom Edison would approve of that adage.

"But you got a lot of money out of it, and you still do, don't you?"

That was because he didn't let the subject of money prey on his mind. The whole purpose of the expansion was "to do as much good as possible for everybody."

Meaning?

"Well, to make money and use it, give employment, build factories, and send out the car where the people can use it." Almost as an afterthought, he repeated, "And incidentally to make money."

Stevenson pounced. "*Incidentally* make money?"

"Yes, sir. Business is a service, not a bonanza." Fresh echoes of Edison.

"But your controlling feature, since you have all the money you want, is to employ a great army of men at high wages, reduce the selling price so that a lot of people can buy your car cheap, and give everybody a car who wants one?"

"If you give all that, the money will fall into your hands. You can't get out of it."

Counsel tried a change of tack. Now, about Ford employees. How were they affected by rises or falls in profits when they had no share in them? "Did you tell them they had to hustle more because you had reduced the price of the car?"

Yes, Henry had said that. Stevenson's patience snapped, or perhaps it was theatrical pretense. He demanded a fuller response than this "mumbo jumbo." He closed in on the witness, jabbing with his spectacles. "Didn't you state that $5.00 a day and an eight-hour workday made them hustle so that they did not have any more hustle left in them at the end of that time?"

Incorrect. Henry's own temper began to rise. "What do you know about how they hustle?"

"I am asking you," Stevenson countered. "I am not on the witness stand. I am not a manufacturer."

The tight smile showed on Henry's face. "That's easy to see."

Interrogation turned to the internal workings of Ford Motor. "Your directors are very accommodating. Whenever you ask them to ratify anything, they usually do it?"

"They usually do. Yes."

"And if they don't do it, they wouldn't be there, would they? They haven't done anything for you to turn them out."

"I don't turn anybody out."

"Because they have always done what you have asked them to do?"

"Not always."

"Tell us some instance where they haven't."

Henry took cover again. "You look it up, and you will find it."

"Just give us a single thing that the board of directors have refused to ratify that you recommended."

"I don't know of anything," Henry admitted.

Stevenson pointed a finger at his victim. "This is the board of directors, right here."

It was as difficult to nail down Henry as jelly to a tree. He pitched his responses so softly at times that only the court stenographer could hear him. He would insist that Stevenson "separate the question so I can understand it." When his own counsel, Alfred Lucking, a professional associate of Mayor Maybury, prompted him with written records, Ford was quick to comprehend; if Stevenson reread the words, Henry didn't quite grasp their significance.

The Dodges' attorney held out to him a ledger to sharpen his memory of some real estate Henry had bought. Henry scowled. "I don't need it."

"Just take the book."

"No. I don't need the book at all. Just take it along with you." He deposited the tome on the rail in front of the stenographer.

Stevenson's anger erupted. "I will get a direct answer from you, and don't you forget it."

Henry mumbled that he would not be able to read the figures, anyway, but yes, he *could* read—sometimes.

"You can't always?" the lawyer demanded. "You can read *sometimes*, you say?"

"Yes, but not in the dark."

"Do you consider it dark now?"

"No, no." The way could not be found to have him open the book.

About the original investments in the company. Was it true that he had put no more money into the business than John and Horace Dodge? "You started with a model of a car, didn't you? A pretty poor model, too, wasn't it?"

"It seemed to sell all right, and I put fifteen years of work into it."

"And who made the first cars?"

"Dodge brothers made part of them."

"They made the motors and frames. They made the whole thing except tires and bodies. Isn't that right?"

The witness resented the impugning of his reputation. "From our drawings," he said sharply. With them to work from, any capable mechanic could have built the Model A.

Stevenson continued in his scorn. "Mr. Ford had a barn—a carpenter shop. The completed car was taken to the carpenter shop, wasn't it, Mr. Ford, and there the body was put on, and you sold it? Dodge brothers spent $60,000 to $75,000 to re-equip their plant to do the work, to retool. They jeopardized everything they had."

"I don't know what," Henry interjected.

"Well, you didn't have anything to risk, did you? . . . And the Dodges gambled with their business to undertake the manufacture of an undeveloped car, didn't they? . . . You have forgotten that they produced the cars that brought the money to make you a success. There isn't a doubt of it, is there?"

A reluctant, muttered "No." He could not wait for an opening before he sprang on Stevenson. "If you sit there until you are petrified," Henry growled, "I wouldn't buy the Dodge brothers' stock."

"I didn't ask you to buy the Dodge brothers' stock," the attorney protested.

"Nor any other stockholders' stock. I don't want any more stock."

"Did I ask you anything about that?"

"No," said Henry firmly, "but that is what you are talking for, and nothing else."

Shadow boxing could not cover up the fact that Henry *had* withheld profits from shareholders. That was an "abuse of discretion," Judge Hosmer ruled in his decision, made public early in December, and immediately appealed by Henry. The new Bolshevik master of Russia, Lenin, was then talking peace with the Germans, promising the disintegration of the Allies' eastern front. Ford's business with Washington had spurted in the meantime. The company had orders for complete Liberty engines now, and a contract was in the making for building a fleet of U-boat chasers. Production of Lizzie was down to three hundred a day.

Edsel had not been drafted yet. Ever since February, he had been debating the idea of volunteering, but Henry had dissuaded him. That was his parent's version of events, anyway, related a year later. His son, who tried always to pretend that Henry could do no wrong, would not allow the truth of this. He asked for exemption, he said, because "I believe I will be of far greater service to my country right here in the plant."

Not surprisingly, he and Eleanor postponed the thought of providing baby Henry with a brother or sister. When that time came, it gave signs of careful planning on her part, in keeping with her nature. Benson, their next child, was born on July 20, 1919; their only daughter, named for her Aunt Josephine, four years later almost to the day; and finally on March 14, 1925, a third son, who had to be christened for his departed Grandfather William, no matter what Eleanor's father-in-law might think.

Edsel was aware that there were acceptable methods of keeping out of front-line duty. He could count on receiving an officer's rank in the reserve, for instance, if he simply bought a patrol boat and donated it to the Navy. Or a similar Army commission could have been arranged for him on Wilson's say-so, followed by assignment back to his Highland Park desk.

A Detroit newspaperman, Edwin Pipp, who left the News to work for Henry and soon regretted it, considered, "It took more courage for Edsel Ford not to put on a uniform than it would have taken to put one on."

The White House heard from Henry about the draft board's obstinate treatment of his son, but the issue never came to a head. A change in regulations made Edsel safe from military service on two scores: He had dependents, and he was classified as irreplaceable in a war industry.

A fresh cause for domestic alarm surfaced in 1917: extortion and the fear that little Henry might be kidnaped. The endless publicity that Grandfather generated made the Fords readily identifiable targets. Well-wishers, job-hunters, promoters, curiosity-mongers, and would-be borrowers with tales of heartbreak to tell ambushed the adults of the family whenever the opportunity arose. Old Henry's armed bodyguards had standing instructions to keep them at bay, but he would order his car stopped if the fancy took him to pick up any stranger for a ride. When Clara was away, he liked to have one or two of the more promising trade-school students spend a few days at the house. When his whim had spent itself and he tired of them, they were dropped instantly, bewildered by their treatment at his hands.

The first aspiring extortioner chose Edsel as his intended victim; Jacob Yellin was sentenced to a five-year term in prison. There was soon to be a newcomer on the company payroll who would be more than willing to take on responsibility for protecting the Fords from danger, and he made a skyrocketing career out of the task.

Harry Herbert Bennett wore bow ties because he once came close to being strangled by his own four-in-hand, clutched by the man he was fighting. With Navy service behind him as well as bouts as a semiprofessional lightweight who boxed as "Sailor Reese," bouncy little Harry was entangled in another street brawl near the Battery in downtown Manhattan when Arthur Brisbane, Hearst Newspapers editor and columnist, happened by. The police were about to hustle Harry into a waiting paddy wagon when Brisbane talked them into releasing the tigerish ex-seaman into his custody.

Brisbane had an appointment with his friend Henry at the Ford offices on Broadway. The reformer in Henry was fascinated by ex-convicts and ne'er-do-wells; in his philosophy, a job with him could be their salvation. "If a man can make himself of any use at all, put him on, give him his chance," he would say. Brisbane took Bennett along to the meeting and delighted Henry with an account of Harry's mighty punch and fancy footwork.

"I can use a young man like you," Ford said. Bennett's initial job at Highland Park scarcely suited his special talents. He was employed in the art department, an oddball assistant with the scars of battle on his nose and cheeks.

He came to Henry's notice again when he was transferred, on the strength of his Navy service, to supervise some of the chores involved in building the submarine chasers—"Eagle" boats, as they were called. There was nothing he wouldn't do for Henry, who began using him for any number of extracurricular activities with no specified job, no desk, and no salary except for what Henry paid him from his own pocket; his income dipped that year to $983,931, while Edsel's amounted to about two thirds of that. One of Harry's commissions was guarding the Edsel Fords, whose Iroquois Avenue house afforded them none too much security.

"What I like about Harry," said his taskmaster, "is that if I want something done, he will do it. I don't have to tell him twice." Henry, who found any kind of rigid organization intolerable in his business, made Bennett answerable only to Ford, and after his humiliation in the Dodge suit, Henry set out to assure himself of ever more absolute power.

Edsel's cherished executive committee was disbanded for a start, and expansion plans were momentarily left in abeyance. Anyone who disagreed with Henry was prompted into resigning, even Harold Wills, the key designer of Lizzie whom the industry called the "mechanical genius of Highland Park." Wills and another Ford veteran, John R. Lee, began planning a new automobile to carry Harold's name, with Wills' severance pay of $1,592,000 to draw on for starting-up expenses.

Henry was no more able to chose a single objective at any one time than a greyhound let loose in a meadow full of hares. President Wilson had opened this midterm election year of 1918 by presenting to Congress his Fourteen Points for peace. Every Senate vote he could command would be needed to ensure that postwar Europe would be shaped according to his terms. He asked Ford down to the White House and played shamelessly on his vanity. "You are the only man in Michigan who can be elected," Wilson told him, "and help to bring about the peace you so much desire."

Henry's consent to run was so carefully hedged that, win or lose, no one would believe that he cared much either way. "I shall not spend a cent nor make a single move to get into the Senate," he vowed. "I shall not have a campaign organization nor pay any campaign bills. I do not care anything about parties or politics or politicians. I would not walk across the street to be elected President of the United States. I certainly would not make a public speech to get the nomination or to be elected." This last precaution was essential for his ego's sake. The prospect of uttering even a word or two before an audience appalled him.

The task he accepted from Wilson was to defeat Theodore Roosevelt's onetime Navy Secretary, Truman H. Newberry, in the solidly Republican state. While Henry carried out his lackadaisical promise to the letter, his opponent showered Michigan with gentlemanly speeches and nearly $200,000 worth of campaign propaganda. GOP tacticians kept him aloof from the dirty tricks department, which made mountains out of the draft deferment of Edsel, skulking behind a desk, so it was said, while their candidate's two heroic sons fought in France.

Theodore himself joined in with an endorsement for Newberry. "The expenditure on behalf of pacifism by Mr. Ford in connection with the Peace Ship . . . was as thoroughly demoralizing to the conscience of the American people as anything that has ever taken place. The failure of Mr. Ford's son to go into the Army at this time and the approval of the father of the son's refusal represent exactly what ought to be expected from the moral disintegration inevitably produced by such pacifist propaganda. . . ."

On Election Day, Newberry squeaked in with 220,054 votes to Ford's 212,487, and Henry was convulsed into action. "Wall Street interests" had bought his rival's victory. Henry sanctioned the hiring of platoons of private investigators to ferret out evidence of corruption and bribery. Petitioning the Senate to investigate Newberry's spending, Henry demanded a recount. The second tally showed him the loser by 5,737 votes. Newberry's fate took longer to resolve. In March 1920, he was fined $10,000 and sentenced to two years for conspiracy to violate the Federal Corrupt Practices Act.

But the damage caused to Wilson and his daydreams of permanent peace by Ford's do-nothing campaign was irretrievable. In spite of the slurs on Edsel, a modest effort in time and money to swing fewer than 3,000 ballots would assuredly have seated Henry in the Senate, to make a total of 48 Democrats instead of 47. The 48–48 tie, by giving Vice-President Thomas R. Marshall the tie-breaking vote, would have kept Cabot Lodge of Massachusetts, Wilson's ultimate nemesis, out of the chairmanship of the Foreign Relations Committee.

In defeat, Henry's desires quivered like a compass needle in a suddenly magnetized field. He wouldn't walk across the street to be elected President of the United States? Well, maybe not. Yet what might happen if the sovereign people of this country knew exactly what ideas and ideals he had to set before them? Before November was over, he bought a local weekly, the Dearborn *Independent*, to carry his pristine message to the nation, ungarbled as it had been in the past by "capitalistic newspapers" owned and controlled by his old jousting partners, the greedy bankers of America. He made himself president of the new Dearborn Publishing Company, with Clara as vice-president and Edsel the secretary-treasurer.

For the time being, there was more urgent business to attend to. On the morning of November 11, uncompleted tanks occupied the floor space at the Dearborn factory. Minutes after news of the Armistice came, they had been hauled away, and the machines required for reverting to tractor manufacturing were being wrestled into place. From his office, Henry called Washington to report that Dearborn was back on peace work, effective immediately. At Highland Park, he issued similar orders: "The war is over . . . we should stop this job." In less than a month, a thousand Lizzies a day were rolling off the lines again, but the Michigan Superior Court had still not assessed the rights and wrongs of the appeal in the Dodge case.

Tramping through the frosted woods of Fair Lane, communing with himself while he checked the bird feeders, Henry concluded that he had waited long enough. The strategy he had used before to have his way with Malcolmson ought to work again this time. Henry would break away from Ford Motor and create a rival to Lizzie as a specter to panic his adversaries. On New Year's Eve, his compliant directors accepted his resignation as president of the Ford Motor Company, with appropriate regrets to be recorded in the minute book, and elected the equally compliant Edsel to succeed him. Then Henry took Clara, their son, daughter-in-law, and grandchild off to enjoy some winter sunshine at their home in Altadena, Southern California. They made the journey in his private railroad car, whose splendor surpassed anything Harriman had ever owned. On this trip, Henry did not indulge himself, as he sometimes did, by having the train slowed down before breakfast so that he might work up an appetite by jogging along behind it.

Getting him away from the strife was Clara's doing. He had gone through a punishing year, and the familiar psychosomatic symptoms may have returned. Some hard thinking was called for from father, mother, and son.

Early in February, the Michigan Superior Court upheld the judgment awarded to the Dodge brothers against Henry. "A business corporation," it was noted, "is organized and carried on primarily for the benefit of the stockholders. The powers of the directors are employed for that end. . . ." A different set of rules must be written for Henry's prospective new business.

On March 4, he gave his first interview in months to a newspaperman called to his Altadena home. The following morning's headlines scared the wits out of the Dodge brothers, the other surviving shareholders, the dealers, and the entire automobile industry. HENRY FORD ORGANIZING HUGE NEW COMPANY TO BUILD A BETTER, CHEAPER CAR. The price? $250. How many employees? About 200,000. The design? Completely different from Lizzie. The proprietors? The Ford family exclusively—Henry Ford & Son, Incorporated, would be the manufacturers. Capital? The $12,000,000 that would be Henry's share of the $19,000,000 he was compelled to distribute.

Where were the cars to be built? "We propose to dot the whole world with our factories because I believe that every family should have a car, and it can be done," said the champion of the common man.

The old company? "Why, I don't know exactly what will become of that," he said offhandedly.

Edsel's approach was less hardboiled, though their separate efforts kept the situation rocking like a car being eased out of a snowbank, with Henry in forward drive and his son alternating in reverse. They expected to make the new creation "a competitor of the streetcar rather than the Ford," Edsel assured anxious Ford dealers. A little later, he applied more grease to quiet their alarm. "A new car may be manufactured, but as to when . . . we are not in a position to say, except that we do know a new car could not possibly be designed, tested out, manufactured, and marketed in quantities under two or three years' time." (His spelling was better than Henry's, but his syntax was weak.)

He promised that there would be no interruption in making "the reliable Model T." In other words, the $250 automobile, despite Henry's claim that it "is well advanced for I have been working on it while 'resting' here in California," was no more substantial than flash powder fired to conceal a magician's sleight of hand.

The shareholders feared nevertheless that its ex-president had doomed Ford Motor to eventual extinction. Together, they owned 41½ per cent of the company—8,300 shares. Henry wanted all of them. Otherwise, he threatened that he would buy none. As early as January, he had been in touch with the bankers of the Old Colony Trust Company of Boston, whom he enlisted to carry out the secret negotiating. They met with minimal resistance; the handwriting was all too legible on the wall.

Ten days after the Altadena interview, the Gray estate's 2,100 shares were offered at $9,000 each to another banking house under a fifteen-day option. Two weeks later, John and Horace Dodge granted an investment broker purchase rights to their combined holding of 2,000 shares at $12,500 each. Two years previously, they had rejected a Rothschild bid of $18,000. Henry's bombshell was having double impact, simultaneously softening up the sellers and driving down the price.

Stuart Webb, an Old Colony vice president, began the bargaining at $7,500, then inched the figure up until it reached $11,000. He nudged the Bureau of Internal Revenue into coming forward with a preliminary valuation of a little less than $9,500 a share, and on that basis garnered the whole crop at $12,500 with one exception—Jim Couzens' 2,180 holding.

Couzens would treat neither with Webb nor Henry, but he would listen to Edsel, his favorite Ford, if the price was right. For an extra $500 a share, he agreed to sell. "In executing this option," he wrote knowingly, "I recognize that it is desired by said Ford for special reasons particularly for the purpose of obtaining for himself and his father . . . as nearly complete ownership of said company as may be possible." Like the rest of the sellers, he would be hit with a staggering tax bill when Internal Revenue reconsidered its hasty arithmetic. In his case, it amounted to $9,000,000.

On July 10, Ford Motor declared the dividend that the courts had mandated, plus interest of $1,536,749.89. The next day, the stock deal was completed. Henry, in his delight, danced a jig around his office. He pretended that the coup had all been Edsel's doing.

"All credit for the successful efforts to centralize the control of the company in the hands of Mr. Ford and his son is given to the young president," said the official news release. "He it was who persuaded his father that this was a better method of carrying out their established policies than creating and organizing a new corporation."

It cost Henry just under $106,000,000. The only means of making up such a sum was to go to the banks, which he affected to despise, and borrow $75,000,000. Edsel had to give up his customary weekend golf games—he played left-handed, in the eighties—to sign the wad of notes that were to be put up as collateral. But when the transaction was complete, every stick of the business was finally Henry's, Edsel's, and Clara's, with respective holdings of 95,321, 71,911 and 5,413 new shares. Ford was master of his universe: Lizzie, the tractors, real estate, his newspaper, the lot, merged into a single giant corporation.

He had seventy-two hours to enjoy the sensation, and then he was hailed into court once more. After three years of skirmishing, his suit against the Chicago *Tribune* claiming $1,000,000 for libel was under way in the little town of Mount Clemens, straddling the Clinton River on U. S. Highway 25, twenty miles or so northeast of Detroit, with beetle-browed Judge James Tucker presiding.

Special trains and the automobiles that lined every street had ferried in sightseers by the thousand to clog the square outside the red-brick courthouse. The Park, the Colonial, the Medea, and every other hotel normally occupied by visitors to the local spa were filled to capacity. Half a hundred reporters covered the story, served by the clattering telegraph machines that fed copy direct to the city rooms.

In front of the bench in the stifling, white-walled courtroom, half a dozen Ford attorneys crowded one wooden table. Half as many again jostled each other in the *Tribune*'s cause at another table set up next to it. To enter, Henry had to pass by a homely, hand-painted sign that exhorted seekers after justice, "If you spit on the floor in your own home, do it here. We want you to feel at home." The humor was lost on him. He had no reason to look forward to another roasting at the hands of Elliott Stevenson, and his nose was stuffed up with hay fever besides.

The defense stratagem was to make it appear that not the *Tribune* but Ford was on trial, and Judge Tucker condoned the maneuver. The newspaper had branded Henry "an ignorant idealist." Stevenson was granted ready permission to establish that the witness was a genuine blockhead. Henry writhed in his chair, long chin cupped in his fingers.

"Did you ever hear of Benedict Arnold?"

"I have heard the name."

"Who was he?"

"I have forgotten just who. He is a writer, I think." The press corps behind the courtroom rail scribbled frantically.

"Ever read any of his writings?"

"Don't believe I have."

"Are you not aware that the action of Arnold constituted one of the first incidents of treason in American history?"

"I don't remember." To cover his confusion, Henry stooped to fiddle with a shoelace. The *Tribune*'s string of legal lights flickered congratulations at each other. From Alfred Lucking, appearing again for Ford, came hisses of "Outrageous . . . cruel . . . a shame to subject that man to such an examination"; it was Lucking who had prompted Henry to bring suit in the first place. The judge saw no cause to intervene.

Did Mr. Ford know anything about an American revolution? "I understand there was one in 1812." Any other time? Not that Henry had heard of. Hadn't he learned that the United States was born in the revolution of 1776? No; he hadn't paid much attention to such things. The doors at the back of the room swung open and shut as newsmen tiptoed out to the telephones.

Stevenson sprinkled salt on the wounds with the delicacy of a gourmet confronted with an underseasoned goose. "Men like Pershing are murderers—is that your idea, Mr. Ford?"

"I guess the general will admit committing many a murder. Killing anyone is murder."

"How about Ulysses S. Grant?"

"Yes, I think he said war is murder."

A smiling correction. "I think you are wrong there, Mr. Ford," Stevenson cooed. "General Sherman said war was hell, but neither he nor Grant said it was murder that I ever heard of."

Henry fancied that he had him there. "I think General Sherman said it was murder."

Henry was kept on the grill for eight days. During breaks in the cross-examination, he liked to cool off, attended by counsel and soothed by his staff, along the banks of the river that flowed behind the courthouse. He carried a steel measuring tape, which he would unreel in silence to figure the clearance between any bridge he was standing on and the level of the running stream below.

The most he would permit himself to say for publication was

that water power was a great source of energy and Mount Clemens obviously had plenty of it. Inevitably, word spread through the town that Mr. Ford was contemplating building a dam, a hydroelectric generating station, and a branch factory to provide jobs for Mount Clemens' citizens. If the eleven farmers (one of them retired) and the road contractor who made up the jury did not get to hear about that, it would be a miracle. Judge Tucker, recognizing the work crying out to be done in an agricultural community at the height of the growing season, held court only on weekdays, and for a limit of 4½ hours a day at that. "Out of Mount Clemens by Christmas," groaned the newspaper reporters, who had been here since the trial opened in May.

When the affair was over, a surprised Ford Motor engineer explained why the rumored developments that intrigued the townspeople were downright impossible. The landscape was so flat that any dam across the Clinton would flood the fields. Mr. Ford must have been thinking of something else, of course.

He might have been given some inkling of what to anticipate in the witness box when the *Tribune*'s soldierly publisher, Colonel Robert Rutherford McCormick, was personally leading his cadre of attorneys from his twenty-room suite in the Park Hotel. In Colonel Bertie's muddled mind, military men were heroes and their critics therefore self-condemned as traitors or tomfools. He claimed in his day to have introduced the Reserve Officers' Training Corps into colleges, and machine guns into the Army, though the facts contradicted him on both points.

Edsel, who preceded his father on the stand, had been exposed to fresh taunts about his civilian status in wartime, combined with a commendation by one defense counsel of ramrod Bertie's six months of glory on the battlefields of France. The colonel's martial influence was again unmistakable when Stevenson asked Henry about a statement attributed to him, assessing militarists as inferior beings to professional gamblers.

"One gambles with lives," Henry explained. "The gambler does not do any harm."

"You prefer the professional gambler to the soldier?"

Yes, he did.

An advertisement printed with his endorsement during the

Peace Ship era referred to the militarists' preparedness campaign as "ballyhoo." Would Mr. Ford define that word?

"A blackguard, I guess."

Lucking confounded the confusion with a suggestion of his own: "A barker?" Stevenson jeered, "a shouter to sell his wares."

Henry hopefully picked up the cue. "At a peanut stand or something? There's a lot of blackguarding there."

He was quizzed about a two-hour interview he gave at Dearborn in 1916 to an inventor and professed firebrand rejoicing in the name of Henry Alexander Wise Wood, who was appearing here as a witness for the *Tribune*. Henry had vowed, Wood testified, that when the war ended, the Stars and Stripes—a "tribal emblem," like every other nation's flag—would not fly again over Highland Park. "Patriotism is the last refuge of a scoundrel," Ford had added, without identifying the quotation as the handiwork of Dr. Samuel Johnson. Wood, in his ignorance, attributed it to Henry, "a rotten American."

"Mr. Wood was a gentleman, wasn't he?" Stevenson prodded.

"He did not look free."

"What was there about him? Did he look like a slave?"

"A slave? Yes, a slave to the financiers. I judge so from the things he said."

"What did he say?"

"I don't remember now, but I think he was trying to trap me into saying things."

At the end of each day's ordeal, Lucking would try tutoring Ford in Henry's hotel. The cram course in United States history got nowhere. Henry would stand at the window, gazing at the view. "Say, that airplane is flying pretty low, isn't it?"

Lucking would steer him back to a chair, but within seconds his pupil would be back at his observation post. "Look at that bird there. Pretty little fellow, isn't it? Somebody around here must be feeding it, or it wouldn't come back so often."

In the courtroom, he steadfastly declined to glance at any of the printed matter extended as exhibits by his interrogators, just as he had refused once before to open a company ledger. The day arrived when Stevenson set another snare. "Mr. Ford, I have some hesitation about the question I am about to ask, but in justice to you I will put it." Henry had perhaps unwittingly created the impression that he could not read. "Do you want to leave it that way?"

Henry scarcely blinked. "Yes, you can leave it that way. I am not a fast reader. I have hay fever, and I'd make a botch of it."

The lawyer underlined his point. "Are you willing to have that impression left?"

"No, but I'm not a fast reader."

"You *can* read?"

"I can read."

"Do you want to try it?"

A soft, insistent "No."

"You would rather leave it that way?"

"I would rather leave that impression." Stevenson slid one hand over the other in self-congratulation.

The jurymen took ten hours of the night of August 14 to render their verdict. The *Tribune* was guilty of libel, but nowhere near $1,000,000 worth—only $.06, to be precise. Both sides claimed the victory. Henry would never appear on a witness stand again if he could avoid it. The threat of a subpoena could be depended on to hasten a settlement out of court. He had been stretched on the inquisitors' rack once too often. Now he had to get on with extending his empire on the Rouge.

Will Durant was running hard on Ford's heels, with apparently limitless capital resources to sustain him in the race to overtake Lizzie. In four golden years of war, E. I. du Pont de Nemours & Company of Wilmington, Delaware, had supplied 40 per cent of all explosives shot off by the Allied armies and netted a profit of $237,000,000. For some time, the du Ponts had been casting around for a new venture with growth potential deserving a portion of their riches. General Motors qualified as a conditioned risk for the investments.

This year, General Motors employed nearly 86,000 men and women, and close to $22,000,000 was forthcoming in dividends. The du Ponts owned 28.7 per cent of the business. With authorized capital stock hoisted to more than $1,000,000,000, the company budgeted $37,398,000 in expansion funds to double its output, confident that the postwar boom in automobiles would bring a gratifying return on every penny spent.

Thousands of families were mortgaging their homes lest their

neighbors overshadow them in keeping up with the times. To
ease the financial strain of buying a new GM car, installment purchasing had just been introduced via the credit services of General
Motors Acceptance Corporation. In GM's laboratories, the search
was beginning for a method to reduce a chronic problem of automobile engines, the knocking inside its cylinders caused by the erratic combustion of low-grade gasoline.

A monstrous, twin-towered building commissioned by Durant
as company headquarters was rising fifteen stories high above Detroit's downtown skyline. It was not too fanciful for him to conclude that his progress was commemorated by the world's first
three-color traffic lights, which had been recently installed on the
city's streets.

BOOK
TWO

Chapter Five

To Clear the Eyes of Man

Under the beaver-fur hat, the little, round-cheeked Ford boy bore the look of his father at the same age of three, though not a soul in the crowd had known the family long enough or well enough to be able to spot the likeness. A beaver hat would have been an unimaginable luxury for three-year-old Edsel when *his* father was working nights on the quadricycle in his coalshed workshop off Bagley Road. This morning, May 17, 1920, with Edsel on course to being one of the ten richest men in the world, the hat was a commonplace dress item for his firstborn son's first appearance for public inspection.

For once, Henry Ford II was to be encouraged to play with matches as the principal performer in the ceremony. Blast Furnace A at the company's new colossus on the Rouge River was ready to be lit. Two years ago, the two-thousand-acre site had been marshy wasteland, too remote from downtown Detroit to hold any obvious promise of development. Marking time on construction of a superfactory until he had all the company stock securely in his hands, old Henry had fiddled with blueprints that were largely unintelligible to him, then fussed endlessly with a scale model made with every wall and window reproduced in miniature to help him visualize what he was after.

Lately, work had advanced at the pace set by roustabouts raising a circus tent. Battalions of carpenters, masons, bricklayers, tilers, plumbers, electricians, and painters swarmed everywhere.

The emerging complex of towers and superstructures, smokestacks and bridges resembled nothing so much as a Jules Verne fantasy, a city of the indeterminable future whose inhabitants would commute to the moon. Nothing in the world matched this marvel that was taking shape on the Rouge. It was to be the womb of Lizzies in the millions.

A network of twenty railroad tracks bisected Miller Road on the eastern boundary, laid down to give the Pierre Marquette Railway temporary right of way for incoming trainloads of supplies, which were shunted then over the company's own twenty-four miles of internal rail lines. An overhead skein of conveyors, ramps, and walkways provided means for aerial transit. The crew engaged on the powerhouse with its cluster of eight landmark chimneys soaring into the sky were racing to finish ahead of the gangs laboring on the foundry, which stretched four hundred yards from corner to corner.

Most of the structural steel was already in place. Concrete for the generator and compressor beds was still being poured. Some buildings were roofed; others were no more than partially finished walls or mere foundations. More of the job would have been completed to date but for old Henry's ceaseless prowling around the site, checking on details. The two-hundred-foot wall of one coke oven unit bothered him. The engineer in charge would not agree that it was out of line until Henry's stony stare broke him down. Yes, it was half an inch off true.

"Take it down," Ford commanded.

Engineers of the United States Army had widened and dredged the little river to provide passage for barges and Great Lakes shipping under a providential Act of Congress passed when Henry promised, to the amazement of no one, to make the necessary water's-edge land available and scoop out a turning basin. Overground storage pits, capable of stockpiling two million tons of raw materials in reserve, stood parallel to the company docks alongside a railroad spur.

Riding herd on the whole endeavor was Charlie Sorensen's responsibility. He strode across its acres like a gladiator, tossing back his blond cowlick, ready to kick the backside of any man he caught slacking. One of the troops under his nominal command was Harry Bennett, who had begun recruiting heavy-fisted bruisers of his own kind in the cause of "security" on the site.

On this May morning, Edsel and Eleanor brought along young Henry from their new home on East Jefferson Avenue, a vaguely Italianate brownstone house roomy enough for their growing family. Harry's surveillance of their safety from extortionists and kidnapers continued.

Lighting up a blast furnace differed from the christening of a liner in that only a match was called for, not a bottle of champagne, which Grandfather would not have condoned. Inside the tower, scaffolding had been erected, with a charge of cordwood and coke piled on its top. Wood shavings, saturated in oil, would ignite the kindling once the shavings had been touched off with a flame. Clara stood by at the front of the crowd of Ford staff and overalled workmen.

Young Henry showed signs of careful upbringing in his unfamiliarity with the box of matches. Grandfather took over, and on the stroke of twelve, a thin film of white smoke drifted from the stack; when it had aged enough to receive a full charge of limestone and coke, it would brew five hundred tons of molten metal every day. The Edsel Fords applauded, Clara beamed, and the rest cheered as Henry swung his grandson up on his wiry shoulders. Little Henry clapped his hands, as pleased with himself as everyone else was with his introduction to Granddaddy's institution.

There were almost 9,000,000 automobiles on the highways this year, a record-breaking 220,000 of them built in March alone, gulping down a major share of the 443,000,000 barrels of gasoline produced in these twelve months by a companion industry whose fortunes were linked with the carmakers'. Lizzie remained her old self in virtually every respect but two: She sported a steering-wheel rim of manufactured composite instead of wood, and post-war shortages of materials had forced up her price, to Henry's chagrin. A runabout currently cost a customer $550, almost $50 more than last year. He intended to put an end to this frustration as soon as he could get the Rouge into fuller operation, syphoning in raw ore by land and water for conversion on the spot into the metals of her being, and paying no markups for anybody's profit along the lines of supply.

"No factory is big enough," he insisted, "to make two models of cars. Let them concentrate on one." Lizzie must be an only child.

He smelled that the market for her was bigger than ever, and the latest census figures would confirm his intuition. The tally of Americans stood at 105,711,000, an increase of 15 per cent in ten years. He could picture more than 1,500,000 potential additions to the ranks of Lizzie's admirers. The headcounters disclosed the scale of her impact on those for whom she had been conceived. Farmers and their families were on the move, deserting fields and pastures for the towns. The turning point had come in the past decade, which brought them the wheels on which to travel beyond a few miles from home.

For the first time, city people outnumbered country dwellers, and Americans were joined in a mass migration from eastern to western states, careless of whether or not they resettled themselves close to a railroad. Lizzie had unique abilities for taking them anywhere they might choose to go. In her standard form, she was almost as flexible as the concertina model made in Hollywood as a favorite prop of the Keystone Cops, with the trick of doubling back on herself, front to rear. She could scale mountains and traverse streams with equal ease or even climb a flight of steps, as one or two of her adherents were happy to demonstrate.

These were disturbing times, rife with alarm as entrenched modes of living were washed away by the surging changes of industrialized society. A national search was under way for scapegoats to blame for the erosion of established values. Not a man in a million had the prescience to lay responsibility on the automobile. Wilson's new Attorney General, A. Mitchell Palmer, accused "Bolsheviks" and "anarchists" of plotting to undermine the country. The Red scare had erupted the day after New Year's when police raids in thirty-three cities sent 2,700 men and women to jail. While little Henry played with matches at the Rouge, the raiding, the undercover federal espionage, and the mass arrests continued. Hundreds of aliens had been deported with no pretense of a trial.

Chances of an unprejudiced trial were remote for Nicola Sacco, shoemaker and radical agitator, or Bartolomeo Vanzetti, fish peddler and admitted anarchist, when they were taken on April 15, and accused of killing the paymaster and a guard during a payroll holdup at a South Braintree, Massachusetts, shoe factory three weeks earlier.

Throughout the spring, businessmen in general had great hope for 1920. Labor's efforts to drive wages up to match inflated postwar prices had brought strikes against the railroads, the steelmakers, the mineowners, and some automobile parts manufacturers, but those troubles were over for the time being. On March 1, the Supreme Court had concluded that the gargantuan United States Steel Corporation was not of unreasonable size, and Will Durant shared the relief of fellow expansionists in the business community.

Hunger for new cars seemed insatiable now that installment buying made it possible to obtain delivery from most dealers for little more than $100 down. General Motors benefited more than Ford. Chevy sales would reach 129,525 this year, still far behind Lizzie's, but enough to help close the profit gap between the two surviving giants of the industry. Ford would net $644,830,550; GM, $567,320,603.

If only Henry could forget his prejudices against borrowed money, his company would maintain a longer lead, but Lizzie sales must be strictly cash, in his judgment. Edsel was more flexible, and on this account he worked behind his father's back. Edsel's views went on record in a letter to a major credit company:

"I believe, as you do, that a corporation such as yours is a very necessary adjunct in the financing of motor car sales . . . it may be interesting to you to note that at least 65 per cent of our cars and trucks are handled by the dealers on a time payment basis. I also feel that the time payment plans will become more important as time goes on."

Discontent among workingmen; construction delays at the Rouge; shortages of the materials essential for his cars; a burden of bank debt; the creeping revolution that was degrading his idealized farmers into townsfolk and mechanics—who or what could Henry blame for the mood of unrest that he found everywhere? He could never be one of the handful who recognized that Lizzie herself was helping in the making over of America. So far as he was concerned, the new age aborning was a backward step for the human race, and the culprits were the Jews.

Five days after his grandson's fire-lighting ceremonial, Henry's

newspaper ran an anonymous front-page story under the banner
line, "THE INTERNATIONAL JEW: THE WORLD'S
PROBLEM." Its opening argument was as hackneyed as its pur-
ple prose:

"There is a super-capitalism which is supported wholly by the
fiction that gold is wealth. There is a super-government which is
allied to no government, which is free from them all and yet
which has its hand in them all. There is a race, a part of humanity
which has never yet been received as a welcome part and which
has succeeded in raising itself to a power that the proudest Gen-
tile race has never claimed—not even Rome in the days of her
proudest power. It is becoming more and more the conviction of
men all over the world that the labor question, the wage question,
the land question cannot be settled until first of all this matter of
an international super-capitalistic government is settled."

How long Ford's anti-Semitism had been coming to the boil
was impossible to tell. He personally set the starting date as far
back as 1916, when he was aboard *Oscar II*. "On the Peace Ship
were two very prominent Jews," he told a reporter. "We had not
been at sea two hundred miles before they began telling me of the
power of the Jewish race, of how they controlled the world
through their control of gold, and that the Jew and no one but
the Jew could end the war.

"I was reluctant to believe it, but they went into detail to convince me of the means by which the Jews controlled the war, how
they had the money, how they had cornered all the basic materials
needed to fight the war and all that, and they talked so long and
well that they convinced me.

"They said, and they believed, that the Jews started the war,
that they would continue it as long as they wished, and that until
the Jew stopped the war, it could not be stopped. I was so
disgusted I would have liked to turn the ship back." Here, then,
was the meaning of his cryptic notebook entry: *Learned a lot on
Peace Ship*.

Henry's antagonism intensified after the 1918 Armistice. At the
Dearborn plant one night, he came across a belated staff member
who had bought two candy bars to stave off his appetite while he
worked. Henry, who kept a supply of mints in his own desk

drawer, helped himself to one bar of candy, took a bite, munched for a moment, and then returned the remains to the wrapper.

"This stuff isn't as good as it used to be, is it?"

The employee said that he had not noticed any difference to speak of.

"The Jews have taken hold of it," Henry muttered. "They're cheapening it to make more money out of it."

Intolerance infested his bowels. Nine months prior to the Dearborn *Independent*'s onslaught, he had gone off on one of his summer camping trips with Edison; Harvey Firestone, who manufactured tires for Fords; and John Burroughs, the white-whiskered naturalist whose companionship Henry cultivated. They traveled as usual by motor caravan, made up of Lizzies fitted with special bodies for these excursions. In his log of the trip, Burroughs wrote: "Mr. Ford attributes all evil to the Jews or the Jewish capitalists—the Jews caused the war, the Jews caused the outbreak of thieving and robbery all over the country, the Jews caused the inefficiency of the Navy of which Edison talked last night."

No thermometer could ever be invented to gauge the fluctuating fever of anti-Semitism, but the 3,300,000 Jews living in North America were enjoying rare tranquillity by comparison with the repression and persecution that this same generation had suffered and still suffered overseas. A political reawakening in Europe was leading to rehabilitation of the Jewish population in most countries there. "Even in Russia," as an encyclopedia designed for young readers noted, "the condition of the Russian Jews appeared more hopeful" under Bolshevik rule.

Distrust of them among the *goyim* kept a majority of American Jews clustered together in ghetto sections of most cities, but a hypothetical fever thermometer would have registered no unusual cause for alarm. The virus was quiescent, and Jews could expect the calm to continue. The automobile industry by and large was non-Semitic rather than anti-Semitic. Wagon making, engineering, work in a blacksmith's shop, and the other trades that spawned the horseless carriage attracted only a few Jews. Their number among the grimy mechanics who turned out cars was relatively small, too. Nobody of Henry's prominence had sought to make a reputation for Jew-baiting until he vented his venom in the pages of his newspaper.

The issue of May 29 returned to the theme, and so did that of June 5. For twenty consecutive weeks, there would be no letup in the search for converts to his belief that "the clear eye of the man who sees and understands is something that even the evil powers of Jewry cannot endure."

Neither Edsel nor Eleanor shared in Henry's bigotry, but both son and daughter-in-law were too discreet to say anything in public against him. Edsel would never acknowledge that there were differences between them. "I have not worked out a separate business philosophy for myself," he said later. "It has not been necessary, for on all material points I agree absolutely with my father's philosophy. I do not merely accept his beliefs; I feel as strongly about them as he does." He was dissembling, which was one of his weaknesses.

The ranting of the Dearborn *Independent* every week dismayed him, and not solely on ethical grounds. More and more Jewish firms and individuals avoided buying Ford cars, trucks, and tractors. Out of sympathy or to keep the goodwill of Jewish customers, many gentiles followed their example. Complaints from dealers about the boycott descended on Edsel's desk. Henry's response was to have pressure applied to impel them to buy bulk copies of his newspaper for distribution. Sales of the *Independent* climbed toward the half-million mark.

The few men close to Henry who declined to take their every cue from him tried to find someone other than Ford to blame for his outcries. Maybe the infection had been picked up from Edison, who applauded the weekly series. Or perhaps it was Ernie Liebold, who had promoted himself as Ford's alter ego in much of the company's business. It was Liebold, certainly, who replied when Detroit's leading rabbi, Dr. Leo M. Franklin of Temple Beth-El, sorrowfully returned a car given to him by Henry as a friend and visitor to Fair Lane.

"I sincerely hope," the secretary wrote in smug illiteracy, "that conditions will so adjust themselves as to eventually convince yourself that Mr. Ford's position is correct, as resulting therefrom the world and all its people may benefit thereby."

Liebold *had* joined Ford some time before the Peace Ship

fiasco. Liebold *did* hold opinions about Jews that would have sat well with a Don Cossack. It *was* Liebold who in June presented his master with a copy of that discredited Tsarist forgery, *The Protocols of the Elders of Zion*, and then hired private detectives in a fruitless hunt for more "evidence" of Jewish knavery.

The secretary only fed a fire that had started by spontaneous combustion. Henry's infused hostilities against bankers, Wall Street manipulators, warmongers, and the desecrators of American tradition all smoldered together and burst into flame.

Edwin Pipp, who quit the editor's chair at the *Independent* in disgust as soon as he heard what was being planned, had his own theory of Henry's purpose. "I believe he hoped to win votes by attacking the Jews. He knew there were about 3,000,000 Jews in the United States, and he figured he would gain three or four or five votes on non-Jews for every Jewish vote lost. He knew the feeling existent in thousands of small towns because he was a small-town boy himself. From 1916 one could see his changing mind. At first, he talked only about 'the big fellows' and said he had nothing against Jews in ordinary walks of life. Later he stated, 'They are all pretty much alike.'"

If the rigmarole printed in the *Independent* was to be believed, Jewry was engaged in an international conspiracy to gain control of the world's wealth by demoralizing the gentiles with wars, revolutions, anarchy, and debauchery. Immorality was rampant because Jewish gold was working to render morals "loose in the first place and keep them loose." The Jewish garment industry was hastening the decline by merchandising shamelessly short skirts, complemented by rolled-down stockings and rouged knees. Jewish entrepreneurs produced the debasing trash of Hollywood and Broadway. Jazz bands, gambling halls, lewd nightclubs, and the panting fiction of such incendiarists as Elinor Glyn—"every such activity has been under the mastery of the Jews."

The weapons they employed for world conquest were money and the nation's newspapers, all of them except the crusading *Independent*. "The current press in general is open only to fulsome editorials in favor of everything Jewish while the Jewish press take care of the vituperation." The British Navy's devious mission was to shield the conspirators' maneuvering overseas as part of a secret bargain to ensure Britain a share in the loot. Such overdue revelations would inevitably be greeted by parrot cries of "Persecution!" though the root of all the trouble lay in "the oppression of the people by the financial practices of the Jews."

The sales boom that General Motors might have expected as the boycott of Ford products spread did not develop. Once again, Durant had overextended himself. The shakiness of the American economy sent Wall Street stock prices plunging at the end of April. First to sound the alarm in Durant's headquarters was the company treasurer, John Jacob Raskob, who was a du Pont man and a Jew. General Motors shares had lost 42½ points in a single afternoon.

The backlog of orders that the automakers had regarded as the equivalent of money in the bank melted away in the course of the summer. There were bankers who refused to make any more customer loans for buying a car. General Motors' problems affected a regiment of shareholders. Henry's financial quandary was his exclusive concern. The Rouge had cost him more than $60,000,000 to date; he had paid out at least $15,000,000 to make himself the proprietor of mines and timberland that would supply the raw products for fabricating Lizzie; and his debts to the banks would fall due in less than a year. He resolved the crisis like an autocrat born and bred.

Edsel, Kanzler, Sorensen, and others were summoned into conference. Price cuts were the solution, Henry told them. It would mean losing maybe $20 on every sale, but part of the loss could be made up on selling the parts and accessories that went with Lizzie, like the electric self-starter for $75 and demountable rims for $25; these were always a profitable source of revenue. How much could be lopped off the cost of the cars?

He glanced at the figures that his hirelings jotted down before he tossed them aside. Not good enough. When they tried arguing with him, he pulled out the sheet of paper he had brought along in his pocket. "There, gentlemen, are your prices."

The others passed the page among themselves, heads shaking. Cuts on this scale would bankrupt the business. "Give it back to me." On two of the models, Henry knocked the price down by another $5.00. The discussion was over.

Toward the end of September, he astonished the country and convulsed his competitors by announcing that $155 had been sliced off the tag for the runabout, bringing it down to $395, with similar reductions all along the line. "Inflated prices always retard progress," stated Henry, the pundit. "We had to stand it during the war, although it wasn't right, so the Ford Motor Company will make the prices of its products the same as they were before the war."

For Durant, it was the *coup de grâce*. He made an attempt to buck the trend and hold his pricing firm. General Motors stock suffered a further washing in consequence. The du Ponts closed in on him like hounds after a tired fox. They bought another 2,500,000 shares with funds borrowed from the House of Morgan, bringing their holdings up to 36 per cent. General Motors was saddled with $83,000,000 of new loans, and Will Durant for the second and final time was ejected from the presidency of the empire he had founded. "Well," he joked as he quit, "it's moving day." His personal debts approached $35,000,000.

His successor, Pierre S. du Pont, chairman for almost four years, had been satisfied until now to leave the running of the business in Durant's uncertain hands. With his pince-nez and tonsured fringe of gray hair, Pierre lacked only gaiters and a reversed collar to pass as a bishop of the Episcopal Church. It was doubtful whether his knowledge of automobiles would enable him even to turn an ignition key. As a member of the oldest dynasty in American industry, he had no need to, when there were corps of servants waiting on him.

Yet among the du Ponts, Pierre had been a motoring pioneer, the first to take a flyer by investing in 2,000 shares of General Motors stock at par value during the days when Durant was warming up to Chevrolet. Prudent Pierre saw this addition to his portfolio as "something very risky," not unlike backing hundred-to-one shots at the racetrack.

Generations of his family had run up their munitions business into a vast, tightly held monopoly, while they remained aloof from their fellow titans, isolated on their thirty separate estates in Delaware, cousins often marrying cousins. It took Pierre to open du Pont eyes to the fresh fortunes that might be made by promoting their multifarious projects to the public instead of restricting sales to such customers as the United States Government, which bought whole categories of explosives for the Army and Navy from du Pont alone.

What particularly intrigued Pierre was the phenomenal increase in the number of closed cars he observed on the streets in place of older-model runabouts and touring cars open to wind and rain unless the drivers wrestled up their canvas tops. He interpreted this as a sure sign of an expanding market for paint, varnishes, artificial leather, and other du Pont products available today or in prospect for tomorrow. Artificial leather was already a reality in du Pont laboratories. They were using confiscated German patents in their dyemaking. They had bought out any number of plastics manufacturers to organize du Pont Viscoloid. Their rayon business, du Pont Fibersilk, would shortly be earning $5,000,000 a year.

Pierre's appointment as president of General Motors reassured Wall Street and the banks—and stirred Henry's bile. The du Ponts to him were merchants of death, evil capitalists who fomented war for profit, and now the implacable enemy, out to do him in.

Pierre's benign appearance was a disguise. The subsurface steel had shown itself twice in interfamily feuding over who among them should control du Pont. In the first, he contrived to displace Cousin Alfred as general manager after Alfred divorced his first wife, Bessie, and gave the new Mrs. du Pont, another cousin, a white marble palace of seventy-seven rooms surrounded by a nine-foot wall, built, he explained, "to keep out intruders, mainly in the name of du Pont."

In the second go-around, Pierre bought all Cousin Coleman's stock in the company to the tune of $14,000,000 to give himself complete operating command. Within a matter of months the value of the shares increased fourfold.

Morale at General Motors skidded on Durant's ousting. What would happen under absentee ownership exercised by bankers and munitionsmakers who probably did not give a damn for automobiles, only for arithmetic? The malaise ran through the company from bottom to top. Sloan was one vice president who debated whether this might be the moment to pull up stakes.

Durant's purchase of United Motors had made Alfred Sloan, a boy from Brooklyn, a millionaire at forty-one. That had to be con-

sidered good going when, after graduating with a degree in electrical engineering from the Massachusetts Institute of Technology,
his first job at Hyatt Roller Bearing paid $50 a month. Everything
he owned was tied up in General Motors stock, and the corporation was falling apart. He had an offer to join Lee, Higginson that
he wanted to mull over. He took a vacation in Europe and placed
an order for a Rolls-Royce to keep his spirits up.

He never took delivery. He would try working along with Pierre.
It was a relationship that, from its inception, hummed as merrily
as a top. First came a fresh round of cutbacks, firings, and liquida-
tions to shrink the company to manageable size. For all that, it
would lose close to $39,000,000 in the next financial year, with
Chevy in the red for $1,000,000 in one particularly disastrous
month.

General Motors, Sloan reflected, "was a management by crony,
with the divisions operating on a horse-trading basis." This must
be remedied before health could be restored. What he had to find
was a method of co-ordinating resources without loss of the advantages of having more than one basket in which to carry the
corporate eggs.

Research was developing a host of new products for du Pont, so
research would be made a priority for General Motors, too. Pierre
set du Pont designers and engineers working for his affiliated business and approved the creation of a specific research corporation as
part of automaking.

After meeting Henry three years earlier, Pierre had vowed, "I
would not step on his foot in the production of a small car." President Pierre and Vice-President Sloan reconsidered their situation.
It would be suicidal to compete head on with Ford under the best
of circumstances. Today, they simply could not afford the infinite
expense of duplicating the assembly lines that churned out Lizzies
like razor blades at prices nobody else could match. But they
could, Sloan thought, "take a bite from the top of his position."

In its directors' judgment, General Motors had the means of
doing this in a new engine that the company's house genius,
Charles Kettering, had devised in his Dayton, Ohio, workshop.
His credentials were impressive. For almost ten years, an earlier invention of his, the electrical starter, had been successfully installed
in Cadillacs. Kettering proposed getting rid of a car's radiator and

much of its plumbing by cooling the motor with air rather than water. Copper fins brazed or welded to the engine's outside walls would do the trick, he said, resulting in less weight and reduced cost.

This was it—a Chevrolet with Kettering's copper-cooled motor competing with Lizzie in the mass market, where every dollar knocked off the price meant thousands of new customers. Nearly two years must be allowed to gear up production, but the men of General Motors looked forward to putting a crimp in Henry's sales.

That came about in the fall of 1920 without any effort from his competitors. The Detroit industry was gripped by a recession that put 150,000 men out of work. The postwar boom in automobiles was finished. Price cutting had failed to keep Lizzie out of the same hole into which everybody else slid.

Ford's financial picture looked as dark as it had ever been. Company cash totaled $20,000,000. The $25,000,000 balance of his debt to the banks fell due next April. He had a mind to hand out $7,000,000 in New Year's bonuses to the staff. And he calculated that he owed $58,000,000 in taxes. Edsel and Kanzler together had been struggling for a year to introduce some semblance of organization into the company, which Henry ran like a Byzantine emperor.

Since Lizzie was flawless in Henry's eyes, neither he nor any other man could improve on her perfection. He had no thought of designing another car. There was nothing left to fill his time except his drive to dominate. Ostensibly, he shared responsibilities with Edsel, making himself in overall charge of engineering and manufacturing, while he delegated his son to run the business side, subject to Henry's veto, which was exercised as capriciously as a cat's playing with a captured mouse. He had to control Edsel along with everyone else. Power could rest nowhere but with Henry.

No job with Ford carried an accompanying title, and any man might find a second assigned to do the same job simultaneously. Henry liked to pit one executive against another as a method of making them both work harder. His way of testing an employee was to load him with the semblance of authority. If it went to his head, Henry would see that he was cautioned against overreaching himself, always delegating someone else to issue the warning. The warning in itself was part of the game. If it prompted the recipient to approach Ford personally to find out what was going wrong, the employee would be met with an amiable word of advice to forget the whole incident. A few days later, he might find himself fired, again by an underling, never by the master.

William S. Knudsen, as burly a Dane as Charlie Sorensen, suffered the treatment. Knudsen's star had risen fast following his expert handling of the Eagle boats contract. It was time for him to be humbled. He discovered that Henry was either revoking Knudsen's orders or advising his staff to ignore them. Knudsen would have to fight back or quit. Edsel attempted to save him for Ford Motors by posting him to England to supervise production there. Sorensen, jealous of his onetime assistant's prowess, ran complaining to Henry that the assignment should be his.

Henry was at Fair Lane, nursing a fever, when he summoned Kanzler and told him to get rid of Knudsen. Kanzler argued, as Edsel would, that the man was too valuable to be sacrificed. "I see that you don't want this job," Henry grunted. "I'll give it to Sorensen. He'd love to fire Knudsen." It turned out to be a dependable forecast. Knudsen trod the path that took him and others like him from Ford into General Motors, where he was to wind up as president.

He had something besides superior ability to disqualify him from soldiering on for Henry. Knudsen was one of the little group of key executives whose help Edsel was looking to in his Sisyphean effort to systematize the business. Knudsen believed in teamwork, not in Sorensen-style bullying. Knudsen evoked cooperation from men who worked for him, without teaching lessons in humility, as Sorensen did, by taking an ax to chop up the desk of a supervisor he thought was getting above himself. Henry would not tolerate any line of command unless it led to his throne. He had a soft spot for bullies, provided they deferred to him. Anyone befriended by Edsel would sooner or later be out of a job, usually with no more reward than his paycheck on the day of leaving.

The reorganization plans of Edsel and Kanzler were stillborn in the near panic of 1920. Sales figures for December sagged to fewer than 43,000 cars and tractors. Edsel's search for new markets had put him in contact with the Bolshevik rulers of the Soviet Union eight months after Tsar Nicholas and his family were assassinated in Ekaterinburg, but the only contract signed so far called for delivery of a mere four hundred Lizzies. Taking account of the vehemence of anti-Bolshevik sentiment in the United States, Edsel kept the negotiation strictly confidential.

Henry could not resist an oblique reference to the hoped-for deal in "Mr. Ford's Page," which ran every week in his newspaper. "When every nation learns to produce things which every nation can produce," his ghost wrote for him, "then we shall be able to get down to a basis of serving each other along those special lines in which there is no competition."

With the contract concluded, his latest customers wanted to meet him to prove that "Soviet Russia is inaugurating methods of industrial efficiency compatible with the interests of humanity." The sentiment appealed to Henry, but no meeting ever came about. The *Independent* did carry a subsequent puff for the U.S.S.R., a rarity in those days, headlined "Russian Trade and Industrial Opportunities." Henry had not yet committed himself to lumping communism in with the rest of the targets of his continuing exercise in anti-Semitism.

Edsel and Kanzler hired efficiency experts to work along with them in producing an economy program to cope with the cash crisis. The effort was a waste of time. Henry was in no mood to be orderly when his company was tottering. The ax he swung was as broad as Paul Bunyan's.

First to feel its heft was the Dearborn tractor plant, closed indefinitely. Highland Park came next, shut down on Christmas Eve. Buying of raw materials was abruptly ended. The market was glutted with Lizzies. Behind locked gates, senior managers and superintendents took over caretakers' jobs. Edsel and half a dozen others put in a machine-shop floor. When that was done, some of them had the choice of being let go or serving as watchmen. Others swept the floors to maintain Henry's standards of cleanliness. On roller skates and bicycles, demoted managers went on their rounds up and down the echoing aisles between the silent assembly lines, grateful to have work to do.

Orders for spare parts represented the only source of cash, so spending had to be held to a trickle. The ax fell on most of the office staff; entire departments were obliterated. But more drastic steps were needed to accumulate money. Henry began stripping every office and factory unit of equipment to sell at a store opened by the company on Miller Road. Desks and furniture were shipped out by the trainload. Every refrigerator, cooking range, and counter in the Rouge cafeteria went on the block. Machine tools, file cabinets, typewriters, lamps, and telephones were offered for sale. Not a pencil sharpener remained in any office. If a clerk wanted a point on his pencil, he bought his own knife.

"We are having lots of fun," Henry reported. There were estimates that these bargain days brought in as much as $7,000,000.

It was nothing like enough. To Edsel and others, it seemed that the only salvation lay in huge new bank loans. Henry liked to pretend in later years that the possibility of going begging to bankers again never crossed his mind. Historians found conclusive evidence that his son's exploring was done with his full knowledge. Edsel sounded out financiers in Detroit; Liebold undertook the same mission there and in Manhattan. As word leaked out of what they were doing, the bankers themselves sought audience with Henry. He had Liebold fob them off—all but one, who succeeded in arranging a meeting at Fair Lane, from which Edsel was apparently excluded.

The caller from New York, identified as a vice-president of a House of Morgan affiliate there, came quickly to the point: the loan that the Ford Motor Company would surely require for survival.

"But I don't need to borrow money," Henry objected. "I can finance all my company's operations myself."

The banker thought otherwise. "We know your obligations. We know your cash reserves. And we know you need money." The bank had gone so far as to formulate a refinancing plan, which he had here in his briefcase. The Ford men present—Sorensen and Liebold among them—took their cue from Henry and listened in silence while the visitor read aloud from the typewritten pages.

He interrupted himself with a question. "Who is going to be the new treasurer of your company?" The position was currently held by Vice-President Frank Klingensmith, a onetime assistant to Jim Couzens.

"That makes no difference to you, does it?" growled Henry.

"Oh, yes, it does. We'll have to have some say as to who the new treasurer shall be."

Henry gave a nod to Sorensen, who claimed to know his master like an open book. Sorensen handed the banker his briefcase and with no more than a word or two escorted him to the door. The money changers were seeking again to invade Henry's temple, but he had thwarted them as he had before.

The next morning, Edsel was given an additional job. From now on, he would be the company's treasurer, though it cost him another member of his scratch team. Henry let Liebold handle the firing of Klingensmith, and the secretary welcomed the opportunity. He was proud that he did not "give a damn what happens to anybody," and besides the ex-treasurer was half-Jewish.

"Klingensmith used to line up with a lot of Jewish bankers," Liebold reminisced, "and that's what Mr. Ford didn't like. When Klingensmith got to advocating that we ought to borrow money, why, Mr. Ford thought that these fellows put him up to it."

Henry resorted to a trick he had played before to make good on his promise that "I can finance all my company's operations myself." Fourteen years before, he had forced Ford dealers to pay cash for the cars he shipped out to them on sight-draft bills of lading, fobbing off on them the burden of raising money. He would do the same now. He ordered Highland Park reopened "right away, Monday, getting those cars out to the dealers. People want cars, and they need them. That's where we'll get our money."

Fifteen thousand men reported back for work at the Ford plant at the start of the week, February 1, 1921. The recession was wearing itself out. Packard and Studebaker were already operating again, but Ford's recovery still held elements of risk. A rebellion by enough of its 6,000 or so dealers could spell ruin.

A man who sold Lizzies had to hustle if he hoped to succeed when prices were held at rock bottom, and he never knew when his commission might be chopped again to a scant 10 per cent. At best, he made roughly $60 on a sale. Company policy demanded that his showroom be kept as bright and spotless as Mary Ford's kitchen. Roving agents, some equipped with cameras, checked to make sure that there was no slipshod housekeeping, no backsliding in the hunt for customers.

He was expected to curry his territory with a fine-tooth comb, keeping files of prospects and ringing doorbells as assiduously as any encyclopedia salesman. He was deluged with advice and exhortations from headquarters on providing Lizzie owners with prompt, efficient, and reasonably priced service in line with her procreator's thinking: "It does not please us to have a buyer's car wear out or become obsolete. We want the man who buys one of our products never to have to buy another."

A Ford dealer must operate as a loner, forbidden even to discuss his problems with his comrades in the trade, only with his superiors in the pecking order that finished with Edsel, who was in overall charge of selling Lizzie. The dealer had the benefit of not a single dollar's worth of company advertising. Edsel was a believer in the powers of persuasion in print and promotion. Henry vetoed any such spending. If a dealer chose to advertise Lizzie, that was his responsibility.

The pressure, always heavy, was increased as Ford syphoned in cash to ease the present predicament. It would have been heavier if Henry, content that he had found the right answer, had not lost interest in the implementation of his decree. Outcries of protest from the field led Edsel to send company roadmen to deal with complaints. Unless a dealer buckled down, he would find his territory cut, with a new Ford agency opened up close by to provide him with some therapeutic competition. If he persisted in his protests, he would be put out of business, his franchise canceled.

Only a tiny fraction suffered the extreme penalty. Most banks were ready to extend credit for the carloads of unordered, unexpected Lizzies that stood waiting for delivery on railroad sidings. If a dealer had trouble with a banker, a company traveler would lend a hand in the negotiating. By mid-April, Highland Park was roaring again, taking back more workers every week, with cars rolling off the lines at the million-a-year mark. In that month, Henry had enough cash to pay off all his debts and have some $30,000,000 left over.

There was a little fixing he wanted done to improve the seaworthiness of the *Sialia*, which rolled like a barge in heavy weather, and at the same time provide him with more deck space in which to stretch his legs. He had the yacht cut in two to lengthen her by twenty feet, while diesel power replaced the old steam engines. The tab exceeded $1,000,000, but he still got seasick, and the hull leaked at every seam.

He also continued to make his own bed in his stateroom every morning. He performed the same chore in any other cabin into which he slipped away to take his midmorning or midafternoon nap. It was useless for the chief steward to remind him that the cabin staff was paid to do that.

"I can make a bed and tidy up a place as well as any of them" was Henry's standard reply.

Reconstructing the *Sialia* took four years. Before the job was finished, Henry had launched the first of seven freighters designed to sail the Great Lakes, hauling ore to the Rouge. Sailing in the *Henry Ford II* one morning, Henry ordered cocoa for young Henry and Benson, who were on board with him. After what seemed an inordinate amount of time, Henry wanted to know the reason for the delay.

"With electricity, it takes longer to heat, Mr. Ford," the deck steward explained.

Henry accepted the point. When the *Henry Ford II* docked, he made for the yard where work on the *Sialia* was nearing completion. For her new galley, he had stipulated an electric range as a replacement for the old iron stove, which had been removed as junk and thrown onto the pier.

Henry retrieved the stove. "Forget about the electric range. Send this stove back to the Rouge and tell them to rebuild it. I'm going to put it back in the boat." When Granddaddy ordered cocoa for his grandsons, he wanted it served in a hurry.

Chapter Six

Rue with a Difference

Edsel's problems with a father who would be satisfied only by making his son a facsimile of himself were a subject never to be discussed except with Eleanor. Their children heard nothing said at home about the tyranny under which Edsel worked and lived. In their eyes, Granddaddy could do no wrong. He doted on them. To spend a few days at Fair Lane with him and Clara—known to the family as "Callie" now—was always a welcome break from their cloistered existence in the house on East Jefferson Avenue, shielded from a rapacious world by Bennett and his guards.

Summers at Fair Lane meant swimming in the pool, into which Henry and Clara seldom dipped a toe. She had the surrounding marble benches scrubbed with soap and water every day. In the winter, there were sledding and skating on the lagoon with Granddaddy and the Santa Claus workshop that he had built in the woods when young Henry, called "Sonnie," was four years old. One Christmas, Granddaddy tied antlers onto his farm horses to convert them into reindeer as an extra surprise.

The children could do whatever they pleased at Fair Lane, as though he were making up to them for the material things he could not afford for Edsel at their age and were trying to give them a taste of his own boyhood. As part of the journey into the past, he had them over to sleep in the hayloft, and he led them into the woods to see maples tapped for sweet, amber syrup. The servants thought that he spoiled his grandchildren, but of course that was not to be mentioned to him or Clara.

The children knew nothing of any friction between Dad and Granddaddy. Edsel and Eleanor kept their troubles to themselves, never saying a word against Henry. Now and then, Sonnie and Benson had a feeling that something was wrong, but it was impossible to lay a finger on it.

Their parents' visits tapered off to average one a month. Edsel telephoned his father every evening to report on the business of the day, but under his wife's influence, he was pushing as hard as he knew how to create his own identity, a separateness from Henry's. In her late twenties, Eleanor had developed into a woman of character at least as strong as Clara's.

Eleanor had no inclination to be swamped by Henry, no matter how wily his efforts were. For instance, the nail of the little finger on his left hand was allowed to grow half an inch or more. He explained to a caller, "I've been letting it grow to show Eleanor how silly women look with nails like that. I guess I'll spray it with paint after a while." So far as was known, the experiment did not send his daughter-in-law hurrying in shame to a manicurist.

Henry had a winter home in Fort Myers, Florida, standing among four acres of palm, mango, and grapefruit trees next to Tom and Mina Edison's place. Edsel and Eleanor's choice for a summer retreat was as far removed as was physically possible within the borders of the United States: Seal Harbor, Maine. But she was careful to blur the edge of the decision. In her strong, graceful hand, she wrote Henry, "I am so crazy to have you come up here that I can hardly stand it. You would just love the forest walks revealing the mountain tops where you are unconscious of the existence of anything human." The hint that her father-in-law loved scenic grandeur above humanity may have been deliberate. She had not brought herself to address Henry and Clara as anything other than Mr. Ford and Mrs. Ford.

The Edsel Fords' new stone "cottage" standing on seventy-five high acres of Mount Desert Island above the village of Seal Harbor cost $3,000,000. Their children remembered it with no great joy. The fog rolled in too often, leaving them with little else to do but retire to the playhouse for games of hide-and-seek. Fair Lane and Fort Myers were a salutary distance away. Here, Edsel could pursue the pleasure he found in boats and racing in any kind of vessel, powered or in canvas. He christened the flagship of his little fleet *Eleanor*.

He tried three times to win the international powerboat races on the Detroit River before he quit. One craft sank under him; another had a propeller shaft coupling smashed when he engaged the clutch as the starting gun fired. He lacked his father's instinctive feel for engines and how they should work as well as Henry's urges to tinker with people. Edsel bought five sailboats in Quincy, Massachusetts, and had them delivered in Maine to tempt his neighbors into joining in the sailing races.

In their self-protective reticence, he and Eleanor were two of a kind. Either by choice or by nature, she avoided any glimmer of limelight. Henry was more than welcome to their share. A friend of theirs came up with a partial explanation. "Nine out of ten people they meet want them to buy something or give them something."

Edsel and Eleanor were willing givers to any cause that appealed to them. This, too, divided them from Henry. He held that "philanthropy, like everything else, ought to be productive." He would scrawl an address in his little notebook as a reminder to have a Lizzie presented to some stranger who took his fancy, but his charity usually ended there. Though $200 in cash was perpetually kept on hand for him under the inkwell of his desk, he avoided carrying so much as a dime in his pockets to be given away to anyone. Henry was a taker, not a giver. "I have no patience with professional charity," he boasted, "or with any kind of commercialized humanitarianism."

Clara was rather different. She felt it to be her Christian duty to go to church, along with her reluctant husband. Remembering the Sunday evenings of his youth, when he scanned the pews for pretty faces, he used to joke that churches made the best place to find a wife: "Marry a girl you meet in church." One or two people wise to Henry's character concluded that he might have gone farther than eyeing attractive women if Clara had not kept a rein on him. Clara's contributions to churches were generous—well over $1,000,000 in her lifetime—with particular emphasis on the rehabilitation of unwed mothers and sinners in an assortment of other categories. She liked nothing better than to investigate the case histories personally.

Only rarely could she coax Henry into going to a concert that she thought she ought to attend. He preferred playing the Victrola in the library—Negro spirituals, anything by Stephen Foster, and "Who Put the Overalls in Mrs. Murphy's Chowder?"—taking a turn around the floor alone if Clara was not there to dance with him.

Concerts numbed him with boredom, and the greater the degree of it, the deeper he slid into his seat. He had often disappeared from view before a performance was over. Musicians to him were a species apart: "They tend to their business, and I tend to mine." But his occasional presence once encouraged fundraisers for the Detroit Symphony to approach him for a subscription. They made no other effort when they received his curt reply: "Any top organization of any kind ought to be able to get along on a self-supporting basis."

The Detroit Symphony, the Community Chest, the Red Cross, and the Detroit Institute of Arts were all on the donation lists of Mr. and Mrs. Edsel Ford, eager to make amends for Henry.

Henry insisted time and again that he would not give a plugged nickel for any painting, and he meant it, as the dealer Joseph Duveen discovered when he tried to add Henry to his roster of customers, which included the elder Morgan, Andrew Mellon, and Henry E. Huntington, the railroad heir.

The procurer of old masters for new American rich took it as a personal challenge that Henry, for all his millions, had bought nothing more spectacular to hang on Fair Lane's walls than Currier & Ives prints and an engraving of Landseer's "Stag at Bay." With an abysmal sense of timing, the dealer decided to rectify the situation in 1920, when Ford's finances were at their nadir. Rather than venture alone, Duveen rounded up four Manhattan confrères to share the glory along with the preliminary expense.

Their ploy was to produce three magnificently bound volumes of full-color reproductions of what they proclaimed to be the hundred greatest masterpieces in the world of art, all of which happened to be obtainable at a price. The plan was to convince Henry to buy the lot and establish himself as the instantaneous, indisputable king of collectors. He agreed to receive the five conspirators at his home.

The sight of Fair Lane's bare walls, decorated in the main with

Ford Motor Company calendars, heartened them. So did their host's evident pleasure with the three books they ceremoniously handed to him. "Mother," he called to Clara, "come in and see the lovely pictures these gentlemen have brought." She turned the pages with the same reverence as her husband.

Duveen, as spokesman, felt that the hook had been firmly planted. "Yes, Mr. Ford, we thought you would like them. These are the pictures we thought you should have."

Henry played the hayseed. "Gentlemen, beautiful books like these, with beautiful colored pictures like these, must cost an awful lot."

Duveen hastened to correct the impression that he and his fellow plotters were a species of traveling salesmen. The volumes, he said, had been prepared specifically as a gift for their host. Henry protested that he could not possibly accept such a lavish present. His visitors were stymied. There was nothing left for Duveen but to confess the motive of their mission. "Mr. Ford, these books were gotten up to interest you in buying the pictures represented in them."

Henry's lips tightened. "But, gentlemen, what would I want with the original pictures when the ones right here in these books are so beautiful?" The butler showed the defeated to the front door, dragging their tails and leaving their bait behind them.

The arts were another area where Edsel could emphasize his distinctiveness. The sketches and drawings he had made as a boy were more indicative of interest than of creative ability, but they were enough to build on. He took up painting as a hobby for relaxation after impossible days at his desk, receiving lessons from John Carroll, and going to weekly classes at the Detroit Society of Arts and Crafts.

He began collecting, too, but not as an illiterate who would be preyed on by the likes of Duveen. Edsel and Eleanor realized that to buy intelligently, they must first educate themselves in what to look for. He persuaded Dr. William H. Valentiner, director of the Institute of Arts, to hold a seminar, which husband and wife went to twice a week. They took him with them to Europe during the course of two summers as counselor and guide on their tours of museums and galleries there, learning to appreciate true quality in a painting or a statue.

Edsel made his first donation of a work of art to the Institute in 1920. The gifts followed year by year, judiciously chosen, unobtrusively made, $600,000 worth of them, reflecting Eleanor's taste together with his own. Among other things donated by the younger Fords, the museum's walls and halls would eventually contain a Donatello horse valued at $100,000; a fourteenth-century Pisano marble; a Tang dynasty lion's head; Flemish tapestries and Persian rugs comparable with anything in New York's Metropolitan; paintings by Fra Angelico, Verrocchio, Titian, and Caravaggio; a "St. John" by Andrea del Castagno; and Renoir's "A Cup of Chocolate."

He kept up with golf, as did Eleanor, who made a never-to-be-repeated hole-in-one at their country club. They went to baseball games and took their children along as soon as they were old enough. They played tennis and had Sonnie and Benson join in, usually with Eleanor and the older boy taking on the other two.

They had riding horses at the farm they established at Haven Hill, sixty miles away from the torture chamber in Dearborn, and they went together to the racetrack now and then, where winning a $5.00 bet was a big event for Eleanor. They enjoyed entertaining and being entertained by the young rich of Detroit—the Books, Calkins, Jacksons, Potters, and Macauleys were some of the notable names. She was accessible by telephone if the *News* or *Free Press* society editor wanted to check out a guest list.

She reversed the procedure one morning by making a call to a woman editor. "I thought you might get wind of this and print it. I wish you wouldn't. We'll be in the soup for sure if it gets out that we gave—a cocktail party yesterday." Her listener knew something of Henry's views on alcohol as the root of all evil, not excluding war: "It made the wine-drinking French and the beer-drinking Germans suspicious of each other." Her listener promised there would be no paragraph about young Mrs. Ford's fall from grace.

At Fair Lane, the principal refreshment served continued to be grape juice. Now that Lizzie was selling well again—more than a million Ford cars, trucks, and tractors in 1921 for 60 per cent of the total market—tranquillity had been restored. Henry was reading less and less these days because he disliked wearing spectacles to correct his aging vision, but Clara kept him up with the times by reading aloud to him. Bedtime came sharp at ten most evenings. Every night, he would fluff up her pillow before she climbed under the covers. Their mingled snoring was a favorite joke in the servants' hall.

A taste of revenge increased Henry's contentment. He had waited almost twenty years for the day he received a plea for help from the man who usurped his place in the old Henry Ford Company after Ford insisted on building racing cars instead of salable commercial models. For most of that time, the name of Henry Martyn Leland had been synonymous with that of the Cadillac Motor Car Company. No finer cars had been produced in the United States when Durant added Cadillac to the General Motors roster for $4,500,000 cash in 1909, and its reputation continued to grow.

In an era when unscrupulous managements and untrained labor together doomed many automobiles to spending half their lives in a repair shop, Leland insisted on such precise engineering that Cadillac parts were interchangeable between one car and another. This was hailed as 1908's greatest contribution to motoring when the company was awarded Britain's Dewar Trophy, the most respected honor within the industry. Four years later, Cadillac won again, this time for making Charles Kettering's electric self-starter standard equipment on all its cars, then followed up by producing the first high-speed V-8 engine available in a mass-produced American automobile.

Long before Pierre du Pont took over, Leland had fallen out with Durant and set himself and his son Wilfred up in the new Lincoln Motor Company, intent on turning out cars to surpass Cadillacs in quality. But the old patriarch, in his late seventies now, had been brought to the verge of bankruptcy by the slump that had only just ended. Father and son asked Henry for a loan. He turned them away.

At this point, Clara the Empress intervened. She had received a letter from Mrs. Wilfred, begging for co-operation. It was too late to prevent Lincoln from going into receivership, but Henry telephoned the Lelands, inviting them to Fair Lane. Clara was on hand when he listened to his visitors' account of how they planned to get their plant back in operation. He had let them leave without committing himself when Clara spoke up.

"Can't you do something to help them? It's a shame that all Detroit should stand by and see that company wrecked."

Perhaps there was a more satisfying course than merely to leave Lincoln dying. Henry had another thought to brood on. Edsel was wholly in favor of taking over the moribund company. "Father made the most popular car in the world," he told one of his golfing companions. "I would like to make the best car in the world." The question was, on whose terms?

The Lelands were shopping around for others who might lend them money enough to buy back Lincoln when it went on the block at the receiver's sale, but the day following Clara's appeal, Henry had them back for the first of a series of conferences. Either then or later, the elder Leland outlined what he hoped to do. If he were able to borrow, say, $10,000,000, he would purchase Lincoln, pay off its creditors, and compensate its shareholders at the rate of $50 a share.

Henry had a better idea. "Yes, I know you can get all the money you need to buy the plant, but if you borrow the money and do that, it will take you years to earn enough profits to pay off the loan before you can even take care of the creditors and stockholders. I can do it right away." Let him buy Lincoln unchallenged, and he would leave the Lelands to run the plant as an autonomous unit of his expanding empire.

To the Lelands, this was the happiest solution they could find. Wilfred set about drawing up an agreement pinning down Henry's promises, including taking care of the stockholders. By Wilfred's account, he read the document line by line to all three Fords, then asked for Henry's signature.

"That isn't necessary," said Henry, launching into a totally convincing explanation of why his word was enough. The Lelands contented themselves with that, believing that as part of the deal he was committed to paying off every man and woman who owned Lincoln stock.

Henry bought the company at the receiver's sale for an uncontested $8,000,000, and forty-eight hours afterward the plant opened up again after a three-month shutdown. Old Leland, weeping with joy, would be president of Lincoln, whose shares were now all Ford's, with Wilfred one vice-president and Edsel another. "Insisted upon by Mr. Ford at the outset of the negotiations" was the fact, as the press release stated, that management would remain in the hands of the two Lelands.

Henry went for a drive in one of the fancy new cars that had suddenly become relatives of Lizzie. Their engineering standards were as good as anything the elder Leland had demanded in the past, but in appearance they were homely compared with Cadillacs. Edsel's hope was to upgrade Lizzie by introducing some Leland niceties into her internal works and perhaps refine the contours of a Lincoln. One feature of the automobile in which his father took a ride was condemned out of hand by Henry even before his jaunt was over.

In front of its radiator, the car had a shutter like a venetian blind that a thermostat controlled, keeping it closed while the engine warmed up, then opening it to let air flow in to help cool the motor. Halfway through the trip, the thermostat failed, the shutter clicked down, and the radiator promised to boil over.

Henry had the chauffeur stop by a cornfield. Henry vaulted over the fence and returned with a corncob. "Wedge it open with this." Back at the Dearborn plant, a joker asked him if corncobs were to be standard items on Lincolns from now on. "Thermostats are crumby," growled Henry. No matter what Edsel wanted, Lizzie was to be spared such newfangled nonsense, just as her pristine virtues had been preserved by denying her those faddish backup lights and a gas gauge on the dashboard.

Ford's apparent cordiality toward Henry Leland, which Detroiters took to be as genuine as good King Wenceslaus' regard for his page, lasted a few weeks longer. On February 16, 1922, the old man reached seventy-nine, and his savior presented him with a check for $363,000. At the birthday party held in the Lincoln factory's restaurant, Ford was overheard urging Leland to "show it to them, show it to them; tell them that they are all going to get them just the same."

The figure on the check that Leland happily fluttered happened to be the par value of his shares in the defunct Lincoln Motor Company. Those of the staff who also had stock in that company imagined that Ford was signifying his intention of reimbursing every shareholder. In the wrangle that developed in the months ahead, Ford Motor identified the check only as payment for special services rendered by the elder Leland in getting Lincoln production going again.

"We are not going to throw away any more money on this company" was Henry's dictum when he sent in droves of Ford executives to overrun the Lincoln plant. In a year when well over a million Americans once again bought a new Lizzie, the Lelands' operation was producing only thirty cars a day. Edsel considered the organization "very stagnant" whereas "mobility" was the up-to-date virtue that automobiles had engendered. Kanzler, lawyer turned efficiency expert, thought that the whole plant was antiquated. Sorensen stormed in, issuing orders right and left, only to find that the Lelands countermanded them, bristling over the infringement of what they understood to be their rights.

If the father and son had been able to read Henry's nature correctly, they would have known from the start that they had no chance of succeeding. He must enjoy absolute control of everything and everyone he felt he owned. Ford money had salvaged the Lelands; therefore Ford methods must prevail at Lincoln. As for the stockholders, he planned to pay them nothing.

He may have felt that he made this clear over a luncheon with the senior Leland. Henry mentioned that Clara had asked what was to be the fate of the previous owners of the company. "You know what I told her?" Henry said. "I told her if they would come out to Dearborn we'd give them a badge and put them to work." The old man, blind to Henry's style, fancied that he was joking. But Henry had a way of sometimes saying exactly what he meant with a grin that led a listener to believe otherwise.

He was deliberately misleading when the Lelands finally protested directly to him about the "insolence" of Ford executives toward themselves. "You mustn't let them do it," he admonished the two of them. "You are in charge here." But Sorensen and his men still kept their fingers stuck deep into the Lincoln pie, and Henry made no move toward sharing any plums with the previous stockholders.

In the latter part of May, Wilfred set down the Lelands' complaints in a long letter to Henry. The Lincoln automobile, he declared, was the culmination of his father's working life. Rather than be swallowed up by Ford, the Lelands were ready to buy back the company for the $8,000,000 Ford had paid "plus a reasonable interest rate." Whether Henry read the letter was problematical. Liebold screened all requests for appointments and all incoming mail, responding as he saw fit. When Wilfred received no answer, he wrote again three days later and again twenty-four hours after that. He heard nothing from Henry.

In desperation, he drove to Fair Lane, passed the scrutiny of the guard at the gates, and spent two hours talking with Ford. "Mr. Leland," said the master of the house, "I wouldn't sell the Lincoln plant for $500,000,000. I had a purpose in acquiring that plant." He promised to take Edsel over there the following morning to "make the Lincoln an independent organization, and you and your father will be in full control." Wilfred, by his own account, left satisfied with that.

Henry kept the appointment alone. It was inconceivable that Edsel approved of the machinations any more than he did the Dearborn *Independent*'s diatribes against Jews. Making "the best car in the world" might prove difficult without the services of the worried old man who had developed it. Edsel would have chosen a more humane course, but he could not cross his father.

Henry pledged himself to spend two hours every working day with the senior Leland, but that was the last time he was seen in the patriarch's office. Ford's staff had the impression that he had heard more than enough from Wilfred, though Henry Ford still "had a lot of respect for Henry Leland."

Letting other men tidy up in his tracks was a habit of Henry's. On Saturday morning, June 10, he had a job for Liebold, his chief executioner, and William Mayo, who had been senior engineer until Sorensen overtook him. "You'd better go over and tell Wilfred that we don't want him any more."

Liebold would be willing to oblige. When the father heard that his son was out, the senior Leland resigned immediately, but Henry could claim that this was none of his doing. Mayo made a date for the Lelands to meet Henry in his office on Monday. Henry did not keep it. Edsel and Kanzler stepped into the Lelands' shoes at Lincoln, and within a month some parts that went into Lizzie's more imposing relation were being turned out at the Rouge.

Henry was soon to pay off Lincoln's commercial creditors to the tune of more than $4,000,000. When he showed no sign of providing anything whatever for the shareholders, the Lelands filed suit on their behalf, promising through their attorney that the case would be "largely based upon the word of Henry Ford against that of Henry M. Leland. Mr. Ford will be called to the stand to tell his story." Had Henry ever bound himself to compensate the owners of Lincoln's original stock? Before the legal maneuvering by both sides could be resolved, and the question answered, old Leland was dead, short of his ninetieth birthday.

Parting with money except in accordance with his spasmodic principles came hard for Henry. At the climax of his squeeze on the Lelands, a glowing biography appeared in the bookstores, *The Truth About Henry Ford* by Sarah T. Bushnell, who had Clara's co-operation on the project. One paragraph caught the eye of Andrew Mellon, appointed Secretary of the Treasury by Warren Harding, who had delighted Detroit by being the first President to ride to his Inauguration in an automobile—a Panhard twin-six. Henry, wrote the author, had already kept his word that he would make not a cent of profit on Ford's wartime production and had returned $29,000,000 to the federal government.

Mellon ordered a search made of Treasury Department records, then personally notified Henry that not a nickel had in fact been received. Liebold fielded that one. He wrote Mellon that Mr. Ford knew nothing about the book and therefore "feels no responsibility in connection with its circulation."

Precisely what Henry's war profits amounted to was a calculation that only a corps of accountants could determine. Henry had asked for an official expert to work out the figures shortly after the Armistice. Now the years had gone by, and his interest in the subject had vanished. The maximum estimate was $27,000,000. Sixty per cent of Ford Motor's floor space was devoted to war work, so the same percentage should apply to his $45,000,000 share of the company's after-tax profits for 1917 and 1918. At the lowest end of the scale, the arithmetic performed by his most eminent latter-day biographers satisfied them that the sum involved was $926,780.46. Having a check issued for that kind of money would impose no strain on Henry's resources—it would bear Liebold's signature under power of attorney, since Henry never signed such things. Yet after all his solemn affirmations, he chose to refund the government nothing whatever.

A further consideration overshadowed his dealings with the Lelands. Henry debated with himself whether he should run for the presidency of the United States. In the spring of his Inaugural year, Harding had accepted Ford's invitation to join in a camping trip, designed ostensibly to demonstrate how safe automobiles were these days and coincidentally provide Lizzie with priceless free publicity. Two of the veterans of these expeditions, Edison and Harvey Firestone, went along. John Burroughs had died a little earlier, and his place was filled by Bishop William Anderson, a jocular Episcopalian divine whom his host once rattled with a question: "Do you think God wanted me to make cars?"

Henry had personally voted not for Harding but for his opponent, James M. Cox. This early, alfresco view of the amiable Babbitt from Blooming Grove, Ohio, against a background of camping gear and baggage carried in a cavalcade of Lizzies could leave no better impression on Ford than did the scandals within the Administration that began coming to light two years afterward. Harding was already baffled by the magnitude of his job. "I knew that it would be too much for me," he confessed to one caller, and to another, "I know somewhere there is a book that will give me the truth, but, hell, I couldn't read the book."

There, anyway, he shared common ground with Henry, as he did in one more important respect: Harding took an ingenuous pride in the technological advances that were revolutionizing the nation even though most people still paid homage to the old farm-and-fireside values, but neither President nor carmaker understood the implications or the demands of change.

By the spring of 1922, enough citizens of Dearborn had grown disillusioned with Harding for a "Ford for President" club to be organized and cardboard hats distributed bearing the legend, "We Want Henry," price $1.00. This group of the faithful rented an office, from which exhortations were mailed across the country, urging others to follow their example. In little more than twelve months, more than a thousand similar clubs had sprung up, campaigning to put Henry in the White House in 1924.

The movement seemed to be spontaneous. Only skeptics detected the influence of, and perhaps cash contributions from, Liebold. He had a matador's gift for flourishing a crimson lure to start Henry heading in a direction of Liebold's choosing. Power fell into his hands by his master's default. As another employee saw it, "He was one of the persons Mr. Ford could ask to do things he wouldn't ask other people to do. Mr. Ford knew the others weren't hard enough." Among the softies, Henry was beginning to include Edsel.

Liebold felt confident that the control he exercised would sooner or later be recognized by his appointment as general manager of the company, but his ambitions rose higher than that. He had made himself Henry's gray eminence already. What if he could act as kingmaker and see Henry in the White House?

The dream of holding supreme political office was not entirely farfetched in Ford's judgment, though in the beginning he repeatedly dismissed it as "a joke." For reasons explained to no one, he abruptly ended the attacks on the Jews, which had been printed without interruption in the *Independent* for nearly two years. "Put all your thought and time to studying and writing about this money question," he ordered W. J. Cameron, who had followed Edwin Pipp as editor.

Henry had concluded that one cause of the world's disorders was the gold standard, which pegged every major currency to the price of that revered metal. Edison had persuaded him that a nation's resources in energy provided a sounder basis for monetary values. More mundane reasons may have prompted him to forego anti-Semitism for the time being. Without the electoral votes of Ohio and the state of New York, with its powerful proportion of Jewish voters, no man had ever won a presidential election.

Liebold was dismayed by Henry's turnabout. The would-be vizier had contrived to have the *Independent*'s series reprinted as brochures under the generic title of *The International Jew* for broad distribution in the United States as well as sales in Europe; as early as March 1923, when Adolf Hitler was in prison writing *Mein Kampf*, German translations flooded the Weimar Republic.

Jim Couzens was much more distressed by the possibility, however remote, that Harding's successor might be Ford. Couzens was a United States senator nowadays, filling the Michigan seat resigned by Henry's senatorial conqueror of 1918, Truman Newberry, one jump ahead of a movement to expel him. Couzens laid into his old associate and fellow tycoon before the Republican Club of Detroit.

"Ford," he thundered, "wants to be President. . . . Why does he refrain from announcing his candidacy? Because he is afraid. He realizes that it would prove just as great a fiasco as his peace ship." Couzens was flaying himself into one of his red-faced rages. "He has never gotten over his defeat as a candidate for United States senator. . . . This man who has made more unfulfilled promises than any man in America is now trying to guide or to criticize others." The speaker seemed mad with everybody. "Why Ford for President? It is ridiculous. How can a man over sixty years old, who has done nothing except make motors, who has no training, no experience, aspire to such an office?"

Opposition served only to fuel Henry's desires. Liebold sent an *Independent* staff reporter off to assess the strength of Ford's support in the "We Want Henry" clubs. He came back convinced that a gratifying number of influential citizens preferred Henry to Harding, while the Democrats were split every which way, with Cox bowing out of politics and no obvious other champion in sight. Ford, with no cause but his own, agreed to let events shape their own course, including the entering of his name in state primaries.

Cessation of the *Independent's* attacks on Jewry was followed by a Ford announcement that gladdened the hearts of workingmen, even if labor unions could not gain admission to Highland Park. the Rouge, or any other automobile factory: Henry put all his employees on a five-day week. The interview he gave for the newspapers was a calculated vote-catcher. "Every man needs more than one day a week for rest and recreation. The Ford Company always has sought to promote ideal home life for its employees. We believe that in order to live properly every man should have more time to spend with his family."

No bandwagon was ready to roll as yet, but one appeared to be in the making. The *Wall Street Journal* seriously examined the possibility of Ford's election. The New York *Times* got around to recognizing Henry as "a powerful and enigmatic figure on the political horizon." James Gordon Bennett's New York *World* found that "the astonishing growth of popular sentiment for Ford for President is causing deep concern to Democrats and anxiety to Republicans." The tenor of the mail pouring into Dearborn lent credence to that judgment.

Henry did not raise a finger or utter a public word to escalate his chances. At home, Clara, who had initially dismissed the whole thing as a joke, began to show concern. In Washington, more and more congressmen were heard predicting that if the country voted at this time, Henry would undoubtedly be swept into power. A national weekly magazine, *Collier's*, polled 250,000 people, announced that Ford led Harding, eight to five, then invited Henry to compose an article, "If I Were President." He farmed out the job to Cameron.

The candidate with neither a platform nor a clue about political machines privately mentioned only one Cabinet appointment he would make: Charlie Sorensen as Secretary of War. Henry's ideas of living up to the office he fumbled for were as hazy as his identification of Benedict Arnold during the *Tribune* trial. "I'd just like to be down there about six weeks and throw some monkey wrenches into the machinery," he said.

He believed that nosing around Treasury, State, Commerce, War, Navy, and other federal departments, hobnobbing equally with Cabinet officials and men on the street, would teach him all he needed to know about running the country. "I'd get to the bottom of things," he promised Liebold.

"No, no. The way the presidency is set up, you don't have much time to get out of the office," explained his none-too-knowledgeable, self-appointed manager.

"You fellows could handle all that. That's just correspondence to be answered and things of that kind."

But the legend of Henry's mastery of men and machines inspired the opening of campaign headquarters in Manhattan and a mass parade down Broadway. Why did he need a program when seasoned politicians and aspirants eager for the spoils of high office were offering to paste up one for him and conduct a third-party campaign on his behalf, much as Theodore Roosevelt's Bull Moosers had done a decade ago?

Then, in June 1923, Harding packed Nan Britton, his mistress and mother of a child of his, off to Europe and bore his wife Flo away with him from Washington. On August 2, he died in San Francisco, mourned at first but soon disgraced, and Cal Coolidge became the country's thirtieth President. It took Henry four more months to conclude that the boom for him was indeed over. Clara moved more rapidly. She had some sharp words for Liebold on the telephone one day. "Since you got him into it, you can just get him out of it. I hate this idea of the name of Ford being dragged down into the gutters of political filth. My name is Ford, and I'm proud of it. If Mr. Ford wants to go to Washington, he can go, but I'll go to England." She had retained her admiration for country gardens and the style of the landed gentry.

Accordingly, it was Liebold who, in December, let it be known that Henry would vote for Coolidge the next time around. Henry attributed his withdrawal from the race entirely to Clara. "She put her foot down, and that was that," he said, disarmingly.

He had not waited to have his newspaper open up again against the Jews with even more venom than before. When a farm vote could be vital for him, he had reached the conclusion that his idealized American farmer was the victim of a Jewish plot to seize control of United States agriculture. Starting in the spring, the *Independent* gnawed at the theme every week, pinpointing as an archconspirator a hot-blooded Chicago attorney, Aaron Sapiro, who was active in organizing a Midwest co-operative to market wheat at prices better than the prevailing lows.

Along with the usual rigmarole about "Jewish international bankers," the names of financier Otto Kahn and Albert Lasker, a giant among Manhattan advertising agents, were dragged in. They took the abuse calmly, but when Sapiro was specifically accused of bilking his clients, he filed suit for the inevitable $1,000,000. His character had been defamed, he said, in exactly 141 instances. The series continued.

If the outcome of his dawdling try for the White House was a defeat, which he would never admit to, Henry could show the disdained socialites of Detroit that, President or not, the world acknowledged him as an equal of the foremost. In the autumn of that election year, the Prince of Wales, heir to the British throne and an international darling, paid a state visit to America and a personal visit to the Fords, staying overnight at Fair Lane and dining and dancing at Edsel's.

Eleanor had her mother at the house on East Jefferson Avenue to share in the glory. She sent Henry and Benson to bed with a promise that the prince might drop in at the nursery if they behaved themselves. Fifteen-month-old Josephine slept in a room of her own.

Mrs. Clay fluttered upstairs and down in her finery, increasingly nervous as the appointed hour for dining came and passed with no sign of the guest of honor. By the time he turned up, ninety minutes late, she had lost her nerve and fled to the nursery. Murmuring apologies, His Royal Highness ventured to say that he would not want to disappoint Henry Ford's grandsons and so was escorted upstairs. The giggling that went on behind the nursery door died as the knob was turned.

"What is this all about?" Edsel asked as they walked in. Henry was unawed by the trim young man who was briefly to be King Edward VIII of England. The boy pointed straightway at Benson. "He was so excited he threw up. . . ."

"Quite a few people do," the prince reassured him.

"And grandmother is hiding behind the screen."

In black velvet, pearls, and a maribou boa, Eleanor carried off the evening in ducal style, unassuming, well-informed and as engaging as such young ladies of the theater as Gertie Lawrence and Bea Lillie, whose company the prince was provided with on the Long Island estate of a host on another occasion.

Edsel undertook to deliver the prince to a private club for a luncheon at which Henry was making a rare and valiant appearance. Edsel left his passenger at the door, declining to go in, since he had not been invited. "Thanks, thanks greatly, but here it's Father's party," he murmured and slipped back into the car.

The protective walls around him and his family that Bennett's security battalion manned had recently been tested when a band of criminals threatened to blind the young Fords' children unless their father met demands for an even $1,000,000. The Detroit police had traced the men and had them behind bars. But Edsel carefully followed instructions to drive on through red lights after nightfall to avoid the risk of kidnapers waiting for the car to make an expected stop. Seven-year-old Sonnie and his five-year-old brother were starting to feel the frustrations of confinement.

Four guards lurking in the shrubbery had not saved Eleanor from being robbed of $100,000 worth of jewelry on a June night earlier that year. After their two dinner guests had left around midnight, she and Edsel went upstairs to find her jewel box and its contents gone—two ropes of pearls, a platinum wedding ring, and a guard ring—together with a gold-cased clock.

The police theorized at first that the thief must have rowed across the Detroit River with an accomplice who had deposited him on the rear lawn, allowing him to creep between the sentries and shinny up the porte-cochere, then make his haul before he slipped out in the darkness as the guests' car drove away. But the grounds proved to be devoid of any footprints to corroborate these guesses.

The detectives concluded next that the burglar was one of the servants in the house. That hypothesis was demolished when fingerprints were checked against those left behind on Eleanor's dressing table. With Edsel's consent, the police tapped his telephones for weeks, hoping for somebody to call him to strike a bargain for the return of the loot. No such call was made, and the insurance company offered to close their files with a cash payment of $89,000. Edsel declined; he preferred to wait.

As the story cooled and progress reports faded from the newspapers, Detroiters fabricated their own solution. Henry, in the middle of his peculiar election campaign, had pocketed the jewels himself to tease Eleanor, or perhaps as a warning to her not to leave them around her bathroom, or maybe to protest her extravagance in owning such baubles by tossing the lot in the river. The flaw in all this was that Edsel had seen the stuff at ten-thirty, and his father had not been a guest at dinner on the night of the crime. Nevertheless, the gossips stuck to their conviction that, all in good time, Henry would hand over the jewels to his daughter-in-law. Neither he nor anyone else ever did.

He had particular reason to feel gratified by royal patronage. The prince had not stayed with Pierre du Pont or any of the Delaware tribe of warmongers. The prince had been kept safely out of the hands of the Grosse Pointe crowd, who Henry thought "weren't the future of America." The prince had not been entertained by Alfred Sloan, who had followed Pierre as president of General Motors a year ago, still with a touch of Brooklynese in his speech.

In an industry where social rank was determined solely by the number of cars a man could sell, Sloan's reputation had risen as high as his stiff white collars. In a single year, 1922, General

Motors had wiped out its $82,000,000 worth of bank loans, made a net income of another $54,000,000, and was never again to return anything but profits.

The providentially interrupted White House term of Warren Harding had coincided with the best days yet for the car manufacturers: 318,000 hands employed in the factories; a billion dollars spent on improving highways; and a dazzling range of innovations to add to a driver's comfort and convenience, like four-wheel brakes, power-operated windshield wipers, baked enamel finishes even on inexpensive models, and headlamps that could be dimmed by a tap on a foot switch. Most of the developments came out of General Motors research. Ford had nothing comparable; Lizzie did not need it.

While the police were floundering after Eleanor's missing jewel case, GM had taken off on another tangent that would shortly bring radical change in the performance of automobiles. A fifty-fifty partnership with Standard oil of New Jersey created the Ethyl Gasoline Corporation, formed to market a product identified as tetraethyl lead, which was manufactured by none other than E. I. du Pont de Nemours & Company.

This, too, was a General Motors discovery. On top of the ailments from which many of Lizzie's competitors suffered—misaligned bearings, loose nuts, and inaccessible wiring and plumbing—every car was susceptible to engine knock. A young man, Tom Midgley, Jr., who had worked as an assistant to Kettering in Dayton, Ohio, before joining GM research, accidentally found the solution in "ethyl," a chemical compound to be added to gasoline.

Midgley took a sample of the powder in a test tube to New York City in January 1922, and dumfounded the Society of Automotive Engineers at its annual meeting there. No one immediately understood why, but the stuff worked, either poured by a gas station operator into his storage tanks, which was how it was handled at first, or introduced by the oil companies before deliveries were made to him. Measured on the octane scale, which was one more device pioneered by General Motors, ethyl stepped up the "punch" in gasoline. Octane ratings, which hovered around the fifty mark before, soon began to climb. With most knocking eliminated, horsepower could be increased. The new cars were faster—

and deadlier—than their predecessors, and Henry had to swallow the fact that any Lizzie owner who tried out ethyl gas owed something to General Motors.

At the time of the prince's descent on Dearborn, Ford had a new competitor to contend with. Walter Chrysler had his name on a car at last. He had left his job as $12,000-a-year works manager with the American Locomotive Company to take on the same responsibilities at Buick during the interval when Durant was first pushed out of GM. As soon as Will had reinstated himself, he promoted Chrysler to the presidency of Buick and also put him in overall charge of GM operations. The ham-fisted engineer with the no-nonsense look of a machine-shop foreman was paid $500,000 a year, most of which he salted away in company stock.

That lasted until 1920 and the collapse of the parent company. Chrysler fell out with Durant when the value of Walter's shares cascaded, and one ham fist nearly shook the door off its hinges as he made his final exit from Durant's office in the old General Motors building on New York's Fifty-seventh Street. Walter wanted his own business. He had the qualifications of ruthlessness, experience, and engineering background but not as yet the financial resources. He accepted the challenge of getting the Willys-Overland Company back on its feet after the 1920 slump bowled it over. As executive vice-president, he doubled his previous salary.

John and Horace Dodge both died that same year. Their widows straightway sold the company founded by their husbands on dividends from Henry to the New York investment house of Dillon, Read for a neat $146,000,000. Here was a ready-made embarkation point for Chrysler. Conditions of sea and weather became precisely right for him. The quick rebound in automobile sales made investors bullish about the car industry in general. Dillon, Read wanted to unload a business that was completely strange to them. Walter had come up with a high-compression, six-cylinder engine that could make effective use of this peppy ethyl gasoline.

It was built into a demonstration model that in itself was something new—lower slung than most contemporary styles, and brilliantly finished in baked enamel. "Through the public's reaction to its smarter lines, to its smooth and vastly greater power," Walter reminisced, "we had hoped to make the bankers change their minds about the loan." They were to, soon enough. A corporation funded by them and named for him was organized to buy Dodge for $170,000,000 in new Chrysler stock.

The first Chrysler went on sale in 1924. "A high-compression engine was something all automobile men appreciated," Walter recalled later, "but until our car had appeared, they had treated it as a racing driver's luxury that would be offered to the public far in the future."

So another kind of race got under way as other manufacturers pressed ahead with designs for faster and faster vehicles to catch up with Chrysler for a prize that was spelled out as "share of the market," meaning how many people bought what brand of car. The industry as a whole was accelerating past a perilous milestone. It was no longer enough, as it had been in pioneering days, simply to demonstrate a car to find customers. It had to be advertised, merchandised, and serviced, sold in terms of its looks and its *speed*.

Dependability, which Henry saw as Lizzie's supreme virtue, was losing its appeal, as was virtue itself in the jazz age. Under her homely hood, her four cylinders still produced only twenty horsepower, which limited her top performance to forty-five miles an hour. She could still trundle unconcernedly across fields and up mountains, but the expanding network of good, hard highways made such feats a rare necessity. She continued to be clad in durable black when Chrysler was finding an army of customers who preferred colors as bright as a parakeet's.

This year Chrysler's company was too young to pose any threat to Ford, and Henry outsold Chevrolet, 1,870,000 to 280,000. A more realistic man would recognize the element of blind luck in that. General Motors had backed a loser in the air-cooled engine for the car that was supposed to overtake Lizzie. Its scheduled debut at the New York Automobile Show in 1922 had been canceled. After twelve more months of work, it still ran so hot in testing that gasoline preignited in the cylinders. In the end, GM felt compelled to blaze one more trail for the industry. Every air-cooled Chevrolet that had been sold was recalled for assignment to the scrap heap. To direct its stultified pursuit of Lizzie, Chevy was provided with a new president in the person of mild-mannered

Bill Knudsen, who gave credit to his years with Henry for teaching him all he knew about the business. "I just adapted Ford methods," he explained afterward.

Insulated by his ego, his staff, and his money from what was happening around him, Henry responded in the only way he knew. The enormous productive power of Highland Park and now the Rouge made it simple for him to go on undercutting everyone else in the low-price field. He reset the price of a Lizzie runabout at a record, unbeatable low of $260. What would Chevrolet do about that?

Chapter Seven

The Heir of Fortune

Some of Ford's men thought that the odds were perpetually loaded against his heir. "Edsel had a pretty hard row to hoe," Cameron of the *Independent* said on one occasion. He "never seemed to be very happy," said the head of the purchasing department. He needed help, his sympathizers realized, but in the steel-bound autocracy of the company, they were slow to offer it. That was too dangerous. Henry was so eternally jealous that anyone who tried to help gambled with his own job.

Edsel was the Ford in touch with reality, a rational being whom everybody could reason with. He stood ready to listen to any problem and do what he could to resolve it up to the point where his father put him down. To Henry, he remained a softhearted lad in knickerbockers, incomprehensible because Henry imagined all men to be made about the same as he was.

In truth, his son scarcely resembled him at all. Edsel had the artistic taste that was as rare as a five-cylinder motor in automobile society. He had compassion, which was possibly even scarcer. He was logical in his decisions, where Henry trusted only his own instinct. "I can't prove it, but I can smell it," he would boast.

Henry felt that he owed nothing to any man, no matter what had been done to help him; Edsel tried to repay every act of kindness. One was devious, the other direct. One exploded in fury if he was thwarted, the other tightened his lips to control his temper, and only the tense muscles of his neck revealed the effort.

Henry loved himself and his wife to the exclusion of all others; their son put his family at the head of his list but respected the sensitivities of everyone who came his way. One was normal, astonishingly so in light of his upbringing, and one was not.

There were Ford executives who decided that, by comparison with his father's single-track concentration, Edsel was easily distracted. That made no allowance for the number of duties he was laden with in a job that gave him little effective authority. Liebold and Sorensen had more power than the president of the Ford Motor Company because they had accurately sized up their opportunities to influence Henry.

With his brother-in-law and steadfast confidant, Edsel had nominal charge of the Highland Park plant while Sorensen ruled the Rouge. Edsel and Kanzler also ran Lincoln, where interference from Henry was minimal. Selling Ford cars, trucks, and tractors at home and overseas was Edsel's ultimate responsibility, though he was allowed next to nothing to say concerning their design. Dealers, agencies, and the supervisors of domestic branches all reported to him; Henry did not want to hear about them except in a crisis or on a morning when nothing else had come up to engross his mind.

He loaded his son like a willing camel with one straw after another in what could be interpreted as a plan either to test his mettle or break his back when the company was so loosely organized and job turnover so chronically high that he was uncertain from one week to another just what staff he might call his own.

To pursue the dream of making every component of Lizzie a Ford product manufactured at bare-bone cost, Henry bought vast tracts of timberland, limestone quarries, iron mines, coal mines, and a railroad—the Detroit, Toledo, & Ironton—to deliver ingredients to the Rouge. He acquired a glass factory because Lizzie's windows had to be crystal clear. When the price of tires rocketed, he procured 2,500,000 acres in Brazil to establish his own rubber plantations.

He plunged into action like a terrier into a pack of rats, snapping up properties, then tossing them over his shoulder into Edsel's care. The trade school was another Edsel responsibility; some of the finest technicians in Detroit graduated from there, and the faculty included some of his own onetime high school teachers.

When Liebold's Prussianism antagonized the staff, Edsel moved in to supervise the running of the Henry Ford Hospital, his father's major gift to the city to date; Henry poured in over $11,000,000 and laid down the rule that prince or pauper must be given the same treatment there, the same standard room with private bath, and the same bargain-sized bill on discharge. The hospital had Edsel's financial support, too—$4,000,000 worth. Eleanor had her appendix removed there before her son William was born.

At little more than thirty years old, with no formal commercial training, locked into an organization that lived according to the whims of its owner, Edsel was simultaneously president, treasurer, and whipping boy. He had grown accustomed long since to humiliation from his father, but privately or in public he would return time and again to unpalatable subjects that he knew must be faced for the sake of Ford's future.

Faster speeds called for safer brakes than the two-wheel, mechanically operated versions that had been standard for Lizzie and every other mass-produced automobile. Buick came out first with four-wheel brakes in 1924, and the next step was hydraulics, activated by fluid pumped under pressure through rubber hose lines. Henry thought as little of these as he had of thermostats for Lincoln radiators.

Edsel sometimes trod ahead of the angels. At the executive luncheon table, he undertook to raise a question on Sorensen's behalf: "Now, Father, I think the time has come to take up the matter of hydraulic brakes."

No one else dared speak until Henry had been heard from. His face was flushed as he pushed back his chair. "Edsel, you shut up!" He stalked away. Sorensen had found nothing to say.

But Edsel's sensibility about changing times told him that the topic must be pursued; Lizzie needed something better than mechanical brakes. He had ten cars fitted with hydraulics without telling Henry, who was invited to try one of them out when he showed up at the engineering building one morning. Edsel watched from an upstairs window.

His father habitually drove as though the road were his alone, wandering left, right, and center, turning in and out as he pleased, paying only casual attention to any speed limit. He had not gone far that morning before he decided he should slow down. As he pushed on the brake pedal, a hose line gave way, leaving a trail of hydraulic fluid. Just as he had insisted, these gimmicks were no good. When the car coasted to a halt, he abandoned it in disgust. Edsel's hopes for safer brakes on Lizzie were set back for a year or two longer.

"Ten cars, and we'd pick that one!" Edsel said when he heard what had happened, but he would not let his gloom linger on for long. Only a stoic or a masochist could survive the life of Edsel Ford. "We never know what direction it's coming from, do we?" he would say. His face grew as hollow-cheeked as Henry's, but the spells of ill health he suffered were another subject excluded from discussion outside his immediate family. Stomach ulcers were part of the job, but he would arrive home to play baseball or touch football with his sons or help run their miniature railroad with a real, coal-burning locomotive and drive their little, scaled-down automobiles. Most winters, he and Eleanor would take the children down to Hobe Sound, Florida, in search of sunshine. He paid $307,000 for his 125-foot houseboat *Onika*—twelve in crew, Chippendale living room, Hepplewhite dining salon, and staterooms furnished in French provincial comfort for eight passengers —which was kept down there.

Wherever they were, the children were as secluded as in an isolation ward. "At Maine in the summer," young Henry remembered later, "I never saw anybody outside of the family except the men who worked at our stables." Granddaddy's fears for his grandchildren were turned to good account by Bennett. "Never mind the plants," Henry told him. "If anything happens to them, we can build new ones. But we've got to make absolutely sure that nothing happens to the children." With that, Bennett set off to visit every major city where crime was rooted, looking for stool pigeons who could be counted on to tip him off if local hoodlums were planning to horn in on any Ford.

Edsel achieved some successes in the 1920s. Under his influence, the company started advertising again in newspapers, national magazines, and on billboards. Halfway through the decade, more advertisement dollars were being spent on Lizzie than on any other single product of American industry, and she outsold Chevrolet four to one. But Edsel scented danger. Lizzie's share of the total market was slipping. From a peak of 60 per cent, it was down to 45 per cent.

Alfred Sloan had thought long and hard about how General Motors might take over the lead. Since Henry's prices were unbeatable, perhaps Lizzie would prove vulnerable in the matter of looks and luxury. The new Chevy "K" cost more than three times as much as she did, but for his $825 a customer got a car with a longer body, a one-piece windshield, a dome light, an improved clutch, and sparkling, baked-on Duco, the nitrocellulose lacquer discovered by chance at du Pont, which made it possible to finish a car in hours instead of waiting two weeks and more for coats of paint to dry.

It would be kept on display in dealers' showrooms for no more than twelve months, starting in the fall, when buying was briskest. This was the crux of Sloan's master plan, a simple matter of evolution, as he interpreted it. If car buyers could be led to believe that the current model was inevitably superior to last year's and that next year's would be better yet, there was no telling how many extra sales could be clinched.

The number of significant improvements in engines and equipment would be small, and the pace of their development slow. Oil filters came along in 1924, safety glass embodying layers of fine wire or celluloid in 1926. The following year saw chromium plating used on stock cars, then a similar interval brought synchromesh transmissions (in Cadillacs) and mechanical fuel pumps.

But even if the engineers had no worthwhile changes in mind, the general appearance of a car could be altered and promoted as the last word in motoring progress. A different line for the fenders, a sleeker cant to the hood, a fancier radiator, a wider choice in colors and upholstery fabrics—so long as a customer could be persuaded that his last year's automobile was mysteriously out of date, Sloan's scheme might work wonders.

The turning point came on July 29, 1925, at a meeting of GM's general sales committee. President Sloan was a firm believer in group decision-making at every level, not in one-man dictatorship, like Ford. Sloan heard out every objection to his annual-model concept, and there were plenty of them. Making the changes as he proposed was pointless when a soundly built car lasted an average

6½ years—Lizzie did better than that, with a life span of 8. The cost of this cosmetic treatment of automobile bodies would push prices up out of reach.

Sloan had the answers ready. He was certain that a new age was dawning in the industry. Most men with money to buy a car owned one by now. Future growth depended on convincing them that to stay abreast of the times they must make a practice of trading in the older model for a new one. Fashion, not function, must be the determining factor. Of course, the retooling necessary for annual change would be expensive, but installment buying and easy credit would overcome that problem. In his philosophy, profit alone was not the measure of a company's achievement. What counted was the size of the profit in terms of invested capital.

"We had no stake in the old ways of the automobile business," Sloan reflected; "for us, change meant opportunity." The plan, which was approved that day, would be copied by Ford, he felt sure. In this respect, Sloan knew too little about the compulsions that governed Henry to realize just how fortunate General Motors was going to be.

The past, not the present, intrigued Henry. In his presence, few people dared to bring up the name of General Motors unless it was to relate—or invent—some preposterous blunder that company had made. Ford considered any man his enemy if he found a good word to say about what Sloan was attempting. At Mr. Ford's luncheon table one day, Sorensen was pulled up short when he mentioned some new developments at GM without remembering to mention how absurd they were.

"Well, I see they got you, Charlie," said Henry, eyes glinting. "They sold you, eh?"

Of his two principal competitors, Sloan's organization was a tool of the du Ponts, in Henry's view, while Chrysler was a creature of Wall Street and eastern bankers. In his increasingly erratic thinking, both manufacturers were part of the labyrinthine conspiracy commanded by "international Jewry" that was intent on destroying America and him along with it.

He sought refuge in the past. The catalyst may have been the ridicule he suffered on the witness stand during the Chicago *Tribune* trial. The scorn had been overwhelming when he was goaded with his declaration that "history is mostly bunk." He had been made to appear a fool, which was unbearable when he was sure he was infallible. On the way back to Fair Lane, he had said to Liebold, "You know, I'm going to prove that and give the people an idea of real history. I'm going to start a museum. We are going to show just what actually happened in years gone by."

There was only one place to start—with a memorial to Mary Ford and his own beginnings. In that same year of 1919, he began restoring to life the farmhouse in which he was born, down to the last hook in the walls and antimacassar on the rocking chair. Edsel was conscripted to assist, and Ford dealers everywhere were enlisted in the task of finding furniture and fittings.

Father and son were discovered digging in the sand of a Lake Michigan bay one day after Henry had spotted a half-buried iron stove that had been dumped there. "No, not it," said Henry morosely after they had shoveled it clear.

"Sure? It *seems* to be a 'Starlight.'"

"Oh, it's a 'Starlight' all right, but a smaller model than the one we used to have." They climbed back in the car and drove away. Henry unearthed a true duplicate eighteen months later in a small-town doctor's house and bought it for $25. Henry's memory could be elephantine in its power. He remembered the roses that were woven into the carpet on the floor of the old farmhouse living room, and he had his men search through curiosity shops from coast to coast until one just like it turned up, in New York. To reproduce the exact pattern of his mother's china, a team of excavators delved into the earth at the site to find the shard of a dinner plate, from which he had a complete set reconstructed, from soup bowls to egg cups. As soon as the home he thought of as his mother's alone had been reassembled down to the last tea kettle, he would have Edsel and his family over to cook them breakfast on the "Starlight" that looked just like the grandmother's they had never known.

Collector's mania possessed him. With Cameron or Frank Campsall, who Henry kept in tow as goad to Liebold, he would drop in at an antiquary's store, pretending to be a Mr. Henry or perhaps Mr. Robinson. After looking over the stock, he would sidle out alone, leaving his companion to ask, "What are you asking for everything here?" Henry bought anything that caught his eye, regardless of period or style, so long as the piece was *old*.

One of his aides reminisced, "There was a time it wasn't safe to pass a rusty plow. If I managed to see the plow first, I'd draw his attention to the other side of the road. If I didn't, he'd be out of the car and up to the farm door to dicker for that damned scrap." Then Henry would have his blacksmiths at the Rouge hammer out the missing pieces and repaint the keepsake to look as good as new.

Carloads of relics went into storage at Dearborn—magnificent antiques, artless souvenirs, gimcracks, and pinchbeck. Among the items for the mother lode were silver by Paul Revere; a stuffed owl from an oldtime barbershop; shaving mugs and Apostle spoons; a gate-leg table at which Lafayette sat; Hepplewhite, Chippendale and Duncan Phyfe furniture; and what was reputedly the oldest hostelry in the land.

The Wayside Inn stood at Sudbury, Massachusetts, on the old Boston Post Road halfway between Boston and Worcester, a day's coach ride in either direction when a horse could average twenty-odd miles at a time. The Wayside Inn dated back to 1702, when it consisted only of a downstairs barroom and a bare upstairs dormitory for drivers and drovers. Half a century later, two more bedrooms, a kitchen, and a front parlor were added. George Washington, of course, stayed there, and so did Lafayette on his way to Boston to lay the cornerstone of the Bunker Hill Monument. Henry Wadsworth Longfellow retreated to the front parlor from his home in Cambridge after his wife Frances was killed by a blazing drop of candle wax that set her dress on fire. There he wrote his *Tales of a Wayside Inn*, which increased the patronage of the place until railroads squeezed the life out of stage coaching. The old hostelry had fallen into disrepair again when a committee of townspeople, anxious to preserve the landmark, contacted Henry, whose passion for Americana was as well publicized as all his other ventures.

Washington, Lafayette, and Longfellow, who was one of his favorite poets (he liked to recite, "Life is real, life is earnest . . .") made the Wayside Inn irresistible. He bought it for $65,000, then acquired nearly three thousand surrounding acres of fields and woods to keep the landscape sacrosanct. But he could not restrain himself from tinkering with everything, including antiquity. He had a new, north wing built with a dining room, ten guest rooms, and a ballroom until he had spent upward of $1,600,000. The idea in the back of his head was to make the place self-supporting; it lost him almost $3,000,000. He was afraid that vibration from the cars and trucks of the new America whose birth he had assisted in would shake the foundations of his plaything, so he had a·four-lane stretch of highway built at a cost of $380,000 as a bypass road, then sold it for $1.00 to the Commonwealth of Massachusetts.

To Edsel, it seemed that the hostelry might provide the means for emptying one or two of the warehouses full of treasures and trivia that Father had collected. The risk of fire increased with every fresh delivery. "We really ought to get the stuff out of here, Father. Let's make a museum of it." Henry wasn't quite ready for that yet. He had to refurnish the inn first, and he set off on another shopping spree.

Prices meant nothing. What he charged for Lizzie he determined before he listened to what it cost to produce her. Once he had fixed the figure, it was up to his senior staff to engineer a profit into the price tag somehow. Paperwork was fundamental to Sloan's approach to magnifying General Motors; Henry's men heard from him either in person or not at all. "My idea," he said, "is that a man ought not to have to give an order more than once in six months, but when that order is needed, he ought to know it will be carried out."

Shortly before he was named president, Sloan distributed a bible of accounting throughout GM to unify methods of calculating profit and loss. This was an essential yardstick for control when the company was made up of a dozen and more scattered units, with divisions like Chevrolet assembling cars here, there, and everywhere. Henry had no time for accountants, job classifications, or organization charts. The Ford Motor Company had to be an extension of himself, a tense, organic thing inspired by instinct, not fettered by logic.

Kanzler irritated him with his harping on the benefits to be gained by cost accounting and inventory control, especially after Edsel managed to have his brother-in-law elevated as second vice-president in 1924. Kanzler would have reason for equating his contribution to a snail's, climbing one foot up a garden wall by day, then sliding back the same distance overnight. Anyone who spent much time on figuring income and outgo was suspect. He might be inclined to become "a banker's man," a self-proclaimed expert who would dare to advise Henry what was right for the business and what was wrong.

"We have found it most unfortunately necessary to get rid of a man as soon as he thinks himself an expert," Henry acknowledged in his ghosted autobiography.

Assurance of his income lay in the immutability of Lizzie. So long as she remained basically unchanged, she could be endlessly duplicated without heavy costs in retooling the machines that made her. Once Henry had set her latest price, his underlings would begin to contrive the profits by hammering down the suppliers with threats to cancel orders or by cutting dealer discounts.

He begrudged paying more than subsistence percentages to dealers, who, in Edsel's thinking, played a role equal to that of the 150,000 hands who toiled on the assembly lines. "They are all getting fat and lazy sitting on their fat asses," said Henry, agreeing with Sorensen that slashing discounts would get them working harder.

More than in anything else, the secret of extracting profits was found in driving the men who built the cars. The harder they were pushed, the greater the tally of their day's labor. When 9,109 Model T's could roll off the lines in a single day, as they did on October 31, 1925, to set a record that stood for thirty years, the cost of producing each one of them was lowered and Henry's income thereby increased. But the era of good feeling between master and man had vanished. Ford Motor had the reputation of being one of the worst sweatshops in Detroit.

"The work and work alone controls us," Henry boasted. In practice on the shop floor, it meant continual speed-up of the moving line to shave a few seconds more from the time taken in each operation, with supervisors enforcing the pace with threats of layoff or dismissal like imperators cracking the lash over the backs of galley oarsmen.

The imperator-in-chief was Sorensen, who set the style for everyone at the Rouge. From top to bottom, the world's largest single manufacturing plant was a place of fear. No executive was allowed an office or a chair, only a desk at which to stand amid the din of the machines. Legend had it that if he showed any sign of resentment or had outlived his usefulness, he would find that desk smashed in with a sledgehammer when he came to work one morning. A workman who spoke up for himself might be kicked across the floor, then find his tools mysteriously missing.

The keeping of records was forbidden. Sorensen's work ethic, picked up from Henry, branded that a waste of time, which must be spent only on keeping the plant rolling at capacity. Talking was prohibited, not only among laborers on the line but among supervisors, too. Sorensen wanted to see everybody on the go and running rather than walking. His harassed subjects would try to duck out of sight if they saw him coming.

The toilers on the line were each allotted minimum space consistent with effective performance. The sheer speed of the work that passed under their hands made loafing impossible. Henry's abhorrence of cigarettes extended to chewing tobacco until so many hands suffered the ill effects of gulping down a wad when a supervisor approached that it was deemed politic to make cardboard cuspidors available, priced at a penny apiece to anybody who felt the call for one.

Another bit of Rouge folklore said that Sorensen paced so fast through the aisles of the Rouge as a precaution against having a wrench thrown at him. One day, a massive casting falling from an upper gallery missed him by a whisker, which one way or the other could be described as an accident. On occasion, his senior subordinates had to save him from being beaten up by men he had pushed around.

The climate that Edsel established at Highland Park was less hostile. The line there was continually speeded up, too, but the figurehead president of the institution refused to condone bullying on the Sorensen scale. Liebold, nobody's fool, detected the contrast. "Edsel felt that people ought to be given certain responsibilities in certain positions and their authority should be designated. Mr. Ford didn't go along with that line of thinking. He often said to me that if he wanted a real job done right that he would always pick a man that didn't know anything about it. The reason was that if he picked a man who didn't know anything about the job, the fellow never got away from Mr. Ford. . . . Of course, you couldn't get Edsel to agree to that line of thinking. If Edsel wanted a thing done, he would pick a man he thought was capable of doing it."

Edsel never farmed out a job like firing a man, no matter how repugnant it was to him. "I'll do my own dirty work," he would say. He saw factory life as a co-operative effort between labor and management. "An honest day's work must precede an honest day's pay," he declared, "and the worker who cheats at his end or the employer who cheats at his end are both doing injury to the general welfare."

"Forditis" was the name that employees invented for the endemic ailment that afflicted many of them. A stomach so upset that eating was impossible, twitching muscles, inability to think straight—these were the symptoms. As often as not, a week or two of rest would restore a sufferer to the point where he could go back to work, ready to face the strain again. Edsel, a classic victim, seldom had the chance to leave his desk for that length of time.

By steeling himself to accept his father's slurs and with the background of calm that his home life provided, he could chalk up another singular victory. He cajoled Henry into agreeing that Lizzie should be a somewhat more stylish creature. Father at heart was a woman's man. Males were to be dominated, females respected. He once listed the four women in his life as his mother, his wife, his mother-in-law, and his sister Margaret. Yet he was too old and absorbed in himself to recognize that women were becoming a profound influence in contemporary living, far more influential than his mythical farmer in voting whether a family should choose this automobile or that.

Listening to Eleanor, who personally gave up trying to drive when she stepped on the gas pedal instead of the brake and crunched into a stone pillar at Seal Harbor, Edsel recognized the importance of women in car buying. "The object," he told an interviewer, "will be to build into the minds of women the impression of Ford cars as a quality product; to imply its social standing and the fact that it answers all a woman's requirements in comparison with any other car."

The slicked-up Lizzie fell far short of what Edsel and the dealers wanted. A six-cylinder car with better brakes, better steering, and up-to-date equipment was essential to fend off the challenge of

Chevrolet. Henry would have none of it. "I've no use," he said, "for a motor that has more spark plugs than a cow has teats." Besides, he argued without a shred of evidence to back him, no six could be balanced properly for smooth running.

His idea of a new power plant to be put into production someday was a radical affair of eight cylinders set like a letter "X," four on top of the engine block and four beneath. He had long since filed the first patents and had his engineers trying to cure the flaws in one prototype after another. They put together an air-cooled version, then reverted to a conventional radiator. He wanted to use the flywheel as a supercharger, but it lacked the power to force enough gasoline into the cylinders. The experimenters labored in secret and in vain to keep dirty water from fouling the lower set of plugs when test cars hit puddles on the road.

Edsel brought a group of unhappy dealers to Highland Park to meet his father and say their piece. High on the list of improvements they asked for to make Lizzie more salable was the abandonment of her antiquated ignition system, operated by a magneto in her flywheel. "You can do that over my dead body," he snarled. "That magneto job stays on as long as I'm alive."

He chose to sit by the door, chin jutting, arms folded, and legs crossed, rather than up front facing the audience. He listened in silence as one man after another pleaded for the transformation of the Model T in looks, comfort, and performance. As the discussion reached its end, he stood up. "I think that the only thing we need worry about is the best way to make more cars." That was his summation and his exit line.

His love affair with Lizzie seemed destined to last through eternity, a destination he had approached one day in his hurry to get back home after a seventy-two-hour camping trip at North Harbor Beach, Michigan. His driver was taking it cautiously down a sandy hill road, but Henry grabbed the hand throttle and yanked it open. The car's nose dipped, and she cartwheeled over, end for end, dumping Henry into a ditch, lucky to be no more than dazed.

Two others in the party, following in a second car, took off to find a new front end. Repairing the damage, they discovered that the front wheels had buckled in the sand because of the frailty of the radius steering rod. Clara sat up for her husband, worrying over whatever had made him so late. When he arrived, he told her nothing. On his own accord, one of his engineers designed a stronger rod that withstood the strain when a car fitted with it was driven headfirst into a sandbank, but Henry would not allow it to become part of Lizzie.

"Don't you think your dad made a mistake?" Edsel was asked by a Ford executive when the abortive dealer meeting was over.

"Yes, he did, but he's the boss," was his reply.

Lizzie never was equipped with safety glass, either. It took a head-on collision between a Model T and a test car that pitched one driver through the windshield, putting him into the Ford hospital for a month, to bring Henry around to seeing some merit in glass that would not shatter. It may have been that Edsel, who inspected the wreckage with his father, pointed out the unmistakable moral of the crash.

So Lizzie in her 1925 dress was scarcely changed except in appearance, but Edsel had his way in that. Eternal black persisted as the only color for runabouts and touring cars, but closed models could be had in blue, gray, or brown. Nickel-plated radiator shells replaced black-painted steel. Seats were lowered to provide a roomier interior, bodies were lengthened, and height was reduced, but the chassis remained unchanged.

Henry was satisfied that the venerable old girl was still herself at heart. He signified approval of what Edsel was attempting to accomplish by deeding him the sixty-five acres that he and Clara had bought long ago on the Michigan shores of Lake St. Clair, fifteen miles from downtown Detroit. The care and planning that went into the young Fords' new home arising on Gaukler Pointe left Fair Lane looking ever more clearly the architectural hodge-podge that the owners had wanted. Eleanor and Edsel's architect had sailed to England as a start to tour the mellowed stone villages of the Cotswolds and immerse himself in the style they were seeking.

He produced for them a manor house of thirty major rooms and a vaulted gallery to hold their art collections. There were tennis courts, a pool, and a games pavilion for the children (four of them now, with the birth of William). The shoreline curved back on itself in a natural lagoon for Edsel's little fleet, and the yacht club lay a mile away. Best of all, Gaukler Pointe was protected by water as well as by a guard in the entrance lodge. Fear for his family haunted Edsel. When he dropped Sonnie and Benson off at the Detroit University School, which they now attended as he had, he was trailed by a couple of Bennett's armed guards in another car.

Sales of Lizzie in her new garb perked up, but not for long; Chevy continued gaining on her. Except for Henry, everyone in the industry, in or out of the Ford Motor Company, knew that she had become as obsolete as a stagecoach and had been for two or three years. Little about her appealed any more to young people, who demonstrated their taste for the better things in life by strumming ukuleles and downing bathtub gin. An open runabout was no place for necking on a wintry night. She was a car fit only for hicks, a funny prop in slapstick movies, a curiosity when she trundled down a Manhattan avenue.

Sloan could scarcely believe his stroke of fortune. "The old master," he wrote, "had failed to master change. . . . He left behind a car that no longer offered the best buy, even as raw, basic transportation."

Since Henry could lay no blame on himself or Lizzie, the fault must rest in selling, which meant Edsel and Kanzler. Not surprisingly, Sorensen agreed with that assessment. "If the sales department was any good," he said, "they could sell them. . . . They used 'sales resistance' as an alibi."

Henry, prophet of the apocalypse, reflected that maybe the present generation was so demoralized that it was blind to true virtue. "I sometimes wonder," he said, "if we have not lost our buying sense and fallen under the spell of salesmanship. The American of a generation ago was a shrewd buyer. He knew values in terms of utility and dollars. But nowadays the American people seem to listen and be sold; that is, they do not buy."

He resorted to his usual home remedy: price cuts and more price cuts. Down went the tags on all Lizzies, including those already delivered to dealers. There would be no compensation for them. Seven out of every ten were running up losses. Some of the best deserted to Chevrolet. Ford's answer was to open up ever more dealerships in territories already overcrowded with showrooms and lots where cars gathered dust. Sheaves of protest telegrams crossed Edsel's desk.

"Most of your troubles at the present time," Henry informed the sales organization, "is a question of your mental attitude." He refused to believe the figures on automobile registrations broken down by car name that the R. L. Polk Company prepared as an industry service. The statistics were rigged, he complained; it was another General Motors plot.

With the walls of the empire crumbling around them, Edsel talked endlessly with Kanzler about what might be done. So long as Henry's one-man rule prevailed, there was little long-term hope. Both young men saw that the first vital steps were to start development of a six, and the establishment of rational lines of command that led to Edsel. Then common-sense management demanded action to end the reign of terror at the Rouge under Sorensen, whose methods appalled Kanzler. The vice-president undertook to present the plain facts to Henry. Kanzler composed a six-page memorandum, with no assurance that it would ever get read or that he would not forfeit his job if it were, and submitted it on January 26, 1926.

"It hurts me to write it," Kanzler avowed, "because I am afraid it may change your feeling for me, and that you may think me unsympathetic and lacking confidence in your future plans." His words were a calculated mixture of tact and courage, their frankness softened with flattery. They were written, he said, because "it is one of the handicaps of the power of your personality which you perhaps least of all realize, but most people when with you hesitate to say what they think." He refrained from naming Sorensen as a notable offender.

Time did not allow waiting for the elusory "X" car to be developed, said Kanzler, too wise to imply that Lizzie's days were numbered. "Won't you permit the organization to develop a refined six-cylinder motor?" For an outlay of only $100,000, that could be done, providing Ford with an automobile competitive with but cheaper than any Chevrolet. Then Kanzler laid the truth on the line as no one else had ever dared:

"We have not gone ahead in the last few years, have barely held our own, whereas competition has made great strides. . . . In the past twelve months, the other manufacturers have gained tremendously. Our production and sales in 1925 were less than in 1924. Our Ford customers . . . are going to other manufacturers, and our best dealers are low in morale and not making the money they used to. . . .

"We are losing our position because the world has learned from you, and with its combined efforts, each learning from the other, it has now developed a product that is alarmingly absorbing the public's purchasing power. The best evidence that conditions are not right is the fact that with most of the bigger men in the organization there is a growing uneasiness . . . they feel our position weakening and our grip slipping. . . . With every additional car that our competitors sell they get stronger and we get weaker. . . .

"Inwardly we are alarmed to see our advantages ebbing away, knowing that the counter-measures to prevent it are not immediately at hand. . . . This feeling exists not outwardly, but I will stake my reputation it exists in every important man in the company."

There was no doubt that Henry read the memorandum, though he wrote no reply. From then on, Kanzler was victimized, ignored by Ford on some days, ridiculed on others, or brutally interrupted if he tried to say a further word around the executive luncheon table. Edsel suffered with him until he had to leave his brother-in-law to face the freeze alone and go to England that spring; General Motors was surging ahead of Ford overseas, too. With Edsel out of the way, Henry had Kanzler fired. Sorensen applied the hatchet again. But that was not the end of Kanzler. He would stay so close to the Edsel Fords that he and his wife Dody were neighbors at all three homes, Grosse Pointe, Seal Island, and Hobe Sound. Kanzler, resourceful and unabashed, was to influence the future of all three generations of Fords.

The year ended with Chevy sales up to 692,000, a catastrophic fall-off in demand for Lizzie, and Henry still insisting, "We have no intention of introducing a six. . . . It is true that we have experiments with such cars, as we have experiments with many things. They keep our engineers busy—prevent them from tinkering too much with the Ford car." He finally ordered all work stopped on the "X" engine without admitting that the experimenters were right: It was a dud.

In the next few weeks, Henry decided that Lizzie was done for.

The anguish it caused him was never recorded. Neither were the circumstances that brought him to relinquish her. The sales figures he saw spoke for themselves. Reports made personally to him by headquarters men back from tours of the branches told of Chevrolet's staggering gains—he would have trouble hearing all the details, though, since he was growing deaf. Sorensen, the best witness, accorded the victory to Edsel. Sorensen remembered afterward, "Edsel had quite an argument with Henry Ford lasting a long time, but he finally forced his father to give up the Model T."

Henry's behavior toward his son from this time on was consistent with that account. The perverse program of humiliation was expanded as though the father was impelled to work off his regret and resentment on Edsel for proving himself so butterhearted that he refused to fight for Lizzie's right to live.

News that the death warrant was soon to be signed had to be held secret, or the bottom would fall out of the market for the hundreds of thousands of cars the dealers had in stock and the flood of Model T's that still poured off the production lines. What would succeed her? With the "X" car forsaken, there was as yet no inkling of an answer. No new model existed, even as a completed design. For all the gadgets Henry carried around in his remarkable head, he could not visualize any love but Lizzie.

His soul probing coincided with trouble from another quarter. In March, the trial of Aaron Sapiro's libel suit opened in Detroit. Process servers tried for weeks to trace Ford and subpoena him; he personally was being sued for the million, not his newspaper. In his absence, Cameron spoke as chief witness for him, making the incredible claim that as editor he was solely responsible for the *Independent*'s anti-Semitism. Mr. Ford, he said calmly, had never discussed "any article" or "any Jew" with him, never saw copy in advance, and never so much as read the paper in his presence. When one of Henry's seven attorneys tried to establish that his client had not even heard of the plaintiff up to now, the opposing side produced a former member of Cameron's staff to testify that Henry had vowed to him that he planned to expose Sapiro.

Toward the end of the month, Ford had a subpoena tossed into his lap as he sat at the Ford Airport, opened in Dearborn two years earlier as part of Edsel's intense desire to push the company into a new business; all-metal, trimotor Ford-built planes were currently flying mail between Detroit, Chicago, and Cleveland. Henry was summoned to appear for something he dreaded as much as anything in the world: cross-examination on the witness stand on Friday, April 1, April Fool's Day.

The Sunday evening before his appointment in court, Henry set off alone in a Model T coupé to drive to the engineering laboratories at Highland Park. He recalled seeing two men hanging around outside the gate. On his way home, up Michigan Avenue, two men in a heavy Studebaker touring car sideswiped his coupé not far from Fair Lane's entrance gates and drove on. Henry's automobile was forced off the road, over a narrow stone curb and down a fifteen-foot embankment. A tree that it struck saved it from plunging into the Rouge River. He had an idea that the pair in the Studebaker were the same couple who had been loitering outside the laboratories.

Dazed from concussion, with ribs cracked and spitting blood, he arrived at Fair Lane's gatehouse. The guard telephoned Clara; instinct told her that this was an attempted holdup. Harry Bennett moved fast and obscurely, working hand in glove with the Dearborn police, with whom no formal complaint was ever filed. Henry was bandaged, splinted, and put to bed until the surgeon-in-chief of the Ford Hospital had him removed there. X rays showed no broken bones, but he certainly had been battered.

Rumor took over in Detroit. The victim was quoted variously as saying the hit-and-run collision was "deliberate," "an accident," and the work of "drunks." One newspaper story conjured up a murder plot. Detroiters heard that Ford was dead and two suspects arrested. Two youngsters were found who said they had seen him standing outside his car before it rolled toward the river.

Bennett discounted their testimony just as he belittled any premeditated effort to harm his boss. As chief of Ford's "service department" of guards, watchmen, plainclothes heavyweights, and private detectives, Bennett impressed reporters as a voice of authority. "Our connections with the Detroit underworld," he assured them, "are such that within twenty-four hours of the hatching of such a plot as this has been called, we would know of it. I believe this is one of those accidents that will never be solved."

On the eve of his scheduled court appearance, Henry was taken home from his hospital room, impatient over having been hemmed in for days on end. Bennett had a second, decoy ambulance provided to divert the crowd's attention from Henry's rear-door exit. The forecast that the case would remain a mystery turned out to be entirely accurate. On April 2, Robert Toms, Wayne County prosecuting attorney, reported opaquely that "on the basis of statements made by Ford detectives" the identity of the duo in the Studebaker was known, "but no action will be taken."

Henry's admiration for Bennett soared after his effectiveness in handling the whole incident and keeping him out of the witness box. Two weeks later, his doctors declared him still unfit to testify. Sapiro's attorneys were ready to demand his examination by a court-appointed physician when Bennett's investigators helped to abort the trial. They had kept the movements and conversations of all twelve jurors under surveillance and singled out one of them, a woman, for particular attention. They produced affidavits charging that her husband ran a speakeasy, that she had perjured herself under oath, and that she had accepted what might well be a bribe from an agent of Sapiro's. Defending herself in a newspaper interview, she complained, "It seems to be that someone is trying to keep this case away from the jury."

At that, Judge F. S. Raymond immediately declared a mistrial. Justice, he scolded, had been "crucified upon the cross of unethical and depraved journalism." The case was adjourned for six months, and Henry grabbed the opportunity to settle out of court. Without a word to Edsel, he chose two envoys to make peace with the Hebrews—an intriguing selection of Joseph Palma, of the United States Secret Service, and Earl Davis, a former Assistant Attorney General of the United States, both contacted initially by Bennett. They got in touch with Louis Marshall, head of the American Jewish Committee, and Nathan Perlman, vice-president of the American Jewish Congress.

Henry was terrified of being served with another subpoena half a year from now, and an intensified Jewish boycott was more than the company could stand. He was prepared to recant his anti-Semitism, call off his newspaper's attacks, halt circulation of the pamphlets, and make amends to Sapiro on condition that he withdraw his suit. Whoever wrote the apology sent to his friend

Arthur Brisbane for public release, it wasn't Henry, who signed it without reading it.

> In the multitude of my activities [its key paragraphs said] it has been impossible for me to devote personal attention to their management or to keep informed as to their contents. It has therefore inevitably followed that the conduct and policies of these publications had to be delegated to men whom I placed in charge of them and upon whom I relied implicitly. . . .
>
> Those who know me can bear witness that it is not in my nature to inflict insult upon and to occasion pain to anybody, and that it has been my effort to free myself from prejudice. Because of that I frankly confess that I have been greatly shocked as a result of my study and examination of the files of the Dearborn *Independent* and of the pamphlets entitled "The International Jew."
>
> I deem it to be my duty as an honorable man to make amends for the wrong done to the Jews as fellow-men and brothers, by asking their forgiveness for the harm I have unintentionally committed, by retracting as far as lies within my power the offensive charges laid at their door by these publications, and by giving them the unqualified assurance that henceforth they may look to me for friendship and goodwill. . . .

Cameron knew nothing of his master's act of atonement until he read the newspapers. "I cannot believe it is true," he gasped. Henry's principal counsel in the case, the venomous Senator James Reed of Missouri, telephoned from Texas: "What in hell is this I see in the Dallas paper?" Aaron Sapiro accepted a payment of $140,000 for legal fees, and Henry saved his final words for a good friend in Dearborn: "The Jews have gone along during the ages making themselves disliked. Right? They ignored their own splendid teachers and statesmen. Even they could not get their people to change some of their obnoxious habits. I thought by taking a club to them I might be able to do it."

He closed down his newspaper in October and packed Cameron off to Ireland, where all future production of Ford tractors was to be concentrated. Bennett was promoted to head of all personnel at the Rouge.

The slate was clear for the work that must be done before Ford had a new car ready. In the interval for public repentance that Judge Raymond had provided, Lizzie, aged nineteen, had drawn her last breath as a product in manufacture. Father and son walked down the Highland Park conveyor line as the fifteen millionth Model T took shape during the afternoon of May 26, 1927. Looking as uneasy as ever, Edsel took the wheel, and Henry rode as the front-seat passenger as the car pulled out into the chilly rain in the lead of a motorcade making for Dearborn. There waited Henry's horseless carriage of 1896, along with a 1909-vintage Lizzie. Henry took a turn around in each of them, then afterward stretched his arms to ease his fatigue. "Now, we've got to do it," he said contentedly. There was nothing else to do but somehow devise a car that Americans would buy by the millions again.

The era of the Model T—sometimes known as the flivver, the galloping snail, the Spirit of St. Vitus, the Detroit Disaster—was over, though some 10,000,000 of her still chirped to and fro along the onward-stretching highways, hauling men, women, children, furniture, groceries, animals, and their feed. The jokes about her lingered on. For example: "Have you heard the last story about the Model T?" a Ford official is asked. "I hope so," he replies. *There, little Ford, Don't you cry,* wrote one versifier, *You'll be a jitney bus, By and by.*

Tin Pan Alley hurried to exploit the mood of nostalgic regret with one song that asked, "Poor Lizzie, What'll Become of You Now?" Of the hundreds of printed elegies, a Massachusetts newspaper's editorial possibly spoke with the greatest poignancy: "Each year will see fewer veterans on the road. Junk yards will give but eloquent testimony to the passing of the great American car. But the world moves. And as far as motor vehicles are concerned, it is as heartless as the polyps which build coral isles. It rises on the dead bodies of worn-out autos to higher things."

Henry forecast that no total shutdown would be called for before the car now identified as Model A followed in Lizzie's tracks. Layoff of workers would be brief, he said, "because we need the men, and we have no time to waste." He was wildly optimistic. Starting that May, the Rouge was closed almost a year for retooling, and the bills would run to more than $100,000,000. At Highland Park, production stopped completely after engines and replacement parts had been turned out as a reserve for cars that would use them for a generation to come. The Rouge was designated as the key to success for Ford's new undertaking. Assembly lines would be torn out of the concrete at Highland Park and installed together with banks of new machines in the plant where Sorensen was in command, with Bennett his understudy. Edsel would have to struggle harder than before to apply a law of reason instead of fear.

His father gave him a vote in settling the dimensions of Model A and agreed that it should ride closer to the ground than Lizzie —three quarters of an inch closer. Edsel wanted to apply his own taste in the car's interior, and stipulated conservative slate-gray trim until the sales department objected, "It's got to be dolled up."

"I don't like gingerbread," he argued, but he was willing to compromise on a dashboard of simulated walnut. In the excitement of creating a brand-new Ford, Henry could overlook the defects he saw in him. "We've got a pretty good man in my son," he remarked. "He knows style—how a car ought to look—and he has mechanical horse sense, too." Edsel's teen-age enthusiasm for imported racing cars and pepped-up Lizzies had guaranteed that.

Styling was a minor problem compared with the challenge of evolving a new engine—no more than four cylinders, Henry ruled —that would meet his exacting inspection and outdo Lizzie's in speed and efficiency. He wanted every step in designing explained to him in chalk on a blackboard cloth, interjecting himself along the way. "Well, now, that's too big. Take a quarter of an inch off that. . . . That cylinder wall is too thick. Reduce that a sixteenth of an inch. . . . Oh, that flywheel looks too heavy."

The company had no test laboratories in the true sense of the word with scientific instruments to assess the strength and performance of component parts, as General Motors and Chrysler did. As the ingredients of Model A emerged, they were pounded and bent until they cracked in a rule-of-thumb appraisal of whether they would serve. The fragments were returned without explanation to the designers if they broke down under torture.

Henry wanted to see things *work* before he passed final judgment. Experimental cars by the score were put together for approval. Ford also lacked private testing tracks, such as Sloan had constructed. Over police protests, Model A prototypes were tried out on the highways of Dearborn and Detroit. Henry and Sorensen rode as passengers in one of them as it barreled down Oakwood Boulevard at better than sixty miles an hour one day.

"How are your brakes?" asked Henry above the wind roar. The driver discovered that the car had none. A mechanic had forgotten to connect them.

In August, Edsel announced nonetheless that the new Ford was "an accomplished fact." The next day, he had more valid grounds for enjoyment when Charles A. Lindbergh, nonpareil of heroes, took him and Henry up for a flip from the Ford Airport in his monoplane, *The Spirit of St. Louis*. Taking his ease at the Wayside Inn that fall, Father sighed, "My work is all done. That's why I'm here. Edsel is taking care of the rest of it."

Not until December did Model A appear on public display in the showrooms, heralded by a $1,300,000 advertising campaign and almost as much free newspaper space as had greeted "Lucky Lindy's" lone flight across the Atlantic. In the twelve months now ending, the company lost more than $30,000,000, Chrysler shareholders received $10,000,000 in dividends, and Chevrolet had brought out a new six.

Chapter Eight

How Firm a Foundation

Ten million people, so the estimates said, went to catch a glimpse of Ford's new automobile during the first few days after it went on display in major cities. "There hasn't been as universal a desire to see anything since Lindbergh came home," noted the Pittsburgh *Press*. Henry was sure that Model A was due to match Lizzie in longevity. "There is nothing quite like it in quality and price," he crowed. Edsel was more guarded, to his father's inevitable exasperation: "There is nothing radical about the new car. In fact, it is more conventional than old Model T." But Henry's name on it was enough to bring in 400,000 orders within two weeks, and the country had a new catchphrase to bandy around: "Henry's made a lady out of Lizzie."

The trouble was that, hard as Sorensen drove machines and men at the Rouge, production dawdled. He had consolidated his power by purging the company of some two thousand foremen and dozens of senior men who might conceivably challenge his authority after Highland Park was phased out. "All the Model T sons-of-bitches" had to go, he said. Loyalty to himself was the prime qualification he demanded of the new generation of supervisors that he installed. Foremen at the Rouge staged a silent rebellion by slowing down work on the line. The orders could in no way be filled when the plant resembled conquered territory with guerrillas on the prowl until Bennett could subdue them.

Model A had teething problems with its flywheel because

Henry ordered his engineers to experiment with a home-built starter that continually stripped the gears. If the four-wheel mechanical brakes should fail—still no hydraulics for Ford—there was no means of stopping the car. It took official protests from fifteen states and from overseas to win his agreement that an emergency hand brake should be fitted. In spite of its new forty-horsepower engine, Lizzie's heir would make no more than sixty-five miles an hour, five less than Chevrolet's.

Delays in deliveries started some dealers crying bankruptcy, but most customers were prepared to wait. They could buy on time now. Edsel had succeeded finally in getting Ford's into the installment business with the setting up of the Universal Credit Corporation, jointly owned by the company and the Guardian Trust group, whose executive vice-president chanced to be Ernest Kanzler. Edsel also remembered a much older relationship: Senator James Couzens of Michigan received a complimentary car.

The orders continued to roll in—800,000 of them by the spring of 1928. Franklin Delano Roosevelt, crippled by polio but angling for the governorship of New York, wanted a car in Niagara blue that could be equipped with special hand controls. In his case, the fire-sale prices set by Henry were not a factor. The two-door sedan sold for the same as a similar Lizzie, $495; Ford lost more than $300 on every one of them. Company losses exceeded $70,000,000 that year. At General Motors, where old Pierre had gone into retirement, profits after taxes barely missed $300,000,000. A third competitor appeared in the low-price market, Walter Chrysler's first Plymouth, which could be churned out in a specially constructed factory at the rate of 1,000 a day. Henry's only chance lay in forcing up output and shaving costs.

Problems or not, there was always time for his grandsons. On Saturday mornings, he had Sonnie and Benson over at the engineering laboratories, "raising more hell than you could shake a stick at," as one executive grumbled. "They'd get into the Model T or any other car that was around there and drive around the center of the building, zigzagging in and out of the columns, seeing how close they could come without hitting." Young Henry was twelve years old.

He enjoyed pulling employees' time cards out of the rack next to the clock and shuffling them before he put them back. When a man came to punch in on Monday morning, he might waste half an hour trying to find his own card. "Boy, we used to get peeved at the tricks," said the same executive. "His grandfather told him to go ahead. He thought it was fine."

One day, the two brothers commandeered the cash register in the plant cafeteria and handed out more money than they took in as the loaded trays were pushed along for inspection, which tickled Granddaddy no end. "Let them alone," he grinned. "They run wild when they're with me because the rest of the time they're cooped up like caged lions."

Mostly, he was supremely unconcerned by the riddle of how to restore Ford's profitability. The headaches, literal as well as metaphorical, were left for Edsel. Henry found something new to divert him all the time. Approaching seventy, he was intent on personal immortality. He was also a firm believer in reincarnation: Didn't he personally bear the spirit of Leonardo da Vinci? He found support for his theory in what he knew of the Bible. "Jesus was an old soul," he decided. "He felt that the essence of knowledge passed on with the soul." Perhaps Tom Edison was a being like himself. One of Henry's treasured possessions after his friend's death in 1931 was a glass vial, stored away in a cardboard shoebox and labeled, "Edison's last breath."

To preserve his sturdy growth of hair, Henry combed it with salt water. Along with tobacco and alcohol, granulated sugar was to be shunned because the sharp edges of its crystals cut into the blood vessels. That was the cause of Clara's arthritis. "You tell her not to eat sugar with her grapefruit," he admonished her doctors.

His boyhood hatred for farm living simmered on. He would like cows, for example, to be made obsolete, together with jails and hospitals, all of which could be done away with "if people would learn to eat the things they should." He provided a little rationale: "We could make milk commercially and get by without eating meat and so would cut out these wasteful animals." He could not bring himself to get rid of the dairy herds on his own farmlands, but the milk they gave was good, pure, old-fashioned milk, not modern, pasteurized stuff.

Exercise was equally important for a near-septuagenarian who would like to live forever. He tried to run three miles as soon as he was out of bed most mornings. If the day promised to be tense, he postponed breakfast until 1 P.M., because he worked better on an empty stomach, which may have explained the soda mints he carried around in his pockets. He persisted in bounding upstairs two steps at a time. "That is dangerous for your heart," he would be warned. "Make your heart get used to it," he replied.

Clara had little interest in his food fads. Her simple rule was to shun cream or butter in an unrewarded attempt to hold down her weight. Her husband was enthused by the nutritional qualities of weeds and coaxed some of his staff into joining him in chomping on what they called "grass sandwiches" while Sorensen stuck to steak-and-kidney pie. She was not to be tempted, and, most particularly, she kept soybeans out of her kitchen.

The seeds contained in the hairy, brown pods of the soybean plants impressed Henry as a potential source of flour, oil as a base for paints and sauces, and fiber for clothes and plastics long before scientific research vindicated his apparent crankiness. He found a job for his friend Edsel Ruddiman, doctor of pharmacy, testing the seed's food value on white rats and promising Michigan farmers that Ford Motors would market the beans if only the farmers would raise them as a crop.

Though he refused to engage a valet, Henry was a natty dresser, partial to pepper-and-salt tweeds and handmade, lattice-topped shoes. In fits of abstraction, he might go around in unmatched jackets and trousers, picked from a wardrobe that grew by four or five new outfits a year, most of them selected by Clara, who bought all his ties and shirts. The soybean suit and four-in-hand he wore were his choice entirely, like the menu of the dinner he ordered served to his guests at the company exhibit at the Chicago Century of Progress in 1934.

The previous year, it had been carrots—twelve courses of them. This year, in the building redecorated with soy oil paint, the meal began with tomato juice spiked with soy sauce, salted soybeans, and celery stuffed with soy cheese. The soup was purée of soybean, served with soybean crackers, followed by soybean croquettes and buttered green soybeans. Pineapple ring with soybean cheese and apple pie with soybean crust were offered for dessert, rounded off by cocoa with soybean milk. For those who had not had their fill, bread, butter, cakes, cookies, and candy were also available, all made from the versatile beans.

Paint manufactured at the Rouge must have a soy oil content. Gear-shift knobs, horn buttons, gas pedals, door panels, distributor housings—there was no end of uses for Henry's pet vegetable. Behind Ford Motor's laboratories, he put in an experimental, showpiece garden devoted to the crop; in two years, he laid out $1,250,000 on it. Before he was through, Ford would be growing 100,000 bushels of beans in a season.

Memories of the cheap violin he had taught himself to play just before he met Clara at the Martindale House set him off collecting masterpieces by Stradivari, Guadagnini, and Bergonzi. His first major acquisition cost him $15,000, but the prize of the collection was the fiddle of his courting days, which had vanished from its hook in the barn after he and Clara left the farm for Detroit. A humble sweeper on Ford's payroll returned it to him, apologizing for having swiped it as a boy of ten.

Husband and wife got to thinking about the dancing they had done together at the Martindale House in their courting days. "Do you realize, Henry Ford," she said, "that we have danced very little since we were married?" It would do them both good to try again, stepping it out in the quadrille and polka as they had nearly forty years ago, not in these new-fashioned foxtrots and tangos.

Henry tracked down an instructor, Benjamin Lovett, with a studio in Worcester, and invited him out to the Wayside Inn to meet himself and Clara. "I hope you'll help him," Clara urged Lovett. The offer Henry made him was not to be refused. With his wife, Lovett moved to Dearborn as the Fords' personal tutors. Their new pupil had soon signed up four oldtime players as a house orchestra —violin, cymbalum, sousaphone, and dulcimer—and had a special, sprung floor laid in the engineering laboratory. "The old American dancing was clean and healthful," Henry said. "The old dances were social. The modern dances are not."

Executives and their wives attended by dictate on the first night that the repertoire and the canvas-curtained ballroom were ready, and Lovett had done his best to memorize some square-dance calls. By the time midnight arrived and the quartet of musicians had wound up the proceedings with "Aunt Dinah's Quilting

Party" and "Good Night, Ladies," confusion had triumphed. "I'll tell you what we'll do," said Henry briskly. "We'll have lessons every night until we get it right."

Instruction was compulsory for two weeks, like attendance at subsequent dances, which continued until Japanese bombers ravaged Pearl Harbor. Henry might drop in on an employee the morning after he had fumbled a movement in the middle of a dance. "You didn't seem to get that step last night," he would say sadly. "Watch now and I'll show you," and he would take off in a demonstration *pas seul*. Or if he knew Lovett happened to be around, he would have him throw in some extra tuition for the stumbling offender.

When Henry wanted more couples on the floor, he would send cars to collect staff members and their ladies from their dinner table or perhaps a card party. Some days, he escorted his executives from noontime luncheon straight into the ballroom. There he would select a partner and gravely lead him through the turns and twists of an intricate dance to the accompaniment of the house quartet. The Varsovienne, which had been a favorite of Louis Napoleon's court, was especially tricky to catch hold of. Henry conscripted hulking, red-faced "Cast-iron Charlie" Sorensen to take a fellow employee's arm to teach him that one as they danced together.

At the Rouge, Sorensen was getting equally successful results. Production was in high gear now that Bennett had perfected the techniques of law-enforcement to impose Henry's idea of proper order. With Herbert Hoover five months in the White House, the bull market on Wall Street had spread a flush of Republican prosperity across the country, and the Big Three carmakers could sell virtually everything they could manufacture. Chevrolet had built a million of its new six, priced at $595 and introduced with only a forty-five-day interruption when Ford's was in the doldrums. Overtaken by Chevy in 1928, Ford was doing much better than that, with twice as many cars produced by the end of July. It was at once a tribute to the productive power of the Rouge and the effectiveness of Bennett's methods in motivating men.

Cocksure and cynical, he operated from a tightly guarded office in the basement close by the main entrance, with a push button under his desk to unlock the door and a light board showing where each man in his force was located. In the desk drawers, he kept a brace of pistols. Henry was fascinated to hear that one day his most dependable henchman disposed of the cigar in a prying union official's lips with a single shot after warning him that smoking was not allowed. The subterranean violence in Henry became more obvious as the years went by; in Bennett, violence was as visible as the scars on his nose and cheeks. "Harry, let's you and him have a fight," the old man would chuckle, then sit back to watch the outcome; Harry had been known to flatten an opponent twice his weight.

Bennett kept up his marksmanship by popping the tips off a row of pencils standing on his desk and by firing pellets from an air pistol into a six-inch steel target set up on a file cabinet at the far end of the room. To Clara's alarm, he drew Henry into a contest shoot at least once. On another day, Bennett accused a soon-to-depart veteran of Highland Park of calling him a liar and was pulling out a gun to underline his point before he got knocked against a door.

Jeered at in secret as "Sorensen's little puppy dog," Harry enveloped himself in an atmosphere of mystery and covert peril. A workman who omitted to wear his identification badge or tried to sneak a cigarette faced a roughing up from one or two of Bennett's service department janizaries, but Harry might do better than that. Frank Kulick, the third-oldest employee, who had been honored as such in the ceremonies attending the fifteen millionth Model T, was an example to bear in mind.

When he was fired without reason in the Highland Park purge, he appealed to Henry, who sent him back to Sorensen, who told him to repair a faulty car for Bennett. The bouncy young chief of personnel complained that the motor still clattered after the old mechanic had worked on it. "We'll take it for a ride," Bennett snapped, telling Kulick to lie on the running board with an ear against the hood to diagnose the trouble. Bennett, who was a gear-grinding driver, gunned the car out through the main gates and turned onto the highway so fast that Kulick was pitched off. He was left lying there while Bennett whipped back in behind the steel-mesh fence through another entrance. The grayhead got to his feet and walked shakily back to the gates. On the boss's orders, the guards refused to let him in.

Harry found recruits in the same places where he laid spy lines for the protection of Mr. Ford and his dear ones—subterranean hideouts in Detroit, Chicago, and Los Angeles. Hiring jailbirds complied with Henry's belief that hard work was every man's salvation, even the likes of the professional bruiser, on parole from San Quentin after serving eight years for murder, who came to work for Bennett. "They're a lot of tough bastards," Harry said, "but every goddamn one of them's a gentleman."

The heavyweights stayed undercover most of the time, to be let loose only in an emergency. The élite of the corps, none of them in uniform, were pleasant-faced ex-baseball players and retired athletes. Last Saturday's football game, crime and rough justice, or who looked good for the World Series were the mainstays of conversation at Harry's personal table in the executive luncheon room, whose staff waited for Henry to appear exactly at twelve fifty-nine or not at all. Bennett knew next to nothing about making automobiles, and he had no impulse to learn so long as Henry ordered him to play cops and robbers.

FBI men, police captains, and gangsters all shared in Bennett's patronage. Joe Adonis of the East Coast Mafia was on the list, and so was Tony D'Anna—both had company contracts for transporting Ford cars in fleets of haulaways. Chester Lamare, the stubby Sicilian with a record of seventeen arrests, was a junior overlord of crime in Detroit until he was awarded the fruit-supply concession at the Rouge. It was so profitable as to make his rum-running and highjacking operations a mere sideline. The story went around that he was hired as a bodyguard for Henry after he was sideswiped during the Sapiro trial. "Chet didn't know a banana from an orange," Bennett acknowledged after his protégé wound up on his kitchen floor with two Mafia bullets in the brain.

Since Harry was exempt from writing reports, keeping records, or filing expense sheets, no one could tell the precise size of his battalions. Guesses ran from four hundred up to three thousand and more, counting straw bosses who had authority to fire any hand without explanation, informers hoping to curry favor, the spies planted among the company's 90,000 employees, and the secret squad that kept tabs on his own Service Department men. The company was not unique in its espionage. General Motors followed the same practices. Meticulously maintained records showed outlays for "security" there bounding up toward $1,000,000 a year, but, like everything else, it was conducted more discreetly by its purring management.

What was verifiable about Bennett made him formidable enough. For a while, he had two caged tigers on view in his office, a gift from Clyde Beatty, the circus king, who trained animals rather than men. Harry was so contemptuous of straw hats that he put a couple of shots through one visitor's boater.

Hearsay magnified Bennett's reputation. Five toughs in a car had tried to crowd him off a highway until the little man in the perennially blue shirt drew a gun and threatened to blow their heads off. A tipster gave advance warning that an armed gang was on its way to hold up the Rouge pay office, and Harry posted guards with machine guns to wait for them. When the stickup car stopped for a red light on Miller Road, he beckoned one mobster over to the fence to describe what lay in store, and they took off in peace, grateful to be spared a massacre. A stranger got off two shots at one of Bennett's three daughters when she opened the front door of his house, built in Ypsilanti, Michigan, while he bedded down for two years in its basement, too short of cash to afford better quarters. That possibly had to be written off as another legend. In Henry's service, Harry maintained five homes simultaneously, and no one could be sure who paid for them.

Tales about these dwellings enhanced Bennett's image as an avenger as resourceful as any dark menace in a weeknight radio serial. In one fortress, it was said, an escape hatch concealed in a bathroom shower stall led to a forty-foot tunnel opening into the garage. In his pseudo-oriental sanctuary on Grosse Isle, in the middle of the murky Detroit River, picking up a certain bottle on the bar would reveal a secret stairway, which Harry could nip down to the covered dock, where his steel-hulled yacht awaited him in case of trouble.

"Harry gets things done," his master said after the results were in for 1929. General Motors had sold a monumental billion-and-a-half dollars' worth of automobiles, but Ford was out front again with 1,710,734 customers for Model A, 400,000 more than for Chevrolet. Henry's unprecedented income barely missed $14,000,000. Edsel's aircraft division was prospering, too, with sales of eighty-six trimotor planes to its credit. If he could keep his father's fingers out, Ford pioneering might well make the company a giant in this new business.

Detroit as a whole had never enjoyed such a year—well over 5,000,000 new cars on the road, more than $700,000,000 paid out in wages, and considerably more than three billion coming in from the customers. Car manufacturing had taken first place on the list of all American industries in sheer dollar value.

A committee of experts assembled by Hoover to examine the impact of change on the social scene agreed: "It is probable that no invention of such far-reaching importance was ever diffused with such rapidity or so quickly exerted influences that ramified throughout the national culture, transforming even habits of thought and language." One such transformation was diminished respect for the value of human life. Only Ford's soft-pedaled speed as a lure in its advertising, and speed spelled increasing death on the highways.

Through the summer and into the fall, 1929 gleamed as bright as gold. In October, Henry saw one more of his engrossments with the past take shape as a minor wonder of the world. In one swoop, he memorialized his idol, Tom Edison, and fulfilled his promise to prove his point about history by showing people "what really happened in years gone by."

A few minutes' walk from Ford Airport, a painstaking, full-scale replica of Philadelphia's Independence Hall had arisen, complete with a replica of the Liberty Bell, as a kind of entrance hall to acres of museum floor space. Here, Edsel had been in charge of putting on display most of his father's magpie accumulation of Americana. This was the core of what was termed the Edison Institute. Close by, a neverland village had been constructed, vaguely Colonial in style, but limited to no specific period of time.

Restoring the Wayside Inn had sparked Henry's imagination. The Edison Institute should provide more than a breath of yesterday, however. It must be a pantheon of the heroes and virtues that Ford worshiped, as much a projection of himself as Lizzie had been, but more enduring, and who was to care if the bills ran up to $25,000,000?

He bought and uprooted buildings across the country and overseas. A shepherd's cottage from the Cotswold Hills of England to demonstrate how the Pilgrim Fathers lived before setting sail and a Cape Cod windmill to show what they did after they landed. The blacksmith's shop from Uxbridge, Massachusetts—without the spreading chestnut tree—commemorated by Longfellow. The courthouse from Springfield, Illinois, where Lincoln practiced as a young lawyer. The whole cluster of structures from Menlo Park in which a host of Edison's discoveries had been made, plus an acre of New Jersey clay for ground cover and Sarah Jordan's boardinghouse, where electric light had flickered for the first time in an outside test.

An inn was transported from Clinton, Michigan, and from elsewhere a log cabin, a general store, a tintype studio, the office of Luther Burbank, and the birthplace of Stephen Foster. Since everything possible must be restored in toto, Henry wanted the body of Old Dog Tray exhumed for stuffing, but he compromised by having a living substitute, another setter, loll around the Foster cottage.

All the brick-and-clapboard importations, close to a hundred of them, served to complement the central purpose of the astonishing collection: telling Henry's life story from its beginnings not in words but in *things*. Here in the two hundred or so acres of the place they called Greenfield Village, future tourists would find the farmhouse where he was born, the schoolhouse he went to as a seven-year-old, the Bagley Avenue coalshed in which the quadricycle was built, and examples of every Ford automobile, burnished as bright as on the day it was made. If Henry could not guarantee personal immortality, he was making sure that he would be remembered.

Monday, October 21, was simultaneously dedication day and the fiftieth anniversary of the discovery of electric light. The guests invited to the Institute for the celebration ranged from Jane Addams to General Electric's Owen D. Young, with such luminaries as Eve Curie, Albert Einstein, Will Rogers, and Orville Wright added for good measure. William Green, the accommodating president of the American Federation of Labor, was flattered to attend, though union organizers were no more welcome than before at the Rouge and Highland Park.

An eternal flame struck Henry's fancy as an appropriate symbol of his desires. Taking no chances, he arranged for three to be

lit, one in the Stephen Foster cottage by a granddaughter of the
pauper composer, one in the Lincoln courthouse by President
Hoover, and one in the transplanted Menlo Park laboratory by
old Tom in person. Edison had only one fault to find with that
section of the Institute. "It's too damn clean," he wheezed. The
long arm of Ford was responsible for letting the whole country
know what was happening. Lights dimmed everywhere for a moment before Edison re-enacted the scene when, aged thirty-two,
he discovered a new means of brightening the night.

A different kind of darkness fell over the land three days later.
This was "Black Thursday," when a drastic lurch in share prices
cracked the façade of Hoover prosperity. On Friday, the market
rallied after worried bankers, meeting at noon, pledged millions of
dollars to support it. On the following Tuesday, the most devastating twenty-four hours in Wall Street's history, stocks slumped by
fourteen billion dollars. By the hundreds of thousands, optimists
who had bought on margin in the belief that the bull market
would last forever were wiped out in the nationwide stampede to
unload. The roaring, razzle-dazzle twenties were fading away in a
whimper.

Henry at first was confident that the Depression would soon be
over. All the company need do was take a dose of its time-tested
elixir. In November, he trimmed the price of every Model A, then
surprised those who fancied they knew him by consenting to join
in a conference of industrial kingpins, led by Treasury Secretary
Mellon, which Hoover convoked to lend weight to his forlorn as-
sertion that "the fundamental business of the country . . . is on a
sound and prosperous basis." The meeting sat Henry in the same
room as Pierre du Pont, but if they said a word to each other, it
went unnoticed.

Similar conferences called by the President produced no action
whatsoever, which was what could be expected when Administration policy was simply to hold the line until the storm blew
over. Henry, the maverick, would never go along with any herd,
especially this bunch. To their dismay, he announced as the conference closed that he aimed to raise Ford wages to a minimum of
$7.00 a day, effective December 1, no matter what was advocated
in the White House.

Edsel supplied a bland explanation: "Lately, we passed on the benefits of some of our economies to our customers in the form of reduced prices on our cars; and now we share up with our work-ingmen." Relying on his parent's love of a grandstand play, he had been able to do something toward sweetening life at the Rouge under Cast-iron Charlie and his personnel director.

The dealers came off less fortunately. Henry and Sorensen, equally hostile to the Sales Department, reasoned that they had just enjoyed a season on easy street, when all they'd had to do to sell cars was to keep their showroom doors open. They could live off their fat for a while. All 8,300 of them suffered the hardest winter of their association with Ford, compelled to last out if they could on the slimmest margins in the industry. Discounts were re-duced to 17½ per cent, while other manufacturers stuck to 20 per cent or more, and still Ford's outlets could scarcely move their stock. The consequence was as inevitable as before: mass deser-tions of able, embittered businessmen to the ranks of Chevrolet and Chrysler, until Henry was compelled to yield and restore most of the cuts.

By May of 1930, Hoover was confident that "we have now passed the worst and with continued unity of effort we shall rap-idly recover." Ford spent $8,700,000 in advertising to dispose of 1,256,600 Model A's that year and was gratified to finish well ahead in the desperate contest to beat General Motors, while Chrysler tailed along behind.

Then the Depression really hit home in Detroit. As the months went by and the country spiraled downward, nobody, it seemed, was interested in Model A. Sorensen ranted about dealer de-featism, but production at the Rouge fell by half. The $7.00-a-day minimum was a luxury that had to go. Mass layoffs were all a worker could look forward to, with the most senior hands first on the lists because they were the better paid. Those who remained were driven more ruthlessly than ever to get more work out of them. Something more than 500,000 cars had been sold by August 1931, which meant that, when the statisticians completed their annual arithmetic, Ford's share of the sinking market had dropped to 28.15 per cent, while GM's had risen to 43.26 per cent. It was time to forget about Model A and come up with a grand-daughter for Lizzie.

Hard times were growing harder yet when Sonnie was sent off

to school. Banks were closing, businesses collapsing, factories shutting down. Cars stood idle in garages because their owners could not afford gasoline. Texas oil prices fell to $.04 a barrel. Unemployment hit twelve million, with nearly 750,000 out of work in Detroit alone. Young Henry was as shielded from that kind of knowledge as from all other discomforts when Edsel and Eleanor enrolled him at Hotchkiss in Lakeville, Connecticut, a congenial establishment with sufficient tone to fit the son and grandson of multimillionaires.

He was roly-poly, nicknamed "T," and painfully aware that the Fords' millions might cut him off from his classmates. Money, a subject never mentioned at home, appeared to impress him as more of a handicap than a reason for lording it over anybody. There were no signs yet that he had acquired much of his mother's strength of character or his father's capacity for applying his nose to a grindstone or a book. "This boy," his headmaster recalled, "was not notable for his intellectual brilliance." He made up for the lack with his good humor and a respect for his teachers that matched Edsel's deference to Henry.

The kidnaping and killing of Lindbergh's twenty-month-old son had alarmed the elder Ford. If there was no alternative to his grandson's being sent away for a high-class education far beyond the guarded gates at Gaukler Pointe, surely Bennett should provide long-range protection for him. Edsel would not commit himself to that. When yet another extortion letter turned up in the mail, he reported it not to Bennett but to the FBI.

A calm young agent arrived at Hotchkiss to assess the risk involved there for young Henry. With the headmaster's assent, he passed himself off as a swimming coach, helping to get the team into shape. The conclusion he reached was that the little Connecticut village was safe enough for the boy to be given a taste of freedom. Young Henry spent the rest of his schooldays unrestricted by bodyguards.

The company was left once again without an entry in the race in the low-price field. In August 1931, Model A was done to death, and the lines at the Rouge were halted. Ford could not make up his mind where to turn next. A beefed-up four-cylinder engine? His engineers labored over what he thought was a "corking good" one, then he hesitated. "We found it was not the new effort which the public is expecting," he said. What about a six? He had parts ordered for some prototypes, then backed off again, getting madder by the week with everybody in orbit around him.

What Edsel wanted was a car with eight cylinders to give it a fighting chance against the competition and restore Ford's place in the market. It was December before he could get his father to agree, and then Henry was off and running here, there, and everywhere around the plant. This was more than Edsel had bargained for. He was disturbed by the reckless pace at which the designs were whipped out, suppliers' contracts signed, and new machinery ordered. He was afraid of the company's lack of experience with an engine of this size, the neglect of experimentation and trial. "He was fearful that we would have trouble," said the chief designer on the project, "and we did have trouble. We were using the public as our testing ground."

After three hectic months, the Ford V-8 went on display. Any objections from Edsel had gone unheard, but the engineers clung to their respect for him. He had a reputation among them for a special kind of awareness. He could hear noises in an engine that nobody else could detect, they said, because he had "an ear tuned higher than anyone else's." His father gave up pretending that he left everything to his son. "I've got back my old determination," Henry grinned. Business depended, he said, "on the man on the bridge"—himself.

His treatment of Edsel took an uglier turn. "Edsel just isn't tough enough" was the refrain. Henry ordered Cast-iron Charlie to rectify that, and Sorensen shut down the aircraft division for good. Sorensen's method was the same as Henry's—humiliate, knowing that the luckless president of Ford Motor Company would not carry tales to his father and that Henry would side with Sorensen if he did.

Top management understood that any order from Edsel was likely to be countermanded and any proposal vetoed. If he discharged a man, he would find him restored to the payroll at some other job. If he befriended anyone, it was as bad as demanding the man's resignation. With Kanzler gone, he had nobody of comparable resourcefulness to turn to within headquarters staff, though his brother-in-law continued to be one of the handful of people who shared Edsel's confidences.

Bennett stood waiting for his turn in downgrading Henry's heir. "He was a nervous man," Harry jeered later. "When he got angry, he threw up. He was just a scared boy as long as I knew him. Mr. Ford blamed himself for this. He had always overprotected Edsel."

Callousness and courage were both part of Bennett. In the few weeks before the V-8 made its debut, he had an unexpected chance to prove his spunk. One man of every two in Detroit's automobile industry was out of work by now. Five thousand of them came along Miller Road one blustery cold March morning, marching on the Rouge. Mayor Frank Murphy, who would be a Supreme Court Justice one day, judiciously cautioned Detroit police to give the parade free passage through the streets of Detroit. At the Dearborn boundary, a different set of blue-uniformed lawmen took over. Tear gas greeted the marchers there, but the wind was with them, and they pushed on, hoping, some said, to take over Ford's factory and barricade its doors.

Among the spectators looking down from windows in the Rouge was a group of Soviet engineers, who had been given offices there. Henry still hoped that a contract with the Soviets calling for them to buy $33,000,000 worth of Ford products might be lived up to, though he was adamant about offering easy credit when their purchases lagged far behind schedule.

"Russia is beginning to build," he said cheerfully when his hopes were highest. "It makes little difference what theory is back of the real work, for in the long run, facts will control. I believe it is my duty to help any people who want to go back to work and become self-supporting." This March day put a deeper dent in his buoyancy. Like many others, he blamed Communists for what developed next on Miller Road.

He and Edsel were at lunch when Bennett got word that the Dearborn Fire Department had aimed its hoses on the march. Bennett pictured to himself the devastating publicity if the newspapers printed photographs of that. He raced out the gates to have the fire chief turn off the hydrants. Then, single-handedly, he drove to the head of the sodden parade, confident that he could persuade the defiant crowd to go on home.

"We want Bennett, and he's in that building," screamed a woman with a brick in her hand.

"No, you're wrong. I'm Bennett." As he fell under a shower of brickbats, he pulled a nineteen-year-old organizer of the Young Communist League down on top of him. Police bullets instantly killed young Joe York. Three more were dead and fifty injured, police and fire fighters among them, before the melee was over. Bennett scrambled to his feet, to be knocked unconscious in the crowd. As soon as the police had dragged him clear, he went to his office, dabbed Mercurochrome on his cuts, and presented himself for Henry's certain approval.

Most of the defects in the V-8—engine vibration, faulty ignition, and leaking piston rings—had been corrected toward the end of the year, but nothing could raise sales much above 250,000 cars. Wages at Ford's were dropped to a minimal $4.00, among the lowest in the industry, but losses of $70,831,153 placed it far ahead in the downhill slide of the Big Three; Chrysler's were something more than $10,000,000, and General Motors' a comparatively piddling $4,559,000.

As November's Election Day approached, a notice was posted in Henry's factories: "To prevent times from getting worse and to help them get better, President Hoover must be re-elected." The assembly line itself promised to become a peculiar source of parapolitical power. Bennett was willing to offer a deserving candidate its facilities by sending a petition along its path for signature by obliging workmen. In Wayne County, Michigan, home of most Ford workers, Franklin Delano Roosevelt received 100,000 more votes than Herbert Hoover.

The deepening Depression during the four months' interregnum before the new President took office brought near disaster to Detroit. To ward off a run on the banks, Senator Couzens sent an intermediary to suggest that he and Ford provide a massive joint loan to shore them up. Henry was not inclined to forgiveness. "You tell Couzens," he replied, "I wouldn't have anything to do with anything he proposed." Edsel, a director of several local institutions, had a counterproposal to make along with Henry. They were willing to put up all the necessary capital for the opening of two new banks, though they would want to choose the men to run them. The financial establishment turned them down.

Relations between Roosevelt and Ford were a study in two-sided duplicity. Swift White House action to buttress the country's collapsing banking system in March 1933 appealed to Henry, who bought advertisement space in May to sing the praises of the President: "On Inauguration Day he turned the Ship of State around." But before long, Henry had his mouthpiece Cameron sitting in front of the microphones on the weekly "Ford Sunday Evening Hour"—fifty-four minutes of music, six for editorializing —delivering such oracular tidbits as, "We have had no Napoleons in this country, and we need none. . . . Spectacular thunderclap characters leave no lasting mark. . . . The public as a whole or in good part has not been deceived by would-be guides who are themselves misled."

For his part, Roosevelt believed that, once they sat down together, he could convert any man, even a character as antipathetic as Henry, to his point of view. Roosevelt tried repeatedly to lure him along with Clara to Washington or, better yet, to the so-called Little White House at the polio treatment center in Warm Springs, Georgia, where they could relax in peace. Henry wanted a lot of coaxing. Edsel had already donated $25,000 to the Warm Springs Foundation toward building an indoor treatment pool, and FDR knew that in him he had an ally, unique among the hard-shell Republicans who ran the auto industry. This was another thing Henry could hold against his son.

Even on the eve of the Second World War, when King George VI of England and his Queen, Elizabeth, were in the United States drumming up sympathy for their country, Henry begged off dining with them in the White House. Clara, he said puckishly, had a prior engagement with her garden club.

Once in a great while, he did allow himself to be wheedled into accepting a Roosevelt invitation. After one encounter, he was asked what he and his devious host had talked about. "Well," Henry said, "he took up the first five minutes telling me about his ancestry." He could not make out why, "unless Roosevelt wanted to prove he had no Jewish blood."

Edsel went down on the night train with him for another uneasy luncheon with FDR, who had his brother-in-law, Hall Roosevelt, and Marriner Eccles, head of the Federal Reserve Board, with him. The President aired a notion of his for lending government funds to deserving borrowers, to be repayable over a thirty-five-year term.

Henry put his spoke in as soon as he had the opportunity. "You know, Mr. President, nobody pays a debt after thirty-five years."

Roosevelt was not to be put off when he was spinning dreams. Three hours later, when the coffee was cold and his powers of persuasion had temporarily dried up, Ford had the parting words: "Before you leave this job, you're not going to have many friends, and *then* I'll be your friend."

Of all the laws passed in the avalanche of New Deal legislation designed to "soak the rich," the Wealth Tax Act of August 1935 posed the gravest potential danger to Ford's empire. Surtax on individual incomes of $50,000 or more was increased, as it was on estates valued at more than $40,000. The heirs would have to pay the tax collector 50 per cent of anything over $4,000,000, and 70 per cent if the inheritance exceeded $50,000,000. The implications were instantly obvious to Edsel. The death of himself or his father would automatically terminate exclusive family ownership of the company. The only possible method of raising tax money in the necessary millions would be to sell a sizable hunk of the stock.

Only Eleanor in all probability knew whether or not Edsel had some presentiment about his future that fall when he and Henry began talks with Ford's longtime attorney, Clifford Longley, about writing intermeshing wills. Progress was slow. Henry's ingrained distrust of lawyers and his refusal to accept his own mortality made him a reluctant client. Hadn't the company just taken on a marvelous new lease on life and forged ahead of its rivals in a suddenly expanded market, with twice as many customers as Plymouth and almost 200,000 more than Chevrolet?

After months of dickering, the documents were finally drawn by Longley with Edsel's help. The company's 172,645 shares were split, 95 per cent of them designated as "Class A" nonvoting, the balance as "Class B" voting stock. On the death of either the father or the son, his nonvoting block would be inherited by an enterprise known as the Ford Foundation, established, as its charter stated, "to receive and administer funds for scientific, educational, and charitable purposes, all for the public welfare and for no other purpose."

Voting stock, key to control of the business, was bequeathed by Henry in equal shares to Edsel and his four children. Similarly, Edsel left Eleanor and their children one fifth apiece of his voting stock, and he put in some of his own cash as seed money—$25,000, which seemed to be his standard contribution to a foundation. Not until a dozen years later did the world catch on to what he had accomplished: the establishment of the largest trust fund ever known to mankind, celebrated in verse by one of its first directors, Robert M. Hutchins:

> How firm a Foundation we saints of the Lord
> Have built on the faith of our excellent Ford . . .
> How firm a Foundation; we've three times the dough
> And ten times the brains that any other can show.

No lawyer could contrive a means of cushioning the impact of another piece of New Deal legislation, signed by the President a month before the Wealth Tax Bill. With the National Labor Relations Act, the government recommitted itself to support labor's right to organize and bargain collectively. In theory, union activists had been empowered to busy themselves at Ford's since 1933, but company defenses had held firm against them. Unions were anathema to Henry, secure in his conviction that he knew what was best for a workingman. Average pay for a Ford hand was down to $.88 an hour—$35.20 for a forty-hour week.

The second clash at the Rouge began taking shape at Atlantic City in October, when John L. Lewis of the hunger-stricken United Mine Workers stumped out of the American Federation of Labor's docile convention there to form the fighting Committee of Industrial Organization. The United Automobile Workers of America, young and untested, soon quit the AFL to join him.

General Motors was its first target. Ten days after 140,000 workers walked out on strike in February, Sloan capitulated and recognized the union. Chrysler came next. There, 60,000 men, following a strategy developed in France, barricaded themselves inside the plant. Victory took somewhat longer, but Chrysler capitulated in April and signed with the UAW.

Bennett had no need of his early-warning system to tell him what was ahead or to stir him to prepare for it. Carrot-topped Walter Reuther, head of the Detroit local, intended to move cautiously against Ford's citadel. The plan for the afternoon of May 26, 1937, was to do no more than pass out handbills at the Rouge gates as shifts changed at four o'clock, with permission granted for the exercise by Dearborn's city hall. Wives and other women volunteered to help.

That morning, an aide of Bennett's tipped off a union man he knew: "I don't want you to go out there today. . . . It's going to be extremely unpleasant." Press photographers were waiting when Reuther and four others arrived an hour early. Bennett was finishing his lunch elsewhere.

Reuther and his mates clattered up the iron steps to an overpass leading from a streetcar stop into the fenced enclosure of the Rouge to take a preliminary look at the terrain. A platoon of pluguglies, wrestlers, and professional musclemen blocked their path, with Angelo Caruso, lord of Detroit's Down River gang, in the forefront. "This is Ford property," Caruso snarled. "Get the hell off here." The union men turned to retreat, but their exit was cut off by a second gang of Ford troopers.

Then the beating began. Reuther's jacket was tugged over his head to bind his arms before he was struck down, kicked again and again in the body and face, then dragged to his feet for another dose before he was thrown down the steps. Another man was kneed in the scrotum to bring him down, and have boot heels ground into his belly. A third was mauled and mangled in much the same fashion. The fourth, the union's Richard Merriwether, had his back broken.

Down below, two dozen desecraters of Ford territory escaped with kicks and punching. At the foot of the stairs, a girl vomited, clutching her stomach. "You mustn't hurt these women!" a policeman on horseback yelled as he pushed into the crowd. Out of sight, Bennett answered a telephone call. "Nobody is going to storm Mr. Ford's gates," he barked. The roughnecks moved to snatch cameras out of the photographers' hands, but enough of them got clear for pictures to cover the front pages of the morning newspapers.

The shambles at the Rouge touched off trouble at Ford subsidiary plants across the country. Police everywhere either turned their backs on the sight of men being beaten up on streets and parking lots, or else picked up union members for handing out pamphlets. In California, Massachusetts, Texas, and Missouri, the pattern repeated itself: union buttons ripped from shirts; incursions by goon squads; threats; tar and feathers; floggings with cat-o'-nine-tails and with a novelty in the strong-arm business, a whip made of plaited cable wire and rubber stripping.

Before the year ended, the National Labor Relations Board found Ford guilty of applying deliberate terror to break the union. The federal examiner wrote a scarifying report: "The company gathered and financed the most vicious and experienced thugs in its employ who accepted an opportunity to indulge sadistic desires in lieu of additional compensation upon any person pointed out to them as a CIO organizer, member, advocate, or sympathizer. . . . The company decided the only way to defeat the workers in their organization efforts was to sow seeds of distrust of unions and fear of reprisals for followers if they joined the union."

Old Henry, seventy-four this year, professed not to believe it. "Anybody who knows the Ford Motor Company," he argued, "knows the things the Board charged never happened and could not happen here." But enough of the public accepted the established truth for Ford's precarious lead over General Motors to be endangered by an additional hazard—a consumer boycott of everything Ford made. The surge of unionism had been turned back by the barricade of brutality. Bennett's reward was a new office and expanded powers. But the barricade might as well have been built of sand, and Henry, like Canute enthroned on the beach, could only wait for the next tide.

Edsel's forbearance toward his father was wearing thin. Walter Reuther had become international president of the UAW when he recalled that era. Edsel, he said, "hated with every drop of his blood what he knew was going on there at the plant. . . . He was a decent man, and he cared." Henry's hostility toward his son's compassion poisoned the atmosphere between them. It grew more noxious when the old man suffered a minor stroke. To prove to himself that it had left him unimpaired, his interference in every detail of the company's operations increased until it reached unmanageable proportions. Working at the Rouge was like living under martial law as plainclothesmen sniffed in every corner for the scent of rebellion.

Young Henry was in his freshman year at Yale when Reuther was beaten on the overpass. As a student, he had regressed if anything from his lusterless Hotchkiss performance. He was still too lardy for active sports, still bursting with good humor, still as re-spectful of his grandfather as he had been when two Hotchkiss schoolmates tried to tempt him into running off to sea.

"I'd like to, but I just can't," he told them. "Why, my grandfa-ther would get out the militia!"

In retrospect, Yale seemed wasted on him. "I didn't learn any-thing in those courses except maybe one, which was kind of fun—a course in psychology. I took them because I had flunked in en-gineering. The other guys said sociology was a snap course, so I figured that was for me. I flunked *it*, too."

Chapter Nine

An Orchid from Edsel

What he wanted more than anything else just now was to be married. There was no doubt in his mind that he had found the right girl. He had known her since the summer of his nineteenth birthday, when Granddaddy and Callie took him off on a vacation in Europe to celebrate his graduation from Hotchkiss. He met Anne McDonnell, blond and exquisite, homeward bound aboard the French Line's *Normandie*.

In every respect but one, she promised to be an admirable match. She was one of the thirteen children of William McDonnell, utilities magnate and founder of the Wall Street house of McDonnell & Company, and a granddaughter of James Murray, an inventor overshadowed only by Tom Edison in the number of patents held in his name. Money had cradled her life so far. Her upbringing had been as sheltered as young Henry's by nannies, governesses, and now the nuns of the Convent of the Sacred Heart, which stands on a quiet headland overlooking Long Island Sound at Noroton, Connecticut.

Religion was the problem. The McDonnells were Catholics, and Granddaddy, a Mason who never went to lodge meetings, lumped Catholics along with the du Ponts, Jews, bankers, warmongers, union bosses, and Communists as creatures of darkness. Young Ford was not deterred. His parents might be classified as Methodists, but questions of faith carried no great weight in Edsel's tolerant philosophy.

The courtship of Anne began virtually as soon as the boy entered Yale. A weekend run down the Merritt Parkway from New Haven in his Lincoln convertible was routine, like switching courses. They met in the McDonnells' Fifth Avenue triplex, where the servants had one floor to themselves, and at the summer place near Southampton, Long Island; Wickapoque Cottage East was a mansion of fifty-four rooms on fifty acres, the center of a tennis-swimming-dancing social set that Scott and Zelda would have envied.

Edsel and Eleanor raised no known objections to the romance, and they treated old Henry according to the principle that for the present what he did not know would not hurt him. In the young couple's circle of acquaintances, there was speculation that Henry might disinherit his grandson, but this was a meaningless conceit when he was an heir of Edsel's, not Granddaddy's under the terms of the unpublicized wills.

Ernest Kanzler used to say of Edsel, "He had a hundred thumbs stuck in as many holes in the boat." If Edsel had had one to spare, it might have gone into his son's performance in college, where he was known as "T" after his grandfather's departed Lizzie. "T" seemed destined to amount to no more than a playful dilettante with an inherited passion for automobiles but no trace of business acumen. His attainments to date could be listed as managing Yale's rowing crew and membership in Book and Snake, a social club. The most serious venture undertaken so far was to receive instruction as a Catholic from the persuasive Monsignor Fulton Sheen for Anne's sake.

But Edsel's hands were filled with the attempt to cut down Bennett. Harry had authority now to hire and fire at all but the topmost levels and was ambitious to extend his control by listening to Henry's suspicions of any executive who questioned Bennett's powers.

Any transfer of staff from one job to another was subject to Harry's approval. His signature was required on all expense accounts, which were paid without question to his personal allies, held up in the case of his adversaries. He was lavish with awards of cars, bonuses, commissions, and agencies to spread his influence. The guards who worked for him allowed truckloads of materials to leave the Rouge unchecked; when inventories were ultimately taken, the shortages totaled $100,000,000. His income was a mystery. Henry rewarded him with handouts of extra cash, then refused to raise other men's salaries.

"The loyalty you had was because of Edsel," one of them recalled. "You really worked there hoping and praying for the time when Edsel would be in charge." That prospect dimmed as the months passed and Ford lagged into last place behind General Motors and Chrysler in its share of the market, with no ray of sunlight to be seen.

Bennett's team had infiltrated key positions in most departments. Liebold had long since fallen out of favor with Henry. The old man's personal secretary nowadays was Frank Campsall, who opened his mail, screened visitors and telephone calls, and reported back to Bennett.

The company secretary and treasurer, B. J. Craig, was another follower, anxious to drop whatever he was doing to answer a summons to Harry's new quarters in the towering Rotunda Building in the Rouge. Self-preservation was the governing rule when it looked as though the future would inevitably fall into Bennett's grasp. But first he must fence in Henry's natural heir and then, if possible, dispose of the last remaining challenger, his nominal superior, Sorensen.

Cast-iron Charlie had given up his appointed task of toughening Edsel. As something of an alley fighter himself, he could scent danger from Harry's direction, and he wanted every bit of support he could get in the event of a facedown. The scent at first was faint but unmistakable. Without his permission, soft-drink dispensing machines were installed overnight at the Rouge.

"Who put those in there?" he asked when he saw them.

"Mr. Bennett."

"He and I used to talk over those things," Sorensen grumbled. "What's getting into him?" To prove that the pecking order stood intact as of now, he ordered them taken away. He really had no time to spare for intrigue on this petty scale. Keeping production rolling at the Rouge with new models mandated every year was Cast-iron Charlie's responsibility; conducting the rest of the business was Edsel's. They quietly agreed to forget the past and try as a team to curb Bennett, who knew of every move they made toward that end. Sorensen's secretary, Russell Gnau, was on Bennett's side.

Apart from telephone calls with Henry and the perpetual chore of fending off the union, Bennett could devote much of his day to extending his power. The technique was simple. He spoke in the name of his greatest admirer. "Mr. Ford says—" and "Mr. Ford wants—" usually brought whatever action Harry desired. In the rare instances when a man queried an order and sought out the old despot himself, Henry would invariably side with Bennett, who according to Henry's dulled perceptions was no less than perfect.

Edsel was equipped neither in mind nor body for this kind of contest. Bennett, who was anything but a liar, bragged of his relationship with Henry: "I became his most intimate companion, closer to him even than his son." A look of permanent melancholy settled on Edsel's taut face, and his clothes sagged on his skinny shoulders.

Somehow he managed to shoulder the company into taking after GM by offering cars for sale in a broad range of prices instead of having only Fords at one end of the market and Lincolns at the other. The dealers had been pleading for years to be provided with cars to fill the gap. The Lincoln Zephyr was the first of his responses. For a while in 1939, it pulled ahead of General Motors' Buick and soon-to-die La Salle in the middle-price field. The outlook seemed bright for his latest entry in the race. The Mercury was an Edsel idea, designed to give GM's Pontiac and Chrysler's Dodge a run for the money, and another concept of his was being worked out on drawing boards and on the shop floor at this time. He hoped that the handsome, hand-built machine that would be called the Continental could soon be produced in sufficient quantity to rival Cadillac in his frustrated wish to create "the best car in the world."

The company's facilities were pathetic by comparison with GM's. Sloan had been stressing the importance of style in selling since 1921, catering to the buyer's unspoken desires, not his needs for a durable car. He enticed Harley Earl away from Don Lee's custom body shop in Los Angeles, which grew rich by fancying up standard automobiles for motion-picture stars, and put him in charge of the styling section at the moment of Lizzie's demise. At

General Motors as in Hollywood, looks counted for more than anything else. There were no better engineers to be found in the industry, but they played second fiddle to the designers. A new model's style was determined first, the fit of its running gear second, and the judgment of the market place showed that Sloan's policies worked. In the matter of engineering, too, Edsel was poorly served. In the turmoil at the Rouge, nobody devoted the time to produce a first-class twelve-cylinder engine for the Continental.

Henry's attention had wandered elsewhere. Maybe a *five*-cylinder engine would set the industry on its ear. His experimental department got to work, skeptical about its chances. When a prototype was hitched up to a dynamometer for testing, the din was enough to shake dental fillings loose. "Isn't that the smoothest thing you ever heard?" he asked. The engineers could not make out whether he was joking or stone deaf, but he kept them pursuing his fancy.

The dream, older than Lizzie herself, of supplying the farmer with a cheap, serviceable tractor returned to haunt him. "I don't care if we can't make a cent of profit," he declared. "The main thing is to get something started." Nothing his own men came up with had satisfied him when a peppery Ulsterman, Harry Ferguson, arrived at the Dearborn farm to demonstrate a model he had developed. The results so delighted Ford that, by this newcomer's account, the two men shook hands on a gentlemen's agreement for Henry to mass-produce the machine, while Ferguson would sell it "throughout the world." Sorensen rated it as too frail and probably too expensive to manufacture, but as usual he would not cross Henry, who proceeded to spend $12,000,000 of his company's dwindling cash reserves on tooling up the Rouge for the job. By June 1939 the first run of the Ford-Ferguson tractor was ready for its public debut.

At this point, other thoughts were revolving in Henry's head. The Depression had put Hitler and his Brownshirts into power in Germany, and now Der Fuehrer's armies were marching over Europe. If, after Munich, the British and the French could steel themselves to oppose him, there would be war. The best preventative so far as Henry could see was "moral rearmament," the cause espoused by Dr. Frank Buchman, the beaming, moon-faced clergyman with whom the Fords had been in touch for the past three years. In midsummer, he induced Henry to sign a statement for public distribution: "There is enough good will in the people to overcome all war, all class dissension, and all economic stagnation, when that good will shall be hitched to the affairs of men and nations."

On August 28, when the Germans were concentrating tanks and planes to batter Poland, Henry maintained, "They don't dare have a war and they know it." On September 25, when the Poles had been defeated and Hitler was turning his sights on the Low Countries, Ford's confidence remained unshaken. "If I were put on the stand," he asserted, "I'd say there isn't any war today." For months to come, he kept up the theme. If *he* would not acknowledge that a war was actually being fought, America could never be dragged into it.

The early days of battle coincided with a test of strength in Dearborn between Bennett and Edsel. Managers from branches had been brought in for a round of exhortation about the new 1940 models. "Ford for '40," as the sales slogan trumpeted, included the Mercury for the first time. On windup night at the country club, Jack Davis, chief of sales, was interrupted in midsentence by one of Bennett's especial favorites, Harry Mack, once promoted straight from managing the box factory to taking charge of the Rouge assembly line.

Davis survived the exchange, finished his speech, and went home. Mack and half a dozen friends retired to the locker room to continue their drinking. There, Bennett's crony provoked a fight with one of Davis's staff, once a tackle for the Chicago Bears, and landed in the hospital for patching. Edsel and his ally Davis had been looking for the chance to be rid of Mack, whom they suspected of spiriting a car away at Bennett's instruction in his hireling's latest appointment as Dearborn branch manager. With Edsel's blessing, Davis fired him.

In no time, Bennett was on the telephone to Davis, accusing him of provoking the locker room brawl and calling him over to his office, where Mr. Ford wanted to see him right away.

The sales manager's attempts to tell Henry the truth about the night of the country club dinner were constantly broken into by Bennett, who had his own version to relate. In turn, he was cut off by Davis when his patience evaporated. "Harry, you're a liar." Bennett shouted, "Nobody calls me a liar!" and clenched his hands. Henry slipped out, content, Davis thought, that Harry was about to be matched in one more brawl. "Why don't you hit me?" Davis goaded, but Bennett said no more, lowered his fists, and let his opponent leave in peace.

Edsel had already heard from Henry when he asked Davis in to talk a little later. "Father," he said, "is in a terrible state of mind." Bennett, taking care of his own, refused to let Mack's firing stand. Unfair or not, it was Davis who would have to suffer in exile, managing the Ford branch in Long Beach, California. Mack would simply be given a new job, in charge of service and parts, where he could continue to take care of Harry's friends.

The company had lost the services of one of the best sales managers it had known, and the pleasure due to Edsel on the Mercury's launching had been soured. He hadn't a finger to spare for plugging holes in his son's education, though he was wise to his shortcomings. To one rose-colored report that young Henry was doing well at Yale, he answered dryly, "It is almost time for him to do so, having but a few more months left at New Haven."

"T" flunked graduation. Taking his chances with Grandfather, he announced his engagement to Anne McDonnell before he tackled his final examinations. "Folkways and Thomas Hardy" was the subject of the required thesis in sociology, and he had skipped reading enough of Hardy to have any hope of writing it. "I got a guy to help me," he explained afterward. The professor immediately detected that the paper turned in was too good to be the work of young Henry.

"They said I couldn't graduate unless I wrote another theme on an entirely different subject. I said the hell with it. I was in a hurry to get out and get married." But he stayed on after the class of 1940's commencement to manage the crew's last big race.

That spring, Nazi tanks rolled unchecked across the Netherlands and on into Belgium and France. Certain that sooner or later the United States would find itself at war, Roosevelt called on Congress for emergency funds to produce fifty thousand planes a year and pulled Bill Knudsen out of the presidency of General Motors to be sworn in as Commissioner for Industrial Production on the National Defense Advisory Commission. The following morning, Edsel was on a plane to Washington. A sizable slice of this business was exactly what Ford's needed. One reason why Edsel had been anxious to sign an armistice with the UAW from the start was that it would assure the company the federal contracts that had been withheld in retribution for his father's refusal to obey the labor laws.

After little more than a week, a United States Army Air Force pilot landed a fighter plane at Ford Airport for examination by Edsel and his father. Henry reckoned it was likely the company could make more like it. Edsel and Sorensen returned to Washington that afternoon, to find that the situation had changed overnight. The British were desperate for more Spitfires to hold back the Luftwaffe bombers that were softening up the island in preparation for a German invasion.

Twelve hours of talking with Knudsen, and Ford was committed to manufacture 9,000 Merlin Rolls-Royce aero engines, 6,000 of them for the British, the rest for the United States, production to begin as soon as contracts were signed. In London, Lord Beaverbrook, Minister of Aircraft Production, jubilantly announced the news.

Forty-eight hours later, Edsel telephoned Knudsen. "Bill— Father won't do it."

"Aren't you president?"

"Yes, I am, but you know how Father is."

Only once during the countless flights that Edsel made between Detroit and the capital did any sign indicate his failing strength, a subject now added to the never-to-be-discussed list. It may have been on this homeward journey that he trembled, chilled with fatigue, and asked a companion if he might be covered with his overcoat. In Washington, there would be an old friend to turn to: Ernest Kanzler carried considerable weight at the War Production Board, where he served as director general at the automotive division.

Knudsen followed Edsel to Dearborn. Henry greeted him as he joined his son and Sorensen in Edsel's office. "You're all right, William, but you're in with a bad crowd down there." Then, with no further debate: "I won't make any of those Rolls-Royce engines for England."

But he had given his word, Knudsen protested, and Roosevelt was delighted. "We won't build the engines at all," Henry said grimly. "Withdraw the whole order. Take it to someone else."

"There'll be a stink over this," Knudsen warned. Ford shrugged his shoulders contemptuously. Knudsen stormed out, flushed with rage. The deal was dead; Packard would handle the job. Henry wanted only to make planes of his company's own design, for sale exclusively to the United States for defense, not involvement with those far-off Europeans who, he lamented, had been duped a second time by "greedy financial groups." Ford had not a dollar's worth of defense contracts on its books when his eldest grandson was married on July 13.

The ceremony was sumptuous enough to satisfy the bride, who took permanent delight in marvelous parties. More than a thousand guests filtered in and out of Wickapoque Cottage East, tailed by press photographers and reporters who could find no alternative to describing it as "the wedding of the year," while as many spectators gawked on the roads outside. Tomorrow's readers would learn that the gifts on display had cost over $1,000,000, with no mention of the 25,000 shares of stock transferred to the bridegroom by his father "in recognition," said the accompanying letter, "of the fact . . . that after being married [you] will join the Ford Motor Company as your future business, and also because of the fact that you are at the present time a Director of the Company." A subsequent assessment set an official value of $135 on each share. The twenty-two-year-old bridegroom was $3,375,000 better off, with good reason to go to work to safeguard his position.

Monsignor Sheen conducted the nuptial mass in the graystone Sacred Hearts of Jesus and Mary in Southampton; the McDonnells' champagne was inexhaustible; old Henry danced somewhat shakily with Anne and exchanged a word or two with the priest; and the couple took off for a Hawaiian honeymoon. The house in Grosse Pointe Farms to which they returned was another present from Edsel and Eleanor. When they moved in, Anne was pregnant. Their first child, Charlotte, was born on April 3 the following year.

There was no arguing with his father's unequivocal statement that his career must lie with the company, and young Henry reported for duty at the Rouge. Bennett set watch on him from the day he arrived. It was Edsel's wish to have his sons learn the business from the concrete floor up, not from the heights of what Bennett sneered at as "mahogany row." The dynamometer room was the first classroom for the director-apprentice, as well as for Benson, shaken loose from Princeton at the start of his junior year. They had no thought of objecting when Leonard Williams, a no-nonsense black foreman, was assigned to teach them the rough, grimy job of taking engines apart.

Grandfather had nothing in particular to say when he stopped by with Bennett, but later in the day Harry pounced on the department chief, Laurence Sheldrick, ready to stir more trouble for Edsel. Mr. Ford's grandsons deserved something better. It was not fitting for them to be trained by any Negro.

Had Henry put his henchman up to this, or was Bennett operating his usual smokescreen? It did not matter much either way to Edsel. He would stand up for his sons more readily than for himself. When he heard of the ruckus, his response to Sheldrick was weary but resolute: "Don't pay a bit of attention to him. That's good for the boys. Keep them right there." Bennett said no more; there would be plenty of other opportunities when Grandfather, who had doted on his grandsons in their childhood, made it clear to Sorensen and others that he did not care to have young Henry and Benson hanging around the Rouge.

Edsel was willing to argue this out to the end. His health was precarious. He must make sure that his sons learned as much as possible about the business before time ran out and they were all caught up in the war that drew closer to America with every Nazi bomb that fell in the continuing blitz on London.

As soon as they were qualified, he put them to work, assembling the gallant little four-wheel-drive vehicle that would always bear the name it was christened with at Ford's. Willys-Overland was another manufacturer experimenting to Army specifications, but apart from a Willys motor, the Jeep was a Ford design. Edsel drove out after lunch one day to see the first of them tested on a spread of wasteland covered with brush, saplings, and weeds along Rotunda Drive. He stood waiting beside the road when, on a signal from another of the crew, young Henry and Benson brought the new chariot bouncing out of the woods up to his feet.

Sheldrick, who was a stanch Edsel supporter, remarked on the delight that showed in their father's face. "That was the one time I saw Edsel when he was thoroughly enjoying himself. He was awfully proud of his boys." But Ford's final bid ran too high, and the contract for Jeeps was lost.

Knudsen tried again. Would Ford agree to manufacture Pratt & Whitney aircraft engines for the United States Government only? Henry was ready to balk once more, but Edsel and Sorensen played on his vanity. Very well, then, if his engineers could refine the motors as they saw fit, let them get on with it. A huge new factory went up behind the fences of the Rouge.

On January 8, Edsel flew to San Diego, California, home of Consolidated's aircraft plant, taking his sons with him. The proposal from Washington was for Ford to make Liberator bombers. Henry pooh-poohed the idea: "Before you can build them, the war will be over."

Sorensen met them there and joined them on a tour of Consolidated, scornful of the snail's pace at which planes were being produced. Nevertheless, before the day was over, Edsel and his hosts announced that Ford would join in building Liberators under license.

The question was: How? Sorensen worked all night in his hotel room, sketching and resketching plans and layouts. They were ready for Edsel's approval over breakfast. The two men presented the proposition together. If the Army Air Force provided the money—$200,000,000 of it—Ford Motors would build a mammoth factory at Willow Run, on farmland owned by Henry some twenty miles from Dearborn. Once this was done, bombers, each comprising more than two million parts and rivets, would come off the assembly lines like automobiles, one an hour, 540 every month. The proposal was too audacious to be refused. Henry was all for it, but he reserved the right to go on denouncing war and to get his grandsons out of the Rouge, the farther away the better.

On their return from San Diego, he called Edsel in. The two boys could stay on the payroll, but they must return in exile to California. Tense and shaken, Edsel went straight to Sorensen. This time, Cast-iron Charlie agreed to speak up to Henry. He was shocked by the hatred he noticed in the old man's eyes when he walked back in with Edsel.

"Edsel has given me your message about young Henry and Benson," Sorensen said. "I'm opposed to any such action, and if you have any idea that I'll carry it out, forget it. I refuse. Furthermore, if you do this yourself, I'm through. That's all I've got to say."

The immense Liberator project would never be airborne without him there to raise heaven and hell. Henry backed off, but there was no assurance that he and Bennett would not circle back to the notion of banishment. The Detroit draft board resolved the problem on March 4, when young Henry was called for an interview. Though Anne was in her final weeks of pregnancy, he did not ask for deferment on that account.

The Rouge had lain paralyzed for three days when their daughter was born. The firing of a handful of men for trying to organize workers in the rolling mill had sent their mates running through Henry's fortress, shouting "Strike! Strike!," and the cry rang like steel on an anvil. Soon after midnight, cars were parked ten abreast to block every approach road. Daylight brought out pickets in the thousands. "Solidarity!" they chanted, circling out of range of the machine guns set up on rooftops at Bennett's orders to guard the gates.

Holdouts from the union, many of them blacks, were trapped inside, bedding down on the floor on paillasses improvised from piles of blueprints, squabbling over the shrinking food supplies, passing the time by taking cars that had come hot off the now silent production lines and racing them on frantic obstacle courses around and around the plant.

Both sides recognized that this was the conclusive conflict. The union had secured its position under law by filing a request with the National Labor Relations Board for an election to be held at the Rouge to determine the will of the employees. Ford must be forced to come to terms and bargain with the UAW, even though he denounced the union as part of the worldwide conspiracy against him. Detroit was by no means the only city in the land to fear that blood would be shed on Miller Road before the week was over.

On the eve of Charlotte's birth, penned-in employees tried twice to storm out the gates to smash the picket lines. Wrestling hand-to-hand, the strikers drove them back. In skirmishes between Reuther's forces and Bennett's, a knife was slipped between the ribs of Angelo Caruso. Bennett wired the White House for help. He received no answer. Then the latest of a long line of company attorneys, I. A. Capizzi, whose views on politics were close to Ford's, was sent scurrying down to Washington in a second bid for federal intervention. He achieved no more than Bennett. By the end of the day that saw Charlotte enter the world, Harry knew the fight must be settled with no help from outside.

Old Henry was grim. Only Bennett could be trusted to treat the enemy with the ruthlessness they deserved. Sorensen, a realist who foresaw that Washington would dictate peace if necessary to keep production going, was packed off to Florida. Edsel, who was already there to nurse his health, flew back to Detroit. He was alarmed to find that his father planned to issue guns and ammunition to the beleaguered hands inside the Rouge and back them up with tear gas.

Forty-eight hours after his first sight of his daughter, young Henry was notified that he was graded Class I as a draftee. The month was not over before he was commissioned a United States Navy ensign and posted to the Great Lakes Naval Training School in Chicago, as pudgy as ever and hoping for sea duty. Before he left, he talked with his father about something that only recently had been on the agenda between them: the future of Ford's.

"I told him that things were in a mess, and that it would have to be cleaned up." Edsel thought that was impossible, but it was arranged that his son would be kept in touch with developments by way of Sorensen's secretary and Bennett's unrecognized confidant, Russell Gnau. Edsel himself was not certain how much longer he could continue.

Desperation made him bolder in confiding to others. After one set-to with Henry, he burst out, "The hurtful thing about all this is that Father takes Harry's words for all this, and he won't believe mine. Where did he come from? He is nothing but a gob. You know, we built that Navy School down there to keep him out of the service because he was in the Reserve Corps."

Tension only rarely rippled the calm of Fair Lane. Clara kept up her reading, partly for Henry's gain. As he sat with a shawl around his shoulders, *Bambi* was a book he enjoyed hearing, and so was another pastoral tale, Marjorie Kinnan Rawling's *The Yearling*. Clara cared so much for *Gone with the Wind* that, after wading through its pages for Henry, she saw the motion picture, with Clark Gable playing Rhett and Vivien Leigh as Scarlett, five times. Her husband confined himself to the *Reader's Digest*, whose campaigns against smoking and bland tales of homespun virtue suited him down to the ground. Unlike Clara, he did not care much for radio, but he turned on "The Quiz Kids," "Amos and Andy," and, of course, "The Ford Evening Hour." After Pearl Harbor, she tried knitting socks for servicemen, but a maid had to turn the heels.

Neither his fortune nor more than half a century of marriage had changed their rustic habit of eating dinner at noon and a light supper before 7 P.M. Clara took a sip of sherry now and then and, on Dr. McClure's recommendation, kept peach brandy in the pantry to help Henry's occasionally sore throat. At bedtime, they each swallowed a prescribed sleeping pill, and every night he fluffed up her pillow before she climbed into bed, as he had since their wedding day. The most sentimental of husbands would still come up on Clara to clasp his arms around her dumpy waist or invite her, "Callie, sit on my lap."

She found herself tempted more and more to influence him, which she felt was not her place. She wrote herself a reminder in one of the little notebooks she kept long after he had given them up: "I must not interfere with what he is doing."

It was impossible always to hold her tongue. On one of Sorensen's infrequent visits to the house, she blurted out to him, "Who is this man Bennett who has so much control over my husband and is ruining my son's health?" The answer, which would call into question Henry's mental grasp, could not be given. He left her weeping.

Edsel prepared for what might be his ultimate contest of will with his father. Edsel had prevailed before, in ending Henry's enthrallment with Lizzie. In the next few days, Edsel set himself the task of bringing Henry to terms with the union to prevent bloody battling at the gates of the Rouge. On April 11, he succeeded. Ford agreed to allow the election Reuther was asking and to negotiate a union contract based on the results. Bennett placed the blame where it belonged: "Though Mr. Ford and Edsel were far apart on this, Mr. Ford gave in to Edsel's wishes." For a man he considered to be "just a scared boy," it was a surprising victory. The Rouge went back to work again with not a skull cracked.

The results of the balloting were everything that Reuther had hoped for and, in Sorensen's estimation, "perhaps the greatest disappointment" Henry ever suffered. For the Congress of Industrial Organization: 51,866 votes; for the American Federation of Labor: 20,364; for no union at all: 1,958; blanks: 34. By June 18, the contract was ready for signature. The UAW was to be granted its first union shop in the industry. Wages were to match the best paid by any competitor and to be subject to checkoff for union dues. All of Bennett's men were to wear uniforms or badges to eradicate the network of spies.

Bennett carried the document back to Henry, who summoned Edsel and Sorensen into conference. "I don't want any more of this business," Henry croaked. "Shut the plant down if necessary! Let the union take over if it wishes!" On that note, he left for Fair Lane.

There was no reading aloud that evening. Clara had come around to sharing her son's point of view. When Henry related what he had told Sorensen, the seventy-four-year-old woman turned on him in uncommon passion. Unless he made peace with the union, men would die on Miller Road. She refused to see that happen. If the contract was not signed, she would run away; abandon him; and their marriage would be ended. Henry surrendered.

So the signatures went onto the contract, and Edsel wrote the foreword to a new chapter: "As the company views the situation, no half measures will be effective . . . we have decided to go the whole way." Uproar ruled at the Rouge for days. A fifty-gallon vat flowed with celebratory beer. Cigarette smoke floated for the first time over the production lines. The union label would soon be stamped onto a car for the first time ever. Bennett sulked over "a great victory for the Communist Party," and attorney Capizzi agreed that Ford's was held to ransom in a Red drive "to control all American industry."

Henry's distorted perception made Roosevelt the principal villain, bent on taking over or taking apart the empire with the help of those ancient adversaries, General Motors and du Pont. Henry armed the chauffeur of his car and provided a back-up revolver in a holster under its hood for defense against the Army Air Force officers arriving at Willow Run, who he suspected were sent to assassinate him.

The old man paid for the union's victory in a second, more massive cerebral hemorrhage that caused blood-vessel damage in his brain. An elevator was installed at Fair Lane during his convalescence. His memory became as uncertain as a candle flame in a quickening breeze. Lovett, his dancing master for nearly twenty years, went unrecognized. Henry would ask querulously where some piece of machinery had gone "that was right there yesterday" when it had been removed a decade ago. There were minutes when he was eager to hear every detail of company operations, but before the answer could be given, his attention had flickered away. One of the few remaining pleasures in life was to take a drive with Harry Bennett.

When Japanese bombs on Pearl Harbor blasted the United States into war on December 7, 1941, the ceaseless journeys of Edsel to Washington and Sorensen's achievements at the Rouge and Willow Run had set Ford's at the hub of the arms industry, making bombers, tanks, aero engines, and armor plate, with orders in the works for gliders, amphibious Jeeps, and much more. The new spirit of co-operation between union and management steadily cut down the man-hours expended in production. Within a week or so, the trickle of cars down the lines would be dried up completely. On January 12, Edsel put Ford's on a twenty-four-hour, seven-day week, then consented to go into the Henry Ford Hospital to be operated on for ulcers of the stomach.

He was discharged, aware that only fragile hope remained of his living much longer, and Eleanor took him to recuperate at Hobe Sound. Two weeks and three days after surgery, he was back at his desk, working for twelve to sixteen hours a day, his shadowed face disguised by a coating of tan. He could still joke, "They don't give me anything to eat. They just feed me pills." He admitted to getting hungry "once in a while."

Further treatment was out of the question. "I can't spare the time," he said. He had to be back for Sorensen's sake, among other things. Cast-iron Charlie, driving himself harder than he had pushed any man, fainted on two occasions at the Rouge. Bennett had no such problems. Of the two men standing in his path, one was destroying himself, the other was being destroyed.

Neither of them was blind to what was happening. Edsel learned from his doctors that he had inoperable cancer. Sorensen knew that he was toppling when the presidential special pulled into a Willow Run siding in September, and Bennett took over as master of ceremonies, organizing the motorcade, barring Charlie from riding with Roosevelt and Henry, who found it impossible to be civil to his fellow passenger with the permanent, jaunty smile.

Edsel held on for seven more months. His father refused to accept that there was any danger. If Edsel would only watch his diet and cut off his relationships with that fast-living Grosse Pointe crowd, he would be fine. Apart from that, all he needed to do was quit fussing and pay attention to Harry. As a contribution to better health, Henry had some of the pure, old-fashioned milk from his dairy herd sent over to put a little more weight on Edsel's bones. The word spread around Detroit, a city that was looking forward to getting back to building automobiles, "Ford? Why, they're washed up. After the old man dies and the tax collector comes in, they'll pick up Ford in pieces."

By the following spring, Sorensen was in desperate need of a few days of rest. The morning before he was due to leave for Florida, he had a telephone call from Henry. Charlie would have to teach Edsel to respect his father and Bennett, stop interfering in the handling of the union, and realize that when Bennett spoke, he spoke for Henry.

When he heard from Sorensen the next morning what had been said, Edsel, close to death, wondered if he should resign. If he did, Charlie would go, too. But that would defeat Edsel's climactic purpose and leave the business in Bennett's grasp before young Henry could take over.

Symptoms developed that mystified the doctors. The extreme weakness, the pains, and the sweating could not be attributed entirely to the known disease. Then they were identified. The milk sent from his father's farm that Edsel had been drinking was contaminated. Pasteurization would have killed the organism that causes contagious abortion in cattle and undulant fever in man, but Henry did not hold with pasteurization.

Almost to the end, his father insisted to those around him,

"You know, Edsel's not going to die." By then his son's condition had been beyond hope for more than a week. Finally Henry, who believed in himself above any God, paid for prayers to be said. Neither he nor Clara was at the bedside in the house on Gaukler Pointe when Edsel Ford, forty-nine years old, slipped away into death in the early morning of May 26, his hand in Eleanor's. Only sentimentalists would include heartbreak among the sicknesses that killed him.

The letter delivered to Fair Lane began "Dear Mr. and Mrs. Ford"—Eleanor had not broken the habit of addressing them so. There was no date other than "Sunday night." She found it difficult to sleep so she wanted to write her thanks "for giving me the most wonderful husband and father God ever made" and "our greatest treasure in the years to come." She prayed that she might in some way carry on as he wanted her to.

People outside the tiny circle that had any contact thought Henry took the death hard, but on the following day he telephoned Sorensen at Willow Run. He, Henry Ford, two months short of eighty, would step into his son's shoes as president and chief executive. That smelled uncommonly like Bennett's doing. Charlie saved his response for Frank Campsall's ears. He would do nothing to help Ford make over the company. As soon as Bennett had the news from Campsall, he sped to Willow Run. What was Sorensen up to? Was he angling for the presidency of Ford's himself? No, not at all, said Charlie.

He was in tears when Edsel was buried the next morning. Henry seemed made of stone. He had urged Bennett to come, but the brass-knuckled little man was no hypocrite. "I knew," he said, "that Edsel had despised me." Ernest Kanzler flew from Washington to be with his sister-in-law. Clara was damp-eyed but composed when her car drove away. She remembered something she had overlooked. She had Rankin, the chauffeur, turn around to pick up an orchid from the coffin as a remembrance.

"Well, there's nothing to do," Henry said blankly. "Just work harder. Work harder."

There was consternation in the councils of the War Production Board and elsewhere in Washington. The total of government funds advanced to Ford's for expansion to meet the demands of war exceeded $350,000,000. How to protect this investment? From

Kanzler's reports, the board knew that, with Edsel gone, Sorensen's position might very soon be made intolerable. What could be done immediately to ensure that bombers from Willow Run's mile-long assembly line and tanks from the Rouge were delivered on schedule for the battles that lay ahead on the beaches of Normandy and the atolls of the Pacific? Could a senile octogenarian be allowed control when the one voice he listened to was Bennett's? Perhaps the government should move in and seize the Ford Motor Company or else let Studebaker Corporation operate the place.

Henry's dependence was made clearer than ever shortly after Edsel died, when a writer for the *Reader's Digest* sat with Henry and Bennett in a car heading out toward Willow Run. Of all the men Ford had met, said the visitor, whom did he rate the greatest. Henry pointed a thumb at the passenger on his other side.

"Whom do you mean, Mr. Ford?"

"Harry Bennett."

Directly after the funeral, Eleanor had the chance to talk at length with her brother-in-law. Kanzler might be able to provide the key to the dilemma. Young Henry, on leave, was brought in to join them. The most urgent need was to secure some kind of watch over what went on in the board room after the stockholders met on June 1. Otherwise, the Edsel faction might find itself swept away.

The meeting lasted most of the day. Her two elder sons sat with Eleanor. In the morning, she was elected to the board for the first time, and they were reappointed, along with Sorensen. So much to the good, but they were outflanked and outnumbered. Bennett was made a director, as was his adjutant, Ray Rausch, and his confederate, B. J. Craig. After lunch, old Henry was ceremoniously voted in as president, Sorensen as vice-president, and Craig as vice-president and treasurer. For Eleanor to carry on as Edsel would have done, the odds in her favor had to be better than these.

Her eldest son made time to spend a day wandering around the Rouge before he reported back for duty. He had completed his basic courses a month ago and been promoted assistant to the training director at the Great Lakes school. Navy living, his father's lingering death, the birth of a second daughter, Anne, last

January—adulthood had been thrust on him, whether he was prepared for it or not.

He had the tenor voice that denotes nervousness in many men of his size, an inch short of six feet tall. He had inherited much of his mother's graciousness of manner, his father's mildness matched by ability for straight thinking, and some of his grandfather's tenaciousness. One petty officer who served under him remembered, "I was watching a miracle, a boy turn into a man. We had the best barracks in the whole damn station."

At twenty-five, young Henry was maturing at precisely the right time. In his opinion, he knew less about the business than his brother Benson, married now for almost two years to a Grosse Pointe girl and serving in the Army Air Force in spite of blindness in his right eye, but the rule of primogeniture could not be disregarded in an inheritance of these dimensions.

Young Henry had been badgering his contact, Russell Gnau, to keep him supplied with company records and gossip. He missed being on the scene, he wrote, when he "was just getting into a little bit of everything and possibly a little too much of some things." Much of his day at the Rouge was spent with Gnau, sounding him out on how Ford's was faring, as Gnau swiftly reported back to Bennett. The questions of a green Navy officer of the lowliest rank in the service seemed too knowing for him not to have been coached in advance.

What was going to happen after the government contracts were finished? Where were the blueprints for a new car to be put on sale as soon as the war was over? Wouldn't it be an idea for Ford's to recruit college graduates for training as other firms did, instead of insisting that nothing more than a high school diploma was the best possible qualification for a future in management? Then the young ensign took himself back to barracks to await the outcome of events that Kanzler would set in motion.

It could have been this day that galvanized Bennett into a bid to rewrite old Henry's will. One man who had blocked Bennett's path was gone. The survivor could be taken care of one way or another. But something must be done fast to prevent the grandson from moving in when Henry died. The old man's aversion for so much of what Edsel had accomplished did not omit the Ford

Foundation. This was the lever Bennett needed. Capizzi was called to meet him at Willow Run. Mr. Ford, Bennett told the attorney, was fearful of Kanzler's influence over young Henry and was looking for a means of keeping control out of his hands until all the grandchildren were old enough to manage the business themselves.

The lawyer advised adding a codicil to Henry's will, canceling provisions for the foundation by setting up a board of trustees to run Ford's for ten years after his death. On Bennett's instruction, Capizzi drafted that document without the knowledge of Clara or anyone else in the family. Whether Henry knew of it or remembered it if he did was problematical; throughout the discussions, the lawyer never spoke personally with him. It was Capizzi's later recollection that Sorensen was present for the initial conference at Willow Run, which would mean that the secret was shared by two rivals hungering for absolute power.

Bennett's list named himself as secretary of the board and included Sorensen, Capizzi, Campsall, and Liebold as fellow trustees. There were two improbable candidates: Dr. Edsel Ruddiman, who had been dead for a year, and Charles Lindbergh, hired as a consultant and test pilot at Willow Run, who had taught Harry to fly.

It took two more months for Kanzler's arrangements for young Henry to be completed and his release from service with the assent of Navy Secretary Frank Knox. Management of Ford's had deteriorated into travesty. Henry for the most part had given up attending board meetings. When he did, he would creak around the room, shaking hands, then turn to Bennett, "Come on, Harry, let's get the hell out of here. We'll probably change everything they do, anyway."

He went on vacation rather than be on hand to greet his grandson on his return. For a while, young Henry had not so much as a desk at the Rouge. "I didn't have a job. Nobody had any suggestion as to what I might do, so I just moseyed around on my own, visited the plants, talked with the fellows, trying to find out how things operated."

One man who welcomed him was Laurence Sheldrick, happy to fill him in on what Edsel had hoped for in postwar automobile design. As part of the tutoring, he arranged to take young Henry to Washington and on from there to the Army's proving grounds at Aberdeen, Maryland, toward the end of the summer. The day before they were due to leave, Sorensen summoned Sheldrick. The most plausible explanation for Charlie's behavior was that doubt about his own security was impelling him to curry favor with old Ford.

"What's the big idea of you filling the young man's head with all these crazy modern ideas of yours of postwar cars?" he demanded in agitation. "Can't you leave the fellow alone and not keep feeding him full of this sort of stuff?"

Sheldrick protested that all he had done was supply details of Edsel projects that his son already knew of. Sorensen brushed that aside. "Another thing. What's the big idea of you making a warmonger out of him and taking him down to Aberdeen and filling him full of all this ordnance materiel, armament, et cetera? You know how his grandfather feels about that." Grandfather had only recently given up telling newspapermen that there was no war, that it was all propaganda "to get America excited and spend our money on munitions." At this moment on the far side of the Atlantic, American and British soldiers were just starting the series of battles that would take them creeping up the spine of Italy.

Sheldrick answered that he was merely trying to show that Ford's was as ardent as General Motors in working along with federal departments.

"If you think they're so goddamn good, why don't you go work for them?"

It had taken just fifteen minutes to come to this. "All right," said the designer whom Edsel had always counted on, "if that's the way you feel about it, I guess I'm through." He walked out of the office and on through the gates.

Young Henry moved into his father's office, with the same staff that had served Edsel. He was still without any specific assignment. He was answerable to Sorensen, and his dislike of him grew as he got to know him better. Young Henry kept as much distance as possible between himself and Bennett, who had a habit of harassing him by telephone.

Harry had a stranglehold on the executives of mahogany row. He controlled all hiring and firing and the payroll department, too. Transportation and communications came under his rule.

Making a long-distance call or sending a telegram was subject to his approval. No intracompany memorandum was safe from his scrutiny. He made sure of knowing every move of top-level managers. The surveillance system was so complete that if he authorized a man to travel overseas, he would learn with whom that man had dinner on any night he was away.

Young Henry conducted a private investigation of Bennett's methods, which confirmed everything he had heard from his father. "When an important policy matter came up, Bennett would get into his car and disappear for a few hours. Then he'd come back and say, 'I've been to see Mr. Ford, and he wants us to do it this way.' I checked with my grandfather and found out that Bennett hadn't seen my grandfather on those occasions."

The word had spread around the Rouge for more than a year: "Charlie sure is dumb. He can't see the handwriting on the wall." In November, the month when Roosevelt and Prime Minister Winston Churchill of Britain met Josef Stalin of the U.S.S.R. at Teheran in one more effort to agree on the grand strategy for victory, an overstrained Sorensen walked in on Henry. "There doesn't seem anything for me to do, so I guess I'll go to Florida." New Year's Day was set as a suitable date. When Sorensen called to say *au revoir*, Henry muttered enigmatically, "I guess there's something in life besides work."

Charlie drove to Miami in a company car. The fact that he had finally been disposed of did not sink in for another four months. Soon after he left, he had news that his office was being taken over by Bennett's crony Ray Rausch. Charlie tried repeatedly to get in touch with Henry, who was spending the rest of the winter at his plantation in Ways, Georgia, with Clara, but the letters and telephone messages went unanswered.

The truth finally came from Frank Campsall after Sorensen had placed one more bewildered call: "I'm sorry, Charlie, but Mr. Ford says I'm to tell you you're through." Servant of Ford since 1905, conceiver of Willow Run, drill master of the assembly line, Charlie tossed his bags into the car at five-thirty the next morning and started northward. When he reached home, Bennett's plant police repossessed the car from the garage. Mr. Ford had concluded that Sorensen was maneuvering for the presidency of the company. Charlie blamed Clara equally with Bennett for implanting that idea. She had not cared for Sorensen from the time Edsel died.

"When young Henry came in here, the company was not only dying," one official said later; "it was already dead, and rigor mortis was setting in." In Washington, the debate flared again about what to do to revive the corpse, if it was not already too late. Roosevelt had a mind to put in Charles E. Wilson of General Electric. That would make a neat solution for the fracas at the War Production Board, where Wilson, executive vice chairman, was at odds with his supposed boss, Donald Nelson.

But the decision was taken to give Ford's another chance now that young Henry had been elected vice-president just before Sorensen took what he imagined would be a rest cure.

BOOK

THREE

Chapter Ten

The Estimable Power of Women

The new vice-president carried a pistol to and from the job. "With those clunks around," he said cheerfully afterward, "you needed a gun." He was not overcome by enthusiasm for the task ahead or overwhelmed by the size of it. He figured that he could live well enough without it, but it was his duty, in Eleanor's opinion, to tackle it for the family's sake, and that counted more than anything. Grandfather had founded the business, Father had given his life for it. A tradition had been established that could not be discarded. "What else was I to do?" said young Henry.

The front door of Fair Lane was always open to him, but he could not look for worthwhile help from Grandfather. He did all he could to stay on good terms with the old man, but there was never any point talking to him about Bennett. "I won't hear a word against Harry" was the stock answer. Clara, firmly on her grandson's side, had all her wits about her, which was a blessing, now that she was ready to suppress her qualms about interfering in Henry's affairs.

She and Eleanor were both handicapped by ignorance of what exactly was going on at the Rouge. The place was clearly in chaos, and the disorder was getting worse. But rumor, gossip, and the alarms that sounded when one more executive departed were no substitute for precise records, and those did not exist. Young Henry would have to ferret out whatever he could for himself.

The two women, one close to eighty and the other a vigorous

forty-seven, represented the only force capable of curbing Bennett: Clara, by applying persuasion to her pathologically stubborn husband, who wanted her constantly by his side after Edsel's death; Eleanor, by virtue of the stock she controlled.

Eleanor continued the life she and Edsel had made together, in the same style, in the same house filled with master paintings, tranquillity, and flowers; gave to the same charities, concealed by the same withdrawal from public view. A future estimate of her fortune could come no closer than setting it at something between $100,000,000 and $200,000,000, probably twice as much as Henry's or Benson's or William's. No one would guess the wealth of advice she constantly offered her eldest son. She declined to be recognized for her decisive role in shaping the destiny of the company.

Edsel's will and the ages of the three younger children were the crux of the matter. Each of them would inherit one fifth of his estate when they reached twenty-five. Benson, Josephine, and William had not yet attained that birthday, which meant that Eleanor could single-handedly vote a full third of the Class B controlling stock. She would say repeatedly, "This company killed my husband, and it's not going to kill my son." A woman Bennett had never met was to see to it that he was stripped of power.

Her son pressed ahead with his exploring. "I didn't even know what all the buildings were for," he remembered, "but I had to learn how to soak it all up like a Turkish towel takes water." What he found was scarcely believable. A large hunk of Ford Motors' more than $680,000,000 in cash was held in bank accounts bearing no interest. "We don't talk about costs around here" was one dictum of old Henry's, and the cost controls introduced years ago by Kanzler had long since been done away with.

The limited financial records that were kept were devised to be juggled to show a bottom line in red or black, according to whatever was asked for. The white-collar men on mahogany row kept the balance sheets strictly to themselves. No outsider could be allowed to measure the desperate state of the company or their own incompetence. "You never know what someone will do with one of these things," said one nervous auxiliary of Bennett's.

An audit was unheard of. So far as young Henry could make out, a profit was calculated simply as the difference between purchasing costs and selling price. In spite of the wartime resurgence of whipcracking at the Rouge, output had sagged to a third of capacity in some departments in which two thirds of a normal work force was engaged. Senator Harry Truman of Missouri and his committee of investigation into the defense program had found some harsh words for the state of production at the Rouge earlier in the war.

Immersion in the elements of disaster did not dampen young Henry's spirits. He could size up the problem much more clearly now, but he had only the vaguest ideas for coping with it. How close Ford's was to going under he just did not know; there were no accurate figures to work with. All he could do was hope that somehow the situation could be turned around. "It never occurred to me I couldn't do the job."

For the present, that included preserving the legends of infallibility that surrounded Grandfather. Sometimes a joke would serve the purpose. After young Henry had dined as guest of honor of Detroit newspapermen at their Off-the-Record Club, he shut off the mass cross-examination to which he was subjected by grinning, "Now I want to ask you a question. Where's the men's room?" Or else he was willing to dissemble mildly, as he did that summer to dealers in Massachusetts.

"He is in excellent health," he said of old Henry. "He puts in a full working day, including Saturday. . . . He is going along toward our common objective, leadership. All our programs have his complete endorsement."

"Vice-president" was a flattering title to have displayed on an office door, but it was as futile as the presidency had been for his father. Bennett remained the suzerain, old Henry's protector against the forces of destruction. "There wouldn't be anything left if it wasn't for Harry," Ford confided to one employee, and to another, "The Jews and Communists have been working on poor Harry until he's almost out of his mind." A vacation would refresh him. "Then he'll come back all ready to keep on fighting the ones who are trying to take over our plant."

Bennett's program of promotion for friends and defenestration for the rest was the only one that Ford endorsed. A strange new order prevailed at the Rouge, where Rausch, the sharp-eyed Dutchman, designated as a future trustee, spent much of his time

closeted in a private hideaway furnished for him in the old powerhouse, with sleeping quarters, a servant to press his clothes, and
mysterious stocks of equipment kept in the storerooms.

The dismissal of veteran management men went on without interruption. Ernest Liebold, once a giant in the company, had
resigned after thirty-four years of service, according to a company
press release. He telephoned a newspaper to ask for a correction to
be printed. "I did not resign or quit. I was fired."

"Do you want that said?"

"Certainly. It's true."

He wrote a letter of protest to Henry: "The entire manner in
which this episode was handled has proved to be a direct attack
upon my personal character and a direct reflection upon my reputation. . . ." Liebold, as obsolete as the Model A, heard nothing
from the man he had once served as chief executioner every bit as
assiduously as Bennett did now.

Henry Doss, who followed Davis as sales manager, quit in disgust when he discovered that Bennett men had begun some postwar planning on their own account, which called for installing
their friends in profitable dealerships. He apologized to young
Henry, "I don't like to leave you, and I wouldn't leave you if
something could be done with this Bennett situation."

"I don't blame you a damn bit" was the reply, "but there is
nothing much I can do about it now. Someday, I will."

He constantly asked himself, "What would Father have
done?," but he had to go beyond that and fight where Edsel, until
the end, would have compromised to keep the peace. Bennett
misinterpreted young Henry's amiability as a sign that he was as
gentle a being as his father and could be handled with the same
contempt. Bennett began to discover he was wrong when young
Henry found a successor to Doss without consulting Harry.

Kanzler, the gray eminence, recommended Jack Davis, banished
to Los Angeles after Harry Mack's brawl at the Dearborn Country
Club. Davis was disinclined to return to more tangling with Bennett. Young Henry twice flew to California in the effort to change
his mind. "Come back and see for yourself," he begged. "Stay
around a month or so."

His candidate was still hesitant. "I don't even want to do that
if I'm going to be in contact with Harry again."

"Hell, let's put it this way. If Bennett makes trouble and you feel you have to go, I'll go too. If I stay, you stay."

Davis grabbed young Henry's hand, close to tears. "I'll come back," he said.

The day of reckoning was advanced by happenstance when Harry hired a newcomer to his clique. John Bugas, tough-minded and trimly barbered, headed the Detroit office of the Federal Bureau of Investigation. Its war contracts put the Ford company under his surveillance. Investigations he and his fellow agents conducted at the Rouge and Willow Run disclosed multiple instances of theft, black-marketing of parts and materials, and bootlegging. Bugas did not wait to check with Harry before the arrests were made, including some of Bennett's own security men.

Before this hawk could do more damage, Harry had him to lunch at Dearborn and invited him to work for him, dealing with the labor problems that were flaring up again. The agent was curious to know old Henry's reaction to the proposition. "We'll find out right now," said Bennett. A telephone call brought Ford down to the office. Yes, he, too, would like Bugas on the staff. What about young Mr. Ford? Henry II came promptly to Harry's buzz on the intercom.

Bugas was treated at first as one of Harry's own, free to walk in on him any time unless old Henry was closeted with him. "I didn't know how to play him," young Henry remembered. "He was Bennett's man." Bugas' place in Harry's favor lasted only until Bugas fired one of Harry's protégés for incompetence. "The freeze began to set in on me," in Bugas' words. "In time, he had me as isolated as a tuberculosis bug." The conditions were ripe for switching to a different allegiance—with young Henry.

That spring, Detroit was awash with rumors like a river in flood after a winter's thaw. One trade magazine forecast Bennett's imminent promotion as operating head of Ford's. *Fortune* researchers picked up a clue to the old man's will and its codicil for leaving his shares in a ten-year trust. Perhaps Bugas would recall some hint of what was being plotted from the days when he had Harry's confidence. Young Ford showed up in the ex-G-man's office, staggered at the prospect that Grandfather intended to let Bennett control the company once the day arrived when its founder learned that he was not excluded from mortality.

"If this is true," he promised, "I'm resigning, and I'm writing every Ford dealer to tell them what they're up against if they choose to stay with us." He would rather demolish the disintegrating pyramid than watch Bennett installed at its top.

Bugas needed time to calm him. "Wait until I ask Harry if it's true," he said. When he burst into Bennett's office to confront him, Harry was as flustered as young Ford had been. He refused to discuss anything immediately. "I don't want young Henry to be bothered," he said to the mystification of Bugas. "Come in here tomorrow, and we'll straighten the whole thing out."

At next morning's meeting, Bennett took an envelope from an inside pocket and extracted from it two sheets of paper, one the typewritten codicil, the other a carbon copy. He let Bugas glance at the original, then set a match to it and dropped it to burn into ashes on the floor. These he put into a fresh envelope. "You can take this back to young Henry."

Bugas watched in silence, asking himself if the fate of the company had been resolved in the flame. Seconds later, perhaps as an afterthought, Bennett handed over the carbon, too. Only he knew the truth, which he may have been telling in a later admission to Capizzi.

"It wasn't any good, anyway," he said unconcernedly. "Because Mr. Ford had carried the instrument around in his pocket for a long time and had made a lot of scribblings on it, including verses from the Bible." The attorney's conclusion was that the old man had never signed it. Bugas had not been given time to check whether or not this was true.

Bugas arrived for work a day or so later to find his office emptied of its furniture and his two secretaries reassigned to other jobs. Bennett declined to see him or take his telephone call. A sheepish subordinate told Bugas where to find his new quarters. He had been moved into a cubicle formed by dividing Harry's toilet with a flimsy partition, with a desk and chair on one side, the lavatory and hand basin on the other. Bennett was inventive in expressing his opinions.

"My first reaction," Bugas reminisced, "was to get the hell out of there, but Jack Davis talked me into staying on." The nucleus of a team was starting to form behind Henry Ford II.

The most imperative need was to buttress his position. When

the board of directors met at intervals in compliance with corporate law, which held them to be in charge, there was no discussion about how this might be achieved. His appointment as executive vice-president was presented to them cut and dried, like everything else. It could be attributed only to the growing confidence of Eleanor and Clara in his ability to take on Bennett in the showdown that had yet to be scheduled.

He was too much imbued with his father's thinking and too used to saying what was on his mind to avoid letting his guard drop now and then. Bennett passed the word around that Grandfather was "enraged" by one interview his grandson gave, declaring himself in favor of a degree of government control of the American economy right after the war ended "lest the demand for consumer goods be satiated too quickly" and simultaneously to cope with the high level of unemployment, which had to be expected. The article continued as if it were quoting Edsel, not his son:

"I hope some workable solution will be evolved," he said earnestly, "whether industry likes it or not." He hopes this because there is a dynamic, unlimited future for mankind "if politics are forgotten and we settle down and get things done."

That summer of 1944, the twenty-five million Americans who held gasoline ration books were limited to a basic two gallons a week. Liberator bombers, aircraft engines, Jeeps, and trucks still trundled off Ford's production lines. All new cars for civilian customers had disappeared three years ago in what seemed to most of the world to be a war without end. But Allied armies, landing on the Contentin Peninsula and then close by the mouth of the Rhône, had turned the Germans to retreat everywhere, and by the last week of August, Paris was free again. It was inconceivable that victory in the West could be delayed much longer.

In the coming months, Ford's fat contracts with Washington would be canceled. The company would be thrown back into the automobile business, straining to compete head on with General Motors and Chrysler with made-over models that had been obsolete in 1941, as sales figures showed. There would be new runners in the race such as Henry J. Kaiser, with a fortune made in mass-producing cargo ships in California, who would take over Willow Run to convert it for churning out his Kaiser-Frazer.

Compared with GM and Chrysler, Ford's facilities impressed some cynical Detroiters as amounting to little more than a pile of junk. Unlike many a defense contractor, the company had not re-tooled and re-equipped itself at the expense of Uncle Sam.

Worn-out machine tools needed replacement at a cost running into the millions, and they were not immediately available at any price. Research and design, inadequate in prewar days, had come to a standstill.

Worst of all, the very nature of the Rouge made it a handicap in itself. Old Henry's monolith had been created to manufacture most of the ingredients for a single model, then endlessly dupli-cate the same kind of car. Built-in inflexibility had turned the gar-gantuan factory into a mechanical dinosaur when the process of evolution, introduced notably by General Motors, led customers to expect fresh models every year in every permutation of styles and equipment as part of postwar prosperity.

Henry II made no pretense of being a marvel who could single-handedly extricate the company from the mess it was in. "I just don't know enough about manufacturing to run this damn place," he would say. He took fleeting consolation in the fancy that he would retire at forty, which was as whimsical as his notion that he could lead two separate lives, one in the office, the other at home with Anne and their daughters. What he hoped to do as soon as peace returned was to make Ford first on the scene with a postwar car even if it could not gain first place in the market.

Inside the company, there were no more than two men with whom he could share his thinking: Bugas, Davis, and nobody else as yet. He needed someone he could trust to run manufacturing, so he took a chance with Mead Bricker, Sorensen's former assist-ant, who was in charge at Willow Run at present but answerable to Rausch at the Rouge. Bricker could start getting to know the other three over dinner at the Dearborn Inn, red-brick, neo-Geor-gian, installed for old Henry's guests opposite the Ford Airport as what was possibly the first hotel specifically built for plane passen-gers.

"My God, no," Bugas objected. "Every room in that place is wired."

They settled for a quiet corner under the cavernous ceiling of the Detroit Club downtown, safe from wire taps and Bennett's eavesdroppers. As soon as drinks were on the table, young Henry got down to brass tacks. "I've asked you men to come here because I have confidence in you. I want you to help me rebuild the Ford Motor Company," he said briskly, then let that sink in for a moment.

Mead Bricker turned to Bugas, grinning. "You son-of-a-bitch, I thought you distrusted me."

A question from the host came next. One-man rule had been the ruin of the business. "Help me" were the key words in his opening remark. "What the hell can we do?" he asked.

Bugas, a lawyer in Cheyenne before he enrolled with the FBI, could supply the start of the answer. "First, get your grandfather to sign a piece of paper stating that nobody can get fired around here any more without your permission."

"All right. Then what?"

"Then I'd clean house," Bugas said. "Better still, delegate me to do it."

"No." Henry II shook his big-bear head. "If I did that, I'd always be known around here as a guy who passed the buck."

When the meal was over and he was driving home, Henry II was not sure that he could go through with all that had to be done. However, he followed the advice from Bugas to obtain Grandfather's consent and interpose himself as a barrier between Bennett and his hiring and firing. The opening challenge to Harry was presented shortly after VE Day. Bricker walked into Rausch's office, where Bennett's overbearing lieutenant sat with some companions. The double doors closed. When they opened again, Rausch and his minions came out as though a bomb had exploded, and the new chief of Ford manufacturing remained inside. Rausch trod the exiles' route to California; there was nothing Bennett could do about it.

On May 25, 1945, the War Production Board allotted America's automobile manufacturers a quota of 200,000 vehicles to be made during the year, cars that another Washington agency, the Office of Price Administration, ruled must cost the customer no more than he had been charged in 1942. Henry II would have his work cut out to live up to the title just bestowed on him by the Junior Chamber of Commerce, "young man most likely to succeed," when Ford's share of the 200,000 was set at fewer than

40,000 cars. Like the rest of the industry, it would have to scrounge around for the necessary materials without government help.

The strategy that was evolving in discussions with Eleanor and Uncle Ernest required him to emerge as a public presence, a symbol of the company as Grandfather had been but with a completely restyled image, a young man who cared about the community. In the thick of the infighting, Henry II agreed to serve as chairman of the carmakers' unit of the Detroit Community Chest, one of Edsel's charities.

He also made himself available for speeches to any number of organizations, without apology for the fact that, while the sentiments were largely his own, a ghost composed the texts. Sometimes the words came straight from his current experience. He was beginning to enjoy himself. "The unhappiest man on earth is the one who has nothing to do," he told one of his audiences. Sometimes there were undertones of old Henry in his prime: "There can be no bosses in our country except the people. The job of government is to serve, not to dominate. . . . The world ought to have a universal currency for universal economy with a universal market."

Just before the German armies surrendered at Rheims on May 7, he was taking note that, "It is far easier to fight a war than build an economy," which was one lesson he and the company were learning. But one week after Washington defrosted the wartime freeze, Ford had a handmade 1946 model on display to fulfill his ambition to be first under the wire in the postwar industry; a dressed-up 1942, to be sure, but evidence that things were stirring in the company at last in spite of its moribund president.

Before the stirrings could be converted into lusty forward movement, the relationship between the old man and Harry must be brought to an end. Otherwise, they would go on hiding one behind the other while the company died. Henry I would have to be deposed for Henry II to take over completely. Eleanor and Clara had been saying that for months. It was reassuring to find Bugas, Davis, and Bricker echoing them. Old Henry still resisted.

It fell to Eleanor to find the moment when his mind was clear and the words that he could understand. Edsel's eldest son must be the new president of the Ford Motor Company, she said. "If this is not done, I shall sell my stock." What it would fetch would be pure guesswork, but that was not her concern. The unloading of one third of the company would topple the monolith her father-in-law had contrived to raise for the family. The process of selling would mean opening the books to prying strangers and disclosure of the mess that Ford was in. The men he detested—bankers, financiers, speculators—would inevitably buy the shares and invite themselves onto his board of directors, to begin the ultimate takeover.

The threat worked. On September 20, the old man sent for his grandson. Henry I was skeleton-thin now as he huddled in a favorite easy chair, permanently weary but uncomplaining. The high-mindedness of earlier days was lost, along with most of his memory. Clara kept wine in the house nowadays on the doctor's orders in case old Henry felt weakness in the night. He could not remember that Sorensen had been done away with months ago. "Take me over to see Charlie" was a regular plea that Clara had to deal with.

"My grandfather," Henry II reminisced, "told me he was planning to step down and let me be president of the company. I told him I'd take it only if I had a completely free hand to make any changes I wanted to make. We argued about that—but he didn't withdraw his offer."

Henry II drove straight from Fair Lane to his grandfather's office in the Administration Building at the Rouge to instruct the nonplussed secretary, Frank Campsall, to prepare the formal letter of resignation: "May I recommend to the board that it consider the appointment of my grandson, Henry Ford II, as my successor. . . ." A directors' meeting was called for the following morning to ratify the changeover. It would be unthinkable for Campsall to break precedent by omitting to tell Bennett the moment the door closed behind young Henry.

Back in his own quarters, Henry II answered the telephone. "I've got wonderful news for you," said Harry at the other end of the line. "I've just talked your grandfather into making you president of the company."

The old man had to be helped into his chair when the board gathered in the glass-partitioned office of the treasurer, B. J. Craig. Eleanor sat at the table as calmly as if this were a Grosse Pointe tea party. Bricker was also there with Henry II. Bennett's dark face contrasted oddly with his jaunty bow tie. He listened as Campsall began to read the letter, but he leaped to his feet at the end of the first sentence. "Congratulations!" he snapped and made for the door. Others intercepted him and induced him to stay to make the vote unanimous.

Then the new president and the defeated champion were left alone for a few minutes. "Bennett seemed in a state of shock—in a daze," young Henry remembered. "I simply said to him, 'Harry, we've got to part company.' Then I told him I'd keep him on salary for a year and a half until his retirement pay would begin." But he was to stay out of Ford's.

"You're taking over a billion-dollar organization here that you haven't contributed a thing to," Bennett growled and left the room. As Henry II made his way back to his office, Davis buttonholed him.

"He's gone," said young Henry.

"Good. Now can I fire somebody?"

"Who?"

"Harry Mack."

"Go ahead."

Davis placed the call to Dallas. "Harry, you're fired, and this time you can't get back, because your boyfriend Bennett is gone, too." More than a thousand of Harry's appointees would be purged before housecleaning was completed.

Bugas walked into Bennett's office with a .38 automatic holstered inside his jacket. The desk stood at the far end of the long room. "I was ready," Bugas said, "if it looked like my life was involved." Harry watched silently from behind his desk until Bugas reached its edge. Then Bennett jumped up, screaming, "You're behind all this, you son-of-a-bitch!," and, still cursing, pulled his blunt-nosed .45 from a desk drawer. Bugas was confident that he could kill first if he had to. Self-defense would be an accepted plea, but the damage of a court trial to the company would be incalculable.

Bennett slammed the gun down on the desktop and let it lie there until his breath ran out. Bugas began to talk: Harry had no one to blame but himself for what had happened. Bennett was calmer now. How about lunching together, Bennett said. Bugas excused himself from that, then turned and started the long walk to the door. "I guess my shoulders might have been braced a bit, waiting to take a shot. Nothing happened."

Harry spent the afternoon burning documents in the incinerator. The next day, he telephoned young Henry and Bugas and invited himself on a farewell ride around the Rouge and Willow Run. Henry drove the car, while Bennett talked like a guide on a conducted tour—this was what Mr. Ford wanted done over there, these were his plans for that department. He left that night for California, and the Ford Motor Company saw no more of him.

Henry II stopped at Fair Lane on his way home. He expected trouble from his grandfather when he told him that after twenty-nine years the greatest man old Henry had ever known was through. Grandfather said nothing for some minutes; then his words were as hard as flint: "Well, now Harry is back where he started from."

The president, born a year after Bennett came to Ford, received a telephone call from the Community Chest that evening, reminding him of a meeting he was scheduled to attend. "Haven't you heard?" he said happily. "I've taken over the company. Mother and I are sitting here now, making plans for the future."

He liked to work in shirtsleeves, with a collection of photographs of Father and Grandfather standing behind his desk. Through the day, he sipped cup after cup of camomile tea and offered chewing gum to visitors. One family tradition remained intact: Not a harsh word was said about old Henry, who was faithful to his promise not to interfere.

The sages of the Harvard Business School and similar seminaries of free enterprise to which General Motors paid its profound respects preached that the one true purpose of any corporation was to return maximum profits. In the universe of chaos into which Henry II had stepped, only lip service could be rendered to that creed until some indeterminable milestone had been passed somewhere down the road. Profits depended on selling a marketable product, which required an efficient plant run by effective personnel. The company was deficient in all four respects: profits, product, plant, and people.

Operating losses hovered around $10,000,000 a month, but Ford lacked another ingredient of the standard capitalist mix, which gave its president breathing space to deliberate on what to do: There were no shareholders impatient for dividends. If only in that respect, Henry had a unique opportunity in an undertaking of this scale and complexity.

Profit making could safely be disregarded as impossible for the time being. Product, plant, or people—which commanded top priority? The answer was obvious. All must be advanced together, but without income from customers, time could run out before assembly lines had been modernized or the right management men enlisted. Ford had to make all the cars it could and get them into the showrooms, or the Big Three, as one early recruit put it, "would surely become the Surviving Two."

Henry II said in retrospect, "We would have had access to the banks, I'm sure, if we'd gone to the banks. I don't know if we would have had access to the market. We didn't have any stock on the market then, so that was an additional part of the problem."

Production of the revamped 1942 model that was introduced as the 1946 model began in the summer of the preceding year. Young Henry polished some apples by having the first one off the line shipped to Washington, where he presented it to President Truman. Japan's surrender on August 14 tempted Henry II into talking rosily about as many as 85,000 cars and 50,000 trucks being finished by year's end, though the company lost $300 on every one of them.

Would-be customers placed 300,000 orders within forty-eight hours of the 1946's public showing, but fewer than 35,000 of them could be filled by December 31. Nipped by the soaring cost of living, members of the United Automobile Workers were downing tools in a series of crippling, spontaneous strikes. Ford management found limited comfort in the fact that the walkout at General Motors was official and the shutdown there complete.

These were days when, caught between the devil of price controls and the deep of union unrest, Henry II could appreciate for the first time just what his father had endured most of his working life, but ignorance shielded him against self-doubt. "I didn't know enough to be scared," he said afterward. Luck alone would never provide more than seasoning in the recipe for pulling the company through, but he acknowledged that he was lucky in some respects.

The most significant was the national itch to buy a car and recapture the precious, lost freedom that Roosevelt had overlooked in his tally of four at the start of his third term. Being free to move around again wherever you chose to travel was as important to most Americans as freedom of speech and religion, freedom from want and fear. "We could virtually sell anything we could get out the back door," said Henry II.

John Bugas, now formally titled chief of industrial relations on Ford's brand-new Policy Committee, had opened negotiations with the union when another stroke of good fortune came young Henry's way in November. Ford did not know the sender of the telegram signed "Charles Bates Thornton, Colonel, U. S. Army Air Force," and the proposal it contained was outrageous on the face of it.

"Ten guys all wanted jobs at once. Thornton explained in his wire that his group was part of the Office of Statistical Control in the Air Force. Worked under General Hap Arnold. He gave Bob Lovett's name as reference. I knew Bob, at least." Lovett, an Assistant Secretary of War of Roosevelt's, would become Truman's Defense Secretary in 1951.

"I wasn't too impressed," Henry continued. "Cripes, colonels were like pebbles on a beach at that time. But I took a chance and wired him to come out and see us."

"Tex" Thornton, promoted to full colonel in his late twenties, was reputedly the youngest USAAF officer ever to hold that rank. His job, in simple terms, had been "plotting a tidier and shorter war." He had sent dozens of promising junior officers to the Harvard Business School for cramming in management and economics, then tried them out in his "think tank" in Washington and at Wright-Patterson Army Air Force Base, Ohio. When peace came, he told nine of them that, in his judgment, they should continue working as a team, applying to big business techniques they had acquired as servicemen. They agreed and chose him as their spokesman.

Their first invitation came from Robert R. Young to move into his shaky Allegheny Corporation. The majority voted No. Then an August article in *Life* related some of the troubles Ford was in and what its green new president was trying to do about them. The ten talents decided to wire him: WE HAVE A MATTER OF MAN- AGEMENT IMPORTANCE TO DISCUSS WITH YOU. . . .

Before he responded, he checked with Uncle Ernest, who knew Lovett and something about Thornton's background as well. Kanzler arranged a personal conference between his nephew and Lovett as briefing for the team's arrival at Dearborn. One colonel, four lieutenant colonels, two majors, and a lieutenant, all in uni- form, marched briskly into the Rotunda dining room to be intro- duced to the man they hoped to work for; two of the team were absent that day.

The interview was soon over. "Thornton had a lot of ideas that sounded good to me. He believed that military management sys- tems could be transformed into industry. So I hired the lot of them." The hiring, in fact, was postponed for a few days. Henry II liked to chart a course for himself that lay somewhere between Grandfather's acting on hunches and his chronic shilly-shallying, both of which had aggravated the company's plight. His grandson would take time to gather all the information and counsel he could; then when the day arrived to make a decision, it would be done before lunch. He asked Bugas to grill Thornton and his men as only an FBI agent could when Bugas took them to dinner that evening at the Detroit Athletic Club.

Bugas did such a thorough job that he left them wondering whether this would be the climate that prevailed at Ford's. Their combined experience of the automobile industry was nil. They had talked of necessity in generalities without nailing down their terms. As soon as Thornton returned to Washington, he sent an- other telegram to Henry II, spelling out the salary each of them expected. It was accepted without haggling. The ten of them were to report for duty on February 1.

One of the team had to be coaxed. Lieutenant Colonel Robert S. McNamara, on extended leave from Harvard, was eager to go back to the Graduate School of Business Administration as a full professor. The Ford Motor Company seemed a poor alternative to a distinguished academic career. Tex Thornton talked him into changing his mind. Mrs. McNamara had spent eight months in the hospital with polio, and her husband had suffered a light case of it himself.

"Didn't you tell me you're broke?" Thornton asked, and McNamara nodded. "Come with us. You owe it to your wife."

This was the necessary persuasion. On a professor's salary, the medical bills would never be paid. Fourteen years later, the reluctant recruit would be appointed president of the company, with share options worth $3,500,000. Another of the ten, and another academic, was to rise to the same altitude: Nebraska-born Arjay Miller, lecturer in business affairs at UCLA before he put on Army Air Force olive drab.

At one stroke, Henry II had acquired enough talent to fill many of the gaps on mahogany row once the ten men had been given time to learn the ins and outs of the business, but who was there to supervise them? Cetainly not a nongraduating Yalie of the class of 1940. "I'm just a young fellow reaching for answers," he repeated at this time. What he needed was a top-flight executive at his right hand, an industry veteran who could steer both him and the company.

Uncle Ernest did not want the appointment, but he had a candidate: Ernie Breech, son of an Ozarks blacksmith, crackerjack accountant, and currently the president of Bendix Aviation Corporation, of which Kanzler was a director. Forty-nine years old, Breech was of an age to be Henry's father, but the last thing in the world the young man was looking for was a substitute parent; physically, he was twice the size of Ernie, anyway. Breech's pre-eminent qualification was that he had spent twenty-one years with General Motors, "the cleanup man," in his words, before he was elected to a vice-presidency. Trouble-shooting was the specialty that had prompted his appointment to Bendix, in which GM had large holdings. Young Henry was casting around for quick solutions to Ford's crisis. The quickest appeared to lie in making over the empire in the image of General Motors, "the best-managed company in the business," in his estimation.

Thornton's team had been signed on but had not yet started working when Kanzler sounded out Breech. Join Ford? "Not under any circumstances," Ernie replied. When the ten ex-officers did report in, they answered to nobody in particular but Henry II, who gave them four months to study operations before they would be slotted into any organization chart.

They found wandering around the Rouge not unlike Marco

Polo's explorations of Cathay. Nothing they had learned from business school case histories had much meaning here. Invoices in some instances were stacked on a scale and weighed as a means of calculating costs. In most departments, the sharp-edged distinction between "staff" and "line" insisted upon in the armed forces and extolled in business school courses was nonexistent. Decision-making by committee played no part in old Henry's autarchy; any executive worth his salt was supposed to figure on his own initiative what should be done and then go ahead to do it. One Ford shop was still making propellers for the trimotor planes that had been discontinued a dozen years ago. "The Whiz Kids," as they were known around the plant to their disgust, made careful notes, debated their findings far into the night, compiled reports—and wondered who would read them.

Young Henry had decided that Breech was the man, and he would not let him get away. Henry turned up ahead of time to keep an appointment with Ernie at nine o'clock one Monday morning in April, carrying a stock option as bait in his pocket. What about coming to Ford as executive vice-president? The answer remained negative, but Breech agreed to look over Henry's empire and offer some advice if that was what he wanted.

For the present, a cease-fire had been signed with the union. The new contract that Bugas negotiated added $41,000,000 to the payroll, but the UAW undertook to bar illegal walkouts and allow Ford to fire any firebrand who started one. During the armistice talks, Henry attained overnight status as a statesman within the industry.

He had accepted the logic that one of the company's intangible assets was himself, a young man thrown in to battle giants and save an American institution from extinction. One of the first things he had done after succeeding Grandfather had been to engage Earl Newsom of Madison Avenue as his public-relations counsel. Not everything Henry said in press interviews was calculated in advance, but neither were his remarks as ingenuous as they sometimes seemed in print. The image that emerged of a plainspoken, gutsy guy reaching out for answers was accurate enough, but it was only an image. He was more complicated and more calculating than that.

Newsom booked him to speak at the annual meeting of the Society of Automotive Engineers in Detroit at a moment when Bugas was in the middle of bargaining with the UAW, and Newsom masterminded the writing of the text of "The Challenge of Human Engineering." Anne McDonnell Ford grumbled that her husband "kept me up nearly all night, reading it aloud. He practically knows it by heart, and so do I." She would not be going to hear him, she said.

Its keynote was a call for understanding and reason to rule at every bargaining table. "The public is the 'boss,' not management or labor. Both labor and management must accept their share of responsibility to the public welfare and live up to their commitments." If union chiefs were "going to be real leaders, they must accept the social obligations that go with leadership." Walter Reuther went along with that when Henry's words, spread by press and radio, brought him congratulations from both sides. Ford workers would not resort to interring dead rats behind car door panels as they had in Bennett's day.

Some old ways died hard at the Rouge. When he took the tour, Breech was appalled to see a superintendent haul a workman out of their path and push him across the room, then kick a newspaper out of the hands of another mechanic and fire him on the spot for idling. Breech was taken aback for other reasons when he asked to see the balance sheet. It was, he thought, "about as good as a small tool shop would have."

Yet he gave in to Henry's tempting. He explained one reason to his wife, Thelma: "I hate to take on this job, but if I do not I will always regret that I did not accept the challenge." There was another inducement, which Jack Davis proved willing to disclose.* Ernie was allocated 20 per cent of a new organization set up to distribute Ford-Ferguson tractors at a price of roughly $2,000 a share. Davis and Kanzler were both stockholders, too. Twelve years afterward, after a series of transformations of assets, Breech's investment of some $40,000 had grown into $6,000,000 net.

Uncle Ernest took on the task of drawing up the marriage contract binding Ernie to Ford and found there were doubts on both sides. When Breech felt satisfied, Henry wavered. He saw his relative off the premises one evening when the document was ready

* Booton Herndon: "Ford," p. 78.

for signature, then hurried down to his car to catch up with Kanzler on Woodward Avenue. Would Breech overshadow him? "My lawyer," said Henry, "says I'm abdicating when I make Ernie vice-president." He accepted Kanzler's words that this would not happen. The new deputy went to work on July 1.

Young Henry by this time had matched himself against a pair of equally celebrated giant-killers, the Office of Price Administration, whose restrictions on what a customer might be charged for a car eliminated any present hope of restoring Ford to profitability, and the OPA's messianic chief, Chester Bowles. Henry struck first with a telegram to Washington, asking for all price ceilings to be lifted. The government gave its standard reply: Without them, inflation would run wild; there was too much money around and not enough goods to buy. The applause won by his "Challenge of Human Engineering" speech encouraged him to try something similar and take his case against the OPA to the public. He chose the Commonwealth Club of San Francisco as his forum.

He had some reservations about the cost figures he asked for from his staff, but they were as accurate as could be estimated when Thornton's group was still in the early stages of its investigations. Before the war, Henry told his California audience, it needed 87 man-hours to build a Ford; in 1945, it took 128. The finished car that Washington permitted him to sell for no more than $728 now cost $1,041 to produce. "We may lose very substantially in 1946," he said in a calculated understatement. Current losses remained at $10,000,000 a month, but this was a figure best concealed. He likened OPA to a noose around the neck of American industry.

It was Chester Bowles' turn to attack. "The speech was typical of those launched every year at this time by a few selfish groups which have worked continuously to undermine the American people's bulwark against economic disaster." Bowles got in another punch a few days later in testimony before the House of Representatives' Banking and Currency Committee. Ford's losses were not the fault of OPA but the result of the company's failure to step up production. The implication was that Henry was greedy. As recently as the past summer, he had been seeking a 55 per cent price hike, Bowles reported.

If Henry had expected support for his stand from the rest of the industry, he was disappointed. Virtually nobody of consequence had fallen in with him. Should the issue be allowed to cool? Newsom advised not, so one telegram from Henry arrived in Washington that evening for Congressman Brent Spence, the banking committee's chairman, and another for Bowles. They reiterated Ford's argument: OPA regulations led to shortages of parts, which could halt the whole assembly line; it was this that held down production and escalated costs.

A turn in the country's political affairs helped Henry move a little closer to the shore that spring. Rising resentment of controls prompted Congress to pass a new compromise pricing bill so riddled with loopholes that Truman vetoed it, and OPA was doomed. Washington allowed Ford its first price increase in March. On May 21, the President seized the nation's soft-coal mines, which John L. Lewis's United Mine Workers had kept shut for two months, cutting off factories' fuel supplies and dimming the lights of cities. On May 22, the White House granted Henry a second price increase, not yet big enough for him to make money on his cars, but encouraging.

The primary task Breech set himself when he arrived for work was to push the permitted price level still higher to arrest the financial hemorrhaging. In Washington, he found that the government was expecting him to request $150 a car. What he needed to break even was $60. He asked for $80—"we don't want any more"—and was delighted to be granted $62.50. The cool-headed young men of the Thornton team felt that they and Ernie would get along well together.

There was another way of cutting losses and raising a little cash —by disposing of old Henry's pet projects on fire-sale terms. He was so ancient—eighty-three this year—and so shielded now that he had no idea what was being done with the hobbies that had meant more to him than any automobile after Lizzie. The Wayside Inn was the first to go, deeded to a nonprofit organization to operate on revenue derived from meals, guest rooms, and rental of its Martha-Mary Chapel, which he built in honor of Clara and her mother, Martha Bryant.

The rubber plantations in Brazil, where losses topped $20,000,000, were sold to the government in Rio for $250,000.

Farms, mineral tracts, and most of the Great Lakes fleet were put up for bids. The last of the soybean factories went to new owners. The village industries, mostly run by water power, which the old man had created at incalculable cost to make such items as steering wheels and gauges as part of his compulsion to revive a departed way of life, were available if anybody chose to take them over. Uncle Ernest would try to strike some kind of bargain with Harry Ferguson when the gentlemen's agreement for building Ford-Ferguson tractors, on which the company lost $25,000,000, was terminated on Armistice Day in November, but Ferguson was a prickly individual, and trouble had to be expected there.

But all of this was comparative chicken feed. What the company had to focus on was its first real postwar car, not a rejigged 1942 model; something with which it could hope to catch the other Big Three. Everything about it must be new and exciting to the customer. The designers would have to start work largely from scratch, and the bills would run close to $120,000,000 before the job was done. In no sense would it be Henry's automobile, as Lizzie had been an extrapolation of Grandfather's ego. This would have to be a team product, but the responsibility was all Henry's. If the car failed in the race for sales, there would be few more chances left. The company's profits for 1946, $2,000, did not leave room for mistakes.

Ford's styling section, manned mostly by staff imported from General Motors, was less than a year old, where GM set such store by its products' appearance that designer Harley Earl had been a vice-president since 1940. Even Alfred Sloan, who had insisted all along that cars sold on their looks, confessed himself amazed at the American fancy for frills in this pleasure-bent postwar era. It "sometimes seemed to many people to have become too extreme," he reflected. "New styling features were introduced that were far removed from utility, yet they seemed demonstrably effective in capturing public taste."

He shook his head over the rear-fender fins that Earl's men had devised for the 1948 Cadillac, which was now in the works. The fish tails owed their conception to a wartime glimpse of a twin-fuselaged, twin-tailed P-38 fighter plane that Earl enjoyed by courtesy of a friend in the USAAF. It was, Harley thought, exactly what a Cadillac could use for a distinctive touch of pizazz.

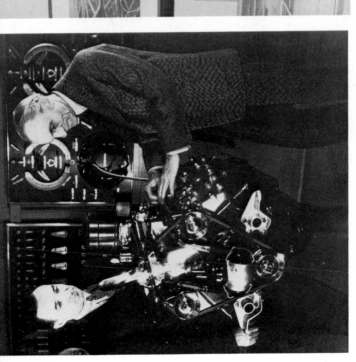

Left: Edsel Ford and Henry Ford examine the first V-8 engine in 1932. *Right:* Henry Ford II, at 26, had become executive vice-president of the Ford Motor Company on the day this photograph was taken – April 10, 1944. He and his 80-year-old grandfather, Henry Ford, are looking over a scale model of the Rouge manufacturing complex in Dearborn, Mich.

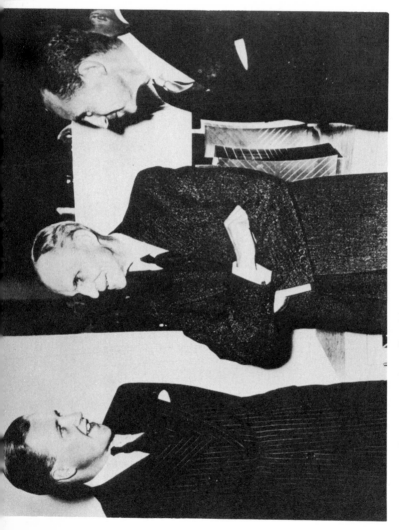

21-year-old Henry Ford II talks with his grandfather, Henry Ford, and his father, Edsel Ford, at the New York World's Fair on May 3, 1939

Thirty-four days before his father, Edsel, died, Lieutenant Henry Ford II stands with his grandparents, Mr. and Mrs. Henry Ford, in the grounds of his father's home on April 22, 1943

Henry Ford II

The three grandsons of Henry Ford became leaders of the company – Henry Ford II (standing), chairman of the board and chief executive officer; Benson Ford (left), vice-president and chairman of the Dealer Policy Board; and William Clay Ford, vice-president, Product Design. In the background are portraits of Edsel Ford (left) and Henry Ford

Above: 1940 Lincoln Continental Convertible Coupé. *Centre:* 1947–8 Lincoln Continental. *Below:* 1956 Mark II

Henry Ford II with the company's new 1978 products – the Ford Fairmont in front, the Mercury Zephyr behind – and with a 1903 Model A Ford in the background

Above: Henry Ford II drives the first Ford off the assembly line on July 3, 1945 a
production was resumed after World War II. Two months later, Henry Ford I
succeeded his grandfather, Henry Ford, as president of the company. *Below:* For
Motor Company produced its 100-millionth vehicle in the United States – a For
Fairmont – during 1977, the company's 75th anniversary year

Earl's painstaking, step-by-step approach was copied by Ford's stylists and Chrysler's too; first, a limitless number of drawing-board sketches, then full-scale drawings from which miniature scale models were built in an assortment of sizes. The next stage called for wet clay, tons of it, from which full-size models were sculpted, their lines easily altered with sweeps of a spatula. Once the shape of the car was agreed on, a further generation of replicas was fashioned from plastic reinforced with Fiberglas. Within this predetermined shell, the engineers had somehow to fit—or contort —the running gear.

The first of Ford's new models were rejected on the basis of hard statistics provided by Thornton's group. "They would have bankrupted the company if they had been produced," McNamara said bluntly afterward. They were "too big and too heavy," Henry II acknowledged. "Ernie said he didn't know anything about styl-ing and suggested we hire some outside designers."

Ford's entry for the postwar stakes was redone and molded in clay before he decided to unveil it to Grandfather. "One Saturday morning, I took him through and showed it to him. I figured he'd probably think it was perfectly awful. I don't remember his exact remarks, but he didn't vociferously criticize it." Clara tried a door handle, and it broke off in her grasp. "It looked so *real*," she apologized. She had seen nothing of the sort before.

She took old Henry to keep warm in the sun at their Georgia estate for two months before they returned to Fair Lane in April. Spring floods had carried the water of the Rouge up into the pow-erhouse, dousing the furnaces, cutting off electricity and tele-phones. The only heat in the house came from log fires on the hearths. He was so infirm now that he could scarcely stand, yet he would still struggle to his feet when Clara entered the room.

She scolded herself for allowing him too much of his own way. "If I'd clamped down from the beginning . . ." She should make him rest more, though that would be a struggle. "He was pretty strong-willed," she admitted.

April 7, 1947, was one of his better days, when his mind was ac-tive and his spirits high. He ate a good breakfast of prunes, oat-meal, bacon, toast, and coffee, then felt like having Rankin take him for a drive. In his pockets, the old man carried a comb, a pocketknife, and a Jew's harp, but in the way of money, not a dime.

They rode as far as the Rouge, but Henry decided that he did not want to call on his grandson, whom he had not seen since returning from Georgia.

He kept interrupting the journey home, first to be helped to take a few steps in his bedroom slippers on the walks of the Catholic Cemetery at Schaefer Highway and Warren, then to watch from the car at Southfield Road as a New York Central freight engine span its wheels getting started. "Let's see if this fellow is going to make it or not," he told the chauffeur. Finally, he wanted to stop at the little family graveyard on Joy Road: "Rankin, this is where I'm going to be buried when I die."

Henry climbed without help from the car when they arrived back at Fair Lane in midafternoon. He rode up in the elevator by candlelight at his usual bedtime, asked Clara for "my little pill," and left her taking down her hair in her dressing room. She had not finished when he wanted water because his throat was dry. She called for her maid, Rosa Buhler, and they went into the double bedroom together. Rosa had no doubt about what she saw in his gaunt cheeks in the lamplight. The two women took a second pillow to prop him higher in the bed, and his head fell against Clara's shoulder. "Henry, please speak to me," she kept repeating. Rosa ran to fetch Rankin, who drove to another telephone to call Dr. John Mateer of the Henry Ford Hospital at his home in Grosse Pointe. A second call was made to bring young Henry and Eleanor.

The old man's breathing faltered. "I think Mr. Ford is leaving us," Rankin muttered. Clara hurried to put on a dress before the doctor came. Old Henry's hands closed together as if in prayer. The maid's voice reached Clara in her dressing room: "Mrs. Ford, we'd both better stay here now." Mistress and maid sat together on the edge of Clara's bed, watching the change come over his face. Rosa felt his pulse and then listened for a heartbeat. "I think he has passed away," she whispered.

He was dead when the doctor arrived to certify the cause, a cerebral hemorrhage, and the time, eleven forty-five. At four o'clock the next morning, Henry Ford I was taken from the house, to lie in state in the Recreation Hall of Greenfield Village. A hundred thousand people were counted passing the bier there before he was buried in St. Paul's Cathedral, while Clara clutched their grandson's arm.

"You ought to get down on your knees and thank God that he went before you did," Rankin the chauffeur told her.

"Oh, wouldn't that have been tragic," she replied. On the turn of the front staircase at Fair Lane, the clock he had brought home after his Peace Ship's cruise ticked on inside the walnut case that carried a plaque with the words engraved in steel:

> *Slowly, slowly, always on*
> *Regrets are vain*
> *When time has gone.*

Chapter Eleven

The Keen Cutting Edge

The event was staged with most of the tricks and trimmings of a Hollywood opening, a New Year's Eve ball, the debut of a daughter of King Croesus. The white-and-gold pillared grand ballroom of the Waldorf-Astoria, where Presidents mingled with visiting princes on other Manhattan occasions, was a dazzle of floodlights, flowers, and banners. Champagne corks popped at half a dozen bars, white-tied waiters juggled traysful of glasses through the crowd, while a black-tied orchestra made a conscientious effort to be heard above the crescendo chatter.

Paid advertising and free publicity had occupied pages of newsprint and hours of air time in advance of this June day when first the news media and then the public were to be introduced to Henry's new cars for 1949, which Grandfather had seen only for a moment in clay eighteen months ago. Now here they were, bathed in light, polished to a preternatural gleam brighter than Loretta Young's, attended by smiling handmaidens and servants flicking feather dusters.

In a matter of days, the order books would provide the clue to whether the stylists had achieved their purpose and given these machines a sufficiently tempting aura of power, glamor, freedom, and social status. Transportation as such was dull as ditchwater, no longer worthy of promotion as a lure to customers. The owner of any old car had means of transportation, so what would prompt him to pay out good money for this year's model? Neither

Ford nor anyone else in the business could prosper if buyers were allowed to let logic prevail and wait until an automobile wore out before replacing it. If the new cars were exciting enough, they would accept a smaller trade-in on the old ones, too.

The 1949 Fords could be sold best in a climate where "new" meant "irresistible." This involved exploiting the rage for novelty, for rejecting the traditional in favor of the sensational, which old Henry and Edison in their generation had provoked in Americans. A latter-day chief of Ford designers expanded on their thinking: "Styling serves to make the public aware that here is a new product with improvements in materials, components, and mechanical design—features that might be hidden to anyone but a mechanic or an engineer. People want to know about these things, and if they buy the car, they don't want its best features to be concealed. They want identification where it is visible to one and all. It's the same sort of urge that causes some girls to wear tight sweaters."

At General Motors, expectations were high for hard-top convertibles, available for the first time in this year's Cadillacs, Buicks, and Oldsmobiles. Top management was less sanguine about the prospects of winning the antitrust suit filed against the company by the Department of Justice. The outcome would have set old Henry jigging with joy: The du Ponts were ordered by the court to divest themselves of GM stock in accordance with a stipulated timetable.

The case for styling versus logic was stated in a nutshell at General Motors: "Seeing is selling." Sloan, chairman since 1937 and a perpetual realist, appreciated the truth that lay concealed by the annual-model razzle-dazzle. "We have today," he said in 1963, "basically the same kind of machine that was created in the first twenty years of the industry."

The new Ford, labeled Model B-A, which tens of thousands of people came in from Park Avenue to see every day for a week, was made up of completely redesigned parts except for its V-8 engine of 100 horsepower. Henry seemed to have inherited his father's keen ear when he took one of the cars for a road test and complained the following day of a tinny sound in its doors. He followed up by going down to the Rouge and slamming doors as cars came off the line.

"Listen to it. Sounds tinny as hell. Know what's probably hap-

pening all over the country right now? Chevy dealers are marching their customers into Ford display rooms, slamming the front
doors, and gloating. 'See?' they're saying, 'that's a Ford for you!'
Man, they're turning the customer around and selling him a
Chevrolet! So let's get these doors fixed. Right now."

More than the doors were in need of fixing on Model B-A. Jack
Davis listed eight thousand faults that had to be progressively
remedied over the succeeding three years, most of them minor,
but one chronic—dust and rainwater seeped in through the join of
body to chassis. But the company booked more orders than could
be filled, though B-A cost $100 more than a Chevrolet, and Davis
was inundated by applications for new dealer franchises. Sales of
the cars that year would top 800,000, the biggest contribution to
an after-tax profit of $177,265,000.

Henry was picking up speed on the highway. "Every time he
turns around," one admiring magazine article said, "his actions
will be fateful to private enterprise in the U.S.A." He was also
providing a successor to himself in accordance with the law of
primogeniture, which had governed the inheritance to date. The
son born to Anne on the day after Christmas 1948, twenty
months after Henry I died, was christened Edsel. He was to be
their last child.

"Beat Chevrolet!" read the signs that hung in the Rouge. It was
a different planet nowadays. One of the first comforts Henry
brought in after Grandfather's departure was to lift the ban on
smoking. A suggestion-box scheme was in operation, paying out
hundreds of thousands of dollars in rewards for practical ideas for
improvement. After seeing how supervisors laid about them with
their fists, Breech commissioned Elmo Roper and his opinion
samplers to sound out Ford workers with a questionnaire: "Do
you believe that you are given a fair opportunity to make sugges-
tions and criticisms about company practices and officials? How
do you think the products of the Ford Motor Company compare
with those of its principal competitors? Please be frank, and
please don't sign your name or identify yourself in any way."

There was no telling whether it was indifference, scorn, or ves-
tiges of Bennett-bred fear that led four out of five workers to ignore the questions, even though the union accepted the poll as a
token of good intentions. Of those who responded, an overwhelm-

ing 84 per cent were critical of the brutal supervisory system, which Breech undertook to reform.

In line with Henry's wishes, Breech was engaged in making over Ford's in the image of General Motors, down to the separating out of divisions for makes of car—Ford, Lincoln, Mercury—on the GM pattern. In spite of the return to profitability, the company still ranked third among the Big Three. Hunger, as always, was the spur to innovation. Ford's pushed ahead among the leaders in the use of machines to operate machines to cut manpower costs and raise productivity.

One of the graduates of General Motors that Ernie Breech imported, Delmar Harder, was credited with coining the word "automation" to describe the process by which electronic sensors and controls replaced the skills and judgments of men on the assembly line. Wartime developments in radar, transistors, and the ABC's of what would emerge as the computer and television industries made it possible to churn out automobile components like cigarettes or candy bars, with scarcely a living soul required except to push start and stop buttons.

Making over the obsolescent Rouge was difficult; the factory had never been intended for such change, which one industrial philosopher, Peter Drucker, considered to be "as great as Henry Ford ushered in with the first mass-production plant fifty years ago." Installing automation as the reason-for-being was easier in the new premises that Henry authorized in Buffalo and Cleveland as evidence of faith in Ford's future.

Substituting machines for men evoked similar unrest in the UAW as in Ned Lud of Leicestershire, England, denigrated by his bosses as feebleminded, who in 1779 smashed two weaving frames to protest the advent of steam power and become the idol of a short-lived workingmen's rebellion. "Speed-up" was the protest raised at the Rouge when the place was struck for twenty-four days in 1949. It was clear to Henry that industrial relations had to be handled as carefully as matches at a gas pump.

The results of Elmo Roper's poll showed how to reduce the risk of further explosions. The poll found that American workingmen had four basic wants: a sense of security; opportunities for advancement; treatment as human beings and not as a mere number on the payroll; and a sense of worth in performing work useful to society as a whole. Satisfying those wants, Henry judged, would provide the recipe for smoother relations with the union.

Looking backward was not his habit, and he could not have remembered something Grandfather once told Walter Reuther, but Henry's mind often worked on similar tracks. After Ford first signed with the UAW, Edsel had introduced his father to Reuther, who had been fired from his $1.10-an-hour job in the Tool and Die Department for trying to recruit men into the union.

"You know, Mr. Reuther," old Henry said, "it was one of the most sensible things Harry Bennett ever did when he got the UAW into this plant."

"I think so, but I didn't think you did, Mr. Ford," Reuther answered with a grin. "How do you figure it?"

"Well, you've been fighting General Motors and the Wall Street crowd. Now you're in here, and we've given you a union shop and more than you got out of them. That puts you on our side, doesn't it? We can fight General Motors and Wall Street together."

Henry II's move was to establish the first pension plan for hourly rated employees in the industry, paying $100 a month to every man who had put in thirty years of service, at a cost to the company of $20,000,000 a year. Benefits had been considerably improved over that when Reuther went on record with a statement that the UAW preferred working with Ford. "Ford," he said, "isn't as smart as GM because they haven't got the depth, but they're a lot smarter than Chrysler, and they're more progressive than both."

In 1949, young Henry had to juggle with an equally fulminatory issue. Kanzler got nowhere with Harry Ferguson in seeking ways of cutting losses in the tractor business. When the agreement that old Henry and the Ulsterman had concluded with a handshake was terminated, Ferguson proceeded to manufacture his own machines, and Ford came out with a new line of its own. Ferguson responded by filing a quarter-billion-dollar lawsuit, claiming damage, conspiracy against him, patent infringement, and unfair competition.

"It'll be a grand fight," he chuckled.

"The blunt truth about this relationship," said young Henry, "is that it made Mr. Ferguson a multimillionaire and cost the Ford Motor Company $25,000,000." If the courts ruled against Ford, much of the progress made to date would be negated and the company would be pauperized, compelled to go begging to the banks.

One more project had been abandoned by this time and nothing whatever substituted for it at the Rouge. Like other makers, Henry and his team had been intrigued by the sudden appearance on the postwar market of cars like the Kaiser and Crosley, so small and light that they looked like dime-store toys compared with the conventional chariots of Detroit. They were an ingenious answer to the problems of materials in short supply: The smaller the automobile, the more that could be produced from given quantities of metals and plastics. Sales were promising when customers would buy anything that was available.

A division designated to explore light-car production was set up with Henry's authorization, and he personally took a look at the prospects for importing the little things when he made a tour of the European plants and agencies in Britain, France, Belgium, Holland, Denmark, Spain, and Germany in 1948. His visit to Germany stood out in retrospect as possibly the most spectacular example of what-might-have-been in Detroit's history. He tried to buy Volkswagen.

Its antecedents dated back to the Berlin Auto Show of 1934, when Adolf Hitler, proclaimed Fuehrer that year, assigned the German industry the task of building "a people's car"—*volkswagen*. The man who conceived it, Ferdinand Porsche, made an inspection of the Rouge to absorb Ford methods and techniques for application in the Volkswagenwerk under construction at Frankfürt-am-Main as the birthplace of the most radical new automobile since the original Lizzie. It was scheduled to share many of her qualities. It would be as low-priced as production in the millions could make it, with minimal changes year after year. Most repairs would be possible by any owner who could handle a screwdriver and a wrench. It would embody Lizzie's slow-gaited spryness and plain looks, and it would generate exasperated affection, just as she had done. One major difference would be the engine, which was to be air-cooled like Charles Kettering's aborted, copper-finned Chevy motor.

Ford's Cologne subsidiary had tried to use Volkswagen as the name for one of its domestic models, but the Reich Government forbade that. Germans by the thousands had paid deposits for Porsche's brainchild, but deliveries, never more than a trickle, dried up completely when the war began.

The Volkswagenwerk, battered by Allied bombing operations, had been back in operation for less than two years, turning out cars for occupation officials, when Henry made the attempt to bring VW under Dearborn's control. Many of his executives showed open contempt. "You call that a *car?*" was the most common reaction.

The legal problems seemed insuperable, among them the question of the rights of those Germans whose deposits had gone up in smoke. Henry was not ready to give up. If he could not acquire the business, perhaps he could tempt its brilliant new manager, Heinz Nordhoff, into joining Ford's. When they met, as arranged, at Frankfürt Airport, Nordhoff decided to stay with what he was doing.

In 1950, Ford-Germany gave up trying to match prices with Volkswagen, which sold 82,399 units during those twelve months. Four years later, the figure exceeded 200,000—38 per cent of the market there—against Ford-Germany's 42,631, and the Beetles' invasion of the United States had scarcely begun.

Henry discontinued the compact-car division after he came back from Europe and put aside the idea of minicars for more than a decade—which was a mistake, in his self-critical opinion. "You win some, you lose some, and some get rained out" was one of his ways of cataloging success and failure in circumstances like these.

Which category covered his marriage was debatable. His devotion—he had great capacity for it—was to his work, and he showed the energy of a man fulfilling himself in his job. He joked about his difference from Grandfather, "a man who drew a sharp distinction between working hard and doing hard work. He believed very strongly in the former and very little in the latter." In an age when the giant corporations of the United States were increasingly managed by salaried business-school graduates, lawyers, and accountants under scrutiny by boards of directors in the professed interests of distant shareholders, Henry II was a *proprietor* who could do exactly as he pleased.

By 1950, the company was thriving again, as the numbers proved: more than $238,500,000 in profits, more than 1,500,000 cars sold for a 24 per cent share of the market, leaving General Motors comfortably ahead, but overtaking Chrysler, which would never again place better than third.

He was at the bedside of Clara, who had been living in seclusion at Fair Lane, when she died of a coronary occlusion early one September morning in the Ford Hospital, only dimly aware of what her daughter-in-law's ultimatum and her grandson's labors had achieved.

Having his name over the door bred the same kind of glow in Henry as the sight of his name on a Broadway marquee brings to every actor. He enjoyed traveling around his properties, toting his own bag and sometimes someone else's, looking more like a custom-tailored yeoman on shore leave than a pillar of Western capitalism. He liked to keep personal tabs on what was going on, continuing to soak up information for storage in his head and his file cabinets. He also liked to play down his role as anything more important than a salesman for Ford.

"I would rather not send any of you home mad," he joked at the close of a convivial evening at the Gridiron Club in Washington. "For if you get mad at me, you get mad at Ford—and we can kiss a sale good-bye. Believe me, I don't want to set the world on fire. I just want to watch those Fords go by."

That was disarming, but not quite accurate. The same audience had already been given a taste of some broader-gauge thoughts circling in his head. "That word 'world' is becoming more and more important to us. For there can't be any real question any more that our own peace and the living standards of this country are closely tied to what goes on in other countries and to living standards of people everywhere around the globe."

Sometimes he sounded off uncommonly like a latter-day Henry I, without the telltale arrogance. "No one can see himself as others see him," Henry II believed, "and it would probably be very discouraging to him if he could." But the old man himself might have said, "The way to keep a good reputation is to live up to it," and, "No idea, and no process to produce the idea, is worth very much if you can't sell what you make."

In his early thirties, Henry Ford II was emerging as the most recognizable figure on the Detroit landscape, but he was willing to talk to an audience like any other run-of-the-mill entrepreneur if he must. "Competition is the keen cutting edge of business, always shaving away at costs" was as platitudinous as the average Chamber of Commerce address, on a par with, "The more we give up relying on ourselves, the more we lose the capacity for being self-reliant." Yet in some of his thinking he was too radical and far-ranging to be accepted as a spokesman by the shellbacks in charge of most car manufacturing.

"What we are shooting for," he said in 1949, "is a nation and a world in which everybody enjoys a higher standard of living—in terms of the human spirit as well as material things." And, "If business is to be a leader and not a whipping boy such as it has been many times in the past, we have no choice but to take a vigorous part in the development of the blueprints on which our future social structure will be built."

This was inflammatory enough to dismay stand-pat management everywhere, but he got worse as he grew a little older and started making speeches about war and peace. "Only when nations and individuals are free from fear of war is it possible for them to prosper. As businessmen, we know that every tank, every battleship, every gun that has to be made is so much less steel for buildings, automobiles, dishwashers, bridges, electric power—even razors. To a businessman, war means only waste and destruction of all he works for."

He returned to the theme when he spoke, as he often did, to a group of Jews; in this instance, the Anti-Defamation League and American Jewish Committee in New York: "Today—having outstripped ourselves in our conquest of the physical world, having probed secrets that go to the very heart of physical creation, having tapped the sources of gigantic power literally capable of destroying the world—we present the picture of a not-too-grown-up child carelessly playing with a loaded shotgun in a packed kindergarten."

He kept himself too occupied for his family to see as much of him as he had of Edsel. Charlotte especially felt as she grew up

that he had been an absentee father, closer to her sister Anne
than to herself. They saw more of him in the summer, when he
flew out to their place at Southampton on Friday afternoons in a
company plane, then sent the pilot home because Henry preferred
to catch the Sunday night train back to Detroit from Grand Central Station. He was leery of publicizing anything about his home
life, which was certainly in line with Eleanor's wishes. Publication
of pictures of Charlotte, young Anne, and Edsel was not con-
donable.

Playing with the children did not always fit into the schedule.
Though he had never bought a car for himself in his life and
scarcely knew a ball joint from a tire gauge, he was a race-car
buff who subscribed to the cult magazines and was pleased to
push a Maserati or a Mercedes as hard as it would go. One of the
stinging little stories that gathered around his head like mosqui-
toes on a sultry night told of his disappearing from a Southampton party they were giving and, to the embarrassment of his wife,
gunning a new car around the greens of a nearby country club.

Close friends detected something of the chameleon in him,
cold-blooded and reserved behind his always clear desk, as boister-
ous as a frat house on rush night when he was off duty. The parlor
psychologists among them attributed that to reaction from the
constraints of an insulated childhood. One element remained constant: No matter where he was, he spoke his mind.

Now and then, he liked to reminisce. "You know, back when I
was a college kid, I went to a dance one summer out in Southampton. It was a hot night, and I was sweating like a pig, so I
went into the men's room to freshen up. There was a guy in there
with his jacket off and his sleeves pushed up and soap clear up
over his elbows. I looked at him, and as I was going out, I asked
somebody, 'Who the hell is that guy in there taking a shower?'
That was the only time I ever saw Howard Hughes."

Henry enjoyed a night on the town in Manhattan when it
could be fitted into the schedule, plumped down on a zebra-
striped banquette at Perona's El Morocco or propping up P. J.
Clarke's Third Avenue bar among its crowd of gray-flanneled Bo-
hemians, depending on how the mood took him. On those nights,
he was as gregarious as a prairie dog, but a stranger risked being
snapped at if he tried to butt in. He rarely mixed with other auto

men or his own executives. Instead, Henry cultivated a circle of friends and acquaintances with a common liking for good talk and a good time.

Actor David Niven was one of them, along with Pat Doyle, police reporter for the New York *Daily News*. Ernest Hemingway was a companion with whom Henry drank and talked a night away. Frank Sinatra joined in the group when he was in town. "I've known him a long time," Henry explained—Sinatra sang with the band at Henry's twenty-first birthday party. Wilbur Mills, who reigned as chairman of the House Ways and Means Committee until preoccupation with alcohol and a strip-tease dancer overcame him, figured briefly on the list of friends.

An evening's conversation with Henry might touch on anything except the automobile business. "Not that it's taboo," he said once, "but anybody that knows you isn't going to talk about it. But we talk about politics, money, people, gossip, or whatever." The stress was on gossip. "One thing that he really likes to talk about is who's sleeping with whom," said Charlotte long afterward.

He could curse like a longshoreman and match drinks with anybody—scotch for preference, but wine, too, and anything else that was being served without worry about mixing them together. When the toll was taken the morning after, Henry was invariably spared any trace of a hangover.

He was an inveterate girl-watcher on his outings, happy to suspend conversation to admire a face or a shape across the room. Jack Davis remembered going with him to El Morocco at the end of a day of sales conferences and being drawn into a $10 bet that Henry could not entice a young woman into leaving her two escorts to take a whirl around the dance floor with him. He needed only two minutes to succeed, grabbing Davis's stake money and his covering $10 from the table as he danced past and pushing the bills into her hand. On the word of friends, Anne Ford remained the only important woman in their marriage.

If she expected that Clara's death would make her *the* Mrs. Ford of Dearborn and Detroit, she was disappointed. The title passed unchallenged to Eleanor, who made no effort toward that end. Her pattern of life continued as though she were Edsel's wife, not his widow. Summers found her at the house overlooking

Seal Harbor, winters at home on Gaukler Pointe, busy with their charities and pastimes. She had succeeded him on the Arts Commission, and the checks still flowed out to the art museum and the symphony orchestra. She was as reticent as ever about everything she did. "Please don't fuss over me" was a constant request of hers, but among the committees she served on, she had a reputation for speaking out as forthrightly as Henry to his staff.

With her gray-flecked hair and brisk walk, in her Mainbocher wool suits, matching hats and the usual two strands of pearls, she looked little different from anybody's rich grandmother. Flowers were too showy to be worn on the person, she thought, but she spent hours arranging them before she entertained. "Nobody," her guests maintained, "sets a table like Eleanor." She would not go so far as to try preparing the dishes herself. That could safely be left to the cook. There were five other servants, and a guard at the gate.

It had taken seven years to settle Edsel's estate while the government wrangled with Eleanor and her lawyers over the value of the stock. Speculation set the tax that she and her children would have to pay as high as $225,000,000. The IRS initially claimed each share to be worth $190; her figure was $58. The two sides compromised on $135, and total federal taxes amounted to roughly $24,600,000.

One of her early donations after settlement was reached was a park and children's playground, constructed on the lakefront at Grosse Pointe Shores not far from her home. Children, including Henry's, received a lot of attention. A summer play school, an art school specifically designed for young talent—she had not lost her pleasure in the next generation since she taught dancing classes as a schoolgirl, and she still loved a dance herself at a private party.

Her open smile was as much a part of her as her quick intelligence, which only her family and the closest friends saw in operation. "She's a brilliant woman with a shrewd mind," one of them said. "She organizes her time the best of anyone I know," said another. There was a religious side to her nature, too, though she was not seen in church every Sunday.

"No interviews" was a standing rule, but occasionally her name turned up in the *Free Press* or the *News*. Gossip writers twittered when she arrived for one birthday party at the Little Club, which was one of the few semipublic establishments on her circuit, wearing the first white mink Detroit had ever seen. The insular capital of the auto trade took its social pretensions solemnly. A committee, inevitably numbering four hundred, was convoked not too long afterward to name the city's foremost social leader. The choice could be no one but Eleanor, "Detroit's Great Lady," as the headlines referred to her.

In 1954, she suffered another family loss. With her robe and slippers left on the edge, her sister Dody was found drowned in the pool at Sea Ridge, the Kanzlers' Florida home at Hobe Sound. Ernest was married the following year to Rosemarie Pavelli Weicker, a native of Mexico who lived in Switzerland. His influence with his nephew was not diminished.

Young Mrs. Ford could not compete with her mother-in-law, whether the wish was there or not. The forces molding Anne's character had been less peremptory than in Eleanor's case: the need to shield a man from his father, her husband's premature death, the drawn-out conflict of willpower to secure an inheritance. Anne lacked the experience of responding to change of the kind that had given strength to Eleanor and was transforming Henry. Anne attended Mass every day and sent Charlotte and young Anne off in her footsteps to the convent school in Noroton, Connecticut, as soon as they were old enough. They would grow up just as she had, if that could be arranged.

She worked hard at being an exemplar of excellence among wives of her rank and position. Clothes demanded attention; she applied such time and taste to choosing them that she would be placed on the fashion trade's fanfared list of the world's twelve best-dressed women, on which her daughters were briefly included, too. Her mother-in-law contributed handsomely to buying a Rubens and a Gerard Terbosch for the Institute of Art; Anne responded by giving paintings by Rembrandt and Picasso. Eleanor spent a small fortune sponsoring the Detroit Symphony; Anne, impatient with Manhattan sneers about Detroit being a shirtsleeve city, arranged to import the Metropolitan Opera for four sold-out performances.

There was some truth in the outsiders' gibes. The fifth-largest city in the land was so wrapped up in itself that it could accept without blinking the admission of Charles E. Wilson, millionaire president and shareholder of GM: "For years, I thought what was good for the country was good for General Motors and vice versa." Because the two interests did not necessarily coincide, he was induced to sell his stock before Congress approved his appointment as Secretary of Defense under Eisenhower.

Combat fever among the Big Three was endemic in executives who worked for them. Off-duty talk over a Stroh's beer or a shot of bourbon had a strong tang of the locker room. Who was on the way up or the way out; how much a pal or a rival was making this year with bonus or commissions; what triumphs or disasters were being met with at Dearborn or at GM headquarters on West Grand Boulevard. "What are they doing over on the boulevard?" was a question that haunted this generation of Ford men. By and large, Detroit males were an exuberant, gung-ho lot who had been sold like the rest of Americans on the benefits of the product as advertised, and they delighted in swapping stories about how fast they had driven the latest model without being hauled over by a state trooper.

Their wives absorbed, or incited, the pugnacity. At a coffee klatsch or around a bridge table, over a sloe gin fizz or a sidecar, which lingered on here long after it had faded from Manhattan bartenders' repertoire, they competed to impress each other with the glories of the new car, their husbands' promotions, and the anticipated joys of the next vacation. What they saw or read about Anne Ford led most of them to suspect that she might be a trifle too urbane for them, too well groomed, much in control of herself.

At parties, where Henry enjoyed clowning around among friends, she watched what she ate and counted her drinks. Overstaying an evening at anyone's house went against the grain of her careful upbringing. Her husband had no such compunctions, so sometimes she left without him. Their own parties had to be perfect; that did not encompass the merrymaking which, on one Southampton night, concluded with Henry, fully clothed, leading the band to wade through the swimming pool in Indian file without missing a beat of "When the Saints Come Marching In." Friends played down reports of tension stirring between Henry and Anne. "There has never been a divorce in the Ford family," said one of them, "and I am willing to bet that not one of them has ever been to a psychiatrist." For the present, he was right on both counts.

The uneasiness between them was no more than that when news bulletins, which received only a flicker of attention, announced that 60,000 North Korean troops spearheaded by a hundred Soviet-built tanks were streaming into South Korea on June 24, 1950. Henry's response was like most Americans'—sluggish. Nearly four weeks passed before he wired the President that "all of us at Ford Motor Company stand ready to carry out any assignment the government may give us."

There were no doubts this time in Washington, as there had been twice before about Henry I's reliability. By September, Truman was galloping ahead with preparations for all-out war, and Ford's was back in the arms business, manufacturing tanks, aero engines, rockets, and machine guns under contracts worth nearly a billion dollars.

It was far from being a winning lottery ticket. The price paid by the auto industry for defense contracts was the return of price controls and federal allocations of scarce steel, aluminum, copper, nickel, zinc, and rubber, with quotas based on 1947–49 production figures, years when Ford ran last of the Big Three. A protest to Washington against the "injustice" of the clampdown brought to light the bitterness of the rivalry among them. Already bruised in the contest, Chrysler complained that Ford was fishing for government help to win a position, second, "which in a free economy it had been unable to attain in the past seventeen years." Both companies' allowances were modestly increased—and Ford outsold Chrysler.

Haggling over the terms of a cease-fire for Korea had been dragging on for months when Henry's attorneys settled out of court with Ferguson. Paying him $9,250,000 to free Ford to make tractors without threat of further lawsuits sat poorly with some of Henry's staff when shortage of supplies was forcing down production and profits equally, but he could always cut short debate on topics like this with one conclusive comment: "My name's over the door."

That fall, he concluded, as a liberal Republican should, that the Democrats had reigned far too long in Washington. He was an early starter in promoting Dwight Eisenhower for the White

House, and he did his bit as a conscientious citizen to help get out the vote for both parties. He was one of the shade fewer than 34,000,000 voters who liked Ike. After his man had been shooed into the presidency, Henry explained some of the reasons for his partiality to an audience in Jacksonville, Florida.

"I think that businessmen in Washington will tread very cautiously indeed to avoid any shred of suspicion that the Fair Deal has been replaced by the Big Deal, the Middle-sized Deal, or even the Small, Economical-sized Deal. Following the leadership of the President, I think most of us today have become dyed-in-the-wool No Dealers."

Henry was not tempted to follow the rocky course of some other corporations, which tripped and fell during Richard Nixon's campaigning. "Ford Motor Company is a business corporation and not a political institution," Henry emphasized on another occasion. "Even if it were legal to do so, the company would not support, financially or otherwise, the candidacy of any person for political office. But what any employee of the company does in his own behalf and acting as a private citizen is another matter and one of his own concern." Lizzie had more relevance to present times than Grandfather's posted signs plugging his preference for the presidency.

Henry II also avoided emulating Eisenhower as "the Great Delegator." In one of his analyses of what makes corporate men tick, Peter Drucker, who was a friend of Ernie Breech's, noted that a perfectly efficient executive such as Ike is usually fated to create a tedious organization. "Effective" was a better description than "efficient" for Henry. Working for him might be exhilarating, exhausting, or, as Tex Thornton found before he quit, frustrating. Tedious it was not.

Henry's labors for Ike were routinely recognized. In July 1953, the month of the Korean armistice, Henry was appointed an alternate United States delegate to the United Nations. Wiseacres who had puzzled over whether Henry was really a playboy or presidential timber decided that he was heading in the latter direction in a new career as a servant of the people.

He had recently jumped into the headlines again with a public appeal for lifting all tariffs on the importation of foreign cars, and this at a time when Volkswagens and other intruders were beginning to bite into American sales. Henry's reasoning was simplicity itself. Ford's overseas operations were doing better than General Motors'. "In order for others to buy from us," he said, "they must be able to sell to us."

As a United Nations delegate, he trod his own paths. He was politely critical of the Soviets, while he looked forward to the day when Ford might resume selling to the U.S.S.R. He dumfounded John Foster Dulles, Eisenhower's chillingly moralistic Secretary of State, by telling Dulles that Red China ought to be admitted to the organization. More than a dozen years later, when the United States was wracked with protests against the war in Vietnam, Henry said, "A lot of water has gone over the dam since, but I have always felt that by talking to people you can at least get a feel of what is going on in their country. I don't know how the CIA works or what information our State Department is getting. Maybe they get all they want. But it seems to me that if the alternative is war, we're better off to talk." Would he sell to Red China? "Sure. Anyone who will pay hard cash. We'll trade."

His new United Nations job overlapped another that had to be tackled now that the revitalized company was generating profits well in excess of $100,000,000 a year. Nearly 90 per cent of them were earmarked for the Ford Foundation under the terms of its legacies from Henry I and Edsel, entrusting it with that percentage of the firm's total assets. The IRS valuation of Eleanor's shares meant that the foundation's worth was approximately half-a-billion dollars. How to make intelligent use of these enormous sums of money was a question that boggled the trustees.

To date, they had been doling out a million or so a year to such unspectacular causes as the Detroit Symphony, Eleanor's godchild, and Greenfield Village. They would have to do far better than that or the accumulation of cash would become unmanageable, providing a tempting target for congressional investigators, Senator Joseph R. McCarthy of Wisconsin in particular, who regarded foundations in general as a flagrant tax dodge and a haven for "pinkos" as well.

Henry took his duties as a trustee almost as seriously as the self-imposed challenge of catching up with Chevrolet. His attendance record at quarterly board meetings was 95 per cent perfect. He endorsed the choice—he had no veto power—of Paul G. Hoffman as first president after Hoffman had headed up Truman's Marshall Plan in Europe, and Ford gave Hoffman a free hand in choosing beneficiaries for the foundation's grants, even if some of them should turn out to be grandiose flops like old Henry's Peace Ship.

One such foundation fumble would be a project to condense all the philosophies of man, to fit between the covers of a single book. After three years and the expenditure of $600,000, the task was given up as hopeless.

Henry made an extended visit of inspection to "Itching Palms," which was Hoffman's name for the office he set up in Pasadena, California. The outcome was Hoffman's departure a few months later. Henry refrained from saying anything in public, but the deposed president clarified the situation: "I felt I'd done a first-class job, and if after two years the trustees didn't agree . . . I'd rather leave."

The turncocks on the dammed-up fortune were opened wider. Hundreds of millions of dollars, half of them channeled into American education, washed across the land. A high-water mark was reached in 1955, when $570,000,000 was pumped out in one go to boost faculty salaries at more than 600 colleges and raise standards in medical schools and hospitals. For three days in a row every quarter, Henry deliberated with his fellow trustees on how the funds should be spent. The experience, on top of his involvement with Ford's worldwide operations, made him, in Bob McNamara's assessment, "one of the best-informed businessmen in the United States on the rest of the world."

In that high-water year, a decision of the trustees pushed the company into another turn as decisive to its future as old Henry's resignation had been. Four fifths of the foundation's income came from Ford stock, yet it had no say in the size of dividends paid or in the management, for better or worse, of the goose that laid the golden eggs. The company was completing a billion-dollar expansion program, which kept returns to shareholders comparatively low. To protect itself from fluctuations of income dependent on whether Ford prospered or faltered, the foundation needed to spread its assets around. The trustees wanted to sell Ford stock to the public for the first time in half a century and reinvest the proceeds elsewhere.

Henry spelled out the consequences. "It meant living in a

goldfish bowl rather than living privately as a corporation. I think it was the right thing to do, because it got us into the market as a way of raising money. Unless you want to be terribly secretive about things, it isn't a great handicap. It's just different."

With Eleanor, brothers Benson and William and sister Josephine as the other sole proprietors, he had the authority to refuse any public offering. "But we agreed to it. I don't remember any great problem, but it was a major decision."

There was no way to circumvent New York Stock Exchange regulations that said that nonvoting stock could not be put up for sale there. Some formula would have to be devised to ensure that effective control was retained by the Fords, despite the escape of millions of shares outside the family. A multitude of consultants was engaged to find the answer. They recommended a shrewd splitting of shares to increase the Fords' equity and ensure that, no matter how much stock was sold now and in the future, Edsel's widow and her children would hold onto 40 per cent of the voting power, enough to stave off any attempt, short of a miracle, to wrest away their mastery.

More than 700 underwriters were enlisted to handle the sale of the initial 10,200,000 shares of common stock released by the foundation, which still kept in excess of 36,000,000 in reserve. The clamor to buy bewildered Henry and many more insiders weeks before the company prospectus, issued late in December, reported assets at $2,483,000,000 and sales for the financial year concluded on September 30 at a little more than $4,000,000,000.

The brokers disagreed, but he thought it best to be realistic about the company's prospects before trading began in mid-January. "We at Ford Motor Company are businessmen and not miracle men," he said bluntly. "I think some people are indulging in wishful thinking about their chances for fast and fabulous financial gains. It's true that 1955 was the best year we and the industry in general ever had. But 1956 will not be as good a year as 1955."

Hundreds of thousands of investors ignored the cautionary words of some investment counselors who felt that at $64.50 the stock was overpriced when a downturn in the automobile market seemed imminent. Wall Street and the other trading floors had seen nothing before like the rush to buy, "a landmark in the history of public ownership," as the New York Stock Exchange's president, Keith Funston, called it. The foundation was richer by $640,000,000; some of the men who had worked with Henry to resurrect the company had options to buy; and roughly 350,000 new owners of common stock, with a vote for every share, watched the quoted price flutter between $70 and $51 in the coming months.

Presiding over the annual meeting of stockholders could never be considered one of Henry's personal pleasures. "Once I get there it's not too bad, but getting prepared is difficult. I live through it." He chose to field most questions from the floor on his own, politely but firmly in the case of the inevitable dissidents. "I'm told they have the right to question management on what has been going on, no matter what it is. I think that is fine and probably right. But I think it's a shame that three or four people take 95 per cent of the time for questions and comments. They scare off the others."

Going public was not about to change the Ford preference for plowing back large hunks of profits for future growth, which interested Henry more than paying maximum dividends, whether some narrow-gauged investors liked it or not. Nothing short of a palace revolution formed around Eleanor and the rest of the family could unseat him. As Arjay Miller said, "He always was the boss from the first day I came in, and he always will be the boss until he decides to retire." With the war in Korea over, Henry grew bossier day by day.

In the eyes of the industry, Eisenhower came close to being a model President, infinitely preferable to his predecessor. Washington did not wait for the cease-fire before it lifted curbs on car prices and controls on production. And before his first term was over, Ike would provide the automakers with a further mark of esteem—the start of the interstate highway system, adding 42,500 miles of smooth, swift concrete ribbon, engineered for driving at unprecedented speed, north, south, east, and west across the United States. At least half of Charlie Wilson's remark appeared to be valid. What was good for America *was* good for General Motors—and Ford, too.

Peace in Korea signaled the resumption of the race between the two companies to dominate the market, though Ford men still nervously asked themselves, "What are they doing over on the boulevard?" Henry had his two brothers working with him now, Benson at Lincoln-Mercury, William handling the Continental Division. Company policy had not changed: Ford would strive to match General Motors in every price range, though at present it had only one car, the Ford, that looked to have a real chance against its GM counterpart, Chevrolet.

Old Henry's insistence on the brand purity of his product had long since gone by the board. Like every other car, a Ford was a hybrid of components bought from an army of suppliers, who in many instances sold identical parts to their competing customers. It minimized the differences between one make and another, but it was a more economical way of doing business than aiming, like Henry I, to produce an entire automobile from the company's own resources. At least Ford had passed the point where it had been humiliated by buying automatic transmissions from GM because it had not developed its own.

At Dearborn and on West Grand Boulevard alike, smaller cars were a dead issue. The Ford Division's own consumer research department reported conclusively to Henry's executive committee that a survey showed, "To the average American, our present car and its size represent an outward symbol of prestige and well-being." Later on, Henry became more skeptical of similar studies —he vetoed a proposal to buy advertising time on a top-rated television show when he pried loose the information that its rating was based on polling no more than a thousand people.

But in this instance, the backup evidence was persuasive. Of all the compacts made in America, only two, Nash-Rambler and Willys-Jeep, were surviving. The rest of them would be assigned to the graveyard holding the nearly 3,000 other makes that had died since the advent of automobiles. Henry J. Kaiser wrote the obituary of the line that carried his name: "We expected to toss $150,000,000 into the automobile pool, but we didn't expect it to disappear without a ripple."

General Motors was first off the mark with a brand-new car in 1953. The low-slung, wide-tracked Chevrolet Corvette with its Fiberglas shell had been sleeked up by Harley Earl's crew to the point where it seemed to be clocking ninety miles an hour standing still. Ford would not let the competition get away with a victory like that unchallenged when the news filtering out from the boulevard was that GM expected to sell 10,000 Corvettes in its opening season. The quick answer was the Thunderbird, calmer-looking but more sumptuously equipped, "more truly a personal or boulevard car," as it was officially described, "for the customer who insists on comfort and yet would like to own a prestige vehicle that incorporates the flair and performance characteristics of a sports car."

If the Thunderbird could not outrun the Corvette, it outsold it, nevertheless. There was, the Ford Division told Henry, "a definite swing toward the Ford." If the right ingredients could be found, "Beat Chevrolet!" would become a reality. In 1954, Chevy, with sales of 1,417,453, was ahead by only those last five figures—17,453.

"We are," said a high-ranking Ford officer on one occasion, "like Chinese bandits. We hit them and run. We can't meet GM head on because of that sheer firepower." Bob McNamara, climbing high in the Ford Division, advocated stressing safety for driver and passengers as an incentive to buy, causing instant discomfiture at General Motors, which felt strongly that this was a theme best avoided; it might unsettle the customers.

Perhaps not coincidentally, Ford announced that seat belts were available as an extra-cost option in the summer of the year when the prospect of the company's going public was beginning to be discussed. At about the same time, Henry pulled off another Chinese-bandit stroke and increased his standing with the UAW by putting up $55,000,000 in trust-fund money in the first contract of its kind in the business to provide extra unemployment pay for laid-off workers. Before much longer, he would work on the other side of the fence and take the company into the fold of the Automobile Manufacturers Association, which it had shunned for fifty-one years.

If the coolly efficient McNamara's judgments were correct, safety features could boost sales. Ford came out with an unprecedented advertising campaign centered on "Life Guard Design." Locks that kept doors shut in collision impact, padded rear-view mirrors to help prevent cracked skulls, recessed steering wheels to reduce the risk of broken ribs or worse—all were standard equipment. Padded dashboards and seat belts cost extra.

When the figures were in, a debate broke out at company head-quarters, where a sizable proportion of the senior staff shared General Motors' doubts about the advisability of safety as a selling pitch. It had done nothing to push Ford into first place. "Safety didn't sell," said one of McNamara's protégés, a thirty-two-year-old troubleshooter named Lido Iacocca by his Italian immigrant parents in memory of the Venetian beach where they spent their honeymoon. Minority opinion held, to the contrary, that without "Life Guard Design," Ford would have fallen farther behind.

Chevrolet had knocked the wind out of Ford's continual boasting that its cars were the most powerful in the low-priced field. Chevy also offered a V-8 now, 180 horsepower to carry a carload of people as fast as the law allowed along the inviting new highways—or maybe even faster. Buyers who would normally have gone for a higher-priced GM car switched to Chevrolet. General Motors' market share fell, while Ford's increased.

Yet at Dearborn and on the boulevard, the catchword was "Safety doesn't sell." If hotter cars were the most appealing alternative, Lido, who preferred to be called "Lee," was Henry's man.

Chapter Twelve

What Shall It Profit?

It cost Ford as much as $350,000,000 to begin to break the habit of emulating General Motors in a magniloquent version of a game which never lost favor with the kindergarten set, "Simon Says . . ."

The Eisenhower years in the White House coincided with a surge in customers' spending. Millions of them put a new automobile in first place on the shopping list, with priority over housing, furniture, educating the children, or taking a vacation. Old Henry's dictum of "any color so long as it's black" was as obsolete as the five-cent cigar. What the vast majority of buyers were interested in was a car, provided it was *big*.

The automakers had cause to congratulate themselves on the creation of this new kind of market, in which price tags counted for less and less, and they hurried to meet its demands. They termed the process "Selling more car per car"—more gadgets, more accessories, more promotable luxuries to give a Lincoln look to a Ford, a Cadillac gloss to a Chevrolet. The more car there was, the bigger the final bill and the greater the profit.

Every manufacturer these days offered "power options"—steering at the touch of a finger and braking at the tap of a toe; door locks, window lifts, and multiposition seats operated off the overloaded battery. Extra mirrors; radio; air conditioning; automatic transmission; bumper guards; special trim—the temptations could be irresistible as the prospect thumbed through one showroom brochure after another, selecting fabric and tones for upholstery and interior, and a favorite color, or combinations of two or three, for exterior paint. The profit on some options was a plump 100 per cent.

If he hankered after something fancier than a two- or four-door sedan, he could raise his sights and the tab, too, for a hardtop, a convertible, or a station wagon. When the industry broke all records to date by selling almost 8 million 1955 automobiles and was confident that the figure could be pushed to 10 million and beyond, 272 American-made models were available, 85 of them from General Motors. By 1963, the two totals had soared to 429 and 138, respectively.

John F. Gordon, GM's current president, calculated all the possible permutations before he boasted, "We could, in theory at least, go through a whole year's production without making any two cars exactly alike. Our objective is not only a car for every purse and purpose but, you might say, a car for every purse, purpose, and person."

At Ford's, where men felt little constraint in expressing their opinions, one vice-president ventured to say in the middle of the boom, "The amount of product innovation successfully introduced into the automobile is smaller today than in previous times and is still falling. The automatic transmission was the last major innovation of the industry."

To Detroit's delight, very few customers could bring themselves to forego all the trimming and buy a so-called "stripped" model, the cheapest, bereft of all extras. Seat belts continued to be available—at a price. In Ford's "Life Guard Design" package, they cost up to $35 plus a $15 installation charge, but more than 400,000 sets were sold. "No option ever caught on so fast," said McNamara, defensively. General Motors still shied away from promoting safety. When it finally fell into line, Chairman Frederick G. Donner, who followed Sloan at a salary of $750,000 a year, justified the decision to make protective features a buyer's choice: "It recognizes what I believe is the basic freedom of the customer to pay the cost of tailoring a car to his own specifications or rejecting whatever he may not want." Safety was put in the same category as white-wall tires.

One more option was always accessible—more horsepower

under the hood. Ford countered Chevrolet's 160-horsepower V-8 by beefing up its own motor to 162 horsepower, and the Big Three tournament to sell speed as an attraction grew more violent. Their engineers contrived to boost the power to be headlined in the advertising for each new model year. Two hundred horsepower, 300, 400—what did it matter if the massive engines burned so much gasoline that an owner was lucky to squeeze a dozen miles from a gallon when the stuff could be bought for around thirty cents?

Power was essential to the aura that the designers strove to have a car exude. This change in the market, the most dramatic since the demise of Lizzie, established them as wizards in the trade. They released their inhibitions and evolved what some Freudian analysts and their adherents in the marketing business recognized as hermaphroditic marvels, womblike in their floating comfort, penial in the forward thrust of hood and radiator grille against the horizon, as mammiferous as Barbarella with a pair of rubber-nippled cusps protruding from their front bumpers. The automobile as sex symbol, stirring unspeakable desire, was the stylists' ultimate conceit.

Sociologists detected a different subliminal appeal. Rolling along a highway with the windows shut, heater or air conditioner whirring, and the radio on, a man felt as good as any other, irrespective of his circumstances. So long as he kept pressing on down the road, poverty, sickness, and anxiety would not catch up with him. For an impressive number of Americans, driving was an addiction, a pain reliever as hard to give up as any habituating drug. Only when the motion stopped could reality intrude. If nothing more than a traffic light interrupted the reverie, the driver could scorch off again when red turned to green. If he had to pull into the driveway of a seedy home or park at the curb outside a run-down tenement that never in the world would look like the sunlit mansions in the automobile advertisements, the impact could be traumatic. The remedy was to get behind the wheel again and escape back into nirvana. Driving a car was a refuge of democracy in an age when the system itself seemed threatened by the launching of Soviet Sputniks and America's lagging behind in exploring the wonders of space. It was no miracle that those who could least afford it, and blacks more than whites, set such importance in having a car, new or old, and the bigger the better, because it heightened the sense of isolated security.

Bigger, faster automobiles spelled longer and longer tallies of death on the highways. Throughout the 1950s and 1960s, the annual count zigzagged upward until it peaked at 56,000. In the age group five to thirty, the car was the principal cause of death in the United States. As a killer at large among the entire population, it was surpassed only by diseases of the heart, cancer, and pneumonia. The first Congressional hearings into the situation were held in 1956, by which time the lives of 1,250,000 Americans had been shortened by the speeding wheels.

Henry, a pragmatist who was leery of long words and the men who used them, had stated his piece on the subject before them at a Dearborn "safety forum." "We are frankly very fond of the people who buy our products," he said. "We would very much like to keep them all alive and thriving." He was also eager to see Ford come closer to matching General Motors in marketing "a car for every purse and purpose." What was clearly called for was a medium-priced car to capture from GM a profitable share of the market between Mercury and Lincoln, where Ford had very little to offer in competition with Buick and Pontiac.

In a business as gladiatorial as automobile manufacturing, the success of a model for which he could claim responsibility was the making of a man's reputation as a manager. Failure shattered it, and he seldom had the chance to try again. Nobody at General Motors, for instance, ever wanted to be identified with the past downfall of its Marquettes, Vikings, and La Salles, but the climbing sales of the Pontiac Division, which he headed, would carry Big Bill Knudsen's son Semon to glory. At Ford's, when the car known as Edsel came to grief, only Henry was willing to say, "I'll take the fault for it, sure." Every other executive passed the buck.

The system of rule by committee that he had fostered made it certain that the Edsel was born by process of deliberation, not sired by a single individual. As early as May 1954, the executive committee approved plans to enter a new contestant into the struggle with GM. It would have its own plant and a fresh lineup of dealers. From its inception, it was referred to as "the Edsel" as a mark of esteem for a man who had always been enthusiastic about innovation—"the E car," for short.

The task of drawing up details for marketing the E car fell to one of the surviving Whiz Kids, Francis Reith, whose earlier assignment had been to work on company budgets. His report to the board of directors reiterated what they were already painfully aware of: "Too large a percentage of our business [resides] in one car and one price bracket"—the Ford accounted for 90 per cent of it. He recommended two types of the E, to do double duty, the lower-priced to be matched against Pontiac and Dodge, the higher-priced against De Soto, Oldsmobile, and Buick. The directors voted unanimously in favor of Reith's program, though Ernie Breech, who bore the new title of chairman now, claimed afterward that his inclination was to oppose it.

The first of the millions of wasted dollars began to trickle down the drain. The engineers prescribed an automatic transmission with pushbuttons set in the steering wheel, safety-rim wheels, self-adjusting brakes, and the biggest engine yet, 345 horsepower, to satisfy the advertising shoguns. The stylists came up with a distinctive body shell that embodied an orifice-shaped grille, which reminded some know-nothings of a horse collar. A national sampling was taken of likely customers, which produced some findings to fascinate the sexists:

"What happens when an owner sees his make as a car which a *woman* might buy but is himself a *man*? Does this apparent inconsistency of car image and the buyer's own characteristics affect his trading plans? The answer quite definitely is *Yes*. When there is a conflict over characteristics and make image, there is greater planning to switch to another make."

A prestigious Manhattan advertising agency, Foote, Cone & Belding, landed the account and, as part of its duties, drew up a list of 18,000 possible names for the new baby, to be tried out for popularity with the public by another team of researchers. Ford company executives gathered in a darkened room to see a slide-projector show of the nominations, so bedazzled that nobody stirred when "Buick" flashed onto the screen.

Henry was off on a Nassau vacation and both of his brothers were absent, too, when the four warmest choices were submitted to the executive committee early in 1956. Breech did not care much for "Pacer," "Ranger," "Corsair," or "Citation." He riffled through some of the rejects again. "Let's call it Edsel," he said.

When Henry took his telephone call, he agreed to abide by the group decision, provided he could get approval from Eleanor and the others. They accepted without enthusiasm.

The bills had shot up to $250,000,000 when the Edsel was introduced in September 1957, the most expensive launching of any commercial product in history. The cannonade of publicity was scheduled to sell a minimum of 200,000 Edsels within twelve months. It had little more effect than the firing of soddened squibs. Dealers and customers found a disastrous number of minor defects in need of fixing in the cars. *Consumer Reports* concluded after road testing, "The Edsel has no important basic advantages over other brands." Calm prevailed at General Motors.

The heir apparent of the Ford Motor Company, whose name sat on the horse-collar radiator grille, was too young to understand words like "corporate failure." He would be nine years old in December, almost ready to follow his father at the Detroit University School. Something else went without comment by the industry at large this year: For the first time in over half a century, more foreign cars were brought into the United States than American cars were shipped out for sale overseas.

The Edsel's span of life lasted for two years, two months, and fifteen days. While it existed, its sales totaled 109,466, it lost Ford a further $100,000,000, and company stock dropped twenty points, with dividends cut from $2.40 to $2.00. Imported cars captured almost 10 per cent of the American market, and the United States, due in large part to John Foster Dulles' playing brinksmanship with Communist China over the offshore islands of Quemoy and Matsu, entered a period of recession, when car buying faltered in spite of Detroit's united campaign with the slogan, "You auto buy now."

Henry, making no apologies, thought the Edsel's timing was wrong. "Hell, we headed into 1958 and right into a recession, and everything went kaput. . . . A lot of people didn't like the styling of the Edsel. We had a very weak dealer organization, and the car's quality wasn't anything to write home about. We couldn't sell them, we were losing money, so we made a decision, 'Let's quit,' which was the right decision, I'm sure. I'd rather admit the mistake, chop it off, and don't throw good money after bad."

The Edsel's obituary was written in November 1959. On December 21, Mrs. Henry Ford gave a coming-out party for her eighteen-year-old daughter Charlotte, whether the girl wanted it or not. Since nothing short of perfection would do, a Parisian designer, Jacques Frank, had been imported for an early start the previous April, along with the incoming flow of Peugeots and Renaults. Local society persuaded itself that the affair would be held at the Ford Museum, but Anne's choice was the Detroit Country Club, starting at 10 P.M. Invitations went out to 1,270 guests: to Mr. and Mrs. Gary Cooper in Hollywood; the Ernest Kanzlers; Lord Charles Spencer-Churchill, son of the Duke of Marlborough; William Talbert of Broadway and his wife; Igor Cassini, Hearst Newspaper columnist, and his lady; and Eleanor, of course. *Time, Life, Newsweek,* and *Harper's Bazaar* would also be welcome to send suitable representatives to watch the fun.

Meyer Davis and his men were engaged to play for as long as there were couples on the floor—he would arrive embellished with gold-and-diamond dress studs, a gift, he said, from the Duke of Windsor. To the mutterings of some displaced club members, five rooms were taken over for two weeks while Monsieur Jacques transformed them into a romantic semblance of an eighteenth-century French château, an undertaking that called for $60,000 worth of flowers alone.

Far too big a turnout of friends in New York, Boston, Philadelphia, and Palm Beach society was invited for Anne to put all of them up in the red-brick Georgian mansion with its thirty-five or so rooms that Henry had bought at Grosse Pointe Farms after he sold the wedding-present house. Eleanor's estate lay a short distance away along the shoreline of the lake. Their new home had been owned before by Roy Chapin, late president of the Hudson Motor Car Company. Anne had been so engrossed by the remodeling that she had a New York decorator stay with them for weeks soon after they moved in.

Henry had the art collector's enthusiasm of Edsel and Eleanor, especially French impressionists and postimpressionists; he had recently tidied up by commissioning Sotheby's of London to auction one Rembrandt, which brought $369,000. "I don't have a particularly large collection," he claimed, but it was of top quality, with masterworks by Matisse, Van Gogh, Degas, Gauguin, Manet, and "a Toulouse-Lautrec that doesn't look like a Toulouse-Lautrec," and it was large enough to give the foyer, where most of the paintings hung, the look of an upstairs gallery at the Louvre. He did not care much for the theater or for anything beyond jazz and "pop" in music. He rarely opened a book except something light to fill in time on a vacation, but he had the same trained eye as his parents for appreciating pigment on canvas.

Anne placed the overflow of guests in other friends' homes in Grosse Pointe and made amends as a hostess by having green orchids, about one hundred boxes of them, delivered to the ladies on the day of the debut. The caterers started early, trucking in 720 bottles of liquor and 480 Dom Perignon '49 champagne; 600 orders of chicken; 280 pounds of bacon; 5,000 finger sandwiches; 2,160 eggs for scrambling; and the makings for 100 pounds of corned beef hash and 2,000 pancakes.

The first arrivals at the mock Louis Quinze château noticed half a dozen sturdy males in matching dinner jackets and tartan bow ties—security police in hired finery, ready to mingle. Later in the evening, Henry spotted a young Grosse Pointer who had rented a more impressive outfit: buckled shoes, silk knee breeches, and long satin coat, as worn at Louis' court. "Mack the Knife!" Henry whispered at the schoolboy son at his side. Two gate crashers who turned up in a ten-year-old jalopy escaped detection, though their tuxedos were Salvation Army hand-me-downs, picked up for $5.00 apiece.

Just back from a spell of schooling in Florence, Italy, Charlotte stood wearing Christian Dior white satin in the receiving line with her father and mother, looking nowhere near as composed as Anne in her splendor. Henry handled the introducing of the big wheels within the industry whose names his daughter had scarcely heard before: "Meet Mr. and Mrs. Gordon—they're our competitors." On the parking lots outside, two dozen attendants struggled with chaos, compounded by the cars that some guests, held up in traffic jams that blocked every approach road, simply abandoned.

Meyer Davis, dress studs sparkling, struck up "The Most Beautiful Girl in the World," and Henry took a turn around the floor with Charlotte before he was tapped on the shoulder by one of her eighteen ushers, each presented with a commemorative gold medallion engraved with her initials. One dowager in the throng harked back to the old days as a blue haze floated up toward the flower-layered ceiling: "Henry Ford wouldn't have liked all this smoking." It was unlikely, either, that he would have approved spending $250,000 on what Cassini in his next "Cholly Knicker-bocker" column felt must be described as "the party of the cen-tury," which included the services of Charlotte's choice as star per-former, Nat "King" Cole.

Eleanor lasted until 2 A.M. before she retired, eyes still shining. The band had obliged Henry with one of his favorites, "It's Only a Paper Moon," and was due to follow up with another, "Hey, Ba-Ba-Re-Bop," which he personally conducted before he sprang onto the floor, chanting and clapping in a display of heels-in-the-air jit-terbugging with Anne, not a strand of whose coiffure was dis-placed in the frolic.

"Henry," she observed shortly afterward, "I think it's about time." It was then twenty minutes after six. Charlotte was still dancing in the crowd of a hundred other couples. As on in-numerable other mornings when the sky turned bright, Meyer Davis and his men signed off with "Auld Lang Syne" and "Good Night, Ladies." Breakfast was about to be served by waiters in Christmas-red mess jackets. "It's a good thing I don't have five daughters," said Henry. "I'd go broke."

His sense of humor stayed alive when newspaper and magazine stories pointed up Charlotte's party as proof of what half Amer-ica imagined about him—that he was an overgrown playboy, a child of fortune who had inherited, as Bennett said in his day, "a billion-dollar organization that you haven't contributed a thing to."

Mulling over the press clippings with some of his public-rela-tions staff, Henry said straight-faced, "Well, there's only one way to prevent stories like this." They waited expectantly, anxious to give effect to his wishes. "Not have any parties like this," he smiled. The playboy reputation did not bother him. Growing in number as the foundation sold batches of new shares at prices that fluctuated between $56.50 and $82, stockholders and public alike could judge him by what he achieved. "I can't do any-thing about it," he explained on another occasion, "so I might as well relax and enjoy it."

He felt no more guilt about owning a 187-ton yacht, built to order at De Haag in the Netherlands, than in treating himself to a night on the town. The *Santa Maria*, with crew of seven and accommodation for six passengers, was more seaworthy than Grandfather's *Sialia*, less ornately fitted than Father's *Onika*. Paying $700,000 for the *Santa Maria* was no strain. She was useful for cruising the Mediterranean as fellow millionaires like Ari Onassis and Stavros Niarchos did. There was not much Henry liked better than a few days at sea, laughing over a good joke, soaking up gossip and sunshine. Uncle Ernest, who added an apartment in Paris to his other homes, sometimes showed up on the passenger list.

Henry was establishing close ties with a broad range of people in Europe, from statesmen like France's Georges Pompidou to celestial bodies such as Gina Lollobrigida and subsonic aristocrats like Spain's Prince Carlos-Hugo de Bourbon, whom Franco installed as the King. "I've had a tremendous number of advantages in my life," Henry commented, "and one of them is the fact that I guess I've met just about everybody." His brothers and sister saw less of him than his friends.

On his travels for pleasure or profit overseas, he tried to slough off the ostentation that most people felt was his due when he came into contact with them. He preferred to stroll around the streets of Rome, Paris, or London as unobtrusively as could be managed, especially London, which impressed him so much that he was to buy a town house there. One of the several reasons for his trips to Europe was the need to keep up to date on manufacturing overseas.

"The best thing that has happened in this business in years, I think," he told Ford dealers at Dearborn when they got their first look at 1960 models, "was the invasion of our market by small European cars. The jolt of it blew through our industry like a fresh breeze, forced us to look for new directions and new guide signs at a time when we felt we had just about run out of good new things to do with automobiles."

The company had a good thing of its own to celebrate in the first compact offered for sale by the Big Three. The Falcon was the godchild of Bob McNamara, a vice-president nowadays and general manager of the Ford Division, a man of ice-cold brain with sheaves of documents to support his contention that logic demanded adding to Ford's range a low-priced, six-cylinder car to appeal to customers who were fed up with tail-finned gas guzzlers.

Falcon's record-breaking sales of 417,174 in its debut season helped Ford's overtake Chevrolet and qualified McNamara as a management hero. The only flaw in the performance was that profit margins on such basic transportation were slim. Ford's needed fat profits to make up for its monumental losses on the Edsel.

The competitors over on the boulevard had been busy developing a compact, too, after reaching similar conclusions as McNamara. This time, there was no copycatting at Dearborn. Chevrolet's Corvair was unique in a number of ways. The block of its air-cooled engine, with origins in Kettering's copper-finned disaster, could be made of aluminum, cheaply and efficiently. Placement of this motor over the rear wheels was a novelty that called for an ingenious suspension system.

Ford and Chevrolet were equally eager to see what the other had come up with, so a swap was arranged, five Falcons for five Corvairs. The simple exchange contained the seeds of a consumer revolution that was to grow like Jack's beanstalk. The Corvairs were taken out for trial on the test track that old Henry had finally consented to build on his airfield, along with some extra models bought through Chevrolet dealers. The results astounded the test drivers.

As Harley Copp, Ford engineer responsible for the 1960 Falcon, reported, "Three Corvairs rolled over during our earlier, customer-type evaluations. None were rolled due to abusive driving, none were considered driver error, and all came as a surprise to the drivers and passengers." Movie film recorded what had happened: Under some turn conditions when tire pressures were out of balance, the Corvair's independently sprung rear wheels folded under the chassis, robbing the driver of all control. However, an independent analysis of the film stated that the drivers of the Corvairs made "unnecessary steering input which caused the vehicle to skid off the road" and the behavior of the Corvairs in the film was not consistent with other test results.

When whispers about the Corvair's inbuilt hazard spread and the first liability suits were filed against Chevrolet, Copp wrote a personal letter (twelve years after the tests) to Senator Warren Magnuson, chairman of the Senate Commerce Committee, underlining the fact that the Falcon was immune to this particular peril.

But this Ford man had stepped out of line in an industry that set its own code of conduct and chose to keep secrets to itself. By the account of some Dearborn staff, Henry telephoned James Roche, president of General Motors in the latest round of changes, to emphasize that Copp had acted without his superiors' knowledge and certainly not with their approval. "Beat Chevrolet!" was Henry's goal, but it must be done according to rule.

Most of his colleagues treated Copp like a case of chicken pox. "Harley's gone off his rocker" was a standard reaction. "You're rocking the boat" was another. Unidentified callers started harassing him with calls to his house. He suspected that he was watched from cars on the prowl outside. "Right now," he was told by one company executive, "it looks as though GM is wearing the black hat and Ford is wearing the white hat. But Harley, you do the sort of thing you've done, and before you know it, both companies could be wearing black hats."

Fred Hooven, who left General Motors to become a senior engineer to the Ford Division, waited until he had retired to say his piece: "I know why the decision was made to keep quiet about the Corvair. Everybody knew the truth would get lost. And Ford's credibility would be challenged, and that would institute an era of dirty advertising and dirty PR, and Ford said, in effect, 'We're in no shape to tell the truth about this.'"

If the word was passed around to ignore a rival automobile's deficiencies, it was Henry's doing. The same silence continued when Chevrolet jazzed up the car with bucket seats, racing colors, and automatic transmission in the likeness of a sports model, then labeled it the Monza. An instant jump in sales convinced General Motors that the public had not lost its taste for big-car style and expensive options. At Ford, the point was taken. The Falcon's girth began to swell and its length extend. The consumer-movement beanstalk started to sprout.

Though Breech still held the chair, Henry was asserting himself increasingly in the board room. Henry would brief himself in advance by having the key points of every subject on the agenda typed on a batch of 3″-by-5″ file cards, but he did not confine himself to these. He had a technique of prodding impatiently for more facts, relying on a retentive memory to toss out questions that caught Ernie and the rest off guard. He foiled yes-men by hinting that he favored a particular position before reversing himself completely. Unless there were opposition opinions, he was disappointed, but any man who argued with him had to be adept in self-defense. Henry, said one executive, "loves a good scrap."

Chairman Breech was flattered by the praise lavished on him in public and private by Henry, but he could not bring himself to quash the proprietor of the business, who was not fond of being bossed in the office or at home. "This is what I'm going to do," he would say at the close of an executive go-around, and that was that. Jack Davis scented what was coming when the question of Francis Reith's future arose following the Edsel fiasco. Davis thought that Breech could resolve the situation and hold onto Reith, and he went to the chairman to say so. Then Henry called Davis in to say, "Why did you go see Breech about Reith? Come to me when you've got a problem." Reith was allowed to depart.

Though Ernie denied it in obedience with the law of discretion that says that board room disputes in every corporation concern nobody but the participants, the business world believed that the break came when he and Henry could not agree on the styling for Ford's 1962 models. Breech saw more and more of Grandfather emerging in Henry's nature. "Henry doesn't need me any more," he said when he resigned on July 13, 1960, protesting that this fitted in with his retirement timetable, anyway. He promptly moved into Trans World Airlines and engaged Earl Newsom, no longer retained by Henry, as counselor in public relations.

Henry, Breech rationalized, "had an innate curiosity and desire to learn, and he worked hard at it. He was there early every morning. He just did it the hard way, learning by sitting in meetings, listening." Ford said that he had not wished to lose his chairman. He asked him to stay on and, when he declined, made Ernie head of the finance committee, with an office in the plant. Henry kept his respect for the little man whom Detroit credited with being the principal physician in the Ford Motor Company's recovery from terminal paralysis. Henry came close to tears at a testimonial dinner for him, and he named a new Great Lakes freighter the *Ernest R. Breech*. He also took over the title of chairman as well as president and chief executive officer until he could find a suitable right-hand man to succeed Ernie.

At the time of parting, Henry had other things on his mind besides the company's well-being. He was fascinated by an Italian charmer of the Lollobrigida marque whom Uncle Ernest brought in from Milan for a party he was giving in Maxim's, Paris. When Henry was briefly introduced to her the previous evening, he asked if they might be seated side by side at the restaurant table.

Maria Cristina Vettore Austin was a genuine exotic: bronze skin, green eyes, warm voice, and as sparkling as spumante wine. She was a doctor's daughter, convent trained, and onetime art student before she was married to Lieutenant William Austin of the Royal Navy. She had been a fashion model and, after her 1955 divorce, an aspiring movie actress, though a New York screen test in the same year carried her ambition no farther than that.

William Austin went to live in Canada; she had no children and fewer inhibitions than a skylark. As for Henry—"When I met him, he was like a lion, full of enthusiasm," she related. His first gift was a small diamond heart on a platinum chain. They hoped to keep their meetings secret and out of range of the cameras of the *paparazzi*. The *Santa Maria* served them well. Cristina would stretch out on deck, toasting her body in the Mediterranean sun until she twitched with convulsions. They laughed together and sometimes at each other. "I never ask him to marry me," she said. "All I want is to be happy."

Henry was sorely troubled with himself. He felt compelled to assess his share of guilt in the decay of his marriage. He wanted to stay close to the children—Charlotte, studying at the Sorbonne; Anne, in school at Briarcliff; and Edsel, who would shortly enter Hotchkiss, as his father had. Henry drove him there in a new-model Ford, then switched to another car with an automatic transmission "and damn near had four accidents on the way back to New York," he recalled.

And the interests of the company he headed could not be minimized. To the world in general, he *was* Ford's. Scandal might boomerang, damaging sales and share values simultaneously. No one could possibly calculate the cost in cash or emotion of the relationship with Cristina. One man he confided in was Max Fisher of Detroit, an admiring friend to Eleanor, a Jew, a philanthropist, and longtime adviser to the government of Israel, who told him, in effect: "Self-reproach will gain you nothing. Find inner security first, and it will open the way to happiness."

No hint of family upset ruffled the surface when Eleanor opened her house for a reception for granddaughter Anne in November, though the act itself could be interpreted as a gesture of reassurance for a shy girl soon to be subjected to stress. Lilies and white lilac imported from the Netherlands predominated among the flowers. The music of Lester Lanin's trio was as sedate as Eleanor's Mainbocher gown. Detroit's finest were met by the butler under the gaze of the Franz Hals portrait in the red-curtained entrance hall before they filed in to shake hands in the caladon-green French drawing room with its long windows overlooking the lake. Then they might filter, if they chose, along the corridor to inspect the paintings in the vaulted gallery until it was time to visit the dining room—more flowers, of course; Waterford candelabra; and Grindling Gibbons carving around the fireplace mantel.

That was the month when McNamara was elevated to the presidency of the company. Like everyone else in the topmost councils, Henry had found the logic of this academic with the gleaming, rimless spectacles to be unarguable. "Even when you knew he was wrong," one ranking committeeman said, "he'd plow you under." McNamara would provide the same salutary counterbalance as Breech to Henry's spells of impetuousness. As well as salary, McNamara was given options on 30,000 shares at $33.

To fill his place at the Ford Division, Henry called Lee Iacocca over to his office. "How would you like to be vice-president and general manager?" At thirty-six, Iacocca had been disappointed in the delay for the past year. He had proven himself a resourceful infighter, as different from McNamara as a rocket from a slide rule. "I was surprised as hell," Iacocca reported afterward, but he promptly went downstairs and drove back to the Ford Division to present himself as its new boss.

He realized there was a mountain of work to do to grow up into the job, but he put his personal stamp on the operation from the beginning. "I told a few people, 'Get with it. You're being observed. Guys who don't get with it don't play on the club after a while.' It worked, because all of a sudden a guy is face to face with the reality of his mortgage payments."

McNamara lasted five weeks. The young man from Brookline, Massachusetts, who had just won a razor-edge victory over Richard Nixon to be elected the thirty-fifth President of the United

States, wanted McNamara in his Cabinet, even if he was a registered Republican who had backed Nixon. John F. Kennedy sent his brother-in-law, Sargent Shriver, out as his recruiting agent. A Sunday-night telephone call to his home brought the news to Henry, who had also voted Republican.

"Sarge came right to the point," he said. "He offered McNamara the job of Secretary of the Treasury in the new Administration. He turned it down, but Shriver wasn't the least bit taken aback. In the next breath, he offered him the Defense Department. I don't think McNamara's answer took too much soul-searching." Kennedy's Defense Secretary drew $25,000 in salary to conduct the $50-billion-a-year business, compared with $159,245 plus those stock options and a supplementary $375,000 stretched over four annual installments at Ford's.

As soon as he was gone, the backbiting set in, a tribal custom in the city that was close to being recognized as Motown, pulsing with black music and black unrest. He had been "a bean counter" in his insistency on cost accounting, whereas "Iacocca has shown he not only can count beans, he can put pizazz in, too." McNamara "wore granny glasses and produced a granny car," jeered a writer in a trade magazine. One senior Ford employee embellished that theme: "You had a Falcon that only had a six. You had big Fords that were sleds. Unbelievable. The kids just didn't respond. No performance, no four-speed transmissions, nothing that made the cars really swing."

Iacocca waited awhile before he chimed in. "I learned from McNamara that if we have to make a choice, make sure we have sufficient alternatives. McNamara was always operating with grocery sheets. He wanted twelve alternatives, even on a simple problem. Hell, that takes time and a lot of paper. All I ask for is A, B, and C. McNamara wouldn't do a damn thing unless he had all the facts, and that's important. But more important is how to interpret these facts." Nothing so outspoken could ever be heard at General Motors, where management changes were normally effected as sedately as Trappists glide to Mass.

Playing with a big Ignacio Haya cigar, Iacocca gathered about a dozen of his get-with-it people together for quiet weekly meetings in a Dearborn motel whose name rubbed off on them—"the Fairlane Group." Their aim was to chart a course for the division by analyzing census figures, population statistics, and market projections. One salient truth came into immediate view. The wartime surge in the birthrate would result in a bumper crop of teen-age drivers in these 1960s. Lee's self-professed gut feel told him what they would be seeking in a car: horsepower, excitement, gratification of ego. In a word, pizazz, and as much of it as they could afford.

His prescription was the Mustang, with taut lines, snappy acceleration, a stripped price of under $2,400, but sold with upward of fifty options to boost the profits and disguise it as a European-class car or a hot rod, as the customer wished. He met with hostility at most committee levels. The Edsel experience still hurt, and dollars in the tens of millions would have to be risked again. But persistence was something Lee had taught himself in high school in Allentown, Pennsylvania, when he had to make up for seven months lost in an attack of rheumatic fever.

When clay models were ready for inspection, Iacocca invited Henry to a preview. Ford was suffering the symptoms of a cold that day, the onset of mononucleosis, which was widely believed to be a disease exchanged in the main between romantic teenagers until medical opinion proved otherwise. He glanced at Iacocca's offering and growled, "I damn well know what you're trying to do—ram the goddamn car down my throat." He walked away. As soon as he felt fit again, he was prepared to reconsider. "We had lots of discussions about it," he said. "Chevy had two products, Corvair and Chevy II, and we sat there with the Falcon." This was the crux of it. "So hell, I said, if they've got two, we're going to have two, or we are never going to be able to compete with them."

He was just shaking off his lassitude when young Anne's turn for a debut came up, like it or not, priced the same as Charlotte's at $250,000. Their mother again summoned Jacques Frank, who turned for inspiration to the Doges and transformed the grounds of the Fords' lakeside mansion into a fairy-tale Venezia with a dance pavilion, two summer houses, and 50,000 red and white roses, planted overnight by a squad of University of Michigan football players. Gondolas were not included, which turned out to be an oversight. The rain teemed down on this June night and the waiters scurried to and fro under umbrellas, serving a fancier menu than before, encompassing Maine lobster Newburg, pâté de foie gras, and strawberries glacé with Bavarian cream. Cars bogged down in the mud caused a three-hour traffic jam.

Meyer Davis was back, with a song composed for the occasion, "Anne—You're the Only Girl." She designed her own dress of white silk organza, and a coiffeur was flown in from New York to style her hair and her mother's, prompting a standard comment from some of the guests: Didn't Anne and her eighteen-year-old daughter look *exactly* like sisters? Henry was more subdued than usual, which they attributed to the after-effects of mononucleosis. His only outburst came when the chattering persisted after Ella Fitzgerald began her first song.

"Damn it, shut up!" he bellowed, then after a pause, "Now I'm going to catch hell from my wife."

Eleanor, in a silk chiffon confection of orange, yellow, green, and blue, remarked serenely of her granddaughter, "She must be tired of smiling so much." That she could smile at all was surprising. Henry had told her the night before that his marriage was breaking up.

The details were dealt with as charily as anything ever attempted in three generations of the family. Lawyers for each side hashed over the terms for a separation. Mrs. Ford would move to New York, into a co-operative apartment occupying the third and fourth floors at 834 Fifth Avenue, taking Charlotte and Anne with her. Each of them would enjoy a bedroom and private bath (rose-colored for herself, eggshell for Charlotte, yellow for Anne) opening off the long hallway. Mrs. Ford was to discover a little additional satisfaction in being exalted as a permanent adornment to the legendary Fashion Hall of Fame, along with Britain's Queen Elizabeth and the Duchess of Windsor. Young Edsel was to remain at Hotchkiss. Except for the servants, Henry was left alone in Grosse Pointe Farms.

He quieted the rumors that had floated into Italian, French, and some American newspapers by calling a temporary halt to his meetings with Cristina. His brothers saw somewhat more of him. He dined with them occasionally, and with intimates on the company staff, at the venerable Yondetega Club on East Jefferson Avenue, "the finest men's club in America" in the judgment of Theodore Roosevelt. If he was at home on Thursdays, cook's day off, he prepared his own dinner, hamburgers and tomato ketchup as often as not. The food served in the company's penthouse dining room was considerably superior. His weight and his intake of scotch increased to a degree, and he worked harder than ever.

While he was losing a wife, he was adding properties to the Ford domain at a pace worthy of Alexander the Great, King of Macedonia—half-a-billion dollars' worth in a year. Henry believed implicitly in corporate gigantism. "The only thing I see wrong with size is when you're afraid to do things because you're big." He had not been afraid in the lame-duck months of Eisenhower's final term to persevere in buying total control of the Ford Motor Company, Limited, of Dagenham, England, for $368,100,000 in spite of the uproar it stirred in Britain's House of Commons and contrary to Ike's appeals to American business to stem the overseas flow of gold from the United States Treasury.

Now Henry prevailed on the board to acquire two more fiefs. For $28,200,000, Ford's obtained a majority holding in Electric Autolite. His fellow directors did not balk; Autolite spark plugs and batteries were profitable items for selling through gas stations and repair shops. The board and senior management also went along with the $100,000,000 exchange of shares that bought Philco. Henry had to be firm about that: "You can't run a company by taking votes."

The electronics firm, manufacturing everything from cheap radios and television sets to hardware for earth-orbiting satellites, had lost money for years. Some market analysts thought that Ford paid at least twice what it was worth. Henry, however, was intrigued by the potentials of the space age, as if turning his back on his previous domestic life had opened his eyes to a more expansive future for himself and for the company. The National Aeronautics and Space Administration had been in existence for three years. Despite its weaknesses, he wanted Philco because it was involved in exciting new technologies in space and defense work, in which Ford's up to this time had been relatively insignificant.

Ten years passed before Henry could report to shareholders that Philco-Ford Corporation had made an operating profit. During the interval, he told them without hesitation that the business was "a can of worms." Privately, he saw the big problem to be getting Ford and Philco people to talk the same language. The

Philco lot "are pretty high-flying characters. We work on internal communications constantly so we can get the benefit of their thinking on basic, earthly modes of transportation, not just on flying to the moon."

He neither conceded error in the acquisition nor pretended to be infallible. "As long as we're 51 per cent right, I guess we are ahead" was a characteristic way of putting it. Yet Ford's quarterly dividends steadily progressed in the unique climate he established as a corporate leader, nagging, self-appraising, boundlessly aggressive, and immensely proud of the profits.

He applied two major principles in developing men: Keep them on the move, and let young rebels and old conservatives compete against each other. "A company needs to be constantly rejuvenated by the infusion of young blood," he maintained. "It needs smart young men with the imagination and the guts to turn everything upside down if they can. It also needs old fogies to keep them from turning upside down those things that ought to be right side up."

The pendulum swept to the "old fogie" sector in the next choice for president, sixty-three-year-old John Dykstra, a veteran of the Hudson Motor Company and Oldsmobile, recruited as Ford production manager fourteen years earlier. He campaigned hard to have his term stretched after he reached sixty-five, but by then the pendulum had taken another swing. He went into reluctant retirement, as prescribed by the rules that Henry was unwilling to bend, to make way for a younger man, Arjay Miller. Three presidents in as many years—Detroiters speculated on whether this mild-mannered ex-lecturer was tough enough to last very long as second in command.

One level down, Iacocca was doing what he could to give the Falcon some instant pizazz—putting in a big V-8 engine and bucket seats, introducing a convertible—while his Mustang was gestated. Automakers figured on three years as the average time that elapsed between first pencil sketches and a car's going on display, and this was the schedule here. The dimensions of the new arrival were calculated and recalculated to fractions of an inch, cost estimates worked out to a fourth and fifth decimal point. "The difference of $.02 per car doesn't sound very much," one industry comptroller acknowledged, "but at current production rates, $.02 a car may mean $10,000 for the model run."

Maximum profit was the ineluctable goal. "There is no such thing as planning for a minimal return," Henry explained to one business audience. "You can't plan to do less than the best you can imagine—not if you want to survive in a competitive market. It's like asking a professional football team to win by only one point—a sure formula for losing."

In the meantime, Iacocca was spinning webs to catch the youth market. "The postwar babies are coming of age," he emphasized. "These kids are our biggest customers." He nudged the company into sponsoring campus hootenannies. Advertisements for souped-up Fords filled pages of hot-rod magazines. And he rekindled Henry's enthusiasm for automobile racing. Protests in Congress about advertising emphasis on speed had led the manufacturers' association to soft-pedal the theme and father a gentlemen's agreement among its members to stay away from racing.

"I withdrew from that agreement," Henry said. "There were just too many breaks of faith to live with it." Pontiac's performance was the sorest point. By making speed the big attraction, Semon Knudsen was happily kiting his cars' sales up to third place in the total market.

John Bugas, who had four more years left as vice-president in charge of international operations, thought, "Racing got us out of the old-maid class." It brought Ford ten consecutive stock-car victories, wins at Sebring, the "Indy 500" engine that proved itself around the concrete at Indianapolis, and a world record when a Mercury-Comet covered 100,000 miles at Daytona at better than 100 miles an hour. It also gave young Edsel a future trip with his father and Cristina to Le Mans to see the racers' triumph there—and it piled up criticism of Henry from the growing group of citizens who were less than satisfied that he had the cause of road safety at heart, even if he was spending $1,000,000 a year on research and development of what one insurance company somberly called "survival cars."

He suffered another kind of scolding in August 1963, when the announcement was finally made that he and Anne had separated. The Christmas before, he had given her $62,000 in diamonds as a good-will offering, which was not exceptional, coming from a man

who would write a $100,000 check for a cause that attracted him,
like Max Fisher's United Jewish Appeal. Generosity also dictated
the settlement when Anne was granted an uncontested divorce in
Fairfield, Idaho, half a year later on the conventional grounds of
"mental anguish." The details were kept private, but she was re-
portedly to receive something between $16,000,000 and $18,-
000,000.

Within two months, domestic pangs were eased when roughly
4,000,000 people flocked into Ford showrooms to admire what
Iacocca had wrought. The ambition he would admit to himself
was to sell 417,175 Mustangs this first season—one more than
McNamara's Falcon. In some experts' opinion, it *was* a hoked-up
Falcon with mediocre brakes, indifferent handling—and marvelous
promotion. *Road Test* magazine jeered that it "abounds with new
and startling engineering features carried over from 1910." But, no
doubt about it, it had pizazz aplenty.

"We sold 50,000 more of them in their first three or four
months of production than all the Edsels we sold in 2½ years,"
said Henry contentedly. "That's the greatest acceptance any new
car ever had, with the exception of the Model A." Iacocca's wish
was granted: Mustang topped Falcon by 625. This was 1964,
when the carmakers spent $361,000,000 on advertising and 47,700
people died on the roads.

The winter was almost over when Henry, forty-six, and Cristina,
thirty-seven, were married in the company suite at a Washington,
D.C., hotel with the legal minimum of people in attendance, one
judge and two witnesses. The bridegroom, automatically excommunicated, shied away from discussing Catholicism or any other
religion thereafter. The two of them flew straight to London,
where Henry telephoned his daughters, inviting them to join him
and their new stepmother on their honeymoon at the Christmas
Palace Hotel in St. Moritz, a sanctuary for the high-flying rich.

The novelty of that impressed both girls. They anticipated
being something akin to wallflowers, but they flew there, anyway.
The choice of a Swiss ski resort during the peak February season
could only have been Cristina's. Henry was not to be seen on the
slopes. He was "not very good on the boards," said a friend. In the
hotel lobby, bulky in black stretch pants and sweaters, he was

accosted by one visitor who identified himself as "your dealer from Dayton." After a polite "hello," the bridegroom departed.

Charlotte and Anne soon put themselves in the category of those who really were fond of Cristina. She was as relaxed as an afternoon at Acapulco: "I have no personal ambition. I am content to be Henry's wife." Both girls had more self-assertiveness in them than that. Anne, the quieter of the two, was just now emerging from behind the grillwork of her upbringing, wondering if she might be in love with a dark young man she had met at a tree-trimming party last Christmas. Charlotte was farther advanced in her desire to discover herself. She'd had dates before, notably with actor George Hamilton and a New York *Times* copy boy, and she had an eldest child's skepticism about the abilities of the youngest. If she had been a boy, she fancied nobody would have questioned whether she was smarter than her brother.

She and Anne agreed that their stay in Switzerland was one of the best times they ever had with their father. One mission Cristina set for herself was to make Henry feel wanted; she would rather listen than rattle on talking gossip and fashion to him. She could not understand independence in a woman. The only improvements she would like to see would be for him to lose some weight and cut down on his smoking.

She had an old-fashioned *signora's* view of a wife's duties. "A feminine woman collaborates with her man," she once said, "tries to help him and be comfortable with him, to relax him and do all the things a man needs. When I am with my man, I like to be affectionate and cuddly." Women's liberation was a concept incomprehensible to her.

Possibly Charlotte felt something of her father's sense of liberation and tried to model her behavior on his. Stavros Niarchos, who came into view in St. Moritz as the irresistible love of her life, was eight years older than Henry, three times married, with four children by his present wife, born Eugenia Livanos, of another family of Greek shipping magnates. The tanker fleet owned by the stumpy, tense-faced Niarchos had made him richer by far than Henry, with a fortune bordering on $350,000,000, largely earned from shipping the oil which, cracked into gasoline, was an automobile's lifeblood. He was a Mediterranean yachtsman like Henry, but the *Santa Maria* was left in the shade by the 190-foot schooner *Creole*, with thirty in crew and $2,000,000 worth of paintings hanging on the stateroom walls.

That summer, when the schooner and her father's yacht both cruised the Mediterranean, Charlotte saw more of the *Creole* and its owner. She was tall, blond, blue-eyed, and, above all, *young*, and she convinced herself that she loved him. The courtship in which Anne was involved with her tree-trimming friend seemed to be considerably less hazardous. Gian-Carlo Uzielli, a Florentine expatriate known as Johnny, made a much more obvious choice for a girl than Niarchos. Like Anne, he was a Catholic, but excommunicated when his first marriage, to a French actress named Anne Marie Deschodt, ended in divorce. His mother was a distant relative of the Rothschilds, a Jewess. He was a Harvard graduate, gregarious, and, at thirty-one, showing promise as a stockbroker with Tucker, Anthony, & R. L. Day of Wall Street. Few of his qualifications would have appealed to old Henry, but Henry II raised no objections to the choice of either of his daughters.

"Whatever Anne wants is fine with me," he said when Johnny, her first romance, went in trepidation to be inspected at Henry's penthouse suite in the Regency Hotel, New York. Much the same held true for Charlotte.

Charlotte was due to serve as her sister's maid of honor at her marriage three days after Christmas, but a more urgent matter had to be settled two weeks in advance of the date. Henry made a night flight to New York City in response to a telepone call from his daughter Anne. After hearing what the two girls had to tell him in their apartment, he made a snap decision. The next morning, all three of them flew to London to talk with Mr. and Mrs. Niarchos. By chance, the first Mrs. Ford was there, too.

On December 15, Eugenia divorced Stavros. On December 16, he and Charlotte were married in the best motel in Juarez, Mexico, by which time he had presented her with a thirty-three-carat diamond. Henry sent a company plane to fly them to Nassau, but that was only a way station, where Niarchos paid $40,000 to charter a Boeing 707 to carry him and his bride to Zurich. A Lear jet completed the last leg of the journey to St. Moritz, and a limousine brought them to the Christmas Palace Hotel. There was a further touch of sentiment. Eugenia and two of his children by her joined Stavros and Charlotte on their honeymoon.

On December 27, the first Mrs. Ford and the second Mrs. Ford were both the essence of their respective kinds of grace at Anne's eve-of-wedding party, though the invitations went out in the names of Henry and his first wife to five hundred guests, comprising such standbys of New York's society pages as Mrs. Albert Lasker, cartoonist Charles Addams, Truman Capote, and William Paley of the Columbia Broadcasting System and his wife. The latest Mrs. Niarchos stayed on in St. Moritz. Apart from her absence, the evening in the Crystal Room of the Hotel Delmonico held little spice for the gossip columns: a hundred magnums of Piper-Heidsieck; music to frug by from The Wild Ones and gentler beats from Emory Davis, son of Meyer, and his orchestra; a bill estimated at a trifling $30,000; and Henry dancing with Cristina and both the Annes in turn. He was still at it when his daughter and Johnny left at 3 A.M.

Later that day, two Ford station wagons waited outside the apartment at 834 Fifth Avenue to carry the luggage of the couple who were to be married there. In a swallow-tail coat, Henry arrived by taxi to give the bride away. Young man and wife were driven off in a chauffeured Lincoln with a built-in television set to beguile them on this first step toward their honeymoon in Acapulco.

Had Henry been in a reflective mood on New Year's Eve, he would have to assess the past year as distinctly spotty. He was more comfortable in his new marriage, and Cristina was wholly convincing when she said, "I do not miss having children." Anne had some growing up to do. How happy Charlotte was going to be remained to be seen.

So far as the business was concerned, it was booming, along with the rest of the industry, which built 9,305,561 passenger cars worth well over $18 billion this year. Something like 100,000,000 vehicles of all kinds moved along the highways, and customers were far more willing to borrow money for buying them—over $28 billion in twelve months—than for any other purpose. Henry was slowly increasing the depth in management strength that he saw as essential to compete with that very model of efficiency, General Motors.

Automaking now was a $25 billion phenomenon, accounting for $1.00 in every $5.00 spent. Ten million people worked at it, and its own shopping list made it a bellwether of American prosperity: more than 20 per cent of all the steel; 46 per cent of the lead; more than 60 per cent of the synthetic rubber, and about the same share of upholstery leather produced in the country. The fallout from gasoline engine exhausts was staggering, too: Burning 100 billion gallons produced 14 million tons of polluting hydrocarbons and 75 million tons of carbon monoxide a year.

The government refused to leave Detroit alone to maximize its profits. Controls were growing tighter. Sterner standards were being set to decrease pollution and driver hazards—needlessly so, in Henry's judgment, when Ford's was offering as much protection as customers wanted. "We can build a tank," he held. "If you want to ride around in a tank, you won't get hurt. You won't be able to afford one, though. Neither will I."

In the past spring, doctors picketed the New York International Auto Show to protest how little Washington was doing to reduce highway death, but another dark young man, this one a lawyer of Lebanese heritage, irked Henry more than any demonstrators. In 1965, Ralph Nader's *Unsafe at Any Speed* was published, and Henry knew on which side that belonged in the ledger for the past twelve months.

Chapter Thirteen

The Patriarch

The commotion caused by Ralph Nader and his instantaneous best seller was as welcome to Detroit as a four-tire blowout. In Henry's opinion, the somber-eyed attorney, who worked without pay for a Senate investigation into the subject, knew very little about cars when he laid the blame for 50,000 and more annual highway deaths squarely on their design, their speed, and their makers' resistance to doing anything about either. Henry took it upon himself to barbecue this critic. Nader didn't think some rear axles were well engineered? "Well, I say we've got jobs for rear-axle engineers, and if he is that good, we'll be happy to give him a job."

Henry kept up the roasting for years. Nader "was just one of those happenstances that needn't have happened. If this industry of ours had been on its feet instead of on its ass, Nader would never have surfaced." Long after the initial tremor, Henry was saying of the safety campaigners' first national idol, "He's full of crap."

He let it go at that, with no thought in this instance of copying General Motors and hiring private detectives to shadow Nader in the wan hope of uncovering secrets in his personal life with which to discredit him. GM president James Roche was summoned before Senator Abraham Ribicoff's Senate subcommittee to eat crow for that. John Bugas, on the other hand, could testify that Ford's "has not been, nor is it now, directly or indirectly involved in any alleged investigation or harassment of Mr. Nader."

Henry, an apostle of free enterprise, heaped more coal on his fire. "I don't expect that everybody will love the businessman," he told a Detroit gathering. "I don't expect business to be immune from investigation, criticism, and regulation. Like everyone else, businessmen are often selfish, shortsighted, and irresponsible and need to be called to account. Nevertheless, after the experience of the past few years, I should have thought that the connection between the pursuit of profit and the public welfare would be somewhat better recognized than it often seems to be. And I should have thought that fewer people would still be building careers by casting themselves as St. George slaying the business dragon."

He unburdened himself of that in May 1966, three weeks before he became a grandfather. Charlotte was delivered of a baby daughter, "the only good part of having been married to Stavros Niarchos," as she swiftly came to believe. It seemed to her that his business was his one true love. Within a year, the marriage was over, and he went back to his Eugenia, the third wife who also counted as the fifth.

Anne Uzielli's life, by contrast, appeared as tranquil as a homemaking page in a woman's magazine. Sharing her husband's 4½-room apartment at 35 Sutton Place South was her first taste of domesticity. These had been his bachelor quarters; a part-time maid came in three afternoons a week and stayed on for dinner if required.

Uzielli marveled at his wife's profound, stainless innocence. He thought, "It's like teaching a child who's been shut in all there is to know about the world." The Saturday morning lessons in cuisine that she had taken at Maxim's when she was in school in Paris were not much help in cooking for two, so she started learning all over again. The style they set for themselves was more suburban than Manhattan: Saturday night poker with three other couples (she had never played cards before); trips to the public library (she had never been inside one); reading stock-market reports and the *Wall Street Journal* (she had no notion of how to handle money until their marriage, her husband discovered).

Henry's home life at Grosse Pointe Farms was usually as tame as his younger daughter's. He pampered his metabolism by allowing himself to arrive at his twelfth-floor office suite at Ford headquarters—the so-called Glass House—later than his staff after a

chauffeur-driven Lincoln had hurried him down the highway
named for his father. "I'm not keen about getting in early. I think
you can get into certain habits that are crazy. If I have a meeting
at nine, I get in at nine. But if I don't have a meeting, why sit at a
desk waiting for someone to walk in and ask a question he ought
to answer himself, anyway?" old Henry's grandson asked.

At the end of the day, he was seldom back before seven-thirty,
always with a briefcase stuffed with paperwork to read, which he
sometimes did in bed. "When he comes home, I try to amuse
him," Cristina reported in an accent that could sound like a put-
on, "not to be heavy, not to say, 'What you been doing? How
long you stay out? You five minutes late!' Nothing! He can come
home at nine o'clock. I smile and say, 'You have a good time?' He
feel that he's free. He's always tied up in the office. He has to be
there every hour, every minute, so at home I make him to feel
free."

Partying had once been a great personal joy; now she could
count on the fingers of a hand how many times they went out together in Detroit during a year, and as for having guests in,
"When I can entertain?" At weekends and on vacation, he might
sleep on through lunch. Most workaday evenings, they watched
television or, infrequently, a movie on a screen in the basement.
Sometimes they had dinner served on trays held across their
knees, most commonly hamburgers. He was partial to the spaghetti that Cristina would cook up in a cauldron for Edsel and his
peers, but Henry "has to be careful of his tummy," his irrepressi-
ble wife explained. Company gossip recorded one occasion when
an aide remarked that eating raw green vegetables stimulated his
procreative energies, and at luncheon that day Henry ordered the
salad.

Weight was a persistent problem. Aggravated by interior stress
in 1976, it put him into St. Joseph Mercy Hospital in Ann Arbor, Michigan, with chest pains diagnosed as angina pectoris, mar-
ring a record of hitherto excellent health and canceling a planned
trip to China. The pounds he shed on excursions to what he
called "the fat farm," a spa in Lacosta, California, soon reap-
peared on his paunch and jowls.

Cristina was a health faddist who relied on riding one of her
three bicycles, a morning massage, a daily hour of exercising, and

private ballet classes twice a week to retain her tiger-cat figure. At the fifty-year-old mark, her husband's principal sport was duck hunting at his marsh at Amesburg on the Ontario shore of the lake. Exercise bored him. "Why should I be bored?" he wanted to know.

She had no more long-term success in reducing his weight than in steering him away from smoking. The solution he reached was to ask photographers not to catch him with one of his preferred Benson and Hedges between his fingers. He found that mint-flavored Tiparillos, plastic-tipped and bought for seven cents apiece, made an acceptable substitute, while Iacocca stuck with his pipes and his big Ignacio Hayas.

Cristina traveled with Henry far more than Anne had, in the United States and abroad. He had no qualms about personal danger coming their way overseas, though the Arab world was boycotting all Ford products in reprisal for his concluding a deal with the Palestine Automobile Corporation for assembling trucks and tractors in Israel. "Nobody's going to tell me what to do," he promised at the time of signing, but later, when he was rumored to be on the list for kidnaping by Black September terrorists, he had to be more careful about security.

At luncheon with Queen Elizabeth II in Windsor Castle, Cristina and Her Majesty's cousin, Lord Mountbatten of Burma, were so struck with each other that he sent over a black Labrador for her aboard the Queen Elizabeth II, to be named "Dickie" in his honor and added to the dozen or so dogs she kept at Grosse Pointe Farms.

After Lyndon Johnson, with Henry's enthusiastic endorsement, commenced his unpredictable reign in Washington, she arrived at one White House dinner-dance wearing a strapless sheath gown, revealing so much more than her shoulders that Henry was visibly nonplussed, and the Washington Star and the Post had a heyday. Doing and saying what they pleased was a pastime of both husband and wife. Grow sideburns reaching halfway across his cheeks and wear Levi belts with his Fenn-Feinstein business suits? There was nobody to question him, any more than to curb Cristina when she startled one society matron with an explanation of how she picked up her tan: "We were cruising on the Mediterranean and sunbathing in the nude."

She nursed her complexion with regular, two-hour sessions at the Kitty Wagner Facial Salon and wore her tawny hair loose and long because Henry did not care for lacquered women. Girl-watching was another habit it proved impossible to break. "He always looks at pretty girls at a party," she confided. "But that is all right. He loves me and I love him." She bought some of her clothes off the rack in the high-fashion department of the J. L. Hudson Company at the 20 per cent markdown that the Fords enjoyed because of Eleanor's family connection.

The mood to let off steam seldom struck now either at home or on their travels. Once, to the music of gypsy guitars, the guests had wound up smashing champagne glasses in the fireplace, while Henry, armed with a soda siphon, dueled with an Italian count who was roosting in a tree, tossing down ice cream. Closer to home, Henry climaxed an evening at a Long Island club by shying a cake at a portrait of the founder, which got him struck off the membership roster. On his own doorstep, he and three companions of his youth showed up at Grosse Pointe's Bronze Door restaurant, where Henry blew an ear-splitting toot on a police whistle to ruffle the diners and interrupt the piano player. But such frolics belonged to the past.

One thing Cristina never could get straight was the identity of the automobiles on the streets of Detroit. She knew she liked smaller cars than his Continental, bearing a "HF II" on the front doors like the monogram on his shirt pockets, but her knowledge stopped short there. "I will say, 'Henry, look at that beautiful Mustang,' and he says, 'That is a Chevrolet. I told you ten times, it's a Chevrolet.'"

His visits to Washington increased now that the Chief Executive there was of a similar mold to himself, a bull male with an outdoor look about him, the same profane humor, and an even greater appetite for power. "Corporations are—or ought to be—politically color-blind," Henry vowed, but as a voter he approved of the principles that Johnson was striving to achieve in the Great Society. Medicaid, federal funds for education, aid to the poverty-stricken Appalachians, assurance of the political rights of blacks—most of this made good sense to Ford, and he was quick to say so.

"As compassionate individuals, we look upon poverty as a blight which deprives fellow men of life's enjoyment," he declared on a speaking trip to Chicago. "As responsible citizens, we also see the poor as a drain on society who should be made into contributors to society. As businessmen, we add a third view—the poor simply are not very good customers for our products, even the most basic necessities."

He was warming up for a second plunge into public affairs. He made no claim to Simon-pure altruism. Manufacturing automobiles as a business was peculiarly like riding a roller coaster, soaring when the economy boomed, diving when it faltered. After record-breaking years of prosperity, sales and earnings went nosing downward in 1967. Concern about car safety, aroused by Nader, had brought about unprecedented federal regulation. Henry had an idea that the credibility of the makers was suffering, too.

Trouble blew in from left and right. Company earnings dipped by 43 per cent in the first quarter and 32 per cent in the second, compared with GM declines of 34 per cent and a trifling 4 per cent. July through September brought disaster. The UAW shut down Ford for fifty-three consecutive days. During the eighth week of the walkout, negotiations dragged on under a news blackout. It was almost midnight when Henry's office telephone rang. He talked with the reporter on the line. How much an hour was the union asking? "I think we can settle for about $4.00 or $5.00 if we care to offer it," Henry answered. After Henry hung up, he worried about whether he had gotten the facts straight and went to check with his vice-president in charge of public affairs. No, he had fumbled it. That was not what the union was seeking. An urgent press release had to be concocted to correct the record.

The strike was directly related to another element in the catastrophe. Simultaneously, Ford recalled its entire production run of 447,000 Mustangs, together with 298,000 other cars—close to a third of the whole year's diminished output—because of "workmanship problems," as the notices mailed to customers stated; postal expenses alone amounted to $260,000. For that quarter, Ford reported its greatest setback in earnings since it went public: a loss of $73,900,000, contrasted with a $65,000,000 profit in the similar period the previous year.

General Motors had reversed its decline into gains of almost 50 per cent, but nobody was smiling on the boulevard. A third variety of trouble tormented Detroit in July. Henry had seen it coming. "The prospect of eliminating poverty," he had warned in the previous summer, "makes poverty all the more intolerable to those who still suffer from it or are offended by it. We should not be surprised, therefore, if they demonstrate their impatience in all sorts of ways that make life uncomfortable for others."

The enormous price of the Vietnam War, which McNamara was overseeing from his Pentagon desk, had forced dramatic cutbacks in relief for inner-city poor and in programs to combat racial discrimination in employment and housing. The consequences rocked the community that in World War II had prided itself on being "the arsenal of democracy." Detroit's black population had multiplied then with the influx of workers for defense production. Now the Army tanks they had helped to build guarded the General Motors Building, fending off waves of rioters intent on burning it to the ground.

Staff in the Glass House could stare out their windows and see a city lit with flames. Arson and looting flared for a week. In the black ghettos, five thousand were left homeless. More than four thousand paratroopers and twice that many National Guardsmen fought to quell the rebellion. By the month's end, at least forty victims were dead, another two thousand injured.

Society was moving into crisis, and Detroit's leading citizen felt obliged to make a start toward countering it in his own backyard. "Real black power," he told an Urban League meeting not long after the flames had been doused, "is not violence in the streets or self-imposed segregation. Black power is the power of the purse and the vote, of knowledge and skill, of self-discipline and self-confidence. Black power is black people and white people working together and voting together. . . ."

In the ghettos of Detroit, he opened two hiring halls to recruit men generally written off as unemployable—blacks who had never held a job or cast a vote, some of them ex-convicts who could scarcely spell their names. Ford took on applicants by the thousands in what the company termed "entry level" jobs as press operators, assemblers, stockroom clerks, and floor sweepers at between $3.25 and $3.80 an hour. Newcomers were handed free bus passes and sometimes lunch money to tide them over until their first paychecks arrived. About half the work force at the Rouge would be blacks within a few years.

The lily-white dealerships were a thornier proposition. "I would hate to be a dealer," Henry admitted. "I'd go broke at the end of the first month." Wheeling and dealing was an innate ability, in his estimation. His credentials as an employer dated back twenty years, when he bombarded his managers with memos underlining Ford's duty to employ minority groups of all races, but personally he cherished no great hopes for a lot of black dealers.

"Now, you can ask our sales people and they'll probably tell you that blacks can do a hell of a lot better than anything I think they can do," he said flatly. "I just think it's a difficult business, and I think unless you're minded that way, you're going to fail." This was Ford speaking his mind as few other tycoons dared to, talking to an interviewer for a black magazine seven years after the experiment with ghetto hiring. The count of black dealerships stood at twelve then, fourteen fewer than with General Motors, seven more than with Chrysler.

Henry looked to employ blacks straight out of schools and colleges as trainees under the company's continuous recruiting process, and in a higher proportion than in the black population of the country as a whole. Black engineering graduates were particularly hard to find, so he pumped donations into training schools to rectify that. When a black would have climbed high enough to be considered for the presidency of Ford's was a question too tough to answer even with a guess. "You know, I always go back and say, 'Well, Rome wasn't built in a day, and you can't change everything overnight.'"

The embers in Detroit were barely cold when he went to a meeting of community leaders, called to find methods of treating the city's sickness. The result was New Detroit, Incorporated, essentially a well-heeled committee that gathered every month to listen to complaints from black militants and try to remedy them. Walter Reuther, Roche of General Motors, and Chrysler's Lynn Townsend were among its thirty-nine members along with Henry, but none of them matched him in exasperation when time was frittered away. "I wouldn't take this crap if you were working for me," he stormed at one fumbling member of the committee staff. "If you were working for me, you wouldn't be working for me any more." While too many local whites still thought of blacks as "jigaboos" and the slump in auto sales persisted, the city's problems could be calmed but not cured. New Detroit's greatest short-term success lay in raising an annual $4,000,000 or so for neighborhood youth groups and similar palliatives. Its longer-range effectiveness was to be tested when a more crippling economic calamity struck in the years ahead.

Just before this dismal 1967 came to its close, Henry suffered the loss of the most important family counselor after Eleanor: Uncle Ernest Kanzler died at the age of seventy-six.

Early in January, Henry answered a White House invitation to apply solutions to the ghetto program on a national scale. For friend Lyndon's sake, he agreed to head up the newborn National Alliance of Businessmen, with a target of hiring and training 500,000 of the hard-core unemployed within a three-year span. The job would necessitate his crisscrossing the country, urging his peers of industry to make good use of the funds that Congress earmarked for the venture. As his executive director, Henry picked Leo Beebe, his chief petty officer during his spell as a Navy ensign.

The latest assignment as a man of affairs would add considerably to the chairman's work load. Was Arjay Miller forceful enough to manage the store in the interim? Henry was pondering the question when it was answered by what he could only interpret as a stroke of luck.

Semon Knudsen, nicknamed "Bunkie" (short for "bunkmate") by his father, was experiencing damaged pride, a painful affliction haunting all executive suites. He had felt certain that Pontiac's record would bring him the presidency of General Motors when Roche was stepped up into the chairmanship the previous November. Instead, his purse-mouthed rival, Edward Cole, was the board's choice. After thirty years of service and holding $3,000,000 worth of GM stock, Executive Vice-President Bunkie was dropping hints about quitting.

Henry was just back from a brief, sunshine break in Antigua, getting into shape for the chores ahead, when the rumor came his way. He telephoned Knudsen to set up a meeting. Grosse Pointe Farms would make a poor site for it because the place was filled with Cristina's house guests. He would drive out to confer with Bunkie at his suburban home in Bloomfield Hills, where GM sachems—and Lee Iacocca—congregated. In deference to an industry that holds its cards tight, Henry made the trip alone, in an Oldsmobile. If Knudsen's neighbors were peeking, they would not immediately recognize Ford plate numbers.

The deal closed with Bunkie made him president of Ford's at the same salary and bonus scale as Henry—$600,000 in all this year—with $750,000 worth of stock thrown in. Knudsen gathered the impression that he was to be granted virtually free rein in the day-to-day running of the company. Arjay Miller was to be rewarded with a backstairs promotion as vice chairman, in charge of public information, the financial and legal staffs, and the Pandora's box known as "corporate development." In the scurrilous gossip of the trade, he was "practically made a bookkeeper." When he resigned the appointment to become dean of Stanford University's Graduate School of Business, he had nothing but praise for Henry.

Iacocca loyalists grumbled that Knudsen was an outsider and a GM chieftain at that, one of a breed apart in their conservatively subdued suits and starched white shirts, with an overlay of superiority that made them look more like bankers than auto men. Not too many Ford executives ever entertained the thought of exchanging the shirtsleeved atmosphere of the Glass House for the regimentation that distinguished GM.

Iacocca had been spreading himself with projects for both ends of the price scale. For the top of the line, he envisaged a Continental with extra prestige and pizazz, to be labeled Mark III and entered as competition for Cadillac's Eldorado, but tagged $200 cheaper. He encountered opposition from management committees who questioned the extravagance until Henry saw a prototype and tried it out on the way home. The Mark III was ready for its debut when Bunkie was recruited; it outsold the Eldorado by 30 per cent in 1968. To stave off the cheapest cars' invasion of the market—Volkswagen and other imports whose inroads grew bigger every year—Iacocca was working on another concept. It was due to be launched as the Maverick, a bargain in stripped-down simplicity but loaded with options if a buyer wanted them.

No timetable for Knudsen's probable tenure could be programmed, but Henry's basic idea was that Bunkie, aged fifty-five, might well serve as president until Lee Iacocca and one or two more men had gathered a few more years of experience on the power pyramid. A General Motors organization chart hung on the wall behind Ford for his press-conference announcement that Bunkie was joining him. Detroit reacted as though this were the second coming. Reminiscences of how old Henry had fired Big Bill Knudsen nearly half a century ago were a mainstay of conversation on the oldtimers' circuit for days thereafter.

Hostility between Bunkie and Lee was discernible from the beginning. Knudsen impressed some of those under him as a stuffed shirt wielding a bullwhip. Possibly, the two errors he made were to imagine that he had been given the keys to the kingdom and to neglect to bring in a team of his own from General Motors, a customary precaution in such circumstances.

He was at his desk by the time the sun came up, scheduling conferences for seven-fifteen, an unheard-of hour in Dearborn. His dawn patrols of the complex of headquarters buildings clustered along and around Ford Road were a sour joke with employees. Engineering and styling were his main preoccupations, and the design center felt a heavy hand. He ordered the Thunderbird bobbed by five inches and equipped with a redesigned front end, which lent the car an air of his old love, Pontiac. Playing with words, Eugene Bordinat, chief stylist, commented, "Knudsen expresses a great interest in our vineyard and helps me *toil it*."

Henry gave Bunkie his way in most things for the present, happy that the roller coaster was carrying the industry up again toward a new peak, giving Ford its best year yet, with 4,744,000 units sold worldwide for profits of $626,600,000. But Henry had a sense of escalating crisis in the division between the races. "We must at last put up or shut up about equality," he said. He found that "there is a curtain between black and white America every bit as opaque as the so-called 'iron curtain' between Eastern Europe and the Western world."

He split away from Johnson on foreign policy. The war in Vietnam struck him as a "disaster"—a popular word with Henry—that was ruining the economy, inflaming domestic problems, and alienating America's young. But he was putting in so much time on Johnsonian causes that he seemed anxious for Cabinet rank or an ambassadorship. Not so, said Henry. "I was never asked to do anything that I thought was very—well, not *very*, not the kind of job I think I'd be good in or was really interested in."

Pentagon brass could be thankful that the *very* appointment that might have tempted him was not Secretary of Defense, taken on by Clark Clifford when McNamara left to preside over the World Bank. Henry held strong views on the importance of civilian rule over that department. "The admirals and generals should be heard, but in my opinion, you are in nothing but trouble if you ride with whatever they might suggest."

He was sorry that Lyndon decided in March to pull out of the presidency, but he turned down an eleventh-hour offer to be appointed United Nations ambassador. "I had been there once, and I didn't want to go back." He backed Hubert Humphrey against Richard Nixon that fall, knowing that whoever won his term would end as chairman of the National Alliance of Businessmen when some 146,000 jobs had been found toward the goal of 500,000.

A palace revolution was taking shape in the Glass House. Managers affronted by Knudsen's high-handedness were forming ranks behind Iacocca. A touch of old Henry's disjointed era was restored when the Iacocca faction went around undoing what Bunkie was attempting. The president himself seemingly misread his chairman's temperament and overstepped the undefined limits of his authority. In September, nineteen months after he had appointed him, Henry had to conclude that Bunkie's presence would sunder the organization Ford had taken twenty years to rebuild. He would not duck what needed to be done. He walked into Knudsen's office to tell him brusquely, "You'll be leaving."

"It just hasn't worked out," Henry told reporters who packed the company auditorium for the news conference. "I had no personal conflict with Mr. Knudsen." On Henry's right sat Iacocca, cigar in hand, a faint smile on his lips. He and Bunkie had no earth-shaking differences of opinion, he told one questioner. Was he sorry to see Knudsen leave? "I've never said 'No comment' to the press yet, but I'll say 'No comment' now" came the reply.

Over drinks that evening, Knudsen mused, "I think Henry was afraid of losing his Tinker Toy." The No. 2 spot in the company was left open for fifteen months. Then it went to Lee Iacocca, who was willing to turn handsprings if necessary to get things done for Mr. Ford.

Henry could be caught thinking like a patriarch as well as the incontrovertible boss of the business. He was talking one day about his son, recognizable already as a car buff in his new prep school, The Gunnery, to which he had transferred from Hotchkiss. "I think he would like to come into the company someday," his father said dryly. "Right now he's majoring in trying to graduate." After Edsel accomplished that, he was admitted to the Babson Institute, an unglamorous educational establishment in Waltham, Massachusetts, and he also signed on as a twenty-year-old trainee in Ford sales. In his sisters' estimation, he had so far relied too heavily on charm instead of perspiration to pull him through. Some girls in his own age group rated him as "just an ordinary young man," which had once been said of his great-grandfather.

The *Wall Street Journal*, priding itself on infallibility, quoted Dearborn "insiders" as saying that "the young son would have to prove his management abilities against seasoned professionals before he could be elevated to a position of power. Rather, they say it is more likely that an experienced manager, such as President Lee A. Iacocca, will become the next chief executive." One faithful reader, Mrs. Uzielli, may have doubted that. Daddy was enjoying himself too much to dream of retiring, though he always made the point with his board of directors that "if the time ever comes when I should step down, they ought to tell me."

He took Charlotte and Cristina along when he flew to the Soviet Union in the spring of 1970, hoping to drum up more business there than two previous generations of the family had ever done. In the course of nine days, he combined duty with vodka-and-caviar hospitality and came home with the news that Moscow had invited Ford to help build the biggest truck manufactory in the universe on the banks of the Kama River at a cost of probably $2 billion.

Russians were a pleasure to bargain with, compared with the Japanese. Japan's grab for a share of the American automobile market irritated Henry and tarnished his faith in free trade between nations, which echoed Grandfather's. "If businessmen want the freedom to compete," he liked to say, "they have to accept the duty to compete." Tokyo wrote its own rules for subsidizing exports and curbing imports.

"We are definitely being discriminated against by the Japanese," he concluded. "The Japanese imports on the West Coast are growing by leaps and bounds. There are so many restrictions against us in Japan that it's really hard to enumerate them. Some of them are not even legal." The company owned two Japanese properties assessed for up to $25,000,000. "We can't take out the yen, but the islands are not expanding, and the land is going up in value. It pays to hang on, and someday we might be able to invest the money there."

Washington knocked the Soviet deal on the head before it could be consummated. At a Detroit press briefing, Nixon's Secretary of Defense, bulldog-jowled Melvin Laird, berated Henry for even contemplating it "when the Soviet Union is sending trucks by the shipload to North Vietnam."

Shareholders had never seen the chairman so mad as he was at the annual meeting in May. Ford took up Moscow's bid, he raged, "because it is the express policy of the United States Government to encourage increased trade with Eastern European nations. The United States Government was advised in advance of our visit and did not discourage us." A question from the floor gave him an opening to put the Defense chief in his place. "I think it was unfortunate," Henry grated, "that Secretary Laird took it upon himself to make the public statement before we had even given complete, serious consideration within our own company. We had not asked them for their opinion; they gratuitously gave it. In my opinion that's a peculiar way of doing business."

The company's principal challenge at present was to earn more money. "When you make a lot of money," he explained elsewhere, "you get a little careless. Our rate of return is not what it should be." He resented any kind of interference from Washington that impeded progress in that direction, though he accepted the fact that if he bought more big operations like Philco, he would probably run into an antitrust suit.

Most of the controls and regulations emerging out of Washington seemed farfetched to him. "They control everything we do, practically speaking. They control the design of our product, both from an operating standpoint and a looks standpoint. They control our prices, control our salaries, control our wages." Controls on profits incensed him more than anything else. "I don't see how you can maintain a position in world markets if you can't increase profits with which to modernize your business and keep it up to date."

No rear-guard action fought against the onrush of government supervision was more resolute than his; Ford's annual outlay of $1,000,000 toward building more efficient, more secure automobiles continued. What he sought was time. Meeting the deadlines imposed by Congress and state legislatures to make driving less perilous and exhaust fumes less noxious involved such spending of capital that it could very well mean bankruptcy. Beyond that, the technology did not exist at present for achieving everything the lawmakers were demanding.

He argued that exhaust pollution had already been cut by 80 per cent as a result of engine redesign—and consequently cars balked and sputtered at the turn of the ignition key and burned crazy amounts of gasoline. "The next 10 per cent is going to cost what the first 80 per cent cost, and how much value is that going to be?" he wanted to know. How in hell could Ford or any other company create clean-running motors when precise specifications for their performance got lost in a maze of bureaucratic muddle? "I don't know how they set standards. They set them in a vacuum."

He could detect no sense at all in some proposals that were being pushed down the manufacturers' throats by Nixon's tough little Secretary of Transportation, John A. Volpe, like the protective air bag, inflating itself to press riders into their seats in a collision, which was supposed to be standard equipment by 1972. That device scared Henry and Iacocca, too. The company did concede one point to its critics—it retreated from auto racing.

If pollution and safety mandates were enforced at their present pace, Henry figured that Lee's latest entry, the perky, pint-sized, easily maintainable $2,000 Pinto, would become a $5,000 car toward the end of the seventies. Inflation, just beginning to smolder in the United States, was to make his forecast fall only slightly short of the truth.

He set Ford's on a voyage of discovery, searching for ways to anticipate what customers might expect in years to come. His motive was constant. "The successful companies in the last third of the twentieth century will be the ones that look at changes in their environment as opportunities to get a jump on the competition." In the simplest terms, Ford versus General Motors.

Over on the boulevard and at Chrysler, they were experimenting with diesel power, but nobody at Ford was particularly smitten with that. A lighter, longer-living, sodium-sulphur battery invented in Ford company laboratories prompted some thinking about an electric car, but Henry was skeptical. "Specifically, I'm not interested in really pushing hard on this project, but I don't want to discourage anyone else at Ford from doing what we are doing. I don't see the electric car as a feasible method of transportation in my lifetime."

Buses? GM held a near monopoly on that market, and he detected few opportunities there. "If you think mass transportation is going to replace the automobile, I think you're whistling 'Dixie' or taking pot." The automobile as such would outlast him. Gas turbines? Yes. Production was scheduled at a plant in Toledo, Ohio. A return to steam engines? Possibly. Research got under way, looking for something more efficient than water to circulate in the boiler.

Among all the explorations, the "people mover" intrigued him most. Automatically controlled transportation was its official name, ACT for short. It centered on driverless, computer-controlled vehicles, electrically powered and gliding on foam-filled rubber tires over aerial guideways. ACT was designed to carry fourteen passengers at a time around airports, shopping centers, downtown malls, and university campuses. Secretary Volpe thought enough of the experiment to give Ford a contract to demonstrate people movers at Dulles International Airport. The pioneer operational model would later be installed at another airport, Bradley International near Hartford, Connecticut.

Henry wondered about putting a people mover to work in a personal project that excited him as a hard-boiled visionary. Detroit Renaissance was his own idea: a $500,000,000 construction job to transform the city's sleazy waterfront and "get the Motor City's motor running again," in his friend Max Fisher's phrase. Thirty-two acres would be made over along the lines of Pittsburgh's Golden Triangle and Atlanta's Peachtree Center, starting with a seventy-story hotel, four office towers, and a shopping-entertainment-restaurant area. Ford contributed $6,000,000 as a beginning, which General Motors quickly felt compelled to match. In less than four weeks, Henry's efforts had raised $24,000,000 of the necessary down payment of $35,000,000.

He hedged himself against disappointment. "Maybe it's not going to work," he admitted. "It's not a sure thing, but we've got to make a start." Rising bills for raw materials and workmen's wages promised to throw the budgets out of kilter.

On the day of its birth announcement, the sweet promise of Renaissance was marred by the bitterness of a personal humiliation sharper than the fiasco of the Edsel. He was on his way to the Economic Club of Detroit for the kickoff meeting when he received the call. "That was a *night*," he remembered. "I didn't know a damn thing about it." He reckoned it to be the nadir of his career.

The company's honor and his own were both jeopardized, he felt, by the disclosure that a few Ford technicians had tested 1973 cars against air-pollution standards established by the new Federal Environmental Protection Agency, then performed unauthorized modifications of the engines before they filed performance records. Now the EPA threatened to withhold approval of the cars, which could mean that none of the line could be put on sale.

A fine of $7,000,000 climaxed the incident; the model year's shortcomings were adjusted; and again Henry let the buck stop on his own blotter: "I must take the ultimate responsibility for what has happened." Possibly some of those who worked for him had been led astray by his constant sniping at exhaust emission controls. "I still don't like the law," he said, "and I think it ought to be changed. But you have to play by the rules. You don't cheat."

He restructured testing procedures, making one of his top-notch engineers directly chargeable for their validity, while he placed some darts in the flanks of his management men. "I think the communications in this company are lousy—up and down. They're bad from the top down because things aren't explained well enough, I guess. And they're bad from the bottom up because things just don't get through."

The $7,000,000 penalty did not dent his regard for the incumbent of the White House. Switching sides again, Henry chipped in $49,726 to help re-elect Nixon that November; Eleanor's contribution topped his by $274.

The Nixon presidency so far had proved benign for Ford. America, it seemed, could afford whatever it liked—a war, an extra car, a heated swimming pool, trips to Europe, clean air, and sparkling water. Euphoria flavored the company's annual reports one year after another.

"Ford's consolidated dollar sales were a record $15 billion in 1970, up from $14.8 billion in 1969," said the opening statement over the signatures of Henry and Lee Iacocca in the gleaming brochure with a golden Pinto pictured on its cover. Another Pinto was starred along with a Courier compact truck and a new Capri the following year: "1971 was a year of record sales and near-record earnings for your Company. . . . Ford's worldwide consolidated net income for 1971 was $657 million, up 27% from the $516 million earned in 1970."

On the next report, dozens of the more than 440,000 people employed by the company here and overseas were portrayed to edify the shareholders, who learned, "By nearly every measure, 1972 was the most successful year in your Company's history." Its hold on the United States car market stood at 25.3 per cent, net income at an unprecedented $8.52 a share.

The first nine months of 1973 shone with an even brighter glow. Never before had Americans bought new cars in such numbers—2,786,000 of them built by Ford in the total of nearly 11,500,000 of them sold before December was over; roughly one in every five was a foreign import, with Volkswagen heading the list. For the sixth consecutive year, Henry could tell the annual meeting in Detroit's Ford Auditorium that records had been broken; the company's worldwide sales reached $23 billion. Profits would have been bigger if Washington had permitted the price of the average car to be increased by the full $106 that it cost to meet the imposed safety and antipollution standards.

Charlotte also had good news for her father one week earlier. As a divorcee she had been out with some celebrated headline-catchers—Henry Kissinger, Frank Sinatra, Jean-Paul Killy—but her choice for a second husband was less spectacular and probably more stable. Eleanor came with the family to young Anne's apartment at 750 Park Avenue to see Charlotte married to J. Anthony Forstmann, whose business was finance, not imperial diplomacy, ageless singing, or downhill skiing. Charlotte had previously ren-

dered similar service to her mother by offering her apartment for
the wedding of the first Mrs. Henry Ford II to Deane G. Johnson,
a Los Angeles attorney, with whom she moved to Beverly Hills.

There were signs that young Anne's lease on marriage was expir-
ing. There were two children to be considered, Alessandro and his
baby sister, Allegra, but in the coming December, Mr. and Mrs.
Uzielli were separated. A year later, she would sue for divorce.
"These things," said Charlotte darkly, "do not happen overnight."
When the decree was granted, Anne pointedly resumed the name
of Ford and kept her son and daughter.

The sparkle of 1973 vanished in its final three months when
Henry's old antagonists, the Arab nations, clamped down on oil
exports and convulsed the industrial universe. The car-buying
spree was done for. Gas prices had been spurting upward along
with everything else as double-digit inflation took hold of the
United States. Now the stuff was suddenly rationed at the pumps,
as precious as water in the desert, and drivers waited in line for
hours to top up their tanks in case it should dry up altogether.
But the year had been kind to him, with its $874,567 in salary and
bonus plus $3,700,000 in dividends.

There was no cure for the energy crisis, only countermeasures.
One step would be for the government to mandate a fifty-five-
mile-an-hour speed limit everywhere in the land. The price of gasoline drove those new-car customers who remained to look primarily for economy and maximum mileage, not for gas burners with
lightning getaway, loaded with fuel-consuming equipment. No
major manufacturer had planned on this. The energy crunch
caught them all off guard, and nothing much could be done about
it in the 1974 model year. New automobiles as obsolete as passenger pigeons still trundled off the lines.

They piled up in showrooms and storage lots, cocooned in protective wax, 1,650,000 of them in the end. Detroit saw a sight as
alarming in its implications as the fires set by rioters had been:
The Michigan State Fairgrounds were jampacked with cars that
nobody wanted. The response among blacks this time was apathy
more than anger. As many as 25 per cent of them had no job in a
city where they made up 40 per cent of the population.

Layoffs of UAW workers had reached 150,000 when Henry,
who stuck to the truth no matter what, caused spasms among his

peers. Sales had slumped to the worst levels since 1958. Ford's payroll had already been cut by 39,900 under orders to pare off every possible ounce of company fat. Car prices had jumped by around one third in four years—the $2,000 Pinto was brushing $3,000 nowadays—but he proposed making driving more expensive yet by hiking federal gas taxes by 10 per cent to raise an annual $11 billion to help the country's poor and unemployed. On top of that, he wanted jobless pay extended from thirty-nine weeks to fifty-two. He knew that in Detroit men and women were foraging through garbage cans, looking for scraps to eat.

"We have to think about the social consequences," he said, "if things continue in the old way. You can't expect people to sell apples on the street corners as they did in the 1930s." The other Ford, President now that Watergate had thrown the country into what Henry recognized as "real trouble," chose to call the situation a recession. Henry's word for it was *depression*. General Motors and Chrysler detested his candor.

Two outside projects of his wilted in the climate of adversity. Runaway construction costs and inflated interest rates demanded finding $100,000,000 in new money for Renaissance Center, where the hotel and two of the office towers were rising on the bulldozed riverfront. He traveled the country, looking for investors, but the full commitment of cash was impossible to raise. The completion date already scheduled—1981—struck him as distinctly remote. "That seems a long time to me. I'll be dead before then," he grinned. Delays beyond that were unthinkable. He committed a Ford subsidiary, Detroit Downtown Development Corporation, to guarantee the balance to close the gap. Writing leases on acres of new office space was a tougher problem, aggravated by fear among some prospective tenants of danger lurking on downtown streets, where trafficking in drugs ran out of control.

"We couldn't foresee this recession," he said, switching to the softer word. "If we planned it today, we'd plan it smaller. But it's too late." Renaissance would have no people mover. "We didn't think we could afford it. I know we can't. I'm ruling them out right now, forever, as far as I can see. We don't have the money."

A second real-estate development, also slowed by hostile wind and weather, seemed a natural place to put in a people mover, though ACT would be indefinitely discontinued for lack of customers after that. Ford's policy committee, paring budgets, could not see laying out $16,700,000 on a single ACT installation.

"They all knew that was my baby, and I'm sure they figured, 'That son-of-a-bitch is going to force his thing through while all the rest of us have to cut.' Well, after some discussion, I asked the other guys involved in the Fairlane project, 'Do you want it?' They all said no, so I said, 'Well, then we won't build it.'" When he had some second thoughts about that, the company decided a people mover would be fine for Fairlane if it could be brought in for around $5,000,000.

Fairlane was to be virtually a town in itself. The company had bought a spread of Dearborn farmland from old Henry's estate, then left it untouched for twenty years, an oasis of fields and woods in the heart of urban spread. "We just paid taxes on it. We pay 42 per cent of the tax base in Dearborn, so we thought we'd better spread that tax base."

The outcome was the 2,360-acre Fairlane Community in sight of his Glass House windows—new roads, office blocks, an enclosed shopping center, a luxury hotel, and more to come, to a mixed reception from the neighbors. One group of them banded together to cling to the past, when part of the tract was Grandfather's bird sanctuary. The Citizens for Henry Ford's Wildlife Preserve got wind of plans to erect condominiums where the old man's cherished flocks of cardinals and finches had nested. The lawsuit they filed promised future trouble for Ford from an already familiar source—Michigan's Environmental Protection Act.

Henry's concern could safely be described as limited. Dearborn was—and is—a community as lily-white as his dealerships had formerly been. So long as Mayor Orville Hubbard remained in office, it was likely to continue that way. The town did not welcome blacks. "What's going to happen when Orville's gone?" was a question that bothered a voting majority of its citizens.

The darkness that settled on Detroit deepened in September, when the 1975 models went on display, with industry dollars in the hundreds of millions staked on their success. Their size had been scaled down to give buyers what they wanted. They were routinely fitted with a catalytic converter fixed to the tail pipe to minimize exhaust emissions and bought from General Motors, where they had been pioneered. According to Environmental Protection Agency tests, the new cars averaged 13.5 per cent more miles to a gallon than any of their immediate predecessors. They also cost about $1,000 more apiece than sixteen months ago, up to $600 of that attributable to safety and antipollution equipment.

The current chairman of GM, Richard Gerstenberg, about to make his exit through the continually revolving door, sounded off like Charles E. Wilson: "When you buy a new car, you help America's economy." His counterpart at Chrysler, Lynn Townsend, echoed him: "A new car is the best buy you can get in America today." The bedeviled United Auto Workers chipped in for some advertising along similar lines.

Henry was reluctant to raise his voice in the chorus. The country's anguish ran too deep to be treated by ballyhoo. "I think the nation had a death wish in a way," he said in retrospect. If it had, it certainly extended to include the automakers. November sales fell to less than half the rate of November 1973.

Old Henry's practice of meeting crises by slashing prices was the last resort. Led by Chrysler, hardest hit of all with 84,000 blue- and white-collar workers laid off, the Big Three tried to lure customers with rebates of as much as $600 off the sticker price, cashing in on sales in the months ahead to save dealerships from immediate calamity. General Motors reverted to another ruse of Lizzie's days by charging for what had previously been standard equipment. Its Olds Omega coupé, for instance, had $219 shaved off its list price when radial tires, the day-night rear-view mirror, and the cigarette lighter suddenly became buyers' options. The competition followed suit.

Dealers came up with some tricks of their own. Some accepted cattle as part of a trade-in. Others went farther and advertised, "We will trade for anything," be it swimming pools, garden tractors, dune buggies, or television sets. Nothing worked well enough. Detroit had expected to sell 9,000,000 cars that year; the final count fell 1,500,000 short of that figure.

Bonuses were a thing of the past. Throughout the city, white-collar workers were being fired or furloughed on a scale unseen since the 1930s. "For Sale" signs speckled suburban streets, bankruptcy claims mounted every week, long lines stretched out of the unemployment offices, and Eleanor donated $900,000 to the Institute of Arts. Henry pursued his own personal economies. The *Santa Maria* had gone to a new owner some time ago. Now Henry gave up his Continental for a compact-size Mercury Grand Monarch Ghia, which had just been introduced together with the Granada. "What the hell do I want to go around the block to dinner in a Lincoln for?"

Iacocca held onto his white Lincoln, and in the executives' underground garage at World Headquarters, a reporter spotted only three other Monarchs. The chairman went around his own house turning out the lights, but the windows of some company buildings continued to gleam long after the staff had gone home. Communication *always* was a headache.

He refused to fault the Arabs alone for the economic mess. "There is much justice on the side of the oil-producing nations," he considered. "The price of petroleum has been kept unduly low, encouraging waste and prodigal use of a limited resource. The benefits of oil exploitation have been unevenly distributed; in most instances the oil-producing countries have had too little to show in return for the depletion of their resources."

A share of the blame lay much nearer home. "We're still living in a fool's paradise in this country. We have always thought that we could have an endless supply of cheap energy, and we can't. We've got a major energy problem, but the American people don't believe it. We waste so much. We waste everything in this country." He was all for terminating price controls to boost drilling of new wells and encourage everybody to save fuel.

By the middle of February 1975, 61,000 Ford workers had been laid off, 134,405 at General Motors, and 59,550 at Chrysler. Nearly four of every ten employed in the industry had no job. The ripple effect stretched much farther. One man or woman of every six in the country's labor force depended on the carmakers for a living in some way or other—in steel, glass, rubber, aluminum, plastics, copper, and auto parts. The catastrophe in Detroit forced the United States into hardship deeper and more prolonged than almost any prophet or computer data bank had predicted.

Henry was the last man alive to conceal his alarm. "In my thirty years as a businessman, I have never before felt so uncertain and so troubled about the future of both my country and my company. It is not too much to say that the very survival of our free society may depend on finding good solutions to these economic problems."

He was not short of schemes for making a start toward solving both sets of riddles. For the company, he commissioned two think tanks to survey its future: the Battelle Memorial Institute of Columbus, Ohio, and the Stanford Research Institute. The Whiz Kids of this generation would be outsiders.

As for the power plant in the next generation of Fords, he shared his engineers' regard for something known as the Stirling, originally invented and patented by the Reverend Robert Stirling, a Scottish clergyman, in 1816, nearly half a century before Henry I saw the light of day. The conventional automobile engine exploded vaporized gasoline inside its cylinders to impel the pistons that supplied motive force. This one embodied a combustion chamber outside the engine itself. It was possibly 50 per cent more efficient than anything in production today, and it would run on virtually anything that burned, including olive oil and old Henry's suggested substitute of Prohibition days, alcohol. The drawback was that the Stirling was unlikely to be perfected before 1985, and it would cost a billion to develop, which would have to be scraped up somehow. The most urgent priority was to argue Congress into declaring a moratorium on writing and rewriting the rules for what a car must be. He delegated Iacocca to apply the persuasion.

At the national level, Henry thought that the country had been caught short too often, exactly like the automobile business. "Take air and water pollution, for instance. Suddenly there is a great big flap, and everybody gets excited, and all of a sudden some law is passed. It's got to be done within a very short time-frame, and it costs you a fortune to do it. You can't clean up the country in four years." By 1977, the company would have to budget $315,000,000 in nonproductive money under those headings. "Ridiculous!"

The answer, surely, lay in setting up a central planning group in Washington with Cabinet status to emphasize its importance. It would assemble and share a mass of information—without authority to issue orders—matching the available supply of food, energy, and raw materials against the size of the population and their demands on the market.

"We will just have one hell of a time making ourselves self-sufficient. And, you know, we just have to rely on the rest of the world. We can't become isolationist and hope that everything is just going to turn out fine for us."

Yet most people had been content to sit back and let federal power grow too much already. "The bigger and more complex government becomes, the easier it is to conceal abuses. The more we rely on government to solve all our problems, the more influence there is to peddle, and the greater the temptation to buy."

Along with every other automobile maker, Ford was draining its resources to redesign its product. General Motors would soon take out loans of $600,000,000 toward a $3,000,000,000 reconstruction program. Henry abided by Grandfather's policy of self-financing as far as possible. Dividends were to be cut heavily to save $75,000,000 for developing ever-smaller cars. So one of Henry's proposals was for a dramatic increase in the investment tax credit, possibly doubling it for a spell from 7 per cent to 14 per cent. For a while like Gerald Ford, he advocated cutting personal income taxes, but he changed his mind about that; too big a dose would demand such federal borrowing that the nation's money supply would be sponged dry.

He had aired most of these thoughts in February when his long-suppressed gadabout streak surfaced during a trip to California. In Goleta, near Santa Barbara, the chairman of the board encountered trouble of a kind to spur fellow directors into mumbling excuses for him. Cristina had taken herself off to Katmandu for the coronation of the King of Nepal.

Henry's companion in the car he was driving on the wrong side of the street was red-haired Kathleen Du Ross, a Grosse Pointe neighbor and mother of two, whose husband had been killed in a car crash sixteen years earlier when she was nineteen. A face and figure like a young Lauren Bacall's had brought her modeling assignments, including work for Ford's. Currently, she was identified as an interior decorator and a friend of a onetime Italian diplomat who occasionally escorted Cristina when Henry was on his travels.

"He was a real gentleman, just as congenial as he could be," said Captain Otie Hunter of the highway patrol after Henry had been pulled over, invited to recite the alphabet to establish his so-

briety, failed at that, and then been taken in handcuffs to Santa
Barbara Hospital. Given a blood test, his next stop was the county
jail, where he was booked on a charge of drunken driving. After
four hours in a cell, he pleaded "no contest" through an attorney
and was put on probation for two years. He posted his own $375
bond to gain release.

"Never complain, never explain" was his only comment, which
did a little to calm his public-relations staff. He returned, un-
ruffled, to expound more of his thinking on weightier issues.
The occasion was his receiving a United Way award for a quarter
century of service, the speech one of his best:

"The problems of minority rights, the problems of the cities,
the problems of crime and drugs, the tragedies of Vietnam and
Watergate, the continuing crisis in the Middle East have exhausted us and left us numb. As a consequence, we have drawn
into ourselves. We have become less concerned about the rest of
the world, less concerned about our country, less concerned about
our communities and our fellow citizens.

"In our communities and in our nation, we have too often
fallen into factions that seem bent on blaming each other for our
problems rather than finding solutions. We raise voices in anger,
we impugn motives, and we seem no longer to believe that men of
good will can compromise their differences and work together
voluntarily for the common interest.

"If we do not reverse these trends, we may indeed lose our
country.

"These are dark days for our country, but my generation can
remember other days that were even darker. In 1932 and again in
1941, we thought the world was coming apart. But it didn't. Our
world need not come apart this time either—not if we can recover
the sense of purpose and unity that has always pulled us through
before."

A few days later, on May 1, the Ford Motor Company reported
losses in 1975's first three months of $10,600,000 by contrast with
a $123,600,000 profit in the corresponding quarter in 1974. If its
methods of accounting had not been changed in the interim, it
would have been $97,900,000 in the red. Henry predicted that
profitability would be restored before June ended, even if the
year as a whole could only be "terrible," and it would probably

take five more years for the industry to recapture its golden days.

He appeared unperturbed as usual at the annual meeting of stockholders, convened this year at the Design Center Rotunda in Dearborn. The news he had for them was a mix of good and bad. Net income totaled $361,000,000 for the past year, compared with something approaching three times as much in 1973. But Ford for the tenth year running had licked General Motors and all other United States manufacturers in selling cars and trucks overseas. Philco-Ford was thriving.

Michigan legal routines allowed twenty-four hours to pass, saving the chairman the embarrassment of appearing on the platform deprived of a valid driver's license. Then it was suspended for sixty days as an automatic sequel to his Santa Barbara spree. Kathleen Du Ross made plans to open a Detroit discotheque.

He grew more sanguine as the year progressed. He looked to invest more than $2,000,000,000 by 1980 in building automobiles different from anything currently on the road, a complete and, he hoped, exciting change. The cars would be about two feet shorter, possibly nine hundred pounds lighter, and a little higher off the ground. Their sides would be straighter cut, and they would still accommodate six people and a load of luggage. Any reasonable standards set by Congress to stipulate miles per gallon and purity of exhaust could be met, provided the timetable was not so Utopian that Ford and everyone else went broke in the struggle to meet it. Right now, Washington could not have it both ways, more miles per gallon *and* even tougher emission standards for the 1977 models. For the present, it was a choice between one and the other. By 1980, yes, both could be achieved.

He was convinced of one thing: He had seen the end of the age of rubber-tired mammoths, growing bigger and heavier every year at an annual cost to the industry of a billion dollars in retooling and to the customer of about $700 a car. The habit of turning out a new model every twelve months would be hard to break, but it had to be done. Changes now would be a matter of evolution, introduced whenever they were advisable during a production run. People would spread repayments of their loans over perhaps four years to ease the bite of higher prices—another nail in the coffin of the annual model.

Where size was concerned, Henry was thinking smaller. Call

them compacts, minis, subcompacts, or whatever, they would make up the bulk of the market. "The big cars," he said, "are going the way of all flesh." They were doomed to disappear. He had missed a bet and let Chevy get a jump on him with the Chevette, evolved on the drawing board as soon as the Arabs turned off the oil—and sold with even the rear seat as an option. But he would try to catch up with a hybrid named the Hondo, Pinto chassis and body, four-cylinder, backward-slanted engine by Honda of Japan. He had another deal worked out with the Japanese, giving Ford 40 per cent of a tractor-building operation there.

The day of the 100 per cent American automobile was over, too. He had another entry for the miniatures' sweepstakes—the so-called International. Parts to be made in Britain, Spain, and France; assembled and body-stamped in Spain and Germany; engine for the United States version coming from Britain. This would be smaller than the Chevette, but one question yet to be resolved in his mind was how much smaller a Ford could become without alienating the buyers. The price of gas would go on rising, yet drivers paid without protest in the same way as nicotine addicts craved cigarettes whether a package cost a dime or a dollar.

"Beat Chevrolet!" seemed likely to be the self-applied flail as long as he lived. General Motors had serenely announced its intention to seize 60 per cent of the domestic market as soon as possible, shrugging aside the Justice Department's deliberations about that company. An antitrust suit to break up his archcompetitor was nothing that Henry would welcome; it would be contrary to the carmakers' code of conduct. Anyway, he did not believe GM could come close to making three of every five cars sold.

He would push Ford hard to capture a bigger share of customers than Ford's present 28 per cent. Failure to do so thus far was "a real disappointment—I don't know what our failure is." He still was not satisfied that he had welded together the best possible management team, but he had young men maturing on the staff who might fill some others' places at every level.

One of them was his heir apparent, Edsel II, twenty-eight years old in 1976 and sharing his father's feeling about family responsibility. He worked full-time in product planning and marketing after trying his hand in Iacocca's former bailiwick, the eighteen-to-thirty age group. Edsel contributed to research and design for the 1976 Stallion, which was basically a Pinto with pizazz, and Cobra II, a tamed version of Carroll Shelby's fiery Mustang. The long-term outlook for both cars depended on the perking up of young adults' appetite for excitement on wheels. Just now, a Washington study in statistics disclosed that they were more inclined to buy a cheap import or no car at all.

"He's got some years to spend learning the business," said Henry, who was pitchforked into it when he was Edsel's age, but Henry had hopes that the fourth generation would head the company someday. If Henry could arrange it, there would always be a Ford in the future and a Ford in charge, as there had been since the dawn of the century.

Chapter Fourteen

L'Envoi

In the corner of the inn's lobby, which it shared with the grand piano, old Henry's old clock managed to chime the half hour. The driver of the airport minibus that was parked outside walked over to the cashier's counter to change a $20.00 bill. A homeward-bound reporter went out through the front doors, holding a suit-case and a tape recorder to wait in the cool afternoon sunlight by the canopy. Four men he had seen lunching in the bar were saun-tering back to their jobs. On the curve of the driveway, they paused to examine a Volkswagen Rabbit as though it had just landed from the moon.

When the driver came out, the reporter paid his $4.50, climbed up into the bus, squeezed into a seat, and eavesdropped without shame. "I took a look at that auto show," one corn-fed passenger was saying. "They all look the same to me except the price tags."

The hiccuping man beside him had been there, too. "They tell me most of the stuff is imported. Engines from Germany, trans-missions from some other goddamn place. How does anybody know what in hell they're buying with their money?"

The bus pulled away from the Dearborn Inn and on to Oak-wood, making for the Ford Expressway. The reporter wished for a moment that he was going in the opposite direction, to Greenfield Village, so that he could check an idea that had come into his head.

Perhaps he scented at last what old Henry had really done

there. It was something more important than a monument to himself. It was a memorial to the American past, the traditional, the virtuous—everything that he and his generation of tinkerers had destroyed as unthinkingly as boys pulling at a butterfly's wings.

Consciously or not, he must have been driven to make atonement after he saw the part Lizzie had played in discrediting the values he had been raised on, rewarding him beyond all reason in the process. Respect for accumulated wisdom was replaced by what someone called "a perpetual, unwholesome rage for the new"—new cars, new comforts, new fads, new emptiness. Lizzie's wheels had run over the roots which nourished qualities that old Ford considered essential for human betterment. If only one or two in the escorted parties of schoolchildren who would be roaming the place now and every day caught a glimpse of his purpose, it would be a victory. They would feel a sense of man's continuity with his past, which had been disregarded altogether too long.

"Imagine," said another rider in the row ahead, "three brake jobs in three weeks. I only had 150 miles on the clock when my mother-in-law passed away. Didn't like to drive all that far to Jersey in a new car. You can't tell if all the bugs are worked out yet."

"Like what I bought," said his neighbor, who wore a Band-Aid on his forehead. "Engine blows up in the first week. Had my seatbelt on, but I hit the sun visor."

"Lucky it was nothing worse," said the man with brake troubles.

It was Ford territory the bus was passing through. The name spilled on to street signs, office buildings, factories, research laboratories, schools, a college, a hospital, a library, and most of the cars in sight through the windows. If you were one of the 250,000 men and women who worked for Ford in America, you had every right to choose your own make, but brand loyalty ran high. So did affection for slambang getaways and tire-squealing cornering, which were other local habits.

The light glittered on Goodyear's giant roadside tabulator, clicking off an up-to-the-moment tally day and night of how many cars had been built in the country so far this year. 453,901 . . . 453,902 . . . 453,903 . . . On this day in 1975 it felt like spring, and the figures promised sunnier weather than had been known since 1973.

The reporter wondered if the kind of talk he was listening to would dampen the outlook. How many cars would have to be recalled for flaws to be fixed? Hundreds of thousands of them, if what had happened before was any guide. The push-button machines that made them were not infallible, and they bred boredom in the men who minded them. Boredom on the assembly line was a safety problem, like drunken driving. As soon as Detroit recovered from its staggers, would every auto worker in this Aquarian age resist the temptation to goof off now and again?

Henry II had no perceptible illusions on that score. He had explained: "There is no Eleventh Commandment that says, 'Thou shalt keep thy nose to the grindstone.' Work is only one value among many, and for most people it stands well down on the list of values that govern their lives."

Maybe the assembly line was as obsolescent as the six-yards-long limousine, and the way to restore a climate of accomplishment on the shop floor was to restore teamwork. That was the system the Volvo group was trying in Eskilstuna, Sweden, letting employees take coffee breaks as they chose and lowering costs per unit by at least 10 per cent, too.

Another method, urged by some union leaders, was to give workers a voice in running a company by way of a directorship. Henry was against that, for sure, being "deeply concerned over any proposal that would take the final say in corporate policy and in the selection of the executive board away from the elected representatives of the shareholders. Such a denial of the basic rights of ownership seems inconceivable to me."

The bus pulled up at Detroit's Metropolitan Airport in the city of Romulus, and the passengers climbed down. At the curb, a grease-streaked taxi driver lay on his back under the jacked-up front end of his cab. "Goddamn shift's stuck in second. Going to have to get a tow."

Footsteps echoed off the floors inside. The building was as barren of life as Carthage after the Punic Wars. On a dais on the upper level, a GM Cutlass waited in solitude, with nothing in view but its next flick with a feather duster. In line at the check-in, the conversations continued.

"We figure we're up around 70 per cent capacity, but we'll have to do better than that to make any real bread."

"I hear Ford's doing okay, but not so good as GM. They tell me Chrysler's picking up some with Townsend gone, but it ain't so at AMC. They've got some good automobiles there, but maybe too small, you know. Seems to me people will go for a bigger car."

"When we get some good warm weather, things ought to look up."

"Always did, but it's hard to tell these days."

For a long time to come, it was going to be hard to predict Detroit's future. Climbing sales in the final year of Gerald Ford's presidency worked like adrenalin among most automakers. Optimism gushed again, and they prattled about setting new records in 1977. Then the union struck Ford, and customer demand for everybody's cars grew sluggish. A familiar pattern began to repeat itself: overstocked showrooms, production cutbacks, worker layoffs, rising unrest in Motown. What the effect would be on the country as a whole after the next President entered the White House was anybody's guess.

Light filtering in through the thick glass-block walls of the corridors leading to the gate was an appropriate shade of pale, plaintive blue. The gloom over Motown was certainly lifting, but the city was not out of convalescence yet. The automakers, second only to stockbrokers in their undiluted optimism, had not recovered sufficient heart to pretend otherwise.

No more than a dozen seats were filled in the BAC 111 jet when it taxied past the blue-green control tower, then took off from the runway in a climb like a fever chart. The white smoke streaming from the stacks of the Rouge might have been the pennants of an empire that stretched around half the world.

Somewhere in the clutter below the plane's belly was the house where Eleanor was married; Boston Boulevard was home now for blacks whose talents made the music of Motown. The house on East Jefferson Avenue where she once had the Prince of Wales for dinner and dancing had different owners, too; the UAW bought the place.

North along the shoreline of the lake was the house she still lived in, a little concerned about her weight, which had increased

moderately of late in spite of the regimen of Elizabeth Arden's
Main Chance spa in Phoenix, Arizona, where the bills added up
to $800 a week plus tips and taxes, shielded by a very proper
Englishwoman secretary, who screened out all but the few calls
and callers Mrs. Edsel Ford wished to receive. Before very long,
she would retreat into an apartment in Parklane Towers West,
Dearborn, to continue the style of her self-effacing life to the end,
which came in October 1976.

The pilot banked, still climbing. Under the portside windows,
the suburbs of the city spread like a carpet of knobby tweed over-
laid with spaghetti strands stretched and looped into highways.
Up and down the strands crept the tiny, glinting things that had
shaped America, stopping and starting in concert as the twinkle of
a light the way toys do on a child's plug-in racetrack. It was too
late to try for a glimpse of the house where old Henry died. The
woods where he and Clara used to wander, calling the birds and
deer, were part of a college campus now. Fair Lane was a site for
seminars, open to any tourist most afternoons on payment of
$1.50.

Somewhere else out of range down there, Henry II would be sitting in shirtsleeves at his cleared-top desk on the top floor at headquarters. He would stop once in a while to pour himself another
cup of tea from the Thermos flask placed there by the butler and
squeeze a lemon slice into the china cup. The tenor voice would
crackle into the intercom or one of the telephones. When a day
went badly and his temper blew up, he could be abrasive.

"Sometimes I am pretty sharp and tear up when I am sharp."
He might ease the pressure by dictating "a blistering, son-of-a-
bitch memorandum," then destroy it if he thought he had gone
too far.

When this February day was over, he would sleep alone in his
office suite. Henry and Cristina had separated. His Detroit attorney declined to say whether the next step would be proceeding for a
divorce.

The airborne reporter enjoyed that detachment, which is a priv-
ilege of those whose feet have temporarily left the ground. Beneath him, the suburbs were giving way to open country, laced
with ribbons of concrete. Old Henry and his kind had drawn this
landscape. The sequence was as simple as one-two-three. They

built the cars, and as a result, the lawmakers built highways. The highways led people out of the cities to homes and jobs, motels and shopping centers, to summer vacations and winter skiing, all of them dependent for existence on the automobile.

In Grandfather's day, Lizzie and her like had tempted millions to quit the farm and head for town. In Henry's tenure, automobiles had reversed the flow and lured more millions to flee the cities—162,000 from Detroit alone—to look for a different patch of the promised land where trees grew, traffic thinned, and crime was as rare as smog. Families were moving out to Arizona, the slopes of the Rocky Mountains, the Ozarks, the Great Lakes, the Carolinas, Southern California, and 92,000,000 cars and 22,000,000 trucks went wheeling along to keep them there. Once more, the automobile was making over twentieth-century America.

Henry imposed himself like a cockleburr on the driver's seat of the industry. He called it time to slow down on new road construction and divert more of the Highway Trust Fund's $6 billion a year to pay for mass transit. People carriers of one sort or another were essential if motorists were to be barred downtown and forced to park at the outskirts.

The massive forehead wrinkled when he talked about it. "Now, if you had little two-passenger things, if the area were big enough in there, and you could put $.50 in a machine and get one of these things for an hour or two to go wherever you wanted . . ."

There might be few alternatives when the word coming out of Washington indicated it would be impossible to make the United States independent of foreign producers of energy, which had been Nixon's daydream. Even if the Arabs and the rest raised prices still higher, to $13 a barrel, nothing could compete with oil in the foreseeable future, and the country burned 17,000,000 barrels every day.

So fifty-five miles an hour was here to stay, which was the best thing that ever happened to save lives on the road. From the era of the horseless carriage to the present, the automobile had killed 25,000,000 people in the world, more than all the deaths in its wars during the same span of time. Here, at last, the body count was falling to its lowest rates in history. Ralph Nader had cause to be pleased, but he didn't intend to let up on Henry or any other automaker responsible for what he saw as "man-made assaults on the human body." He agreed with Ford that the safety and pollution laws and timetables were out of whack, but for different reasons. As he saw it, the laws were too lax and the timetables too leisurely.

Speed, like Scrooge's partner Marley, was as dead as a coffin nail. It was sadly missed by the men who once sold automobiles on the promise of it, delivered by mighty engines with power to turn a car into a battering ram. That sales pitch appealed to something primitive in the human heart. The car represented a weapon, an extension of irrevocable aggression as momentous as a Neanderthal club. Only half of old Henry's slogan for Lizzie was significant in those days of speed: A car got you *there*. Bringing you back was less important.

What most customers wanted to know now was not how fast but how many miles to a gallon. Without horsepower to peddle, copywriters churned out some of the most lusterless advertising Detroit had ever seen. Henry's grumbling about advertisements dated back to a year or two before, when he thought the truth was getting lost. That campaign promised that "no unhappy owners" was Ford's goal.

"You can never build a car that doesn't have problems," he said at the time, "and therefore we'll always have unhappy owners." He did not intervene. "They wanted it, so there it is."

Economy was the overriding theme in the current crop of Big Three ads, when the difference of a fraction more of a mile from a gallon was reason to celebrate in headlines. Chevrolet vowed that its cars "run leaner, run cleaner—and save you money every mile." Of one model, the best that was said was, "What Caprice Classic does so well is make you feel good."

Henry's advertising agents reached out for adjectives like "sexy," "fun," and "practical," but Ford liked to make the point, honest enough, that miles per gallon depended on the driver's skill, conditions of road and weather, and regular engine tune-ups. Cynical readers of every manufacturer's claims for the 1976 models concluded that they were virtually the same as last year's, garnished with two-tone paint and fancier interiors.

The reflective reporter had to conclude that there were some things he would miss in this era of sobriety. The hoopla, for instance, that used to greet the debut of the very latest car, which would lose one third of its market value the minute he signed the sales contract. He had enjoyed the signs that heralded its appearance—the billboards that pictured it as big as a bus and loaded with luxury, ads all over the magazines and newspapers, television spectaculars and banners strung up in the showrooms.

He would miss being escorted by a salesman redolent of antiperspirant and after-shave lotion to inspect the wondrous arrival, glistening like a jewel under the spotlights. He remembered the scents most of all—buffed wax, polished chrome, pristine upholstery, doilies on the carpeting, glass spray that left the windows invisible, virginal tires that would be shamed by a speck of mud. And like musk in a perfume, the enticing smell of clean oil and unsullied metal. Ah, well!

He glanced at his watch and wondered whether he could make it home in time for dinner, and whether Henry in his office quarters would be served hamburger with perhaps a glass of champagne. The reporter had met so many people who harped on about the paradoxes in Henry, the maverick who was also a Renaissance man, the capitalist concerned with the community, the playboy who worked ten hours a day.

At 25,000 feet up, sipping a premixed martini in a flexible container, he realized that Henry had a philosophy like the single-field theory in physics that links electromagnetism and gravity, and it explained a great deal about Henry Ford II. "Conscience and profit pull in the same direction." He had been saying that for years, at least once with some detail:

> There is something in human nature which makes us feel that profit is a poor reason for helping others. But this is a feeling we should resist. To help a man because we think it is good for him is to treat him as an inferior. . . . To help a man because it is in your own interest to help him is to treat him as an equal. It is a way of telling him that you have confidence in him and his ability to stand on his own feet.

The meditative reporter was not certain that the future would permit the survival of men of such belief. Was Henry a species of rara avis, destined for extinction? In this generation, the captains and kings descended from the founders who could still be found running a family business had all but disappeared. Du Pont was no longer headed by a du Pont or Standard Oil by a Rockefeller. There was no Chrysler at the top of Chrysler or a Dodge at Dodge. Henry was left almost alone, independent to the end.

He was a man, take him for all in all, I shall not look upon his like again, the reporter said to himself, reaching up to press the call button for the stewardess to bring along another martini.

Acknowledgments

No such book as this can be attempted without employing as its single, major source the three-volume history of the company, written in the course of almost a decade by Allan Nevins, Frank Ernest Hill, and a team of research associates: *Ford: The Times, The Man, The Company* (1954); *Ford: Expansion and Challenge: 1915–1933* (1957); and *Ford: Decline and Rebirth: 1933–1962* (1963). All were published by Charles Scribner's Sons, New York. The debt is most gratefully acknowledged.

Ranking next in importance for their contribution toward recounting the Ford family's story were: *The First Henry Ford* by Anne Jardin (Cambridge, Mass.: The MIT Press, 1970); *The Last Billionaire* by William C. Richards (New York: Charles Scribner's Sons, 1948); *Unsafe at Any Speed* by Ralph Nader (New York: Grossman Publishers, 1965); *The Investigation of Ralph Nader* by Thomas Whiteside (New York: Arbor House, 1972); *My Years with General Motors* by Alfred P. Sloan, Jr. (Garden City, N.Y.: Doubleday & Company, Inc., 1964); *My Forty Years with Ford* by Charles E. Sorensen (New York: W. W. Norton & Company, Inc., 1956); *Ford* by Booton Herndon (New York: Weybright & Talley, Inc., 1969); *The Turning Wheel* by Arthur Pound (Garden City, N.Y.: Doubleday, Doran & Company, Inc., 1934); *Young Henry Ford* by Sidney Olsen (Detroit: Wayne State University Press, 1963); *American Business Abroad* by Mira Wilkins and Frank Ernest Hill (Detroit: Wayne State University Press, 1964); *From These Beginnings* by William Greenleaf (Detroit: Wayne State University Press, 1964); *We Never Called Him Henry* by Harry Herbert Bennett (New York: Gold Medal Books, 1951); and *The Legend of Henry*

Ford by Keith Sward (New York: Rinehart & Company, Inc., 1948).

Also consulted were: *Duveen* by S. N. Behrman (New York: Random House, 1952); *The Age of the Moguls* by Stewart H. Holbrook (Garden City, N.Y.: Doubleday & Company, Inc., 1954); *Tin Lizzie* by Philip Van Doren Stern (New York: Simon & Schuster, 1955); *Automobiles of America* by the Automobile Manufacturers Association (Detroit: Wayne State University Press, 1962); and *Life of an American Workman* by Walter P. Chrysler (New York: Dodd, Mead & Company, 1950).

Files of the Detroit *News*, the New York *Times*, *Fortune*, *Time*, *Newsweek*, *Business Week*, *U. S. News & World Report*, *The New Yorker*, *McCall's*, the *Ladies' Home Journal*, *Life*, *Look*, and *Black Enterprise* proved valuable, too.

Of the people who have tackled these themes in the past, William Serrin of the Detroit *Free Press* and Bob Considine of Hearst Newspapers provided considerable help. Three others deserve particular thanks: Martin S. Hayden, editor of the Detroit *News*, Joe McCarthy of the New York *Daily News* library, and Janet Aston, who worked a typewriter three thousand miles away.

J.B.

Index

on Edsel's death, 218
education, 6
elected to the board, 219
entertaining of, 136, 147–48
financial background of, 4
Gaukler Pointe house, 167–68
honeymoon, 82
last years and death of, 333–34
marriage of, 4–10, 16–18, 26
philanthropy, 133–36, 263, 264, 268, 322
robbed of jewelry, 148–49
taste of, 5, 6
threatens Henry, 236–37
wealth of, 228
Ford, Gerald, 320, 325, 333
Ford, Henry, 253, 254, 266, 275, 285, 311, 330–31
on accounting and inventory, 162–63
accused of being an anarchist, 25
acquires complete control of company, 101–3
on alcohol, 18–19, 136, 180
anti-Semitism of, 9, 115–20, 128, 147, 159, 201, 229
Sapiro's libel case against, 171–74
artistic interests, 13, 39, 134–35
automobile accidents of, 166, 172–73
Barthel and, 42, 53–55, 61
Bennett and, 97–98, 157, 172–75, 184, 202–4, 210–21, 227, 229, 231, 239, 256
birth of, 31
birth of Edsel, 27–28
builds Edison Institute, 187–89
childhood of, 31–35
collector's mania, 160–61, 182
considers running for presidency of the U.S., 143–47
courtship and marriage, 39–41
Couzens and, 58–81, 144–45, 194
dancing interest, 182–83
on dealers, 163, 166–69
Dearborn house (Fair Lane), 14–15, 25, 82–86, 134–35, 167
death of, 250–51
on denatured alcohol, 18–19
Depression of the 1930s, 189–90, 194–96

Dodge brothers lawsuit, 26, 88, 90–95, 100
early financial problems, 27–31, 44
Edison and, 8–9, 18, 24, 47, 144, 180, 187–89
Edison Avenue house, 4, 14, 72
at Edison Illuminating Company, 27–31, 41–50
on Edsel's death, 217–18
at Edsel's marriage, 7, 10, 18, 25
education, 28, 32–34, 37
estimation of his father, 31, 34–37, 40, 46
exercise, 180–81
favorite slogans of, 9–10
first idea for the automobile, 41
first trip to Europe, 76–77
five-cylinder engine, 205
food fads of, 180–82
gift for Edsel's twenty-first birthday, 3
health of, 53, 73, 103, 107, 171, 216
on history, 160, 187
Hoover and, 189, 194
Huff and, 42, 44, 53, 55, 57
importance of mother's death, 34–36, 51, 160
influence on society, 334–35
Kanzler and, 120, 125, 162–63, 168–70
Leland and, 55, 137–42
Liebold and, 79, 141–47, 155, 160, 203, 230
Malcolmson and, 57–60, 63–66, 69, 100
maximum working hours decision (1914), 8, 93
memory of, 160, 216
Mexican border raid incident, 25
minimum wage decision (1914), 8, 93
notebooks of, 84, 85
one-cylinder engine, 27–30
opens English and technical school, 13–14
orderliness and cleanliness, importance of, 35
pacifism of, 19–24, 80, 85, 86, 98, 99, 105–6, 116, 269
philanthropy, 133, 156
private nature of, 14–15, 98

Ford (Henry) and, 19, 22–23, 98–99

Winton, Alexander, 49, 53, 56, 61

Wood, Henry Alexander, 106

Woodall, Charles J., 59, 66

World War I, 16, 19–25, 80, 86, 89–90, 95–100, 105, 142

World War II, 205–40

Wright, Orville and Wilbur, 87

Yale University, 199–200, 202, 207

Yellin, Jacob, 96

York, Joe, 194

Young, Robert R., 241

Young Communist League, 194